The DIRECTORY includes all species which breed in Europe, plus those which visit, as non-breeders, in reasonable numbers, e.g. the arctic-breeding geese. It does not include vagrants from elsewhere, such as some of the North American waders, even though a few of these occur (in very small numbers) in most years.

In order to present as much information as possible for each species in the space available, some of the facts have been presented in an abbreviated form. The codes have been devised in such a way that the reader will learn rapidly to read off the information with little difficulty.

The brief introduction to each family or group outlines the common characteristics of the species within it. This is followed by some general information about identification, and a final sentence directs the reader to the *key points to look for in order to distinguish between the species within that group.*

In each species account, the English vernacular name appears at the beginning of the entry in bold capitals, followed by the scientific name (see p. 58) in italics, e.g.

WOOD SANDPIPER *Tringa glareola*

As a quick check, a symbol in the margin indicates the likelihood of the species being seen in Britain and Ireland:

● Regular breeder in significant numbers
○ Irregular breeder, or regular breeder in very small numbers
■ Regular outside the breeding season in significant numbers
□ Vagrant or regular outside the breeding season in very small numbers

The absence of a symbol means that the species has not been recorded in Britain or Ireland.

The average length of the adult bird is expressed in centimetres from bill-tip to tail-tip when the bird is stretched out. Even though this only happens to dead specimens, it is nevertheless a useful standard, e.g.

20cm.

Weights of birds fluctuate greatly with feeding conditions, season, geographical race, and with many other factors; in particular, birds lay down large amounts of fat before migration, and some small birds double their weight just before starting on a long flight. A normal range of summer weights is given, e.g.

50–80g.

Following these measurements is a comment on the bird's status in Britain and Ireland, which includes an 'order' of abundance, which can be interpreted as follows:

During the breeding season

order 1	under 10 breeding pairs
order 2	10–99 breeding pairs
order 3	100–999 breeding pairs
order 4	1,000–9,999 breeding pairs
order 5	10,000–99,999 breeding pairs
order 6	100,000–999,999 breeding pairs
order 7	over 1,000,000 breeding pairs

Outside the breeding season

order 1	under 20 records in an average year
order 2	20–199 records in an average year
order 3	200–1,999 birds probably in Britain and Ireland per year
order 4	2,000–19,999 birds probably in Britain and Ireland per year
order 5	20,000–199,999 birds probably in Britain and Ireland per year
order 6	200,000–1,999,999 birds probably in Britain and Ireland per year
order 7	over 2,000,000 birds probably in Britain and Ireland per year

Such records may be of individuals which spend the whole of the non-breeding season, or long periods of it, in Britain, or of birds which merely pass through briefly while on migration.

Diagnostic features of the species are given. These are the most obvious and useful points by which the bird may be recognised in the field: most of them concern plumage, but typical behaviour is also mentioned if it helps in identification.

VOICE: the usual call(s) and song(s) are described. Most species give a variety of different calls, and only the most characteristic are given.

The habitat (HAB) normally occupied by the bird in summer (SUM), i.e. the breeding habitat, and in winter (WIN), i.e. between breeding seasons, are given.
NB: many birds on migration are found in atypical habitats (particularly on the coast).

NEST: If the mating system is other than monogamous, this is mentioned first. Otherwise, the information concerns the usual nest site, the materials used in its construction, and which of the sexes is involved in building it. The following abbreviations are used:

♂	Male only builds
♀	Female only builds
♂♀	Both sexes share the building
♀(♂)	Female does most of the work; male may help

For EGGS the usual clutch size is given; figures in brackets are less common clutches, and others further outside the normal range may occur. A brief description of the colour and markings is followed by the average length of the egg in millimetres.

The usual number of **BROODS** reared per year is given. Some species will finish rearing a family to the fledging stage of independence, and then start all over again by building a new nest, laying eggs, etc. (Many species will make a second attempt if their first nest is destroyed; but this is not counted as a second brood.) In others, a bigamous female may bring up two broods, each with a different male who himself only breeds once in a year. This is denoted by:

♀2, ♂1

These figures may vary markedly from year to year and from place to place. For instance, few species breeding in the Arctic have time to raise more than a single brood in a season, whereas the same species might well raise two or even three further south in Europe.

The usual number of days taken in incubation (**INC**) is given, with a comment on the role of the two parents in brooding the eggs:

♂	Male only incubates
♀	Female only incubates
♂♀	Both sexes share the incubation
♀(♂)	Female sits on the eggs most of the time, male only occasionally

The type of **YOUNG** hatched is given as:

| col | nidicolous | } see pp. 206–209 |
| fug | nidifugous | |

and then a figure showing the usual number of days taken from birth to fledging (the time when the young bird can fly to some extent). The fledging period of nidifugous young is particularly difficult to establish. A ' + ' against the figure indicates that the young commonly leave the nest a few days before they are actually able to fly strongly; so the true fledging period can be longer than noted. The role of the parents in caring for the young during this time, or at least for part of it, is shown thus:

♂	Male only cares for the young
♀	Female only cares for the young
♂♀	Both sexes share the care of the young
♀(♂)	Female does most of the caring; male may help

When the young bird has reached the flying stage it has a period of immaturity (**IMM**) in which it often remains in non-adult plumage or plumages for some time, before moulting into adult plumage (p. 218). An indication of the length of time (in months) for which the young birds remain in juvenile or immature plumage(s) is given. This figure refers to plumages which are recognisably different from the adult's by the casual observer in the field; in many cases experts, especially when they have the birds in the hand, can identify young birds for longer. In some species, the juveniles of either sex rapidly resemble adult females, and the time given is for this stage, even though young males cannot be recognised as such until a later stage. When the figure is '0', this means that the young birds resemble adults in plumage as soon as they fledge.

Example:

IMM 10

means that a young bird (let us say one born in May) will achieve adult plumage the following March (after a moult).

AGE: Two or three pieces of information may be given here.

The first figure is the age (in years) at which the species normally starts to breed. (Even when the young bird has acquired adult plumage, it may still not breed immediately.)

The second figure gives the oldest age known for the species in the wild. This is based on information from ringed birds; common, much-ringed species are likely to have an older record age than rare species. So the age is given in brackets when it seems likely that the oldest record so far known falls far short of the probable age achieved by some individuals.

The third figure shows the percentage of adult birds which survive from one year to the next; but this is known for only a limited number of well-studied species (page 284).

Example:

AGE 2, 20, 95%.

indicates that the species normally starts breeding at the age of two, that the oldest known individual reached the age of twenty, and that 95% of the breeding adults survive from one year to the next.

The preferred **FOOD** of the bird is given. Again, there may be wide variation with time and place.

In a separate column, cross-references direct the reader to further information on the species or group, to be found in the other sections of the book.

In the distribution-maps,

yellow represents breeding range

blue represents winter range

Where the two ranges overlap, and green appears on the map, this means that in that region the species is present throughout the year.

Collins

New Generation Guide

TO THE

BIRDS

OF BRITAIN AND EUROPE

A clear and careful Introduction tells the story of the appearance of birds on the earth from their reptilian origins. Afterwards they evolved in many directions, and a lucid analysis of their anatomy and movement explains much of the background to modern classification.

Armed with this understanding of how scientists classify birds into orders, families and species, the reader is ready to use the Directory, in which all the birds of Britain and Europe are set out in systematic order. Illustrations of each species, in their different plumages depending on age, sex and season, may be used in conjunction with advice in the text to identify the birds that are seen. Only after putting a name to a bird is it really possible to take an interest in it, and many details of the bird's status, habitat, calls, behaviour, breeding habits, size and age, are given in handy reference form.

A special column of cross-references directs the reader to the third, and longest part of the book, where every stage of the life of the bird is considered in great depth. It is an account of survival, of the advantages and disadvantages in the various ways of growing up, moulting, feeding, migrating, breeding – of adapting or succumbing to the multiplicity of threats to its existence and self-perpetuation. Whether it is read as a story, or dipped into, it explains what we see birds doing, and the often hidden reasons why they are doing it.

Overleaf: *A single place can provide a suitable habitat for many different bird species, each of which manages more or less to avoid conflict with the others by exploiting different parts of it in different ways, and perhaps for different reasons. The illustration shows a coastal marshland, with reed-beds, mud and brackish water; twenty-one species of twelve different families are shown.*

Collins

New Generation Guide

TO THE

BIRDS

OF BRITAIN AND EUROPE

Christopher Perrins

GENERAL EDITOR
Sir David Attenborough

COLLINS
8 Grafton Street, London W1

ARTISTS
Norman Arlott
Crispin Fisher
Robert Gillmor
Alan Harris
Martin Knowelden
Bruce Pearson
Philip Snow

First published 1987

ISBN 0 00 219769 3 Paperback
ISBN 0 00 219768 5 Hardback

Copyright © 1987 by Christopher Perrins

WILLIAM COLLINS SONS & CO. LTD

LONDON · GLASGOW · SYDNEY · AUCKLAND

TORONTO · JOHANNESBURG

Filmset by Ace Filmsetting Ltd. Frome

Colour and black-and-white reproduction by
Alpha Reprographics Ltd. Harefield

Made and printed in Great Britain by
William Collins Sons & Co. Ltd. Glasgow

CONTENTS

Part 3: THE LIFE OF A BIRD

Foreword

by Sir David Attenborough

What is a field guide? It is, surely, a small book that you take into the field to help you identify the naturally-occurring things that you may find there – a bird, a flower, a butterfly. The New Generation Guides certainly claim to do that.

But they also aim to do more. Even while we are leafing through the pages of a guide, trying to track down what we have seen, we may be wondering why on earth apparently dissimilar species are grouped together in a particular family, and why the families are listed in the order that they are. If there is no rational explanation, then classification will appear to be arbitrary, incomprehensible and therefore, in the end, dull. But there *are* such explanations. They lie in the way that the group of organisms concerned is thought to have evolved. So the first short section in these new guides explains just that.

The Directory that follows, the central core of each book, contains in a specially concise and tabulated form all the details that are necessary for the identification of what we find.

But having answered the question 'What?' we may then want to know 'Why?' Why is there a difference in the appearance of the sexes in this species but not in that? Why does it occur here but not there? Why does this flower have a fragrant scent, and that one smell unpleasant? Why does this bird migrate over long distances, while that one stays in the same area throughout its life? The books that discuss such issues are for the most part large and heavy, and certainly far too bulky to be carried around the countryside with ease. Yet it is in the field that such questions are likely to come into our minds.

So the New Generation Guides contain, after the Directory, an Encyclopedia. This traces the life of organisms from birth, germination or hatching, to maturity, reproduction and the final death of the individual. And cross-references lead from the Directory, where a species has been identified, to the Encyclopedia, where its features that are of particular interest are explored in detail.

In short, the aim of the New Generation Guides is not only to identify but also to make sense of what we encounter in the countryside. In that way, we hope they will enable their readers to discover a deeper meaning in animals and plants than just their names, and therefore find in them a new delight.

Preface

by Dr Christopher Perrins

There are so many bird-books on the market that one must have a good reason to add yet another to the ever growing pile! Our reason, not merely for this book but also for the whole New Generation Guide series, is that they provide something quite new.

Books dealing with the biology and lives of birds seldom say much about identification; similarly, books on bird identification rarely say anything about how birds live. Here we have covered both these subjects in a single volume.

The book is aimed at interested amateur bird-watchers, either those new to bird-watching or those with a more lasting interest, who would like to know more than just how to identify them. In order to do this within a reasonable amount of space, considerable condensation has been necessary. Readers whose interest has been whetted by what is presented here will pursue the subjects of their interests elsewhere. When they do this, the major purpose of this book will have been achieved.

Many people have helped to make this volume what it is. Norman Arlott's contribution – of the plates in the directory – is so obvious as to be hardly necessary for me to mention to the reader: without his superb plates the book would be poor indeed. In addition he patiently repainted plates to take into account our comments. Equally the illustrations by the other artists listed on page 4 have greatly enhanced the main text.

At Collins, Crispin Fisher combines his experience of publishing with a very wide knowledge of birds which he is usually at pains to hide. This feigned naivety cuts little ice with me since I first met him bird-watching on Fair Isle over thirty years ago! His valuable criticism of both text and plates has added immeasurably to the standard of the book.

My wife Mary helped considerably in extracting data for the directory texts, and many others commented helpfully on text or plates or both. These included Chris Harbard, Dr M. P. Harris, John Marchant, Dr P. K. McGregor, C. J. Mead, Dr I. Newton, Dr M. A. Ogilvie and Dr Sarah Wanless. The levels of abundance in the status sections were derived from material collated at the British Trust for Ornithology by Dr Peter Lack and Robert Hudson.

Part 1

THE EVOLUTION OF BIRDS

BIRD'S PLACE
IN THE ANIMAL KINGDOM

Between about 200 million and 65
million years ago, the land was domi-
nated by reptiles – the dinosaurs.
However, about 195 million years
ago the first mammals appeared,
followed by the first birds about 55
million years later. Small in size and
numerically unimportant to start
with, these families took over as the
big dinosaurs died out.

Both mammals and birds are themselves descendants of the reptiles. The
immediate ancestors of birds were a
group of small dinosaurs called
theropods. Indeed, it has been claimed
that the dinosaurs never really became
extinct since the birds are their living
representatives!

Archaeopteryx

Theropod

ARCHAEOPTERYX

The theropods were a group of
carnivorous, bipedal dinosaurs. Most
early reptiles – and indeed most
modern ones – are cold-blooded and
use the heat of the sun to warm up
and become fully active; but some
theropods may have been at least
partially warm-blooded. In order to
maintain a temperature higher than
that outside the body, an animal
needs to be well-insulated; one or two
fossil reptiles may have achieved this
by evolving scales that overlapped
more than usual. Both feathers and
reptiles scales are made of keratin,
and there seems little doubt that
feathers are modified reptile scales
and that they evolved in order to
provide insulation for a warm-blooded
animal.

Birds are not very large and most
have hollow bones (p. 12). As a result,
they disintegrate rapidly after death;

so the fossil record of early birds is
poor. There is however, one major
exception to this – a famous fossil
bird called *Archaeopteryx litho-
graphica* (literally 'Ancient-wing in
picture stone'). The first of these was
discovered in 1861 in a quarry in
Bavaria. Since then four others have
been found, all in southern Germany.

Archaeopteryx is one of the most
remarkable 'missing links', having
both reptilian and avian characteristics. Nevertheless, it is probably true
to say that, at a casual glance, it looks
rather like a typical theropod dino-
saur and it might well have ended up
– unrecognised – in the basement of
some museum, but for one thing:

clearly visible in the very fine texture of the rock in which it lay were the unmistakable impressions of feathers.

Archaeopteryx roamed the German forests in the late Jurassic period, about 140 million years ago. It was about the size of a small pigeon; it retained many reptilian characters, including heavy jaws and teeth, a very long body and a lizard-like tail. It was also unbirdlike in that it lacked the deep keel (sternum) to which the flight muscles of modern birds are attached. Its most bird-like characters were the covering of feathers and the shape of the forelimbs. The latter show remarkable resemblance to the wings of a modern bird. The flight feathers are in the same positions and indeed there are the same number of feathers as in some modern birds.

We know little of how *Archaeopteryx* lived. It had an opposable hind-toe and so probably perched on branches in the same way as modern birds. It had claws on the elongated forelimbs and so could cling to a branch with these also. There has been much controversy over whether it could fly well or merely glide. In view of the lack of sternum, it has been suggested that it could not have flown as strongly as modern birds. But bats do not have a sternum, yet they fly well. Furthermore, the asymmetric shape of the primary feathers indicates that they were used for flapping flight (p. 38). Perhaps the ancestor of *Archaeopteryx* was an arboreal animal which glided from one tree to another clambering up again before launching itself in another glide. In the earliest birds, any increase in the size of the scales at the rear edge of the arm would have increased both gliding efficiency and manoeuvrability; so a wing may have started to evolve. Once such a gliding surface became large enough, it would have been advantageous for its owner to have been able to flap it – and hence there would have been selection for larger muscles. Much of this is, of course, speculation, since *Archaeopteryx* is already a long way down such an evolutionary road and no earlier bird is known.

THE EVOLUTION OF MODERN BIRDS

The next known fossil birds are from the Cretaceous Period – some 30 million years later. During this interval there must have been great strides forward in the evolution of birds for the next fossils are more obviously like modern birds. A large aquatic bird – perhaps rather like a diver – called *Enaliornis* had forelimbs constructed like those of flying birds, but much reduced in size; it seems that although its ancestors had been able to fly, *Enaliornis* had become flightless.

Late in the Cretaceous, about 30 million years later, more fossil birds appear. These include *Hesperornis*, another flightless bird related to *Enaliornis*, and *Ichthyornis*, a heavily-built tern-like bird, clearly capable of flight.

Only late in the Eocene epoch, which started about 54 million years ago, do we find species that clearly belonged to families which exist today. In the London Clay of the early Eocene, fossil herons and vultures have been found; other deposits from about 10 million years later, in France, yield specimens of geese, rails, partridges and flamingos. By the end of the Eocene, some 40 million years ago, there are fossils of at least thirty modern families of birds. It can truly be said that, by the end of the Eocene epoch, birds had arrived.

Hesperornis *and a flying* Ichthyornis

CHARACTERISTICS OF BIRDS

In general form all birds are very similar to one another. Birds have such a constant form because of the need to be able to fly efficiently. Flight is one of the most useful, but at the same time one of the most energy-demanding methods of loco-motion; in order to make it as economical as possible – indeed in many species to make it possible at all – birds cannot deviate from sound aerodynamic design. Only in a few species, such as the Ostrich and the penguins which have abandoned flight, has it been possible to alter greatly the basic size and shape.

It is possible to see adaptations for flight in virtually every aspect of a bird's anatomy; evolution has made birds as light as possible, and as manoeuvrable as possible. However, since there is also a great need for power for flight, some parts – such as the flight muscles – could not be reduced. In general, manoeuvrability is best achieved by having a compact body with most of its weight close to the centre of gravity (in contrast to the long and rather floppy body of a lizard). Birds have almost all their weight concentrated around their centre of gravity.

THE SKELETON

The bird's skeleton shows a number of marked adaptations for efficient flight, which again can, perhaps, best be looked on as helping to reduce weight or to make the bird as com-pact and manoeuvrable as possible. If we compare a modern bird with *Archaeopteryx* or even a lizard, we can see what changes have come about in the course of evolution.

The weight of the bird's skeleton has been reduced in a number of ways. Some parts have been greatly reduced and many of those bones that remain have been considerably lightened. The skeleton of a pigeon is only 4.5% of the bird's total body weight. Many bird bones are hollow tubes instead of being almost solid like those of mammals; the outer surface of the bone remains big enough to provide adequate attachment for muscles, but its weight is much reduced. In order to prevent these thin structures from kinking like a drinking straw, there are internal struts. The largest birds, such as the storks, have more hollow (pneu-matised) bones than smaller birds. The spaces within these bones are

The skeleton of a bird

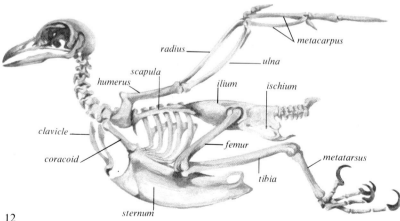

clavicle

coracoid

humerus

scapula

radius

metacarpus

ulna

ilium

ischium

femur

sternum

tibia

metatarsus

Longitudinal sections of the bones of a mammal and a bird (below)

The bones immediately associated with the flight muscles cannot be reduced in size. The breastbone (sternum) has to carry the very large flight muscles which need large surfaces for their attachment.

THE LIMBS

All terrestrial animals use one or both pairs of limbs for locomotion. Most, such as lizards and horses, use both pairs of limbs simultaneously and these are positioned so that the animal's centre of gravity falls between the limbs. Birds, however, have two quite different modes of locomotion – flying, and walking or swimming. In order to do both efficiently, they must have the centre of gravity close to the base of both sets of limbs, and this has led to certain complications.

When in flight, a bird's body hangs from the shoulder joints and the centre of gravity lies just beneath the shoulders. However, this means that the centre of gravity is well forward

air-filled and are connected to the outside by extensions of the air sacs.

The skeleton has been lightened in other ways: heavy jaws and teeth have gone; long, bony tails have disappeared; the body has been shortened and the number of bones in the hands and feet has been reduced. These ways of losing weight have presented birds with other problems. For example, the loss of teeth has had to be matched by changes in the digestive system (p. 16).

A further loss of weight has been achieved by the fusion of many bones, especially those of the lower spine; this does away with the need for ligaments and muscles to hold them in place. The number of vertebrae which are fused varies; rails have fewer fused vertebrae and hence more freedom of movement, probably because of their need to be able to twist and turn in thick cover.

Further rigidity of the torso has been achieved by means of backward projections from the ribs, called uncinate processes, which overlap, and are bound to, the next rib. In some diving birds such as the auks these uncinate processes are very long and overlap two ribs. This protects the body from the high pressures encountered when diving. These pressures may be considerable, since Black Guillemots can dive to a depth of 50 m, Puffins to 60 m, Razorbills to 120 m, and Guillemots to 180 metres.

A diving Guillemot cut-away to show the uncinate processes

13

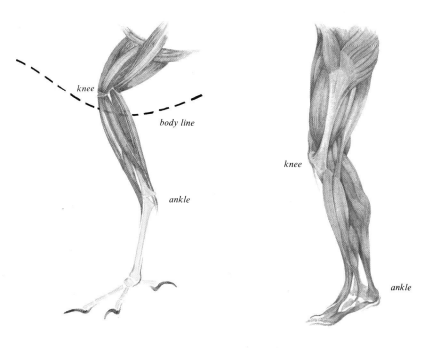

The muscles and bones of a bird's leg, contrasted with those in a man

of the hip joint; so a bird balanced at its hips would be in danger of falling forwards when it walked. The bird's skeleton is adapted to deal with this problem in a unique way. The top section of the leg, the femur, is tightly held along the sides of the body by muscles. The lower end of the femur then performs as if it were the hip joint; because this is nearer to the centre of gravity, the bird has less of a problem about balance when it is walking.

This rather over-simplified description may help to explain why the bird's leg looks odd. In man the knee, at the lower end of the femur, is half-way down the leg. In most birds the knee is held close to the body and is covered in feathers so that it is not visible. The two sections of leg which are visible are a little different from ours. The lower section is made up

from part of the lower leg and upper foot bones. The joint halfway down the bird's leg and which bends 'backwards' is not in fact the knee, but a joint which has no exact equivalent in humans; it is roughly comparable with our ankle.

The forelimbs have undergone the greatest changes, becoming the wings. The upper arm, the humerus, and the lower arm bones, radius and ulna, are still directly comparable with ours, but the hand bones have much modified to form the outer section of the wing. Only three of the original five digits remain and two of these are quite small. One of these, reduced to only a single bone, lies in front of the main wings and holds only three or four feathers; these form the 'bastard wing' or alula which is important in flight (p. 39).

14

THE MUSCLES

In order to power its wings, a bird needs a massive power source and this is provided by the great flight muscles. As anyone who has ever carved a turkey or a chicken knows, these muscles are by far the largest on a bird. In most species the weight of the flight muscles is about 15% of the bird's total weight, but in some this may be as high as 20%.

Muscles work by contracting and pulling the bones – to which they are attached – towards each other. Large muscles need large areas of attachment on the bone. The flight muscles are attached at one end to a specially broadened base of the upper arm (humerus) and at the other end to the very large breastbone (sternum). There are two pairs of muscles, again clearly visible on a turkey; the larger pair (the pectoralis major) pull the wings downwards – the action which requires the greatest effort. The smaller pair (the pectoralis minor or supracoracoideus) lie closer to the sternum; they power the recovery stroke, bringing the wings back into position for the next downstroke.

Muscles vary in colour, being composed of either white or red (dark) fibres, or a mixture of the two. White muscles seem better for rapid bursts of power, but are less suitable than dark ones for sustained power over long periods. Hence light muscles seem better for a quick escape, dark muscles for long flights. We can see these differences in domestic chickens: they still retain the same white flight muscles of their ancestors – used only for rapid, but short, flights – and the dark leg muscles which are their main means of locomotion. Contrast also the pale flight muscles of the domestic hen with the dark ones of the domestic duck whose ancestors flew a great deal.

In order to keep the weight down close to the centre of gravity, there are only very small amounts of muscle in the wings and legs, other than near to their bases; limb movements are controlled by tendons from these muscles. For example, the curling action of the toes of a perching bird is controlled by tendons which run from the upper leg down to the toes, passing round the back of the ankle joint. As the bird lands, it bends the leg, putting tension on the tendon, and as it tightens it pulls in and bends the toes. This action is partly purely mechanical: a freshly-dead bird's toes can be made to open and close by bending and straightening the leg. However, the bird does have some control over the action; the grip is much more powerful in a live than in a dead bird.

The relative lengths of the different bones in birds' wings reflect the style of flying adopted by the species. The muscles involved in flight are shown at bottom right.

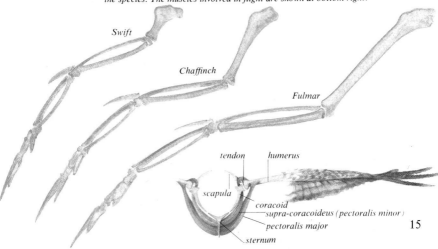

Swift

Chaffinch

Fulmar

tendon   humerus

scapula

coracoid
supra-coracoideus (pectoralis minor)
pectoralis major
sternum

15

DIGESTIVE SYSTEM

Although the weight of a bird's head has been reduced by the loss of the heavy jaws and teeth of its reptilian ancestors, food still has to be caught or torn up and many birds need to use some sort of tool for this – the beak – designed to deal with a wide variety of food. A good clue to the bird's food can be found in the sort of bill it has.

BEAKS

Despite the wide range of form, the basic design of the beak is similar in all birds. The upper mandible is firmly attached to the skull, though in many species there is a small amount of articulation between the mandible and the skull. The lower mandible, like the human one, is much freer, articulating at its base with the skull and held to it only by muscles. The horny outer surface of the bill is, like scales and fingernails, made of keratin. This wears away and is replaced. In some species it grows continuously and is worn away by action against the opposing mandible; damage to one or other mandible may result in there being no opposing surface, so that the bill sheath is not worn away and becomes progressively longer. This is the most common cause of markedly deformed beaks.

VARIATION IN BEAK FORM

Natural selection has resulted in a great diversity of bills, each enabling its owner to cope with a specific diet. The most generalised bill, such as those of warblers and thrushes, is a pointed one of medium length; this can be used for collecting a wide variety of foods from insects to fruits. Warblers do little more than stab their insect prey to kill it; Song Thrushes hold prey such as snails which they beat on a rock; both swal-

The anatomy of a bird's bill and skull

Great Spotted Woodpecker's head cut away to show position of the long tongue; the dotted lines indicate the position occupied by the tongue when retracted.

Hawfinch

Common Crossbill

Bar-tailed Godwit

Icterine Warbler

Marsh Tit

Shoveler

Smew

Red-footed Falcon

Ringed Plover

Shag

16

low their prey whole, as do many other birds. Although the bill of the Starling is similar, it has much more powerful muscles for opening the bill; it probes into soil and forces the bill open so as to enlarge the hole to enable it to withdraw any prey that it finds.

Tits also have beaks that can be used for a wide range of diets; with them they catch insects – often having to break the head capsules of caterpillars – and also open large seeds by hammering them. The Great Tit can even open hazelnuts and has to break the contents into smaller pieces before they can be swallowed. The master hammerers are, of course, the woodpeckers; the Great Spotted Woodpecker often makes a small hole in a tree branch in which to wedge nuts or seeds while it hammers them open. At other times a woodpecker uses its bill for opening up wood to get at burrowing insects. They may even take the young of hole nesting birds such as tits. They have very long tongues with which to reach and grasp the prey, and special adaptations of the skull which reduce the shock of the hammering to the brain. The Green Woodpecker can extend its tongue four times the length of its bill, the Wryneck five times.

The bills of finches have evolved specialisations for opening seeds. The upper mandible has a groove in which the seed can be held by the tongue while it is split by the cutting edge of the lower mandible. The extreme development of this type of bill is found in the Hawfinch which has the largest beak of any European finch; the jaw musculature is also exceptionally large. The Hawfinch is able to split open the stones of cherries and olives, a feat requiring a crushing force of 4 kilograms per square cm or more. The crossbills have unusual beaks which enable them to twist open the scales of conifer cones and scoop out the seeds with their tongues.

The jaw muscles of birds of prey are also powerful; many of these birds use their bill for tearing large prey into pieces small enough to swallow. They may also actually use the bill to kill their prey. The owls do not normally tear up their prey, but swallow it whole; their bill and jaw muscles are less powerful.

The bills of many ducks and geese are broad for grasping the vegetable matter on which they feed, though some such as the Tufted Duck and Eider – which take mainly animal foods – have narrower beaks with a more powerful grip. The so-called sawbills (Smew, Goosander, Red-breasted Merganser) have slender bills with tooth-like serrations for gripping slippery prey. Most other fish-eating birds have either a slightly serrated edge to the mandibles (herons, Gannet) or a markedly hooked tip (cormorants, shearwaters) both of which reduce the chance of the prey slipping out of the bill.

The waders have a wide variety of beak forms. Some such as the Ringed Plover have short beaks with which they pick prey off the surface of sand, while others such as the curlews and godwits have extremely long bills which they use to probe for prey which are deeply buried in mud. These birds have very sensitive cells in the tips of their bills which enable them to feel for the prey they cannot see. The snipes are also well-equipped with such touch receptors and have the further advantage of being able to open the tip of the bill when it is deep in the soil and while the rest of the bill is kept closed; this makes it much easier for the bird to snatch the prey than it would be if it had to open the whole bill. Some ducks also have these sensitive tips to their bills, enabling them to find food in muddy water where the visibility is poor. The Avocet sweeps its open bill through very watery mud, shutting it as soon as it feels its prey. The reflex which snaps shut the bill of the Spoonbill when it touches its prey is one of the fastest known in the animal kingdom.

Among the most specialised bills are those of the flamingos and the pelicans. The former feed with their bill held upside down in the water. There are fine hair-like bristles along the sides of the bill and the birds suck water into the mouth and then

The bill and feeding method of a Flamingo

force it out with a pumping action of the large, fleshy tongue. Small aquatic animals and plants are filtered out of the water on the rows of bristles and are then worked backwards in the mouth and swallowed. The pelicans have very springy bones in the sides of the lower mandible; as they thrust their bill towards their prey, the resistance of the water forces these bones to bow outwards and the pouch to fill with water. The upper mandible snaps down as the sides of the lower mandible regain their normal shape. All being well, the fish is trapped inside the pouch in the water. It takes the pelican a few moments to draw its beak out of the water, for the water in the fully expanded pouch actually weighs more than the whole bird; so the pelican cannot move far until it has drained the water from its bill.

The weakest bills are found in many of the insectivores such as the flycatchers, swallows, swifts and nightjars. These species mostly catch flying insects and rely on a very wide gape to give them the best chance of doing this.

The bills of Nightjar (below) *and Red-breasted Flycatcher*

THE CROP

Many birds accumulate their food, initially, in a thin-walled extension of the oesophagus – the crop. No digestion takes place here. It is simply a temporary storage place and allows a finch, for example, to alight, swallow a large number of small seeds in a short space of time and then retire to the safety of a bush to digest them. The bird can also take a large quantity of seeds to roost with it and digest them during the night, so shortening the period over which it has to go without food. Many birds, such as some seabirds and pigeons carry food long distances in their crop to their young. In pigeons and flamingos, the crop wall becomes thickened during the nestling period and the cells from these thickened areas are sloughed off to provide a milk-like substance for the chicks (p. 270).

THE GIZZARD

Because birds no longer have a set of teeth with which to grind up the food, this treatment has to be carried out elsewhere. Birds that eat insects, fish or meat do not have a great problem since their stomachs have strong juices and their food is easily digested. This is not so true of the birds, such as finches, ducks and geese, that eat vegetable matter. They need to be able to grind up their food into fine particles to digest it properly. They do this in the gizzard, the muscular forepart of the stomach. Hard material to serve as teeth is needed for the grinding process, so these birds take in grit and mix it with the food. They need a regular supply of grit, just as domestic hens do, to replace the fragments that are steadily ground down. Another advantage of this digestive system is that the relatively heavy gizzard is much closer to the centre of gravity than are the jaws and teeth of the lizard ancestor.

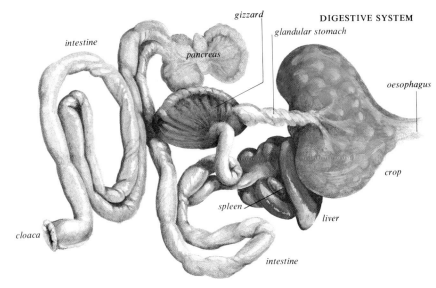

gizzard

glandular stomach

intestine

pancreas

oesophagus

crop

spleen

liver

cloaca

intestine

The digestive system of a goose

DIGESTION

Some vegetable material, such as seeds and fruits, has a relatively high nutrient content and can be more easily digested than green material such as grass and leaves. Several groups of mammals are specialised herbivores; they take in large quantities of vegetable material and digest it with the help of bacteria which break down the cellulose cell walls. In order to do this efficiently, the mammal has to retain the food for a considerable period in what is necessarily a large and heavy stomach. Such an organ would be very impractical for a flying animal. This is almost certainly the reason why there are relatively few birds that are leaf eaters. Among them are some of the grouse and pheasants; the Capercaillie even eats conifer needles. On the whole these birds do not fly much or far.

Wigeon feeding on grass

However, the other major group of grazing birds, the ducks, geese and swans, includes species which feed mainly on grass and which fly long distances. These birds rely on a very rapid throughput of large quantities of vegetable material, from which they get pound for pound rather a small amount of nutrition compared with that which a grazing mammal might extract. By this method waterfowl are spared the need for a very heavy stomach.

EXCRETION

Birds have a very efficient excretory system. Much of the water in the faeces is reabsorbed before defaecation, and recycled. In some groups, such as the grouse, the faeces are characteristically extremely dry, because most of the water in the urine has been reabsorbed. In many species a very dry uric acid is excreted, often visible as a white end of the faeces. Such a system greatly reduces the need for drinking large quantities of water (which has to be carried in flight); the smaller amount of water in the gut can be continuously recycled.

19

RESPIRATION

Energy is obtained from food by making it react chemically with oxygen in a way comparable to that in which petrol must be burned to provide the power for a car to move. Any strenuous activity requires that the animal obtains not only a lot of food but also a lot of oxygen. Flight is one of the most energy-demanding activities in the animal world. A bird in flight may use up energy ten times as rapidly as when it is resting. To fly, it must be able to inhale quantities of air and take the oxygen from it efficiently and rapidly. At the same time it must be able to get rid of the carbon dioxide which is produced as a result of burning up the food. In other words a bird needs a highly efficient respiratory system in order to be able to fly.

Oxygen is absorbed, and carbon dioxide lost, by the lung. At first sight, the bird's lung does not seem to be a very effective one. For example, our lungs take up about 5% of our body, whereas those of a Mallard only take up about 2%. One would expect birds' lungs to be large. However, gaseous exchange takes place between the tiny blood capillaries and the smallest air tubes in the lungs, the alveoli. In birds these are very much smaller than in mammals. As a result, there is a much greater surface area of alveoli in a bird's lung than in those of a mammal of comparable size, and hence much greater opportunity for gaseous exchange.

Further, the bird's lung is of a rather different design from that found in mammals. The spaces within the bird's body are filled with air sacs, thin-walled structures which look rather like inflatable polythene bags. These sacs fill most of the body cavity and even extend between the two big pairs of flight muscles and into all the hollow bones, taking up about 18% of the body volume in the Mallard. They are not directly involved in the uptake of oxygen or loss of carbon dioxide, but they perform a vital role in the way the inspired air flows through the lungs, and in cooling the body. There are nine major sets of air sacs in the body; for simplicity they can be regarded as two groups, those lying forward in the body, the anterior air sacs, and those lying behind the lungs, the posterior air sacs. Air which is breathed in by the bird does not go directly into the lungs, but into the posterior air sacs. From there it goes into the posterior end of the lung and thence out into the anterior air sacs from where it is then expired by the bird.

This system has two major advantages over the mammalian lung. First it means that there is a one-directional flow of air through the lungs rather than an ebb-and-flow system such as is found in mammals. If we breathe very deeply, we can change about 75% of the air in our lungs with each breath; the bird however, changes all of it. The second, and more important, advantage with a through-flow system relates to the way in which oxygen is taken up by the blood in the capillaries. Blood that is low in oxygen readily absorbs the gas, even from air which is low in it. As the blood's oxygen content increases, so its ability to take up more diminishes. Ultimately, it can only absorb the gas from air which is particularly oxygen-rich. A bird's circulation is so arranged that blood in need of re-oxygenation arrives first at the front end of the lungs, where the air is low in oxygen. As the blood flows along the lung walls, absorbing oxygen as it goes, it encounters air that is progressively more oxygen-rich. Consequently blood in a bird's lung takes up oxygen more efficiently than that in a mammal's lung where the air ebbs and flows. The situation is the same in reverse for the loss of carbon dioxide; blood rich in carbon dioxide comes first in contact with air which has high levels of carbon dioxide and,

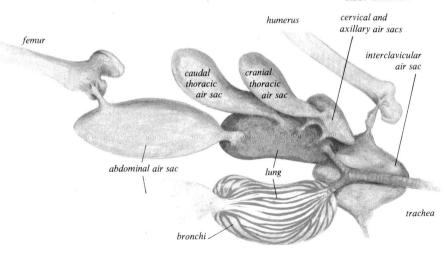

femur

humerus

cervical and axillary air sacs

interclavicular air sac

caudal thoracic air sac

cranial thoracic air sac

abdominal air sac

lung

trachea

bronchi

The respiratory system of a bird

as the level in the blood drops, the blood comes progressively in contact with air that has lower concentrations and so can go on losing it.

This highly efficient respiratory system enables the birds to obtain the large quantities of oxygen they need for flight. However, although the bird's respiration is very efficient, bats also fly and men can run at speeds which require great increases in their oxygen consumption. Where the bird's lung shows itself to its greatest advantage is at high altitudes where oxygen is scarce. If sparrows are put in a chamber with an air pressure equivalent to that on the top of Mount Everest, they go about quite unperturbed, whereas mice put in the same conditions quickly become out of breath and can only stagger around. This ability to breathe at high altitudes has important implications for migrating birds, many of which fly at 20,000 feet or more for part of their journeys. There are even a few records of larger birds flying at altitudes of 30,000 feet or more, heights at which most mammals could not easily exist, let alone be active!

Diagram of the counter-currents in the blood vessels around the lungs of a bird

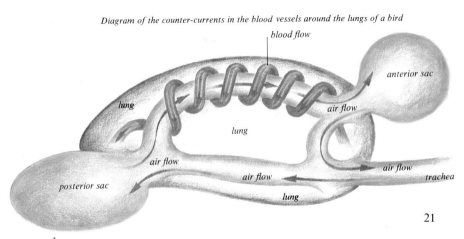

blood flow

anterior sac

lung

air flow

lung

air flow

air flow

posterior sac

air flow

lung

trachea

21

BIRD SONG

A bird breathes in air through its trachea (windpipe). At the bottom of the neck, the trachea divides into two tubes, the bronchi, which carry the air to the two lungs. At the junction of these two bronchi lies the syrinx, a complex organ which produces many of the sounds birds make.

The bronchi are composed of cartilaginous rings joined to each other by connective tissue. In the area of the syrinx, these thin tissues are modified to form elastic vibrating membranes, the tension of which can be altered by a complex of controlling muscles. As air passes over these membranes they vibrate, and this produces the sounds we hear. The quality of the sound varies with the tension of the membranes. Not all the sounds are derived from the syrinx alone; for example the calls made by some of the swans are, at least in part, the result of complex convolutions of the trachea itself.

The design of the syrinx varies markedly in different species of birds and there is still debate as to the exact way in which many of the sounds are produced. However, it is now clear that in certain species which produce complex songs, such as the Chaffinch, the full song is made up of two separate parts, produced by the membranes in each of the two bronchi. How the bird controls the two sets of sound from the two bronchi is not understood.

The musculature of the syrinx is complicated, but birds have been divided into two groups on the basis of these muscles, the Non-oscines and the Oscines; the latter being largely equivalent to the passerines (p. 59).

THE STRUCTURE OF SONGS AND CALLS

The sounds made by birds are used to convey messages to other individuals. Some of the sounds made, especially

The vocal organs of a bird

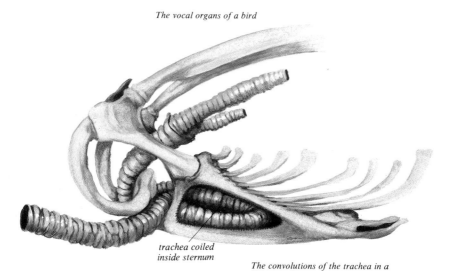

trachea coiled inside sternum

The convolutions of the trachea in a Whooper Swan

some of the songs, are very complex. Birds' hearing is somewhat different from ours (p. 26) and it is likely that they are able to get much more information out of a call than we are able to.

Even so, birds can produce a wide variety of different calls to convey different messages. Up to fifteen different types of call have been identified in the Whitethroat. In some species such as the Chaffinch and the Yellowhammer, the individual birds have a smaller number of elements which they put together to make a song. They tend to keep these elements in the same order so that they produce a song which they repeat. They may have more than one song type, and use just a few over and over again. Such a group of song types is called the bird's repertoire. The Sedge Warbler however, has as many as fifty recognisable elements in its song and draws on them almost at random to pour out long streams of songs which virtually never repeat themselves. Marsh Warblers copy the sounds of other birds and use them in their own songs; individual birds have been recorded as mimicking the songs of up to 40 different species. In Europe the calls or songs of over 100 species of birds have been recognised in Marsh Warbler songs, many of them being of African birds which must have been learned when the Marsh Warblers were in their winter quarters.

Each individual has a slightly different voice so that, in many cases, individuals can learn to recognise the songs of neighbouring birds and the calls of their mates or chicks and distinguish them from other birds (p. 204 Guillemot eggs, p. 210 Flamingo chicks, p. 213 Sand Martin chicks, p. 257 territorial males).

THE FUNCTION OF SONGS AND CALLS

Birds produce calls or sounds in order to convey information to other birds. In certain cases, the same sound may serve two functions. For example the territorial song of a male bird may be used to warn other males to stay away, but at the same time serve to attract a female.

The songs of different species are often clearly different. For example the small warblers of the genus *Phylloscopus* (Willow Warbler, Wood Warbler, Greenish Warbler, Bonelli's Warbler, Chiffchaff) all have strikingly different songs. One of the reasons for this is that songs also provide a valuable way of recognising a species, so reducing the chance of a bird breeding with another of a different species (p. 260). This is especially important in birds which are similar in appearance as are these warblers.

Some types of sound have characteristics which make them useful under particular circumstances. For example, calls of less than half a second duration, within a certain frequency range, which start and end sharply, are thought to be very difficult to locate. (They certainly are to humans.) It may be no coincidence that a wide variety of different species give alarm calls which have precisely these characteristics. Alarm calls are given to warn mates and offspring of the presence of a predator; at the same time, the bird that gives the call does not want to give its own position away if it can help it. By using a call that is hard to locate, it minimises the risk to itself and at the same time warns the other birds. The type of alarm call given depends on the type of predator; so further information is supplied to the listener about the particular danger that threatens it.

There is also some evidence that different types of sound carry better in certain types of environment than do others. For example, those that travel well in woodland are not the same as those which do so in open country. Even the characteristics of the sounds which carry best in coniferous forests may differ from those which are best in deciduous woods. There is some evidence that Great Tits use different songs in these two habitats and that they may be using those types of sounds which tend to carry best in each environment.

SENSE ORGANS

Birds rely largely on sight and sound just as we do. Because of this similarity in sense organs we can, perhaps, share more of a bird's world than we can of a mammal's. The dog, said to be man's best friend, has lived alongside us for thousands of years. When one goes out with us it spends a great deal of its time acquiring information by means of its sense of smell. In spite of our long association we really have virtually no idea of what information they perceive from smell.

VISION

For an animal which moves rapidly through the air, sight is clearly the most important sense. Birds have developed vision to a very high level indeed. Their eyes are relatively far larger than those of mammals. The eyes of a Buzzard or small eagle are approximately the same size as man's even though the bird weighs and bulks far less. In many bird species the eyes take up so much space that there is only a small bony septum between them. The eye muscles, which in mammals take up quite an amount of space in the orbit, are also very small. As a result, birds' eyes are less mobile within their sockets, and they make up for this by moving the head rather more.

Most birds probably see about the same range of colours that we do. They have sharp vision, but the legendary ability of the eagle to see vastly better than we do is probably exaggerated. Birds of prey may have vision that is about two or three times as acute, but probably not much more than that. Other birds, such as the pigeons, may have vision which is no more acute than ours, while some gamebirds may be even less sharp-eyed than us.

The eyes of most birds are not forward-looking, but are positioned on the sides of the head. This gives the bird an enormous field of view, which is very useful if one is trying to keep a look-out for predators. In a bird such as a pigeon, there is only a small area straight ahead where the field of the two eyes overlap, but the bird can probably see a long way round behind it, perhaps through an arc of more than 300 degrees. Some waders may even be able to see all the way round behind them without moving their head. Indeed the Woodcock which has large eyes high in the sides of its head may be able to see not just all round, but right over the top as well, being able to watch the whole of a half sphere without moving its head!

Having the eyes at the sides of the head has disadvantages as well as advantages: there is only a small area of sight where the fields of both eyes overlap. Binocular vision is valuable because it greatly increases the accuracy with which it is possible to judge the distance of an object: by viewing from two different eyes, the bird can fix a position more precisely. In practice the small area of binocular vision possessed by most birds seems sufficient for their needs. However, some birds such as herons, sway the head from side to side when hunting; in all probability, they are moving the head to improve the accuracy of their assessment of the distance to the prey by looking from two different positions. In some birds, such as the owls and birds of prey, the eyes face for-

A bird's skull from above to show position of the eyes

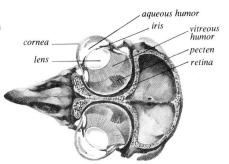

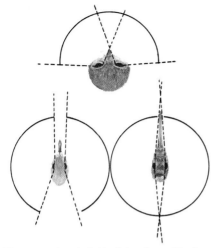

Diagrams to show the fields of view of an owl (top), *a Woodpigeon* (left), *and a Woodcock* (right)

migration; the ability to measure the movement of the sun over a very small period of time may be of great importance to them.

A few birds such as owls have the ability to see well in the dark, though not so well as legend would suggest. They certainly cannot see in total darkness. Compared with most diurnal birds, they have a higher proportion of light-detecting cells (rods) than colour-detecting ones (cones). However, again contrary to folk-lore, they can see well in the day, and at least the Little Owl and the Tawny Owl have colour vision. In the dark they are highly dependent on good detection of sound to catch prey in the dark.

Aquatic birds require some modifications to their vision since light which travels through water behaves differently from light which passes through air. A bird such as a heron or a Kingfisher, which sees its prey from above the surface of the water, has to allow for the difference when aiming at or diving after fish. However, for birds such as grebes or cormorants, which swim after their prey under water, vision can be somewhat modified to enable them to measure distances without difficulty. Birds have a third eyelid, the nictitating membrane, a translucent structure which can be passed over the eye without totally preventing vision and which keeps the surface of the eye clean and moist – especially when the bird is in flight. In certain aquatic birds there is a clear, but thickened area in the centre of this membrane which is kept in front of the eye as a kind of correcting lens while the bird is under water.

wards in much the same way as ours do; these birds have wide areas of binocular vision, but a correspondingly narrower field.

Another important difference between human eyes and those of birds is the area of field which is in sharp focus at any one time. In our own eyes, only some 2.5 degrees of the visual field are in sharpest focus. As a result, in order to be able to examine objects thoroughly, we are constantly moving our eye from one object to another. Birds, in contrast, have some 20 degrees or so of their visual field in sharp focus. This means that they are able to examine objects over a wide field without having to move the eyes or the head. This may be a particular advantage when trying to observe small movements. To tell whether something is moving, it helps to be able to compare it with another object. In our case, if the two objects are more than 2.5 degrees apart we have to move the eye from one to the other and the fact that we are moving the eye makes it much more difficult to observe a small movement. Birds, not having to move their eyes, can probably detect small movements more precisely than we can. This may seem a trivial advantage, but many migrant birds make observations on the movement of the sun and the stars in order to get their bearings for

The nictitating membrane

HEARING

Birds' ears are structurally similar to ours in major details, but there are some differences. There is no outer ear, or pinna, as in most mammals, probably because this would upset the streamlining of the bird in flight. The external opening of the ear is covered by special feathers which lack barbules, probably so as not to impede the passage of sound.

As in mammals, sounds reaching the inner ear are detected by very fine sensory hairs which then transmit signals via the nerves to the brain. There are very much higher densities of these sensory hairs in birds than in mammals. This probably enables birds to differentiate between sounds that occur much more closely in time than it is possible for mammals to do. Birds can distinguish two sounds which occur just two thousandths of a second apart; this is approximately ten times better than we can manage. Hence birds are able to receive a much more complex message from, say, a bird song, than we can because they can break it down into many more small sections.

Apart from this very major difference, the hearing of birds and man is fairly similar. Birds can hear sounds over approximately the same range of frequencies that we can; they can neither produce nor hear ultrasonic sounds. Capercaillie have been shown to produce sounds which are of too low a frequency for us to hear, but it has not yet been shown whether they can hear them themselves!

Diagram of a bird's ear

semicircular canals

cochlea

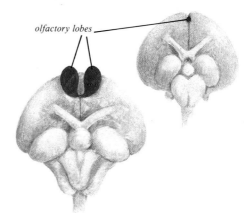

olfactory lobes

Diagrams of the olfactory lobes of a Storm Petrel (left) and a sparrow

SMELL

In the lives of few, if any, European birds is the sense of smell known to be an important factor. One can guess the importance of smell from the size of the olfactory lobes of the brain; it is unlikely that these would be well-developed unless the sense of smell is used. Most birds have poorly-developed olfactory lobes; but these are enlarged in some ducks and geese, suggesting that these birds rely on the sense of smell to some extent. Storm-petrels not only have enlarged olfactory lobes in the brain, but the birds themselves have a very distinctive musty smell. They are nocturnal at their nesting colonies and so a sense of smell might well be of use to them in the darkness for finding their nest-site or recognising their mate.

TASTE

Birds can distinguish the four types of flavours that we can – salt, sour, bitter and sweet. However, they may not be able to do it as well as mammals for two reasons. First, some of the information which contributes to our sense of taste comes from the sense of smell. Since most birds cannot smell well, this may mean that their sense of taste is not acute either. Second, in mammals the tongue carries large

Spoonbill

Pintail

Avocet

Snipe

numbers of taste buds. However, the tongues of most birds are covered by a horny surface in which there are no taste buds. The few taste buds there are lie at the back of the tongue and in the throat. Hence birds have to almost swallow an object before they are able to taste it.

Although the evidence suggests that birds have only a poor sense of taste, they seem nevertheless able not only to distinguish the essential different flavours, but also to assess the concentrations of some substances such as nectar.

TOUCH

The sense of touch is important to birds in a number of ways and they have several different types of receptor cells which are sensitive to touch. These occur in the obvious places such as the soles of their feet and some on the tongue. In most birds the horny covering of the bill makes it difficult for them to have touch receptors there, but some species such as ducks and waders which feel for seeds and small prey in mud or water have good touch-sensitive cells in the tips of their bills (see beaks, p. 17).

Because the surface of the bird is covered with feathers, it would not be much use to have general touch receptors in the skin. However, there are touch-sensitive cells surrounding the base of certain feathers. These record the angle at which the feather is raised or moved and probably tell the bird about the way in which its feathers are lying. Such information may be particularly important during flight.

The sense of touch is important to certain birds who cannot always see clearly the food for which they are searching.

FEATHERS

Of all the adaptations of birds, feathers are the most distinctive. Although biochemically they are similar to reptile scales and mammalian hair and claws, they are quite different in structure. They have proved extremely versatile, providing essential insulation and waterproofing, the large expanses of the wings which provide both lift and propulsion (p. 36), good streamlining and an amazing range of colours – from dazzlingly bright to surprisingly cryptic.

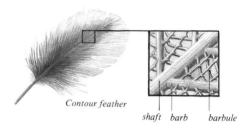

Contour feather

shaft   barb   barbule

The feathers and bones in a bird's wing

scapulars   secondary coverts   greater wing coverts   alula

tertials   secondaries   primaries

FEATHER GROWTH

Feathers grow from follicles, small pimples easily visible in the skin. Inside these follicles, a ring of feather cells is formed; as further cells are produced, these cells are pushed out of the skin in the form of a tube which continues to grow at the base. This tube eventually becomes the feather. The tube is slightly thickened at one point and has a line of weakness along the opposite side. By breaking along this line the tube opens out into a flat surface, the thickened part becoming the central rachis. The main plane of the feather also has many lines of weakness which also fracture to produce the barbs and barbules.

FEATHER STRUCTURE: CONTOUR FEATHERS

There are four major types of feather, body (or contour), flight, down and filoplume. The basic form of the feather can best be understood by examining the normal contour feather.

Contour feathers are composed of a quill (or rachis) from which two sets of barbs grow out, one from either side of the quill, to form the vanes of the feather. The barbs in their turn

Central tail feather

Primary wing feather

have barbules projecting from their sides; those on the side of the barb nearer to the base of the feather are grooved while those on the opposite side are hooked. These barbules lock together and so prevent the barbs from being easily pulled apart. In the Crane, a single barb may have 600 barbules on each side – more than a million barbules on a large feather. The whole structure is remarkably strong and yet very light.

FLIGHT FEATHERS

The flight feathers, the large feathers of the wings and tail, are often called remiges (the wing feathers) and rectrices (tail feathers). These are very similar in design to the contour feathers except for their size. The major feathers in the wings occur in a fixed pattern, although the number varies slightly between species. They are subdivided into primaries (which are attached to the bones of the hand) and secondaries (which are attached to bones of the lower arm). An important feature of these feathers is that they are asymmetric; this is essential for flight (p. 38).

DOWN FEATHERS

Down feathers (or plumules) have a very short quill, topped by a large number of barbs projecting from its end, but not locked to each other by barbules. These down feathers form an important layer of insulation and waterproofing beneath the contour feathers in many birds, especially water-birds because they are very effective in trapping a large amount of air.

Down feathers also provide the covering of young birds both those which stay in the nest until they are fully grown and those, such as the chicks of ducks, waders and game-birds, that leave the nest soon after hatching; the well-camouflaged plumage of these chicks is composed entirely of down feathers.

Filoplume

Down feather

The facial bristles on Spotted Flycatcher (above) *and Cuckoo*

FILOPLUMES AND BRISTLES

The filoplumes are single hair-like structures, sometimes with a downy tuft at the tip. The typical filoplumes are usually intermingled with the other feathers (and are easily visible on a plucked chicken or turkey that has not been singed). These, in combination with touch-sensitive cells (p. 27) provide the bird with information about how the feathers are lying on its surface.

Some birds such as the flycatchers also have a set of stiffer bristles (which lack the tuft of down at the tip) around the base of the bill; these may help by providing information about large insects which they have in their beak or they may protect the bird's eyes from struggling insects. Others like some of the cuckoos have a set of these bristles around the eyes which look extremely like mammalian eyelashes; they are thought to provide protection for the eye.

29

THE NUMBER OF FEATHERS

The number of feathers which cover the bird varies markedly with a number of factors, the most important being the size of the bird. Amongst other factors, water-birds tend to have a more dense covering of feathers than land-birds. However, there have been few counts and the situation is complicated by the fact that many European species seem to have fewer feathers in summer (even when they are not moulting) than in winter.

The smallest species of all, the hummingbirds, have fewer than a 1,000 feathers. Most European birds have more than this: the Treecreeper, the smaller tits, some finches and the Swallow have some 1,400 to 1,500 feathers. An American Bald Eagle weighing 8 kg had 7,182 feathers which weighed 586 g. As might be expected swans have many feathers, the most ever counted on a single bird being 25,216.

FEATHER MAINTENANCE

Birds spend a great deal of time caring for their plumage: preening. The most obvious activities involve the washing of the feathers to keep them clean, and the fine nibbling which is done to re-hook barbs which have become separated and probably also to remove parasites such as feather lice and fleas.

Birds produce two substances which help to maintain the quality and perhaps the waterproofing of the feathers. One is powder-down. Special down feathers – especially on the underparts of the birds – keep on growing throughout their life. As they grow, tiny particles are continually breaking off from their tips. These waxy particles become spread around in the plumage and are thought to improve the waterproofing. Occasionally, when a bird flies into a window, it leaves a clear imprint of itself on the glass; this is made up of powder-down which has been knocked off the feathers by the impact.

Most birds also have a preen gland situated just above the base of the tail. This gland produces a waxy substance which the birds spread around on the feathers during preening. This too is thought to help maintain the structure and waterproofing of the feathers. It may have the additional benefit of providing Vitamin D which may be synthesised when preen oil is spread on the feathers and is exposed to sunlight.

Another way in which some birds care for their feathers is by anting. Birds may fly down onto anthills and sit there with the wings spread and their feather fluffed out. Ants take exception to this and spray the birds with formic acid – their normal defence against attackers. The acid on the birds feathers is thought to help destroy parasites. Some birds even pick up ants and pass them along the sides of their body – apparently making sure that the feathers are well-sprayed.

A Whinchat preening its wing; a Jay anting; a Spotted Redshank preening its underparts

FEATHER COLORATION

One of the most striking attributes of feathers is their varied coloration. These colours are produced by structural alterations which vary the wave-lengths of light that are reflected, or by pigments, or by a combination of these two methods.

Normal (white) light is made up of all the colours of the rainbow; each of these colours has a slightly different wave-length, as can be seen by altering the angle of a piece of glass across a beam of light until the colours separate. If the feather reflects all the wave-lengths of light equally, it will look white, as many feathers do, but if some wave-lengths of the light are cut out or reduced, the feather will take on the colours of the remaining wave-lengths. Most glossy, iridescent colours in birds, such as the purples on a starling or the green on a peacock, are produced this way. The reflective surfaces may be on the outside of the feather; if so they are usually produced by flattening the surfaces of the barbules. However, this reduces or removes the strength of the feather, and so many of the iridescent colours are achieved by reflections from granules of pigment within the feather, without loss of strength.

By far the commonest pigment in birds is melanin. There are many different melanins and, despite the name, melanic pigments are by no means all black; many produce the wide range of browns that we see in birds. Many of the red, orange, and some of the yellow colours that we see in bird feathers are produced by carotenoids. Birds are unable to synthesise carotenoids; they must get them from their diet. Flamingos kept in captivity lose their pink body colours unless they are given carotenoids in their diet.

These basic colours may be modified by combining structural and pigmentary effects; for example, the olive green of a Greenfinch is produced by tiny areas of black (melanin) in the tips of the barbules and patches of yellow (carotenoid) in the base of

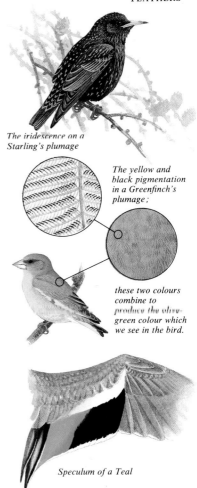

The iridescence on a Starling's plumage

The yellow and black pigmentation in a Greenfinch's plumage;

these two colours combine to produce the olive-green colour which we see in the bird.

Speculum of a Teal

the barbules and in the barbs. Effects of 'texture' can be achieved by varying the surface structure of the feather. For example, the bright green wing speculum of the Teal results from the barbs twisting slightly so that their flattened surfaces give a glossy appearance, while the velvety look of the bird's nape feathers is produced by a dense growth of short feathers standing more or less vertically.

The structure of the feather may affect its strength and this will be one of the factors which will have influenced the evolution of the different colorations of feathers. For example, if one picks up moulted gull feathers in a colony at the end of the breeding season, it is easy to see that the white tips have worn away – down to the black section. Apparently, the white part of the feather is structurally weaker than the black. Possibly this fact has influenced the shape and positioning of the wingtip patterning of these birds, too much white and the wingtips wear away too quickly with loss of flying efficiency.

Various stages in wear of the wingtip of a Common Gull

MOULT

Whatever their colour, feathers eventually become abraded and lose their strength. They need to be replaced. This is a disadvantage since it means that the birds are without some of the feathers while they are being replaced. This leads to loss of insulation in the case of contour feathers, and loss of flying efficiency in the case of flight feathers. In the latter case some species have evolved the habit of dropping all their flight feathers at the same time and so becoming flightless during the moult, rather than trying to carry on flying with an incomplete wing (p. 221). In addition to the inconvenience, replacing a set of feathers requires a considerable amount of energy (p. 224), so the bird must find extra food during the moult period; and as well as needing energy to build the new set of feathers, a bird needs extra energy partly to cope with increased heat loss (because of reduced insulation) and partly to compensate for decreased flying efficiency because of gaps in the wings. (In the Chaffinch, total energy requirements increase by about 25% during the two months of the moult, see p. 227.)

Although replacing feathers requires energy, the ability to replace them gives birds an advantage over bats, which use large flaps of skin for their wings; these are difficult to repair if they become damaged. The bird, however, can replace lost feathers at any time. Another great advantage of moulting is that birds can change their colour at a moult, a feature which they have exploited extensively (p. 219).

Although a feather which is torn out may be replaced at any time,

Four different techniques in wing-moult

Rock Pipit

Spotted Flycatcher

most feathers do not just drop out at the moult. Their loss is precipitated by the growth of the next feather in the follicle which pushes the old feather out of its socket. The replacement of feathers is not haphazard, but takes place in an orderly manner so that large or unnecessary gaps do not appear in the plumage. The feathers of birds are situated in tracts which cover the whole of the body. The body feathers are replaced gradually from one end of each tract to the other. Similarly, except in those species which are flightless during the moult (and in which all the main wing feathers are dropped simultaneously), there is a distinct pattern in the way in which the wing and tail feathers are replaced. The primaries of most species are replaced from the inner one outwards while the secondaries are replaced from the outer one inwards. In each case, one feather is shed every few days so that, at any one time, there is a gap in which three or four feathers are growing. As a result of this pattern of moult, a gap opens up at the bend in the wing and two gaps move away, outwards along the primaries and inwards along the secondaries. Such a pattern is not totally rigid. In some species in which flight efficiency is particularly important (e.g. the vultures and the Fulmar), there may be more centres at which moult starts and fewer feathers may be shed at any one time. Hence, these species may have three or four small gaps in the wing instead of two larger ones. The Spotted Flycatcher differs from most other birds by moulting its primaries from the outside inwards instead of the other way around; no one knows why this species has found it advantageous to reverse the pattern used by other birds.

The other surfaces made of keratin, the horny scales of the legs and the bill covering, are also moulted. Although this is not always easy to observe, there are species such as the Puffin where the summer and winter bill plates are quite different, giving the bird a different appearance. The claws are not moulted, but grow continuously.

Moorhen

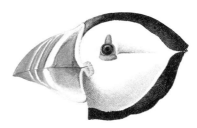

The bill and face of a Puffin in summer (above) and winter

Griffon Vulture

REPRODUCTION

The reproductive system of birds, like so many of its characters, is well-adapted to the need for flight. In both male and female the sex organs shrink outside the breeding season to a minute size and weight.

They must, of course, grow larger for the breeding season and this they do gradually through the late winter and early spring, increasing as much as 1,500-fold in weight (p. 244). The ovary is usually larger than the testes so that the female has to put more into this growth than the male. The sex organs tend to remain enlarged for some time after mating and laying: the birds may lose their nest and need to lay a replacement clutch. However, in the shearwaters and petrels, the sex organs start to regress very soon after laying because these species lay replacement eggs only when the first egg is lost almost immediately after it is laid.

The major adaptation for flight is that the eggs are produced sequentially. An individual ovum, together with the yolk, is shed from the ovary and passes down the oviduct; on the way, the albumen (white) is laid down around it. Then the shell is secreted and pigmented with the characteristic colours.

Each egg is laid before the next egg is shed from the ovary. Although the ovary may contain several individual ova in various stages of development, these are all quite small, except for the one which is to be shed next. As a result, the female bird does not carry more than one full-sized egg in its body at any one time.

This system has a number of advantages. The only way most female birds could fit more than one egg into their body at one time, would be to have smaller eggs. Mammals face the same problem. Those which have more than one young at a time have to have smaller young; there simply is no space within the body for several large young.

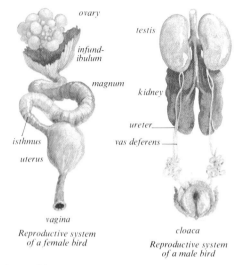

Reproductive system of a female bird

Reproductive system of a male bird

Stages of development of an egg within the female bird's body before it is laid

Ovum breaks out of ovarian follicle and is grasped by the infundibulum, where it remains $\frac{1}{4}$ hour.

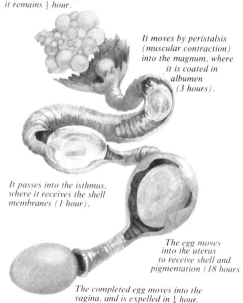

It moves by peristalsis (muscular contraction) into the magnum, where it is coated in albumen (3 hours).

It passes into the isthmus, where it receives the shell membranes (1 hour).

The egg moves into the uterus to receive shell and pigmentation (18 hours

The completed egg moves into the vagina, and is expelled in $\frac{1}{4}$ hour.

34

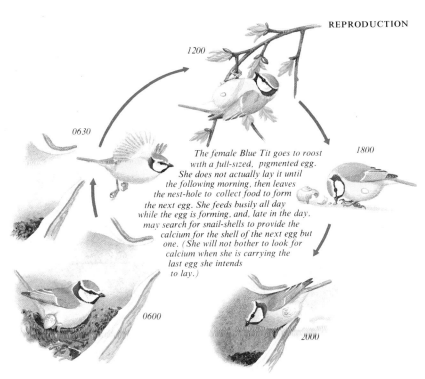

1200

0630

1800

The female Blue Tit goes to roost
with a full-sized, pigmented egg.
She does not actually lay it until
the following morning, then leaves
the nest-hole to collect food to form
the next egg. She feeds busily all day
while the egg is forming, and, late in the day,
may search for snail-shells to provide the
calcium for the shell of the next egg but
one. (She will not bother to look for
calcium when she is carrying the
last egg she intends
to lay.)

0600

2000

A day in the life of a breeding female Blue Tit

By producing their eggs sequentially, birds are able to produce several large ones. These eggs are rich in nutrients which enable the developing embryo to grow during incubation without further supplies of food. One of the reasons why the young bird attains full size so quickly is that it emerges from the egg at a relatively large size – certainly much larger than would be possible if the bird carried more than one egg at a time.

Most birds lay eggs at daily intervals, though in some larger species the interval may be longer; for example swans lay their eggs at two-day intervals and the two eggs of the Golden Eagle are laid three or four days apart. In most small birds the eggs are laid in the morning, in the tits often before the bird leaves the nest-chamber after its night's roosting. By doing this, the birds do not have to carry the load of a fully-formed egg during much of the morning. The next egg develops later in the day, and the bird goes to roost with it fully-formed. One puzzle is how the laying female manages to carry an egg without breaking it, especially during the early stages of shell-formation when the shell is very thin. At this stage, the females of some species seem to be very inactive for part of the day and this may well be to reduce the risk of breaking the shell.

Although this way of breeding is very satisfactory from the point of view of flying, it does lead to other difficulties for the bird. The parents must look after the eggs in a safe place outside the body until they hatch or, as is the case in many species, until the nestlings are ready to fly. Since the parents are unable to move the eggs around this makes the two parents, the eggs, and often the young, very vulnerable to predators during this period.

FLIGHT

LIFT AND DRAG

Flight is achieved by creating lift – an upwards force great enough to counteract the force of gravity on the bird's body. Lift is produced by the wings. When air moves over a stationary wing of an appropriate shape, the air which is deflected over the upper surface has to travel faster than the air beneath the wing, because it has further to travel in the same time. The pressure exerted by air passing over the surface of the wing is inversely proportional to the speed at which it is travelling. So, the air that passes above the wing is at a lower pressure than that beneath, and this produces lift. It may seem odd, but most of the lift produced by a wing comes from the passage of the air over the top of it and not from that which passes underneath. It is easy to demonstrate that air passing over the top of an object produces lift; if a piece of paper is held as shown in the figure, air cannot be blown over the lower surface. However, blowing just across the upper surface causes it to rise.

Several factors affect the amount of lift which is produced by a wing. One of these, clearly, is size. The larger a wing the more lift it produces. Two other factors are also important. One of these is the speed at which the air passes over the wing. The faster it does so, the greater the lift it creates. The other factor is the angle that the wing makes to the current of air. This is called the angle of attack, and the greater it is, the greater the lift it produces. This is because the greater the angle of attack, the greater the distance the air passing over the upper surface of the wing has to travel, compared with that passing under-neath, and therefore the greater the difference in pressure. However, this is only true within certain limits; it is important that the air flow remains smooth over the wing. If it becomes

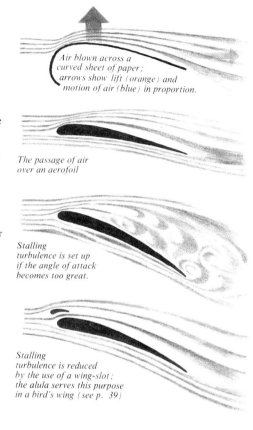

Air blown across a curved sheet of paper; arrows show lift (orange) and motion of air (blue) in proportion.

The passage of air over an aerofoil

Stalling turbulence is set up if the angle of attack becomes too great.

Stalling turbulence is reduced by the use of a wing-slot; the alula serves this purpose in a bird's wing (see p. 39)

turbulent then the lift is lost and the wing stalls. In practice many wings stall when the angle of attack reaches about 15 degrees.

Unfortunately for the bird, there is another force produced by air passing over the wing. As the air hits the wing, the wing tends to be pushed backwards; this force is called drag and this too increases with the size of the wing, the airspeed and the angle of attack.

36

GLIDING

There are two ways that a bird can glide in still air. First it can launch itself from a high perch and use the potential energy provided by gravity; its movement is comparable with that of a toboggan on a snowy slope. It can maintain its speed for as long as it is above the surface of the ground; but since it is losing height all the time, the length of time that it can stay airborne will depend on the height from which it launched itself.

The second method of gliding is the reverse of this – maintaining height by loss of speed. Such a glide can only take place when a bird has already achieved a reasonable airspeed; it is using kinetic energy. The moment the bird stops flying and starts to glide it is slowed down by drag. As it slows, it loses lift, since lift varies in proportion to airspeed. The bird can maintain its lift by increasing the angle of attack of its wings. However, this in turn increases the drag and so the bird slows down still further. It is not long before the bird has slowed down so much that it has reached stalling speed. Then it can no longer stay airborne. It may seem that such a method of gliding is not much use, but in practice birds use it regularly every day, for it is the way in which they land. By approaching a branch or other landing site in more or less level flight they can, if they judge it right, slow down to the speed at which they stall, just as they land, thereby minimising the shock on their legs.

Up to now we have been looking at the rather special case of a bird gliding in still air. Often the air is by no means still and birds have learned to use air currents to great advantage. Perhaps the most famous of all gliders are the vultures which soar high in the sky for long hours during the day. These birds have very large, broad wings and they can stay aloft because they find air which is rising. In still air a vulture would, as we have seen, slowly lose height until, eventually, it would come down to land. However, if the air is moving up-

wards, then the vulture will take longer to descend. It is as if a toboggan is descending on a hill which itself is rising. For this sort of gliding, it is important to be able to lose height as slowly as possible. The lower the rate of sink, the smaller the rate at which the air has to rise for the bird to stay airborne. This is achieved by having a low wing loading, a large surface area of wing in relation to the weight of the bird.

Vultures and many other birds spend a lot of time gliding in rising air and save themselves a great deal of energy by doing so. The most com-

A soaring vulture glides down to stall just before landing.

The wing movements of a flying bird

mon places to find rising air are above open country on a sunny day where the heat of the sun on the land causes the air to thermal upwards, and where winds are deflected upwards off mountains. Both these situations are exploited to a great extent by birds of prey and by other species such as the storks. Indeed they are so practised at using these upcurrents that they have come to depend on them during much of their migration. Most of these birds have evolved migratory routes that leave Europe for Africa round the two ends of the Mediterranean, and make short sea crossings at the Bosphorus or Gibraltar, thereby avoiding long flights over water where there are no upcurrents and where they would have to rely on flapping flight.

Other birds are also expert at making use of upcurrents; Herring Gulls and Fulmars can hang almost motionless above cliff edges, riding the air pushed upwards by an onshore wind colliding with the cliff. In mountainous areas Ravens and Alpine Choughs, amongst others, do the same. Some seabirds such as the shearwaters can make use of the air deflected off waves to help them glide and in other parts of the world the albatrosses have become greatly skilled at exploiting the changing wind speeds across the surface of the sea.

POWERED FLIGHT

Most birds have to use flapping flight in order to stay airborne. They must produce enough energy to overcome gravity and counteract their rate of sink, so that they stay aloft, and enough forwards force to overcome drag so that they can move forwards.

The flying power is produced by the downbeat of the wing. During this movement, the wing twists slightly because the wing bones are at the front of the wing and the pressure of the air against it causes it to rotate. As a result, the wing pushes the air downwards and backwards, propelling the bird in the opposite directions – upwards and forwards.

The wing-beat is in fact more complex than this. Because the bird is travelling forwards during the downbeat, the movement of the wing-tip relative to the air is not straight downwards, but angled forwards. This makes it slightly more difficult for the bird to get propulsion from the downbeat than if the beat was straight downwards. Propulsion is aided because the large feathers at the tip of the wing are, like the wing itself, supported closer to their front edge than the rear and so, again like the wing, the feather twists during the downbeat. This results in the air being pushed backwards and downwards.

The flight feathers twist under the force of the downbeat

SLOTS AND ALULA

The way in which the feathers of the wingtip separate out from each other is also important in enabling the bird to fly efficiently. On the downbeat, air pressure increases underneath the wing and decreases above it, and air tends to spill round the wingtip so as to equalise the pressure. This happens to some extent in all birds, and results in some loss of lift. One way in which the loss is reduced is by the manner in which these feathers separate; they can have the effect of smoothing the air currents across them and so minimising the loss of lift. Wing tips in which the feathers are most widely spread tend to occur in birds with very rounded wings, such as buzzards and sparrowhawks or those with very short wings such as partridges. The gaps between the feathers are modified by the shape of the feathers which may be either notched or emarginated to increase the gap. Again birds with short rounded wings tend to have more notches or emarginations than birds with long wings, for with a relatively short wing it is more important to minimise the loss of lift at the tip.

A very special device for smoothing the air flow, the alula or bastard wing, is found at the bend of the wing. This consists of a few feathers attached to a very reduced digit (p. 15). During normal flight the alula lies flush with the front of the wing and plays no important part. However, when the bird slows down and raises the angle of attack of the wing, the alula rises off the front edge of the wing to form a special slot. This smoothes the air flow over the surface of the wing, enabling the bird to increase the angle of attack beyond that at which stalling would otherwise occur. Hence a raised alula allows the bird to fly more slowly without stalling.

The wing of a Buzzard showing the alula (a) and the notched (b) and emarginated (c) primaries

39

A Guillemot comes in to land on a cliff.

TURNING

There are a number of ways in which a flying bird can turn. Any unilateral alteration of the bird's shape results in imbalance in the amount of drag on the two sides of the bird and hence leads to the body turning. This can be achieved by the bird sticking a webbed foot out to one side or turning its tail to one side; those species with elongated outer tail-feathers, such as swallows, being particularly adept at rapid turns.

Nevertheless most birds rely mainly on adjustment of wing shape for turning; anyone who has watched a tail-less swallow or martin will know that the bird can still manage well. Slight folding of one wing will reduce the surface area and hence both the drag and the lift on that wing with the result that the wing will drop slightly and move forwards, relative to the other. Equally, increasing the angle of attack of a wing will result in an increase in both lift and drag, so that wing will be slowed and lifted, relative to the other. Either, or both, of these manoeuvres will result in the bird banking.

TAKE-OFF AND LANDING

Taking-off requires a lot of energy. The bird must accelerate to normal flying speed, and gain height; both of these require more energy than normal flight.

For a small bird such as a sparrow or a thrush, the bird alters the angle of its body so that it is flying upwards and increases the wing-beat; nevertheless, taking-off does not seem to be too difficult. This is not the case for all birds however, and some species have special problems with take-off.

Because of their size (p. 43), very large birds cannot just jump into still air and fly away; they need to have a good air speed before they can easily get enough lift from their wings. There are two ways of achieving this. First, many large birds such as swans need a take-off run in order to get up sufficient speed for take off. Second, and far easier but not always possible, is for the bird to take-off into a strong headwind; the speed of the wind immediately gives the wing a high air-speed and hence valuable lift.

Many birds take off from perches

A Mute Swan lands.

A Gannet comes in to land on a cliff.

in trees or on cliffs and this provides another useful way of getting up speed: the bird simply drops off the perch, accelerating with the help of gravity. This is particularly valuable for birds such as the Guillemot which has small wings and a high wing loading and needs a high air-speed to get enough lift.

Landing is achieved by losing the lift. Ideally this is done in such a way that the bird is flying as slowly as possible at the moment of touch-down, so as to minimise the chances of injury. However, those birds which have some trouble taking-off also have certain problems with land-ing. Large birds such as swans prefer to land on water if possible since this reduces the chance of injury. They can also reduce their speed relative to the ground by coming into land upwind, allowing the wind to give them lift when their land speed is well below their normal stalling speed. Birds such as the Guillemot

also land on water, thereby reducing the shock of landing on their legs. Guillemots (and other species such as swifts) landing at their nest sites use a different technique of slowing down. They approach the site from below, rising sharply upwards at the last moment, using the force of gravity to slow them down. If all goes well, they arrive at the site moving very slowly; but the technique requires consider-able skill, especially in turbulent winds.

WING-SHAPES

The shape of birds' wings varies markedly in relation to the type of flight which the species uses. There are basically two types of gliding wing, the long thin one of the alba-trosses and fulmars, and the shorter but much broader one of the vultures. The albatross wing is better for high speed gliding over sea; being longer

A Mute Swan takes off.

and narrower it has less drag. However, it is harder for an albatross than for a vulture to turn in a small circle. The vulture's wing (p. 37) is adapted for manoeuvrability and a slow rate of sink, enabling it to stay airborne in small, weak upcurrents of air.

The gamebirds, such as the Pheasant, have small, broad wings in which the feathers separate more than in most species, each feather twisting independently of the others. With the help of large flight muscles, the Pheasant can rise more rapidly than any other bird of its size. This explosive power is only used for short flights to escape predators and the bird soon glides to earth again.

The seabirds such as the auks, which use their wings as paddles when under water, all have high wing loadings (weight in relation to wing area) and so have to fly with rapid, whirring wing beats. They also have problems with take-off and landing (see above).

In general birds which need high manoeuvrability have shortish wings, and often longish tails, enabling them to turn swiftly. For example, the sparrowhawks which hunt largely in woodland have broader wings and longer tails than the falcons which hunt in the open; they probably fly less swiftly, but they can turn more easily.

Another factor which may affect wing shape is the migratory behaviour of the bird. Many species which migrate long distances lay down large quantities of fat as fuel for the journey (p. 242). For two short, but very critical, periods of the year the birds weigh much more than for the rest of the time. For example the two species Willow Warbler and Chiffchaff are closely similar in many ways. However, the Willow Warbler migrates to central Africa, undertaking long flights across North Africa (p. 234) while the Chiffchaff goes only to southern Europe and North Africa. The Willow Warbler has a wingspan of over a centimetre more than the Chiffchaff. Is this related to its need to carry greater weight during migration?

A Pheasant takes off.

FLIGHT SPEEDS

Every bird can vary the speed at which it flies, within certain limits. The speed at which it chooses to fly depends on what it wants to do. If we drive a car very fast along a motorway, we get to our destination sooner than if we drive it more slowly. However, if we want to cover the greatest distance on a given amount of fuel, it is better to drive at a slower cruising speed. It is the same for a bird; if it needs to escape a predator or to make as many journeys as possible to its nestlings, it may pay it to fly as quickly as possible. If, however, it has to make a long migratory flight without many chances to stop and re-fuel (p. 240), it pays it to cruise at a lower speed because this gives it the greatest range on its fat reserves.

The situation is more complicated for a bird than for a car because the bird is moving through air which

The wings of Chiffchaff (left) and Willow Warbler

Hobby (a falcon)   *Male Sparrowhawk*   *Female Sparrowhawk*

itself may be moving rapidly. If a bird flew at 20 kms per hour into a head-wind of 20 km per hour, it would stay in the same place. The ideal air speed, for a bird to cover the greatest distance for a given amount of energy, varies with the force and direction of the wind; it should fly faster into a head wind and more slowly if it has a tail wind. This is not merely theory: Chaffinches have been shown to adjust their air speed in this way.

Precise measurements of airspeeds of birds are not easy to make, and many accounts are greatly exaggerated. Even a swooping Peregrine is unlikely to be travelling at more than about 180 kph.

Level cruising speeds of birds are very much slower than this, and vary with a number of features of wing shape. In general, larger birds tend to fly faster than smaller ones. A list of some cruising speeds for a range of species is given below. Note that, in spite of its reputation, the Swift flies quite slowly.

Species	cruising speed in mph	in kph
Crane	42	68
Woodpigeon	38	61
White-fronted Goose	34	54
Carrion Crow	31	50
Grey Heron	27	43
Swift	25	40
Herring Gull	24	38
Starling	21	34
Blue Tit	18	29

THE SIZE OF BIRDS

Flying birds vary in size from the Bee Hummingbird which weighs a little over 2 grams to the largest swans and bustards which may weigh as much as 15 kilograms. Different factors of scale affect both these limits of size.

The smallest sizes have to contend with the problems of heat loss, and this issue is fully discussed on pp. 224–7. The upper size limit to flying birds is set by a different factor. As a body gets bigger, volume increases faster than surface area. This means that, other things being equal, larger birds are heavier in relation to their wing areas than smaller ones. One of the important factors which affects the ability of a bird to fly is the wing loading (the weight in grams divided by the wing area in square centimetres). The increase in wing loading with size can be seen by comparing birds of different sizes: it can even be seen within species such as the Sparrowhawk and Goshawk where the males and females are different sizes; male and female Sparrowhawks have wing loadings of about 3·1 and 3·7 respectively, while male and female Goshawks have wing loadings of about 5·6 and 5·75.

A bird with a larger wing loading must either have relatively larger flight muscles than a smaller bird (so increasing still further its wing loading) or it must beat its wings faster. Either way it uses up more energy to fly than the smaller bird does. The upper limit, above which flight seems not to be practical, is some 15 kg.

43

SWIMMING

When not flying, birds move around rapidly on the land or in the water. Swimming birds have had to overcome a number of problems. In order to fly, a largish surface area of wing is necessary. However, the size of wing needed for efficient flight is too large for it to be easily flapped in water. As a result, some of the best swimming birds, the penguins, have given up flight altogether and have evolved a wing well-suited to swimming. The only other group of birds which use their wings extensively for underwater locomotion are the auks. In order to do so, they have had to compromise on wing size. They possess a small wing which they can use for beating under water; in air, this has a very high wing loading (surface area of wing divided by body weight) and has to be flapped very rapidly. The auks, especially the largest ones, are in fact quite close to the state where flight is no longer possible. Indeed, the loss of some of the wing feathers during the moult means that flying is no longer really feasible at all for Guillemot and Razorbill, and it is more efficient to become completely flightless until the wing feathers have grown again. The now-extinct Great Auk was larger than any living species of auk and was totally flightless; a bird of its size could not have flown on a wing that could be used for beating under water.

A few birds such as the scoters and Long-tailed Duck have avoided the problem of needing a small wing for swimming and a larger one for flying. They beat the folded wing under water, thus being able to offer a small surface for underwater propulsion, but a larger one for flight.

The birds that are best adapted for swimming are those that spend longish periods under water, such as the cormorants, divers, grebes, shearwaters, some ducks, some coots, and the auks. All these can submerge from the water surface without difficulty. A second group of birds feed under water, but can only easily submerge by diving from a height; this group

Little Tern

Great Auk

Razorbill

Long-tailed Duck

Gannet

44

includes the Gannet and the pelicans and terns. Many others such as the Fulmar, geese, swans, some of the ducks and the gulls spend a lot of time on the water, but do not dive regularly. Obviously only those that swim long distances under water benefit greatly by being able to use their wings under water. However, all aquatic groups depend largely on their feet for swimming, though some ducks, such as the Long-tailed, use mainly their wings while under water.

The body of a bird that swims well tends to be long, and the legs are positioned far to the back, in the same position as the propellors of a ship. This helps the streamlining of the swimming bird because the large leg muscles are tucked behind the body as opposed to being more to the sides. This is also a good position from which to steer, which is why the rudder of a boat is placed at the rear. The legs of swimming birds are usually powerful and the tarsi and toes are very flattened so that they present very little resistance to the water as they are moved forwards on the recovery stroke. On the swimming stroke the foot spreads out to produce a large surface area.

This area is greatly increased by webbing or lobing of the toes. Most swimming birds have webs between three of the toes; these include penguins, shearwaters, divers, geese, swans and ducks, auks, and the gulls

and terns. The gannets, cormorants and pelicans, which all belong to the same order, differ from the others by having three webs – all four toes are joined by webbing. A few other groups including the grebes, some of the rails (e.g. the coots) and the phalaropes have lobes on the sides of the toes rather than complete webs. Although for the coots and phalaropes, lobing might leave the toes freer for running on dry land, this cannot be the reason why grebes have lobed feet since these birds hardly ever come ashore. Other rails (e.g. the Moorhen, Water Rail) have elongated toes with broad soles, but no webbing at all. A few other species, such as the flamingos and some of the waders (e.g. the Avocet) have webs between the toes. In the case of the flamingos, they often wade out of their depth while feeding. However, with the Avocet the webs are more likely to be for support on the very watery mud in which it hunts for food, rather than to be primarily used for swimming.

The feet of various aquatic birds

Shag

Great Crested Grebe's foot on forward (right) *and backward* (left) *strokes*

Moorhen

Grebe's foot seen from the front, to show low resistance to water

Mallard

Red-necked Grebe

Swimming Mallard's leg on forward stroke

on backward stroke

RUNNING, HOPPING, WALKING, PERCHING

Two-legged animals such as birds and man need rather large feet if they are to maintain their balance easily whereas quadrupeds such as cows and horses can manage with much smaller feet. The possession of large feet enables birds to wrap their long toes securely round branches, and so perch easily.

Since their legs are placed far to the back of their bodies, many of the birds that swim well are not good walkers. Some of the diving ducks waddle rather ineffectively, and divers and grebes can hardly walk at all.

The length of the leg varies greatly between groups. The two visible sections of the leg, the tibia and the tarsus (p. 14), have to be more or less the same length, otherwise the bird could not keep its centre of gravity over its feet; it would topple over every time it tried to sit down. Birds with long legs tend to be those that live in open country and need to run well (Ostrich, Stone Curlew, bustards) or those that need to stand in water to feed (flamingos, herons and many waders).

In contrast, birds that hang upside down from the branches or small twigs of a tree while feeding need to be able to grip strongly. They also need their centre of gravity to be as close to their feet as possible; such birds have short legs. Birds which come into this category include the tits, finches and many of the smaller parrots. Birds that actually spend

their time climbing the trunks of trees do not have such short legs. They tend to hang from their splayed feet, often, as in the woodpeckers and tree-creepers, supported by stiffened tail feathers which they use as a prop. Nuthatches have a different method of climbing. They put one foot ahead of them from which they hang, and the other behind them to steady themselves; they do not use their tail for support. This method can be used equally well for climbing *down* tree-trunks, an ability unique to nut-hatches; in this case the bird hangs from the upper, rearmost foot and uses the other one to steady itself.

Pigeons and the sandgrouse (two closely-related families) have very short legs. They spend a lot of their time on the ground, but neither group can run rapidly; they depend on flight for escape. The birds with the shortest legs of all are the swifts and kingfishers. Kingfishers use their legs only for perching above the streams into which they dive for fish. Swifts, the most aerial of all birds, use them only for clinging to vertical surfaces

Tree-creeper

Nuthatch

Kingfisher

Turtle Dove

46

Fieldfare

Redpoll

Lesser Spotted Woodpecker

Greenshank

or crawling into their nest-chambers.

Most birds need to be able to tuck their legs and feet away in flight so that they do not affect the stream-lining. Usually they do this by folding their legs up and tucking them under the belly feathers, however, birds with long legs cannot do this. Species such as herons, flamingos, cranes and the longer-legged waders have to fly with their legs trailing behind.

Most birds, especially those with long legs, have problems with heat loss from their legs and feet. They cannot easily have legs which are well-insulated with a thick layer of fea-thers, for these would get too wet and sticky as the birds walked around in water and mud, and impede their movements. So their uninsulated, slender legs, and in some species the webs, are a potential source of con-siderable heat loss. Many birds spend much of their day wading or swim-ming in very cold water. Some such as the Iceland and Glaucous Gulls, the Long-tailed Duck, the scoters and some of the waders may swim or paddle in seawater that is below 0°C.

Birds have reduced this disadvan-tage in two ways. First, because there are no large muscles in the lower leg (p. 14), very little blood flows into the legs, and so the legs and feet can be kept at very low temperatures. Even so, if hot blood flowed into them it would be cooled rapidly, so wasting energy for the bird. This does not happen, thanks to a neat adaptation. The outflowing arteries subdivide into very small vessels which interweave with the inflowing veins which are similarly subdivided. Much of the heat of the warm arterial blood is transferred to the returning cold,

venous blood; so a lot of heat is conserved that would otherwise be lost if it were carried farther down the leg.

Birds which feed on the ground either hop or walk (running is a fast form of walking). Most species, indeed most families, stick to either one method or the other. The crow family is an exception; some mem-bers, such as the Raven, usually walk while others, such as the Jay, usually hop; the Magpie tends to walk if it is moving slowly, but changes to long, bounding hops when it speeds up.

Most birds that spend nearly all their time on the ground, such as waders, larks and pipits, run. Those which hop are primarily arboreal – thrushes, tits, finches, etc. When moving from branch to branch, hopping is clearly the best sort of locomotion; the bird half jumps, half flies from a perch and lands on another with both feet together. What is not clear is why such birds do not change from hopping to running when on the ground. It seems as if in some way the adaptations for hopping restrict the ability to run. It has been suggested that the ancestral mode of locomotion for the passerines (p. 59) was hopping, and that walking was a later development. The evidence for this is that in some species, such as the Raven and the Skylark, which walk when adult, the young hop for the first few days after leaving the nest.

NATURAL SELECTION

The birds we see today are of course the product of evolution. Everything we see has evolved through natural selection over the course of a very long period of time. To convey this, we have given our text an evolutionary slant and make no apologies for doing so.

There are many misconceptions about evolution, not least of which is that it is something which happened in the distant past. All the time, in all species, evolution is going on around us. Natural selection is acting on each and every generation moulding the animals and plants that we see about us. Major changes in form may take long periods of time, but as we shall see, the general appearance of birds, their breeding biology and their migratory behaviour can all change in short periods of time and are indeed doing so.

As Charles Darwin was the first to emphasise, individuals differ in many different ways, a fact that we can easily confirm by looking at the people all around us! These differences form the foundation on which natural selection acts – the survival of the fittest. In each and every generation some individuals get through to become breeding members, others perish before doing so. Although many of those that fail may do so by ill-chance, on average those which are more superior in one way or another are going to predominate and leave more offspring, who in their turn will perpetuate their superior traits.

One cannot emphasise too strongly that natural selection is a continuing process. In almost all populations, a high proportion of the young die before reaching breeding age; only a small proportion make it through to breeding.

The 'spaces' in the breeding population are hotly contested. This does not mean necessarily that the birds are in actual physical competition with each other all the time (though such direct competition does occur for certain things such as territories, mates, nesting sites and food), but rather that the individuals are each striving to survive and that, on average, the fittest will be more likely to survive than those which are less fit.

A common error is to think that a species is like it is because its characteristics are good enough for it to be able to do its job in nature; hence the species survives. There are two faults here. First, the species is not the unit on which natural selection works, it is the individual. Second, even the individuals will not prosper if its characteristics are just adequate. Almost certainly, other individuals will appear in the population which are more than adequate; these – and their offspring – will out-compete those that are merely adequate. In each generation, selection will act, favouring some individual variations over others.

A different sort of loose talk is to say that 'such-and-such a species evolved a certain adaptation'. Unlike the previous statement, this is not necessarily wrong, but does involve a certain shorthand which needs to be clearly understood. Strictly, no species evolves anything; this sounds as if some sort of pre-planning was involved, which is not the case. What actually happens is that natural selection will favour those birds which are born into a population with a particular improvement of a characteristic (such as crossed mandibles, longer legs, camouflage, or whatever) over those which are less well adapted; the former will be more likely to survive and leave offspring than the latter. This is a rather long-winded way of putting it and provided the reader is clear what lies behind the statement that 'a species evolved . . .' it is perhaps permissible to use it.

The misconception that, after all this time, animals should have fully evolved and that there is no scope for further evolution is still widespread. There are several reasons why this cannot be so. First, the environment is always changing. One obvious example concerns the Ice Ages, the last of which covered northern Europe and most of the British Isles with a massive sheet of ice only some 12,000 years ago. Since it started to recede, there have been progressive changes to our climate and the habitats. These changes had hardly ended (indeed, perhaps, had *not* ended) when man started to make his mark upon the scene. Hence for one reason or another the habitats in which the birds live have been in almost continual change; inevitably, therefore, the birds have never been able to become perfectly adapted to these habitats.

There is another reason why it is impossible for birds to evolve perfection. There are many circumstances in which more than one conflicting feature may be advantageous for a bird; in such cases, some form of compromise may be necessary. For example, a male Pheasant may get more mates if he is more brightly coloured than his rivals and has a longer tail. However, consequently he may be easier for the fox to find and catch; he is likely to have fewer seasons in which to attract mates. Some sort of balance between his attractiveness to mates and his ability to avoid predators will be required. The actual level of this compromise may vary from place to place or time to time if the risks from predation do so.

Another compromise is necessary during the breeding season. Male birds defend their territories against intruders. Yet, unless they allow a female 'intruder' to become estab-lished, they will not obtain a mate. If they are not aggressive enough, they may not breed at all. Black-headed Gulls setting up territories within their colony need to be as far away from the next pair as possible, because the neighbouring parents will rush in and eat an egg or chick if they get the chance. However, they also need to be close to their neighbours so that they can gang up and mob potential predators, such as Carrion Crows; the more birds mobbing, the more likely they are to be successful. The size of their territories is a com-promise between two conflicting needs.

One essential feature of evolution is that any characteristic on which natural selection is to act must be in-heritable. If it cannot be passed on to future generations, natural selection will not be able to operate on it. Recent studies have shown that a wide variety of characteristics may be inheritable, including body-size, egg-size, clutch-size (p. 270), laying date (p. 253) and aspects of migratory behaviour (p. 232).

Not only are such characteristics inherited, but they can change swiftly if conditions alter. We can infer that this must be true from the speed with which things must have altered since the Ice Ages; bird populations have spread perhaps 4,000 km or more northwards as the ice has retreated in the space of some 7,000–8,000 years. Within this time period, marked geographical races of many species have arisen (p. 60). It is difficult to measure such changes scientifically: although they may be swift in geo-logical terms, they are gradual in terms of the span of a human life. Nevertheless, some recent studies have shown how rapid some changes can be, as the following examples testify.

Despite more or less constant conflict among themselves, the members of a breeding colony of Black-headed Gulls will gang up to drive away a marauding Carrion Crow.

CHANGES IN SIZE AND COLOUR

The House Sparrow was introduced into North America in about 1850, being released in New York and Quebec and one or two other places. As with many successful introductions (p. 311), it spread at a great rate and is now common over much of North America, is still spreading down through Central America and has colonized several Caribbean islands. In some of these places it has been present for as many as 130 generations, but in most much less than that. Already, however, it is showing slight changes in size and coloration between some of these areas. Most interestingly, the sparrows tend to have become paler in desert areas and darker in hot humid areas, which is the same trend as one sees in other species in these habitats. Hence within this short space of time, the sparrows are showing signs of evolving local characteristics.

CHANGES IN CLUTCH-SIZE

Island populations of species tend to lay smaller clutches than those on nearby mainlands. The reason for this is not fully understood, but may be related to population densities (p. 293). The Little Owl was introduced into Britain from continental Europe in the early part of this century. At first, the birds seem to have laid clutches similar in size to those on the Continent, but after a short time, they became somewhat smaller.

A Black-tailed Godwit on its breeding-grounds on a Dutch polder

The House Sparrows introduced to the New World also show changes in clutch-size. There is a tendency for clutches to be smallest in the tropics (often only one or two eggs) and to become progressively larger the further north one goes (p. 271). The House Sparrows breeding in Costa Rica usually lay two eggs while those in Canada have larger clutches than those in the United States. Again these changes have evolved in fewer than 130 generations.

CHANGES IN BREEDING SEASONS

In the Netherlands several species of waders, including the Black-tailed Godwit, now start to breed about two weeks earlier than they did fifty years ago. The increase in agricultural mechanisation has lead to hay being cut progressively earlier and this results in the late broods being killed. Hence there has been increased selection for early nesting and the breeding season has shifted.

CHANGES IN MIGRATORY BEHAVIOUR

Migration patterns must have changed markedly since the Ice Age. In Germany it has been shown that in Blackbirds (which are partial migrants – p. 236) the proportion of migrants in the population can be related to the severity of the previous winter. Cold weather kills; migrants who have removed themselves to milder areas for the winter will return the following spring to find that the numbers of those which stayed put have been reduced. Migrants are then in the majority. However, during mild winters, the residents thrive and the dangers inherent in migration take their toll. The following spring, residents are in the majority. Since the tendency to migrate or stay for the winter is inherited, the migratory tendencies of a local population can change quite swiftly if the winter weather changes.

SPECIATION

THE NEED FOR THE TERM 'SPECIES'

Nature is a vast assemblage of animals and plants and if we are to be able to describe any one of these to another person we need some way of doing so. It is obviously easier to say 'I saw a Robin' than 'I saw a small brown bird with a red breast'; we need to be able to put names to the organisms that we see. By common consent the most convenient unit to describe has proved to be the species.

WHAT IS A SPECIES?

We all know that a Robin and a Blackbird are different species. Perhaps the best definition of a species is 'a group of actually or potentially interbreeding natural populations, which is reproductively isolated from other such populations'. No definition is fool-proof as we shall see, but this one does nevertheless provide a useful rule of thumb which covers the great majority of cases. If one views the problem from just a single place – say Europe – there is usually little difficulty. However, when one takes the wider view it may become more difficult. For example we regard the Great Tit as a species; it is obviously distinct from the Blue Tit which is a different species. However, outside Europe the Great Tit has a wide range. Birds similar to the ones we know range across Europe, through the forest belt of northern Asia. Throughout this area, a bird-watcher would immediately recognise the birds as Great Tits. East of the Caspian Sea, the green-and-yellow *P.m.major* overlaps and interbreeds with the grey-and-white *P.m.cinereus*, which in turn overlaps and interbreeds in China with the slightly more colourful *P.m.minor*. The northern extremity of *P.m.minor* in Russia overlaps with the eastern limit of *P.m.major*; the two populations live alongside one another and *do not* interbreed. An eastern Russian ornithologist might be forgiven if he saw the birds as two clearly distinct species! This kind of difficulty occurs in a number of species where at one point two forms of the same species meet, but do not interbreed: they are usually referred to as ring–species. (This circle of sub-species is complicated by *P.m.bokharensis* which ranges diagonally across, and whose interactions with its neighbours are not clearly understood.)

The breeding distributions of Blue Tit and various forms of Great Tit

Great Tit
Parus major major

Parus major
bokharensis

Blue Tit
*Parus
caeruleus*

Parus major
cinereus

Parus major
minor

There are many other situations where it is difficult to know whether one is dealing with one or more species because one cannot tell whether the two populations would interbreed if they met. One of these is where there is a population of birds breeding on one area of land and another population on an island nearby. The latter may be clearly distinct in appearance from the former, but at the same time, obviously very closely-related. Does one call them different species or not? An example of this sort of difficulty is found in the Willow Grouse, a species of gamebird that is widely distributed in northern areas of Europe and Asia where it is known to change from a basically brown summer plumage to a Ptarmigan-like white for the winter. However, on one group of offshore islands there is a bird which is clearly very similar to the Willow Grouse except that it stays in its summer-like plumage the whole year round. Should it be considered a separate species or not? In this case, the islands are the British Isles and the bird is the Red Grouse. Once described as the only species which was endemic to Britain, the Red Grouse is nowadays considered to be only a form of the Willow Grouse and not a separate species.

In the case of the grouse, the two groups of birds do not meet in the wild. Another difficulty occurs in the crows. In Scotland and other parts of Europe there are two types of crow, an all black one, the Carrion Crow, and another – with a mostly grey body – the Hooded Crow. Over most of their range in Britain (and outside it), these birds behave as two perfectly good species. However, in a belt across the middle of Scotland the ranges of these two birds overlap and there they interbreed. In this zone, there are not only large numbers of hybrids, but also descendants of the hybrids, and crosses between the hybrids and one or another of the pure forms. This hybrid zone has been present for over a century although its position has changed slightly. So, does one call the two types of bird different species, or does one, because they interbreed along a narrow belt at the edges of their ranges, consider them to be the same species? There are many cases of this sort and there is no simple objective answer; for the most part it is a matter of choice and different authors make different choices.

These are the sort of difficulties which face the person trying to decide what is and what is not a species. Why not try to make a simple

Breeding distributions of Willow Grouse and its British subspecies, the Red Grouse

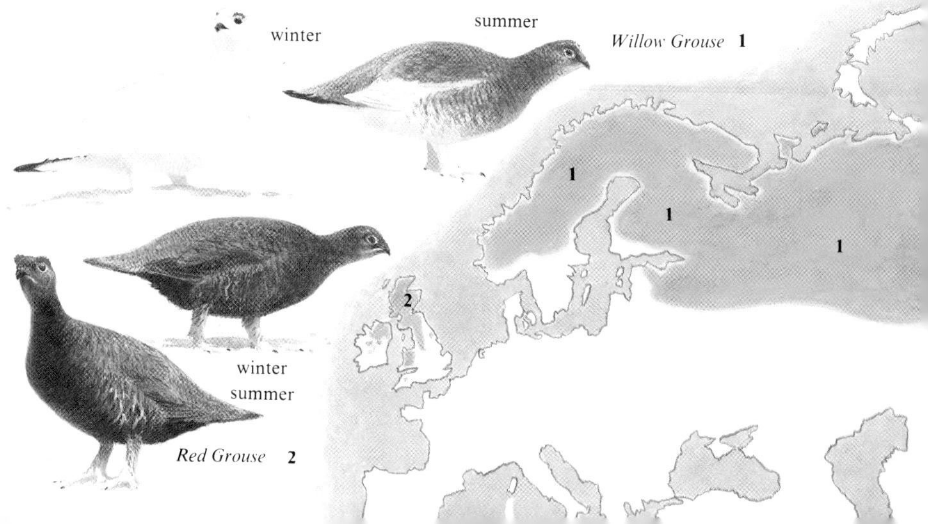

winter

summer

Willow Grouse **1**

1

1

1

2

winter
summer

Red Grouse **2**

Carrion Crow

Carrion × Hooded hybrid

Hooded Crow

such as the Willow and Red Grouse mentioned above – would or would not interbreed if they met. The only way that one could find out would be to put them together in captivity. To try to do this for all pairs of species that one wanted to know about would be an impossible task, even though this only arises where the ranges of the two species do not overlap (we say that they are allopatric). Where the ranges of species *do* naturally overlap in the wild (sympatric) we can observe that, normally, different species do not interbreed. To see why there is no simple definition of what a species is, the next section looks at how species arise.

Scaup

Scaup × Tufted Duck hybrid

Tufted Duck

Tufted Duck × Pochard hybrid

Pochard

definition of a species and then stick to it? The answer is that many people have tried to achieve this ideal and none has succeeded; all definitions have exceptions. Usually included in such definitions (as in the one given above) is some statement about the species being a set of animals which does not interbreed with any other set. This is, biologically, a very necessary feature. Unfortunately it is often not much use to the taxonomist; there are two major difficulties with it. The first is that there are far too many occasions when it is obviously not true! For example if one looks at any large wildfowl collection one will find that there are many hybrids between different species of ducks and geese, birds that are normally held to be perfectly good species. To make it even worse, such hybrids are often fertile and so there may be many intermediate forms (though note that such hybrids are much more common in captivity than they are in nature).

The second difficulty concerns how one can tell whether two populations of birds that live in different places –

HOW SPECIES EVOLVE

Species do not evolve overnight, but over very long periods of time, probably many thousands of years, so that we cannot actually see them evolving, but must deduce from their distributions and other evidence how they evolved.

For birds it is thought that new species arise only when a single species becomes divided into two by a geographical barrier. One example of the way in which this can happen is thought to have occurred during the last glaciation (Ice Age), which reached its peak around 15,000 years ago, covering vast areas of Europe and Asia with ice. This sheet of ice spread gradually southwards over many thousands of years. As it did so, the habitats moved further south as well, each dying out on its northern border as the climate became progressively colder, but spreading on its southern one. The birds that lived in these habitats were forced to move southwards at the same time. During the Ice Age most of the birds that we know in Britain today survived far further south, in refuges in the Mediterranean region or in North Africa. These species were not neces-sarily distributed in one continuous belt across areas of Africa and Asia; the lands of southern Europe, the Middle East, India and south-east Asia are separated from each other in several places by expanses of sea. Consequently, populations of many species would have been broken up into pockets in these different refuges. The most extreme of these would have been those species that survived only at the two ends of Eurasia: in south-west Europe and in south-eastern Asia. One species which may have done this is the Azure-winged Magpie and it still has a distribution of this sort. Almost inevitably, the birds in the separate areas would have changed slightly over long periods of time, becoming better adapted to their local environment. However, in most cases, as the Ice Age ended and the northern areas became habitable once more, these birds would have extended their ranges northwards once again.

As the species moved northwards and spread out across Europe and Asia, in many cases populations from different Ice Age refuges would have linked up eventually. The interesting thing is what happened then. There are two possibilities:

Breeding distributions of the two forms of Black Redstart (black-bellied and orange-bellied) and the two forms of Bluethroat (white-spotted and red-spotted), and the areas of intermingling

Marsh Warbler→

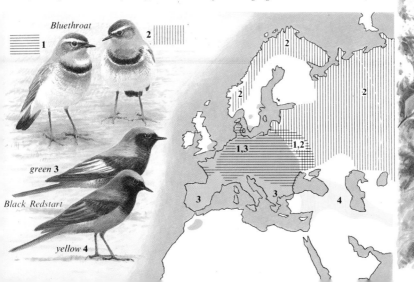

Bluethroat

1

2

green 3

Black Redstart

yellow 4

2

2

2

2

1,3

1,2

3

3

4

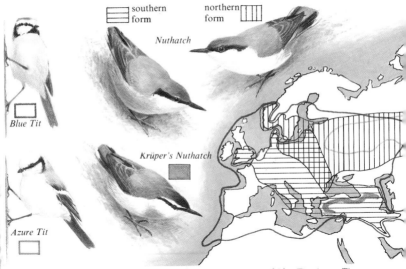

southern form
northern form

Nuthatch

Blue Tit

Krüper's Nuthatch

Azure Tit

←*The Reed Warbler occupies a different habitat from the Marsh Warbler.*

Breeding distributions of Blue Tit, Azure, Tit, two forms of the Nuthatch, and Krüper's Nuthatch

(a) They joined up, intermingled, interbred and carried on as if they had never been apart. The less they had changed during their period of separation, the more likely it would be that this would have happened. If they intermingled completely, then there is no way that we could see any signs of them having separated and come together again. However, in a few species the intermingling has been incomplete, and in these the evidence is there to see. Two such species are the Black Redstart and the Blue-throat; each of these has two forms which are clearly distinguishable in the field – except in the area of inter-mingling.

(b) They had evolved sufficient differences in their long period of isolation so that they would or could no longer interbreed. When this was the case, there were again two possibilities:

(b¹) One of the populations proved more successful than the other, and took over the area completely, so that the other failed to survive. In this case, we would be able to see no evidence that this had happened.

(b²) The two populations came to live alongside each other. In this case, we have a new species. The two

groups of birds (now separate species) will compete for the same resources (see niches p. 296) and, if they are to continue to live alongside one another, natural selection will favour the development of differences between them such as, say, the habitats they live in or the foods that they take. The Marsh and Reed Warblers provide a good example of a pair of very similar species whose ranges are also very similar, but who live in different habitats: whereas the Shag and Cormorant live in much the same habitats, but take different foods.

Thus although we cannot see evolution occurring in any one species, we can see the whole range of situations described above: species whose ranges have become sub-divided, but where the two popula-tions do not yet show any clear differentiation (Marsh Tit); species where two distinct forms have met up again and are intermingling (Nut-hatch); cases where the two forms which have met up are overlapping but not interbreeding, in other words have become different species (Blue/Azure Tit; Nuthatch/Krüper's Nuthatch); species where the two forms, which apparently arose in eastern and western refuges, have

55

Pigeon Guillemot

Horned Puffin

Black Guillemot

Puffin

now overlapped almost completely (Black and Red Kites).

Land masses create geographical barriers for seabirds in the same way that the seas do for land-birds. Hence we find similar, but different, species in different seas. Both the Puffin and the Black Guillemot have become subdivided by North America into two separate populations, one in the Atlantic and the other in the Pacific. In both cases, the forms in the two seas have become different (Horned Puffin and Pigeon Guillemot respectively).

One of the factors which is thought to influence whether or not the two groups of birds will stay separate, or interbreed and merge, is the success of the hybrids between them. Suppose, while the two populations have been apart, they have developed differences in their bill sizes to cope with foods of different size. This has happened in the Reed Bunting where there is a thin-billed and a thick-billed race. When such pairs of subspecies meet up again, each will tend to feed on that type of food to which it has become adapted. What happens to the hybrids, with medium-sized bills, becomes crucial.

One possibility is that the hybrid offspring can cope as well as those of either parent stock (or perhaps even better: they may be able to eat both ranges of food). In this case, birds which mate with the 'wrong' stock will not be selected against; indeed if the hybrid offspring are more successful than either parent, selection would favour cross-matings between the stocks. The second possibility is that the hybrid offspring are not as successful as either of their parents, perhaps because they are less competent at feeding than either of the two types. In this case any parent birds which interbreeds will leave fewer offspring than if it mated with its own stock. Whenever this happens, selection will favour those birds which do not make this mistake.

Atlantic and Pacific breeding distributions of Puffin and Horned Puffin, and of Black Guillemot and Pigeon Guillemot

Tufted Duck on fresh water

ISOLATING MECHANISMS

Whenever the hybrid offspring between two stocks are less successful than either of the parent stocks, natural selection will favour the evolution of what are called isolating mechanisms, characteristics which enable the birds to choose the right sort of mate. To start with, such isolating mechanisms may be quite small and difficult for the human eye to perceive; but in the course of time such differences tend to become exaggerated.

Almost all closely-related species have characteristics which make them quite distinct from each other. Usually we think of birds as being very different if they have strikingly different plumages (such as for example the Tufted Duck and Pochard), but to the birds it is just as useful if the differences are vocal ones. It is common among closely-related birds to find that if they look alike, their songs will be quite different (e.g. Willow Warbler and Chiffchaff; Marsh and Willow Tits).

In practice, birds probably use a number of different cues rather than just a single one. Isolating mechanisms work pretty well, and hybrids between most different species are rare. The ability to distinguish between species often breaks down to

some extent in captivity and this is one reason why one finds hybrids quite commonly in bird collections such as that of the wildfowl cited on p. 53. The number of cues which the captive birds can use – such as the types of habitat, flight displays, etc. – are reduced. In addition, many species occur together in captivity which rarely or never meet in the wild; hence there has been little or no selection for the two species to evolve isolating mechanisms. For example the Tufted Duck and Scaup look rather similar to us. However, they take up their mates in the winter flocks; in the Tufted Duck these are almost invaiably on fresh water whereas in the Scaup they are at sea. Hence the Tufted Duck has had less need to evolve isolating mechanisms from the Scaup than it has from the Pochard which occurs in the same waters.

Hence the evolution of new species comes about through a series of stages – geographical isolation, changes through time, often followed by re-meeting but not interbreeding. In the latter case there will be further changes in ecology (see evolution of niches, p. 296) which enable the two species to co-exist, accompanied by changes in songs, behaviour or appearance to reduce the chances of individuals pairing up with the wrong mates.

Scaup on the sea

NOMENCLATURE AND CLASSIFICATION

THE NAMING OF A SPECIES

Every species of animal and plant has its own scientific name. This name is unique and is based on Latin and/or Greek. The system which we use was formalised by the Swedish botanist Carl Linnaeus (1707–1778).

Linnaeus's idea was that every organism should be given a name consisting of two words that were, to some extent, descriptive. This binomial system was gradually accepted.

The full formal scientific name includes more than just the two words. For example, the full name of the Blue Tit would be written:

Parus caeruleus Linnaeus, 1758, Syst.Nat., ed.10, p. 190 – Sweden.

This tells us the name of the bird, the man who named it, the year he named it, the scientific journal where it was published, and the locality where the type specimen was collected – or the species thought to occur. (Syst. Nat. refers to *Systema Naturae*, where Linnaeus published the names of plants and animals; the 10th edition is used, since prior to that there were minor changes in the system used.)

Of the two words of the name, the first is called the generic name (see below), and the second is the specific name because it denotes that particular species. It is conventional for the genus to start with a capital letter, and for the species name to start with a lower-case letter, and that both words should be in *italics*.

Once a bird has been given a specific name, this cannot be changed except, in exceptional cases, by the International Committee for Zoological Nomenclature. This rule refers only to the specific name, not to the generic, whose function is to indicate the immediate relatives of the species

in question, all of whom have the same generic name. From time to time, detailed research may suggest that a species is more closely related to a different group of birds from that in which it is currently placed. In this case, the bird may be moved from one genus to another. This should happen less as time goes on; but it has happened a great deal in the past. For example, many of the sandpipers were once given the generic name *Tringa*. Nowadays it is recognised that there are distinct differences between these birds and the true *Tringa* (the 'shanks'); so the sandpipers are put in a separate genus *Calidris*.

Only rarely does this rigidity run into difficulty. One such instance arose when early ornithologists were sent some downy seabird chicks with the information that they were young Puffins. Dutifully, the ornithologists labelled one as *Puffinus puffinus*. Unfortunately, the young bird was later shown to be a young Manx Shearwater; the young chicks are superficially similar. The fact that the Manx Shearwater, and not the Puffin, is called *Puffinus puffinus* is somewhat confusing.

A result of this system is that somebody reading today's literature at any time in the future can be certain of which animal is meant. The local language name may have changed; but the scientific one should not have. In addition, by using the scientific names, people of all nationalities can communicate without confusion.

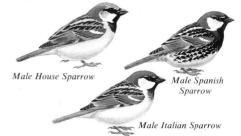

Male House Sparrow

Male Spanish Sparrow

Male Italian Sparrow

CLASSIFICATION

We have seen that the species is a very useful unit for describing animals. However, we need to have more than just one sort of unit, we need to be able to bundle up the units into groups. This has been done by producing a Classification for all Organisms. The main levels which concern birds are as follows:–

Kingdom	Animalia	(Animals)
Phylum	Chordata	(Chordates)
Class	Aves	(Birds)
Order	Passeriformes	(Passerines or Song-birds)
Family	Ploceidae	(Weavers and sparrows)
Genus	*Passer*	(Sparrows)
Species	*Passer domesticus*	(House Sparrow)

Such a classification makes order out of what would, if there were no groupings at all, just be a jumble of species. More importantly, it does not do this arbitrarily: the animals are grouped in ways which the taxonomist believes display their true relationships. All the species in the genus *Passer* (which also includes, for instance, the Tree Sparrow *Passer montanus*) are considered to be more closely related to each other than to any other birds. All the members of the family Ploceidae are thought to be more closely related to each other than to the birds in any other family; and so on.

What the taxonomist is saying is that his classification tells us something about the degree to which different groups have separated in the course of evolution; those species in one family are all descended from a common ancestor whereas those in another family will have different ancestors. The classification is some sort of image of the family tree for birds.

Taxonomists also use other subdivisions, usually groupings or subdivisions of the above list, such as Super-family or Sub-order. These are used where it is thought there is some merit in further grouping within the overall classification. For example, the Order to which the waders belong is a large and very complex group. The waders with which we are most familiar are classified in four sub-families as follows:–

Order Charadriiformes

Sub-Order Charadrii
    (There are two other sub-orders.)

Super-family Charadroidea
    (There are six other super-families.)

Family Scolopacidae
    (There are five other families.)

Sub-family Tringinae
                (curlews, etc.)

Sub-family Scolopacinae
                (Woodcock, snipe, etc.)

Sub-family Calidritinae
                (godwits, sandpipers, etc.)

Sub-family Arenariinae
                (turnstones)

Similar subdivisions are also used for species. The term super-species is sometimes used to emphasise that the members of it are still plainly very closely-related and have only recently evolved from a common ancestor. They may also be referred to as sibling species. The House, Spanish and Italian Sparrows form such a group, and produce another instance of where it is difficult to draw a line between species. Although most authors accept that the House and Spanish Sparrows are sufficiently distinct to be considered separate species, the status of the Italian Sparrow is less certain. Since there is a stable zone of interbreeding with the House Sparrow in northern Italy, it seems best to treat it as a subspecies of House Sparrow, as is done with Hooded and Carrion Crows (p. 52). However, Italian Sparrows also interbreed with Spanish Sparrows in Sicily. It is therefore difficult to produce simple, tidy nomenclature for this group of birds: the convenience of the term 'superspecies' is obvious.

SUBSPECIES

Where a species is represented by two or more distinguishable forms which in the breeding season occupy different geographical areas, these forms are given the status of subspecies or 'races'. The differences between them are usually difficult to recognise in the field, but are discernible by, say, bird-ringers when they have the birds in the hand. Such diagnosis tells us something about where a particular bird breeds. For example, some of the Wheatears which pass through Britain each autumn are markedly larger than those which breed here; these birds belong to the Greenland subspecies, birds which have already made a long flight south towards their winter quarters.

Where a species is subdivided into subspecies, these are described by adding a third name to the other two. For example, the British race of the Lesser Black-backed Gull *Larus fuscus* is different from the one that breeds in Scandinavia and they have been named *Larus fuscus graellsii* and *Larus fuscus fuscus* respectively. These long unwieldy names are only used when absolutely necessary and even then are often abbreviated. In the case of the Lesser Black-backed Gull one could often write *L. fuscus* if it was clear one was talking about a gull species, whereas if one was writing about the races of this species one might write *L. f. graellsii* and *L. f. fuscus* or even just *graellsii* and *fuscus*.

INTERPRETATION

A natural classification such as the one described here has other purposes than just to pigeon-hole nature. If it is done properly, and the relationships are correct, it enables us to make certain generalisations about birds that we do not know much about. For example, if we know something about the nesting habits of some of the finches, it is fair to guess how some of the species that we do not know will nest; the more closely they are related to the species we know the more likely we are to get it right.

Although a complete classification of a group is valuable, there are pitfalls in producing one; many of these are all too apparent. If one looks at several different bird books, we find that the orders in which the families are listed and the number of species in each family may differ. There are a number of reasons for this and the reader should be aware of them so as to make his own judgement. In some cases, we simply do not know enough about the groups to be confident of the relationships, and so groups that may not be closely-related get put together. For example, the Order Gruiformes contains the hemipodes, cranes, rails, bustards and a number of foreign families; by no means all these birds look as if they are close relatives!

The most difficult problem concerns the numbers of species. There is a widespread belief that one ought to know how many species of birds there are. In practice, as we have seen, it is often impossible to draw a hard and fast line between whether two populations of birds are of separate species, or merely sub-species of the same species.

This really should not worry us at all. If we think of evolution as a continuous process which is still going on, then all stages in the formation of new species will be present at any one moment, and there is no simple way to draw a dividing line. One should be surprised, not that there is disagreement about how many species there are, but rather that anyone should think he knows. A classification is a necessary and a valuable tool, but by its very nature it has its limitations, and we must not ask too much of it.

Part 2

THE DIRECTORY OF SPECIES

The preceding pages have explained the systems and judgements underlying the classifications of birds into groups and ultimately, within those groups, into species.

The DIRECTORY of species which now follows is ordered according to the taxonomic work of the distinguished Dutch ornithologist Prof. Karel Voous (though, for the reader's convenience, we have occasionally made slight changes to the order, so that similar species appear together on the same plate). It includes all the species which breed in Europe, plus those which visit as non-breeders in reasonable numbers, such as the arctic-breeding geese. It does not include vagrants from elsewhere, such as some of the North American waders, even though a few of these occur in most years, albeit in very small numbers.

The paintings by Norman Arlott are arranged in a manner designed to facilitate identification. But identification is often very difficult, and two-dimensional representations cannot always enable the naturalist to put a name to every bird he sees perhaps fleetingly, from an odd angle, or in bad light. It is nevertheless hoped that the inclusion of a wide coverage of the variations of plumage with sex, age and season will be of the utmost assistance in distinguishing among the great diversity of species that can be seen in Britain and Europe.

A complete key to the symbols and abbreviations used in the text can be found on the endpapers of this book.

The term 'juvenile' or 'juv.' in the plates denotes the first complete set of feathers worn by the young bird after fledging. The term 'immature' or 'imm.' denotes subsequent plumages between juvenile and full adult.

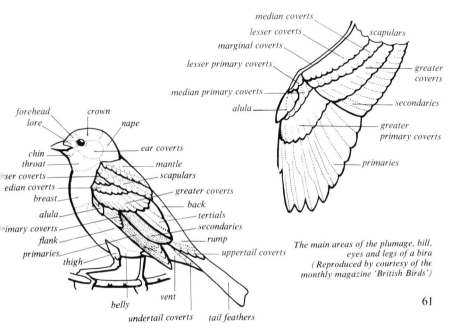

The main areas of the plumage, bill, eyes and legs of a bird (Reproduced by courtesy of the monthly magazine 'British Birds')

Order Gaviiformes

DIVERS family *Gaviidae* 5 species in the world.

A small family of largish diving birds. They have webbed toes to aid swimming and their legs are positioned far to the rear of the body. Hence they walk poorly and are rarely seen away from the water's edge. They dive from the swimming position. They fly rapidly on smallish wings.

Swimming under water p. 44; Feet and walking p. 45, 46; Hatchling p. 218; Spring moult p. 220, 223; Migration p. 237; Nest site and material p. 263–5.

● ■ **RED-THROATED DIVER** *Gavia stellata* 50–60cm. ♂ *c.* 1,750g. ♀ *c.* 1,500g. Regular breeder in north (order 4), offshore in winter (order 4). In winter like Black-throated but has finer, more up-tilted beak and back is finely spotted. VOICE goose-like 'kuk-kuk-kuk' rapidly in fast flight; song a haunting, far-carrying wail. HAB SUM freshwater lochs, some nesting on tiny pools, usually feeds at sea; WIN at sea. NEST on ground near water; shallow scrape, lined with vegetation, ♂♀. EGGS 2, greenish- or brownish-olive, spotted blackish, 75mm. BROODS 1. INC 26–28, ♀(♂). YOUNG fug, 43. ♂♀. IMM 4. AGE 2–3, 24. FOOD fish, often sand-eels.

Baby bird p. 208; Moult p. 223; Incubation p. 248.

● ■ **BLACK-THROATED DIVER** *Gavia arctica* 60–70cm. ♂ *c.* 3,500g, ♀ *c.* 2,500g. Rare breeder (order 3), offshore in winter (order 3). Straighter, slightly heavier bill than Red-throated; in winter lacks the fine speckles on the back, and often shows white patch at rear of flanks. VOICE deep 'kwok kwok'; song a mournful rising wail. HAB SUM largish freshwater lakes; WIN at sea. NEST on ground near water; shallow scrape, lined with vegetation, ♀(♂). EGGS 2, greenish- to olive-brown, spotted blackish, 85mm. BROODS 1. INC 28–30, ♀(♂). YOUNG fug, 60–65, ♂♀. IMM 4. AGE 2–3, 27, 90%. FOOD fish.

Moult p. 223; Pairing p. 259.

○ □ **GREAT NORTHERN DIVER** *Gavia immer* 70–80cm. *c.* 3,800g. Winter visitor (order 4). Though larger, similar in outline to Black-throated, but bill heavier, forehead steeper, crown darker than back. VOICE goose-like 'kwok' – similar to the other species; song a mournful wail, rising. HAB SUM freshwater lakes; WIN at sea. NEST on ground near water; shallow scrape, lined with variable amounts of vegetation, ♂♀. EGGS 2, greenish- or olive-brown, spotted blackish, 90mm. BROODS 1. INC 29–30, ♀(♂). YOUNG fug, 70–77, ♂♀. IMM 4. AGE 2–3, (8). FOOD fish.

Moult p. 223.

□ **WHITE-BILLED DIVER** *Gavia adamsii* 80–85cm. ♂ 5,750g. ♀ 4,500g. Rare vagrant. Much scarcer than Great Northern; bill yellowish-white (Great Northern's can look pale grey) and appears up-tilted because lower mandible is angled. VOICE similar to Great Northern. HAB SUM coastal lakes; WIN at sea. NEST on ground near water; shallow scrape, sometimes lined with vegetation. EGGS 2, buffish- or greenish-brown, spotted darker. 90mm. BROODS 1. INC ?, ♂♀. YOUNG fug, ?, ♂♀. IMM 4. AGE 2–3. FOOD fish.

Moult p. 223.

Order Podicipediformes

GREBES family *Podicipedidae* 19 species in the world.

More dumpy than divers and most species have relatively longer necks. Their feet are placed well to the rear of the body and they find walking difficult, so rarely stray from the water. They have lobed not webbed toes. Their nests are floating mats of vegetation, anchored to waterside plants or roots.

Vision p. 25; Swimming under water p. 44; Feet and walking p. 46; Baby bird p. 207–8; Hatchling p. 218; Spring moult p. 220; Migration p. 237; Nest design and material p. 266.

● ■ **LITTLE GREBE** *Tachybaptus ruficollis* 27cm. 100–200g. Common resident (order 5). The smallest grebe and the one with the stubbiest bill; although only rarely seen in flight, it is the only grebe without a white trailing edge on the wing. VOICE high 'whit'; song a shrill whinnying trill. HAB widespread on fresh waters, especially those rich in aquatic vegetation. NEST floating heap of vegetation anchored to reeds; roots, etc. EGGS 4–6, white when laid, becoming stained. 35–40mm. BROODS 2 (3). INC 20, ♂♀. YOUNG fug, 44–48, ♂♀. IMM 2–3. AGE 1, 13. FOOD small fish and aquatic insects.

Hatchling p. 218; Clutch weight p. 245; Multiple broods p. 250.

DIVERS

Other than divers, the only groups which dive from the water's surface are the grebes (pp. 60–63), cormorants (p. 66), diving ducks (pp. 80–87) and auks (pp. 130–133). Divers are longer, larger birds than any of these except the cormorants which have hooked beaks. Divers fly more rapidly with their head and neck outstretched and hanging slightly below the line of the body, giving a hunchbacked appearance.

Look for size and shape of bill, back plumage, and proportions of light to dark on throat, neck and flanks.

adult summer · adult winter · ad. win.

GREBES

Grebes are usually silent outside the breeding season and are rather rarely seen in flight. When flying they hold their necks outstretched and just below the line of the body. Most show conspicuous white patches in the wing.

Look for head pattern, especially amount of white on side of face.

adult summer · adult winter · nestling · ad. win.

63

● ■ **GREAT CRESTED GREBE** *Podiceps cristatus* 48cm.
750–1,200g. Common resident (order 4). The largest grebe, with
the most 'upright' look because of its long neck; in winter its
cheeks are whiter than other species' and there is a thin white line
between the eye and the dark crown. VOICE shrill barking notes;
song crowing and moaning calls. HAB SUM well-vegetated freshwater; WIN same, but also on open water and at sea. NEST floating
heap of vegetation anchored to other plants. EGGS 3–4, white,
becoming stained, 55mm. BROODS 1 (2). INC 28, ♂♀. YOUNG fug,
71–79, ♂♀. IMM 6. AGE ?, 10. FOOD fish.

Feet p. 45; Baby bird
p. 208; Moult p. 221;
Breeding season p. 253.

☐ **RED-NECKED GREBE** *Podiceps griseigena* 43cm. 700–900g.
Rare winter visitor (order 2–3). A large grebe, stockier than Great
Crested, with a black and yellow bill, greyer cheeks and much
greyer neck; black crown comes down to level of eye. VOICE high-
pitched 'kwek'; song a loud wailing or squealing. HAB SUM small
lowland waters, rich in vegetation; WIN on more open waters,
estuaries and sea. NEST anchored mass of floating vegetation. EGGS
4–5, white, becoming stained, 50mm. BROODS 1 (2). INC 22–25, ♂♀.
YOUNG fug, 72, ♂♀. IMM 6. AGE prob 2, ?. FOOD fish, crustaceans;
mainly aquatic insects in summer.

Swimming under water
p. 45.

○☐ **SLAVONIAN GREBE** *Podiceps auritus* 33cm. 375–450g.
Rare breeder (order 2), winter visitor (order 3). Largest of three
smaller grebes, very similar to Black-necked, from which distinguished by smaller, well-defined, dark cap, paler sides to face, and
straight bill. VOICE mainly silent outside breeding season; song a
squealing trill. HAB SUM shallow, well-vegetated ponds and lakes;
WIN more open waters such as reservoirs, estuaries, shallow coasts,
saltmarshes. NEST anchored pile of floating vegetation. EGGS 4–5,
white, becoming stained, 45mm. BROODS 1 (2). INC 22–25, ♂♀.
YOUNG fug, 55–60, ♂♀. IMM 6. AGE prob 2, ?. FOOD crustaceans and
aquatic insects in summer; mainly fish in winter.

○☐ **BLACK-NECKED GREBE** *Podiceps nigricollis* 30cm. 250–
350g. Rare breeder (order 2), winter visitor (order 2). See Slavonian,
than which has greyer cheeks and neck, upturned bill. VOICE soft
peeping notes; song a shrill chattering. HAB SUM shallow ponds and
lakes; WIN more open waters, including reservoirs, estuaries,
shallow coasts, saltmarshes. NEST floating mass of vegetation,
anchored to other vegetation. EGGS 3–4, white, becoming stained,
43mm. BROODS 1 (2). INC 20–22, ♂♀. YOUNG fug, ?, ♂♀. IMM 6.
AGE prob 2, ?. FOOD fish, crustaceans, insects.

Nest site p. 262.

Order Procellariiformes

SHEARWATERS family *Procellariidae* 53 species in the world.
This family contains the shearwaters, fulmars and petrels.
Relatives of the albatrosses, they are superbly adapted for life at
sea, many such as the Fulmar being able to soar for long periods.
They are, however, poor at walking on land and many, including
the shearwaters, are vulnerable to predators when they come to
land to nest; as a result most are nocturnal on land and so rarely
seen. All species lay only a single egg and have long incubation and
fledging periods.

Bill p. 17; Sex organs
p. 34; Flight p. 38;
Swimming under water
p. 44; Feet p. 45;
Hatchling p. 218; Lack
of replacement clutch
p. 250; Egg size
p. 268; Incubation and
egg chilling p. 272.

● ■ **FULMAR** *Fulmarus glacialis* 47cm. 700–900g. Common as
a breeder, and in winter, along coasts (order 6). The only white
(some northern ones grey) shearwater in Europe; gull-like, but
holds its wings much straighter in flight; usually gliding rather
than flapping, often soaring along cliffs; close-up, tube-nose conspicuous. VOICE wide range of growling and chuckling noises.
HAB SUM cliffs in breeding season; WIN at sea. NEST colonial, cliffledge; no material. EGGS 1, white, 75mm. BROODS 1. INC 52–53,
♂♀. YOUNG col, 46–50, ♂♀. IMM 0. AGE 7–9, 34, 95%. FOOD crustaceans, fish, squid, offal, carrion.

Moult p. 33; Flight
and wing shape p. 15,
38, 41–2; Migration
p. 238, 240–1; Clutch
weight p. 245; Breed-
ing season p. 249, 253;
Food for egg forma-
tion p. 246, 269;
Incubation p. 248, 272;
Egg size p. 268; Food
for young p. 275;
Survival and popula-
tions p. 285, 289–90,
292, 303.

adult summer
nestling
adult winter
ad. win.

adult summer
nestling
adult winter
ad. win.

adult summer
nestling
adult winter
ad. win.

adult summer
nestling
adult winter
ad. win.

SHEARWATERS

The shearwaters are long-winged birds mostly blackish above and white below; they skim the waves (hence shearwater) with a series of flaps followed by a bank or glide; most need considerable experience to identify. The Fulmar is the only white member of the family in Europe and is diurnal.

Look for head pattern, rump pattern, amount of white on underside; if possible size in comparison with other species.

adult
nestling
ad. blue
ad.

65

□ **CORY'S SHEARWATER** *Calonectris diomedea* 46cm. 700–800g. Vagrant, especially in autumn (order 2). The larger of the two common shearwaters in the Mediterranean, paler above and without dark 'cap'; commonly seen following fishing boats; see also Great Shearwater. VOICE silent at sea, loud wailing cries at colony. HAB SUM nests on offshore islands; WIN at sea. NEST colonial, in burrow or under rock; no material. EGGS 1, white, 70mm. BROODS 1. INC 54, ♂♀. YOUNG col, 90, ♂♀. IMM 0. AGE prob 6–7, ?. FOOD mainly fish and squid.

Incubation p. 272.

□ **GREAT SHEARWATER** *Puffinus gravis* 46cm. 800–900g. Vagrant, especially in autumn (order 3). A large shearwater from the South Atlantic, sometimes seen off western Europe in late summer and autumn; distinguished from Cory's by dark cap and white patch at base of tail (faintly present in Cory's). VOICE silent at sea. HAB open sea. NEST colonial, in burrow or under rock; no material. EGGS 1, white, 79mm. BROODS 1. INC 55, ♂♀. YOUNG col, 105, ♂♀. IMM 0. AGE ?6–7, ?. FOOD mainly fish and squid.

Migration p. 240.

□ **SOOTY SHEARWATER** *Puffinus griseus* 41cm. 400–800g. Vagrant especially in autumn (order 3–4). The only European shearwater which is dark on the underside (there is a pale band along the underwing). VOICE silent at sea. HAB another southern species which occurs off western European coasts in late summer and autumn. NEST colonial, in burrow or under rock; no material. EGGS 1, white 74mm. BROODS 1. INC 56, ♂♀. YOUNG col, 95, ♂♀. IMM 0. AGE ?5–7, 10. FOOD mainly fish.

Migration p. 240.

○■ **MANX SHEARWATER** *Puffinus puffinus* 35cm. 350–450g. Locally abundant summer visitor (order 6). In flight looks black above and white below (Mediterranean race is browner above, greyer below); unlike Cory's usually ignores ships. VOICE silent at sea, at colony a range of wild caterwauling cries. HAB SUM marine, nests on islands; WIN at sea. NEST colonial, burrow usually in soil, sometimes under rocks; no material, or small amount of vegetation. EGGS 1, white, 60mm. BROODS 1. INC 51–54, ♂♀. YOUNG col, 70, ♂♀. IMM 0. AGE 5–7, 29, 90%. FOOD fish, squid.

Parental care p. 210, 212; Migration p. 242; Pairing p. 260; Nest hole p. 265; Food for egg formation and young p. 246, 269, 275; Survival rate p. 285; Competition for nest holes p. 296; Status p. 301–2.

STORM-PETRELS family *Hydrobatidae* 20 species in the world.

Also related to the albatrosses, these are the smallest seabirds. Although more manoeuvrable on land than the shearwaters, they too only come to land after dark to avoid predation. They also only lay a single, large egg, and have long incubation and fledging periods.

Development of young p. 210, 212; Egg size p. 268; Egg colour p. 269; Incubation and egg chilling p. 272.

●□ **STORM PETREL** *Hydrobates pelagicus* 15cm. 23–29g. Locally abundant summer visitor (order ?5). Very small; black with a white rump; flutters low over the surface of the sea. VOICE silent at sea, at colony makes churring noise ending with a hiccough. HAB SUM nests on offshore islands; WIN at sea; sometimes strong onshore winds bring it close inshore. NEST colonial, in amongst boulders on storm beaches or scree, sometimes in rabbit burrows, stone walls; no material. EGGS 1, white, 28mm. BROODS 1. INC 38–50, ♂♀. YOUNG col, 56–73, ♂♀. IMM 0. AGE 4, 20. FOOD plankton, tiny fish.

Smell p. 26; Migration p. 238, 240–1; Breeding season p. 253; Nest hole p. 264–5; Egg size p. 268; Food for young p. 275; Status in Britain p. 301.

●□ **LEACH'S PETREL** *Oceanodroma leucorhoa* 20cm. 40–50g. Very local summer visitor (order ?4). Larger than Storm Petrel, with forked tail and more obvious grey mark across the wing; flight more buoyant and bounding. VOICE silent at sea; at colony high-pitched churrs and screams. HAB SUM nests on offshore islands; WIN at sea. NEST colonial, in burrow, more often in soil than Storm Petrel; no material. EGGS 1, white, 33mm. BROODS 1. INC 41–42, ♂♀. YOUNG col, 63–70, ♂♀. IMM 0. AGE 4, 24. FOOD small plankton, including fish.

STORM-PETRELS

Storm-petrels are black with white rumps, and flutter over the surface of the sea, dipping to pick up food items (they rarely alight); usually not seen close inshore unless there have been very severe gales.

Look for tail shape.

Order Peleceniformes

GANNETS family *Sulidae* 7 species in the world.
CORMORANTS family *Phalacrocoracidae* 30 species in the world.
PELICANS family *Pelecanidae* 7 species in the world.
 These are all largish, fish-eating birds, mostly marine; all obtain their prey by diving. They have webbed feet, with all four toes joined by three webs.

Bills p. 16–18; Vision p. 25; Swimming under water p. 44; Feet p. 45; Hatchling p. 218; Brood reduction strategy p. 273.

●□ **GANNET** *Sula bassana* 90cm. 2,800–3,200g. Locally common breeder (order 6); some present offshore all year (order ?4). Very large white bird with black wing tips, juveniles dark brownish grey. VOICE silent at sea except when feeding, at colony harsh clamorous honking. HAB SUM nest on offshore islands or cliffs; WIN at sea. NEST colonial, on ground or cliff ledge; seaweed and other flotsam. EGGS 1, white, becoming stained, 78mm. BROODS 1. INC 44, ♂♀. YOUNG col, 90, ♂♀. IMM 48–60. AGE 5–6, 21, 94%. FOOD fish, squid.

Diving, swimming under water p. 44–5; Plumage succession p. 219; Incubation p. 248; Territory p. 255; Pairing p. 260; Colonial nesting p. 262; Survival rate p. 285; Status in Britain and Europe p. 301–2.

●■ **CORMORANT** *Phalacrocorax carbo* 90cm. 2,000–2,500g. Widespread resident (order 4 summer, 4–5 winter). In breeding season, white throat and thigh patch, outside breeding season yellowish patch at base of bill; juvenile brown with whitish underparts. VOICE silent on sea, guttural honking and croaking noises at nest. HAB mainly coastal all year round in Britain, though on Continent many live in fresh water. NEST colonial, on cliffs or in trees; seaweed, twigs, ♂♀. EGGS 3–4, pale blue, overlaid with chalky white, 65mm. BROODS 1. INC 28–31, ♂♀. YOUNG col, 50, ♂♀. IMM 12(+). AGE 4–5, 20, 86–91%. FOOD fish.

Speciation p. 55; Migration p. 238, 240–1; Niche p. 297.

●■ **SHAG** *Phalacrocorax aristotelis* 76cm. 1,750–2,250g. Widespread resident (order 5). In summer dark green gloss and forward-pointing crest distinguish it from Cormorant, but in winter hard to separate; juvenile brown with whitish underparts. VOICE silent at sea; loud croaks, hisses if approached. HAB coastal. NEST colonial, on cliffs or rocky islets; seaweed and twigs, ♂♀. EGGS 3–4, pale blue, overlaid with chalky white, 63mm. BROODS 1. INC 30–31, ♂♀. YOUNG col, 53, ♂♀. IMM 12(+). AGE 4, 16, 84%. FOOD fish.

Bill p. 16; Feet p. 45; Speciation p. 55; Migration p. 238, 240–1; Niche p. 297.

PYGMY CORMORANT *Phalacrocorax pygmeus* 48cm. 550–850g. Easily the smallest European cormorant; also distinguished by short neck and longer tail. VOICE short, high-pitched barking notes at colony. HAB fresh water, usually reeded. NEST colonial, in trees or reed-beds; twigs and reeds. EGGS 4–6, pale blue, overlaid with chalky white, 47mm. BROODS 1. INC 27–30, ♂♀. YOUNG col, 70, ♂♀. IMM ?12. AGE ?, ?. FOOD fish.

WHITE PELICAN *Pelecanus onocrotalus* 140–180cm. 10,000–11,000g. Distinguished from Dalmatian by purer white plumage (sometimes with pinkish blush), in flight underwing shows a lot of black. VOICE deep grunts and growls. HAB large freshwater marshes and shallow coastal waters. NEST colonial, shallow scrape on ground or in dry reed-bed; little or no material. EGGS 2, chalky white, 97mm. BROODS 1. INC 30–35, ♂ ♀. YOUNG col, 65–70, ♂ ♀. IMM ? 6. AGE 3–4, ?. FOOD fish up to 600g.

Bill p. 17–18; Feet p. 45; Brood reduction strategy p. 273.

DALMATIAN PELICAN *Pelecanus crispus* 160–180cm. 10,000–12,000g. Some slightly larger than White, plumage greyer; shows almost no black in underwing. VOICE short hoarse bark. HAB as White, but also on smaller waters in hilly areas. NEST colonial, often a large pile of reeds, sticks, etc; ♀ ♂). EGGS 2–3, chalky white, 94mm. BROODS 1. INC 32, ♀ ♂). YOUNG col, 50–55, ♀ ♂). IMM ? 6. AGE 3–4, ?. FOOD fish including some up to 50cm.

Bill p. 17–18; Feet p. 45; Brood reduction strategy p. 273.

GANNETS, CORMORANTS AND PELICANS

Gannets and pelicans are large white birds which plunge into the sea from a height; cormorants dive from the surface; after fishing, the latter stand around with their wings outstretched to dry them.

For cormorants, look for crest, patches of white on face or thigh, neck and tail length; for pelicans leg colour, pattern of black on underwing.

three immature stages

adult

ad.

ad. sum.   ad. win.   juv.

immature

ad. sum.   ad. win.   juv.

immature

ad. sum.   ad. win.   juv.

immature

adult   juv.   imm.   ad.

adult   juv.   imm.   ad.

69

Order Ciconiiformes

HERONS, BITTERNS AND EGRETS family *Ardeidae* 62 species in the world.

A family of medium to largish fish-eating, primarily freshwater birds. They are long-legged and long-necked, and wade in shallow water, stabbing at their prey. They normally nest colonially in trees or reed-beds.

Fossils p. 11; Bills p. 17; Vision p. 24–5; Wading, legs p. 46–7; Copulation p. 261; Colonial nesting p. 262, 302; Solitary feeders p. 262; Brood reduction strategy p. 273; Persecution p. 302.

○□ **BITTERN** *Botaurus stellaris* 76cm. 900–1,100g. Rare local resident (order 2). Presence usually noted by call; rarely seen except in flight, a chunky brown heron with legs only just protruding beyond tail. VOICE powerful, far-carrying booming, sometimes preceded by grunting notes. HAB almost exclusively reed-beds. NEST in reed-bed; a mound of reeds, ♀. EGGS 4–6, olive-brown, sometimes lightly speckled with dark spots, 53mm. BROODS 1. INC 25–26, ♀. YOUNG col, 50–55, ♀(?—♂). IMM 0. AGE 1, 11. FOOD mainly fish, some mammals, nestling birds, etc.

Habitat drainage p. 308–9.

□ **LITTLE BITTERN** *Ixobrychus minutus* 35cm. 140–160g. Rare vagrant. Rarely seen except in flight; ♀ a small brown heron, ♂ a striking black and pinkish buff. VOICE variety of croaking noises; song a short bark. HAB dense marsh vegetation. NEST in reed-beds, shallow cup of reeds, etc. EGGS 5–6, white, 35mm. BROODS 1. INC 17–19, ♀(♂). YOUNG col, 25–30 but may clamber about reeds from 17, ♂♀. IMM 0. AGE 1, (5). FOOD small fish, amphibians, insects.

□ **NIGHT HERON** *Nycticorax nycticorax* 60cm. 55–700g. Rare vagrant (but small free-flying colony in Edinburgh Zoo). Broad-winged, striking black, white and grey; juveniles like Bittern, but base colour blacker. VOICE a deep, hoarse 'kwok'. HAB dense river-side vegetation, may sit out in trees. NEST colonial; in low trees and bushes, sometimes in reed-beds; platform of twigs and reeds. EGGS 3–5, light greenish-blue, 50mm. BROODS 1 (2). INC 21–22, ♀(♂). YOUNG col, 40–50, ♂♀. IMM 10. AGE 1–2, 21, 77%. FOOD fish, amphibians, insects.

□ **SQUACCO HERON** *Ardeola ralloides* 46cm. 250–300g. Rare vagrant. A small brownish, bittern-like heron that suddenly 'bursts' into white when it spreads its wings and takes off. VOICE usually silent, but has harsh, crow-like 'karr'. HAB wide range of marshy country; often rather skulking. NEST colonial; in reeds or bushes; reeds or twigs, ♀(♂). EGGS 4–6, pale greenish-blue, 38mm. BROODS 1. INC 22–24, ♀(♂). YOUNG col, 45, ♂♀. IMM 0+. AGE ?1, ?. FOOD small fish, amphibians, insects.

□ **CATTLE EGRET** *Bubulcus ibis* 51cm. 300–400g. Rare vagrant. Small white egret with yellow bill; legs reddish in breeding season, otherwise greenish; in breeding plumage has buff plumes among the white. VOICE croaks and grunts. HAB often away from water, especially in fields with cattle and horses. NEST colonial; often in trees, may be away from water; twigs, reeds, etc., ♀(♂). EGGS 4–5, pale greenish-blue, 38mm. BROODS 1 (2). INC 22–26, ♂♀. YOUNG col, 30, ♂♀. IMM 0. AGE 2, 15, 75%. FOOD largely insects, often those flushed by cows, etc.

□ **LITTLE EGRET** *Egretta garzetta* 56cm. 450–550g. Rare vagrant. A small white egret with black bill, and black legs with yellow feet; there is a very rare form which is almost black all over. VOICE 'cark'; song a bubbling gargling sound. HAB shallow marshes and open ditches; commonly feeds out in the open. NEST colonial; in bushes or trees; twigs, ♂♀. EGGS 3–5, pale greenish-blue, 47mm. BROODS 1. INC 21–22, ♂♀. YOUNG col, 40–45, ♂♀. IMM 0. AGE 1, 9. FOOD small fish and other animals, many aquatic insects.

HERONS, BITTERS AND EGRETS

Herons, bitters and egrets are distinctively shaped, with long
stabbing beaks. They have fairly broad, rounded wings and fly
with a slow wing-beat, keeping their necks folded back (see crane
p. 107, storks p. 71) and their legs extended behind them.
In egrets look for bill and leg colour.

adult

adult

imm.

ad. ♂

ad. ♀

ad. ♂

ad. ♀

adult

imm.

adult

adult

imm.

juv.

adult

imm.

ad.

adult summer

immature

ad. sum.

ad. sum.

immature

adult

71

☐ **GREAT WHITE HERON** *Egretta alba* 90cm. 950–1,600g. Rare vagrant. The only large white egret; the same size as Grey Heron; blackish legs and feet, bill black with yellow base or almost all yellow (out of breeding season). VOICE a range of croaks and grunts, but mainly silent away from colony. HAB lakes and rivers. NEST colonial, usually in reed-beds, very large; thin twigs and/or reeds. ♂♀. EGGS 3–5, pale blue, 62mm. BROODS 1. INC 25–26, ♂♀. YOUNG col, 42, ♂♀. IMM 0. AGE ?2, 23, 75%. FOOD mainly fish, but in dry season will turn to lizards, small mammals, etc.

●■ **GREY HERON** *Ardea cinerea* 90cm. 1,600–2,000g. Widespread resident (order 4 summer, 5 winter). The common large heron; back and wings grey, underparts pale, whitish; in flight black flight feathers contrast with grey back and inner wing. VOICE harsh 'fraank'; wide range of croaks and gargles at colony. HAB wide ranges of water margins, at times away from water. NEST colonial; usually in tall trees, but exceptionally reed-beds or on ground; twigs; ♀(♂). EGGS 4–5, light blue, 60mm. BROODS 1. INC 25–26, ♂♀. YOUNG col, 50, ♂♀. IMM 10–12. AGE 2, 25, 70%. FOOD mainly fish, but also water-voles, moles, etc.

Air speed p. 43; Migration p. 237; Clutch weight p. 245; Breeding season p. 252; Populations p. 287–8, 293; Solitary fishing p. 293.

☐ **PURPLE HERON** *Ardea purpurea* 80cm. 600–1,200g. Rare vagrant. Black crown, rufous neck and chest; back darker grey than Grey Heron and in flight contrast between flight feathers and the rest of upperparts not marked. VOICE similar to Grey, but higher-pitched. HAB more skulking than Grey, usually in reed-beds or thicker cover. NEST colonial; usually in reed-beds; reeds, ♂♀. EGGS 4–5, pale blue, 56mm. BROODS 1. INC 26, ♀(♂). YOUNG col, 45–50, ♂♀. IMM 10–12. AGE 1, 25. FOOD mainly fish, though some aquatic insects, etc.

STORKS family *Ciconiidae* 17 species in the world.
Storks are very large birds which stand upright, looking rather like heavily built herons. Both European species migrate to Africa for the winter.

Bones p. 12–13; Use of thermals p. 38.

☐ **WHITE STORK** *Ciconia ciconia* 102cm. 3,000–3,500g. Rare vagrant. A large white bird with black wings, red legs and bill. VOICE usually silent except for loud bill-clappering at nest. HAB marshes and wet open ground, often near people. NEST some colonial; high in tree or, more often, on building; large twigs, ♂♀. EGGS 3–5, white, 73mm. BROODS 1. INC 33–34, ♂♀ (latter more often at night). YOUNG col, 58–64, ♂♀. IMM 10–12. AGE 4, 26, 79%. FOOD many amphibians, small mammals; in drier areas large grasshoppers, etc.

Migration p. 238–9, 243; Incubation p. 248; Survival rate p. 285; Populations p. 289; Habitat drainage p. 308.

☐ **BLACK STORK** *Ciconia nigra* 97cm. *c.* 3,000g. Very rare vagrant. A large glossy black bird with white underparts, red legs and bill. VOICE bill-clappering combined with hoarse rasping notes. very variable. HAB wet meadows, marshes; often wet glades in forest. NEST high in tree; twigs, ♂♀; nest may be used for many years, becoming gradually bigger. EGGS 3–5, white, 66mm. BROODS 1. INC 35–36, ♂♀. YOUNG col, 63–71, ♂♀. IMM 10–12. AGE 3, 18. FOOD mainly fish, also amphibians, large insects.

IBISES AND SPOONBILLS family *Threskiornithidae* 31 species in the world.
Largish, long-legged and long-necked. Spoonbills have broad tips to their bills; ibises have decurved bills. Both feed by passing their open bill through the water and snapping it shut on prey.

☐ **GLOSSY IBIS** *Plegadis falcinellus* 56cm. 500–800g. Rare vagrant. Usually looks black; the only large heron-like bird with a strongly decurved bill. VOICE usually silent, may make croaking or grunting noises. HAB shallow marshes, wet meadows. NEST colonial; in trees or reed-beds; twigs, ♂♀. EGGS 3–4, blue, 52mm. BROODS 1. INC 21, ♀(♂). YOUNG col, 45–50 but may wander from nest much earlier, ♂♀. IMM 10–12. AGE ?, 20. FOOD mainly insects, worms.

STORKS

Storks fly with legs and neck outstretched, like cranes, but unlike herons. Often, their legs seem to be slightly below the level of the body in flight. Adults of both European species have bright red bills and legs, though the juveniles do not.

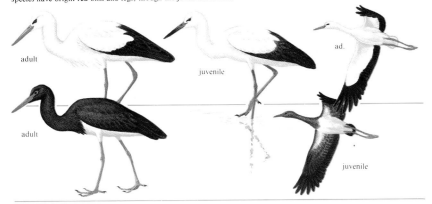

IBISES AND SPOONBILLS

Both ibises and spoonbills fly with their necks outstretched, unlike herons, but like cranes and storks.
  Look for bill shape.

73

SPOONBILL *Platalea leucorodia* 86cm. 1,200–1,700g. Rare vagrant. Large, white, heron-like, with broad, spoon-shaped tip to bill; immature has black wing tips. VOICE normally silent, may grunt. HAB shallow wetlands. NEST colonial; in trees or reed-beds; reeds and twigs, ♂♀. EGGS 3–5, white, sometimes with darker blotches, 67mm. BROODS 1. INC 24–25, ♂♀. YOUNG col, 45–50, ♂♀. IMM 12–24. AGE 3–4, 28. FOOD insects, small fish, etc.

Bill and sense of touch p. 17, 27.

FLAMINGOS family *Phoenicopteridae* 4 species in the world. Flamingos form a distinctive group, thought possibly to be the link between the storks and the ducks. They filter tiny food particles from the water by pumping water into the mouth and sieving the items off onto bristles along the edges of the mandibles from where they lick up the food with their tongues.

Fossils p. 11; Bill p. 17–18; Crop milk p. 18, 276–7; Pink colour p. 31; Feet, wading and legs p. 45–7.

☐ **GREATER FLAMINGO** *Phoenicopterus ruber* 125–150cm (♀ smaller). 2,500–3,500g. Rare vagrant (most seen are probably escapes from captivity). Unmistakeable; tall, pale pink and black birds with bill sharply turned down at tip. VOICE goose-like honkings. HAB shallow salt lagoons. NEST colonial; on ground, usually on low islands; cone-shaped dome of mud, ♀(♂). EGGS 1, white, becoming stained, 89mm. BROODS 1. INC 28–31, ♂♀. YOUNG semifug, in nest for about 10 days, then run around, 70–75, ♂♀. IMM 24–36. AGE 6 or more, many must live much longer. FOOD small invertebrates and plants filtered from the water.

Baby bird p. 208; Crèche p. 210; Incubation p. 248; Copulation p. 261; Nest material p. 267; Survival rate p. 285; Status in Europe p. 302; New habitat p. 311.

Order Anseriformes

SWANS, GEESE AND DUCKS family *Anatidae* 151 species in the world.
An important, widespread group of birds. All have webbed feet and most swim strongly, some spend almost all their lives on the water. Almost all have a moult in which the flight feathers are shed simultaneously, leaving them flightless until they have grown a new set.
SWANS genus *Cygnus* 6 species in the world.

Gizzard p. 18; Grazing p. 19; Voice p. 22; Feathers p. 30; Interval between eggs p. 35, 269; Landing and taking-off p. 40–1; Feet and swimming

p. 45; Baby bird p. 207; Parental care p. 214; Copulation p. 261; Nest material p. 265–7; Egg size p. 268; Conservation p. 301.

● ■ **MUTE SWAN** *Cygnus olor* 152cm. ♂ 12,000g. ♀ 10,000g. Widespread resident (order 4 summer, 5 winter). The only widespread swan; orange bill; wings make a singing noise in flight. VOICE various quiet grunts and hisses. HAB most freshwater lakes and rivers; some on brackish or salt water. NEST rarely colonial; on bank or in reed-bed; mound of reeds and other vegetation, ♂♀. EGGS 5–8, pale greenish-white, 115mm. BROODS 1. INC 34–38, ♀. YOUNG fug, 120–150, ♂♀. IMM 12. AGE 3–4, 20·0, 80–95%. FOOD aquatic vegetation, grass.

Baby bird p. 208; Parental care, young, first breeding p. 214–17, 274; Moult p. 219, 222; Migration p. 237; Clutch, incubation p. 245, 248; Territory p. 258–9; Pair p. 282; Survival p. 285; Arrival Britain p. 312.

■ **BEWICK'S SWAN** *Cygnus columbianus* 122cm. ♂ 6,500g. ♀ 5,700g. Winter visitor (order 4). The smaller of the two swans which are mostly winter visitors, a higher forehead and smaller bill. VOICE musical crooning and honking notes. HAB SUM marshy tundra; WIN freshwater marshes, open fields. NEST on ground close to fresh water; mound of vegetation, ♀. EGGS 3–5, off-white, 102mm. BROODS 1. INC 29–30, ♀. YOUNG fug, 40–45, ♂♀, cared for through winter by parents. IMM 12. AGE 3–4, 22. FOOD grass and aquatic vegetation.

☐ **WHOOPER SWAN** *Cygnus cygnus* 152cm. ♂ 10,000–11,000g, ♀ 8,000–9,000g. Very rare breeder (order 0–1); winter visitor (order 4). As large as Mute, but with long, black-tipped yellow bill. VOICE noisiest of the three swans; loud bugling and whooping calls. HAB SUM northern swamps, marshy tundra; WIN lakes, marshes and grassy fields. NEST on ground on island or near water; mound of vegetation, ♂♀. EGGS 5–6, off-white, 113mm. BROODS 1. INC 35, ♀. YOUNG fug, 78–96, ♂♀. IMM 12. AGE 4, (8). FOOD aquatic vegetation and grass.

Voice p. 22.

ad. sum.

imm.

ad. win.

FLAMINGOS

Flamingos' bright pink colour – especially obvious in flight – and the bill shape, make them quite unmistakeable. At great range they are still identifiable in flight by the very long legs and neck, the neck hanging slightly below the level of the body.

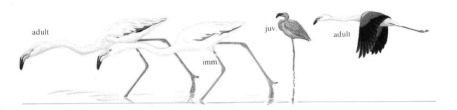

adult

imm.

juv.

adult

SWANS

The largest members of the waterfowl family; most are pure white when adult. Sexes are similar in appearance, though males are larger than females.

Swans' large size and white colour makes them almost unmistakeable. All fly with the neck stretched out.

Note calls and bill colour.

ad. ♂

ad. ♀

imm.

juv.

juv. 'Polish'

ad.

adult

juvenile

adult

adult

juvenile

adult

75

GEESE genera *Anser, Branta* 14 species in the world.
A group of largish birds, mostly black, dark brown or grey in colour. Many migrate long distances, breeding in the high arctic and wintering in more temperate areas. Many are grazing birds feeding on grasslands, though some eat aquatic vegetation; some have benefited from the feeding available on agricultural land. The European species are usually divided into the 'grey' geese (*Anser*) and the 'black' geese (*Branta*). Sexes similar in appearance.

Fossils p. 11; Bills p. 17; Digestive system p. 19; Grazing p. 19; Smell p. 26; Hybridisation p. 53, 57; Flightless in moult p. 222; Fat stores

p. 229; Migration p. 237; Breeding season p. 249; Pairing, pair bond p. 255, 259, 282; Incubation p. 272; Conservation p. 304; Tundra p. 306.

☐ **BEAN GOOSE** *Anser fabalis* 75cm. ♂ 2,600–3,200g, ♀ 2,300–2,800g. Winter visitor (order 3). Large grey goose with orange-yellow on bill and legs. VOICE quieter than most geese, makes rather deep 'bow-wow' call. HAB SUM arctic rivers and lakes, in forested and tundra areas; WIN grassy fields. NEST shallow scrape on ground; lined with moss, etc. and down from ♀. ♀. EGGS 4–6, creamy, 84mm. BROODS 1. INC 27–29, ♀. YOUNG fug, 56, ♂♀. IMM 0. AGE 3 (2), (8). FOOD grass, spilled grain, etc.

■ **PINK-FOOTED GOOSE** *Anser brachyrhynchus* 70cm. ♂ 2,500–2,700g, ♀ 2,000–2,500g. Winter visitor (order 5). Very similar to Bean, which has browner back; Pink-foot also has pink on bill and legs, not orange. VOICE louder than Bean, harsh high honking notes. HAB SUM open arctic tundra and rocky country; WIN farmland and (less) saltmarsh. NEST colonial or semi-colonial; shallow scrape on ground, lined with moss and down from ♀. ♀. EGGS 3–5, cream, 80mm. BROODS 1. INC 26–27, ♀. YOUNG fug, 56, ♂♀. IMM 0. AGE 3 (2), 22, 74%. FOOD in summer grass and aquatic vegetation; in winter mainly on farmland, grass, grain, potatoes.

Breeding season p. 248–9.

■ **WHITE-FRONTED GOOSE** *Anser albifrons* 70cm. ♂ 2,100–2,500, ♀ 1,900–2,200g. Winter visitor (order 4). Bill pink or orange; white forehead and variable amount of black barring on under-parts (both lacking in immatures). VOICE higher than other grey geese, more of a cackle. HAB SUM arctic tundra; WIN wet grassy fields and estuaries. NEST colonial; shallow scrape on ground, lined with vegetation and down from ♀. ♀. EGGS 5–6, cream, 80mm. BROODS 1. INC 27–28, ♀. YOUNG fug, 40–43, ♂♀. IMM 12. AGE 3, 18, 72%. FOOD wide range of vegetation, especially grass in winter.

Migration p. 239–41.

☐ **LESSER WHITE-FRONTED GOOSE** *Anser erythropus* 60cm. ♂ 1,800–2,000g, ♀ 1,400–1,800g. Very rare winter visitor. Difficult to tell from White-front: smaller, white on forehead extends further up, wing tips extend beyond tail. VOICE higher pitch and faster than White-front. HAB SUM bushy, arctic tundra; WIN grassland. NEST shallow scrape on ground, lined with vegetation and down from ♀. ♀. EGGS 4–6, cream, 77mm. BROODS 1. INC 25–28, ♀. YOUNG fug, 35–40, ♂♀. IMM 12. AGE 3 (2), ?. FOOD in summer a variety of vegetation; in winter mainly grasses.

○■ **GREYLAG GOOSE** *Anser anser* 80cm. ♂ 3,400–3,700g, ♀ 2,900–3,100g. Local resident (order 3), but situation very confused; probably only a few hundred wild pairs in Scotland, but widespread breeding elsewhere from feral stock; also winter visitor (order 5). Large, heavy, pink legs, orange bill; in flight pale grey front edge to wing. VOICE loud cackling as in farmyard geese. HAB SUM marshes, lakes; WIN farmland. NEST some colonial or semi-colonial; shallow scrape on ground; little lining, ♀. EGGS 4–6, cream, 85mm. BROODS 1. INC 27–28, ♀. YOUNG fug, 50–60, ♂♀. IMM 0. AGE 3 (2), 17, 77%. FOOD wide range of plant material.

Habitat drainage p. 308.

☐ **RED-BREASTED GOOSE** *Branta ruficollis* 55cm. ♂ 1,200–1,500g, ♀ 1,000–1,200g. Very rare winter visitor. Very small, immediately recognisable by its reddish-chestnut throat and breast. VOICE a shrill double cackle or squeal. HAB SUM tundra/scrub; WIN farmland. NEST colonial or semi-colonial, near river banks, low cliffs; shallow scrape, lined with grass and down from ♀. ♀. EGGS 4–5, off-white, 71mm. BROODS 1. INC 25, ♀. YOUNG fug, *c.* 40, ♂♀. IMM 0. AGE 2, ?. FOOD grasses.

GEESE

Geese are large, often noisy birds which live in large flocks; they often fly in 'V' formation. The black geese are usually fairly easy to identify; each has a distinctive black-and-white (and red, in one species) patterning of the head. Some grey geese are much more difficult and require good views or experience with the calls.

In grey geese, look for beak and leg colour. In black geese, look for face pattern.

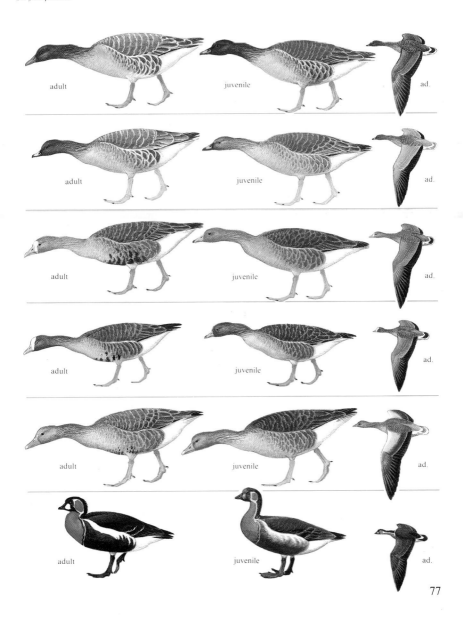

adult   juvenile   ad.

adult   juvenile   ad.

adult   juvenile   ad.

adult   juvenile   ad.

adult   juvenile   ad.

adult   juvenile   ad.

■ **BARNACLE GOOSE** *Branta leucopsis* 63cm. ♂ 1,600–2,000g, ♀ 1,500–1,800g. Local winter visitor (order 5). The only 'black' goose with a completely white face. VOICE rapid notes, sound rather like bark of small dog. HAB SUM arctic tundra; WIN grassland close to sea, saltmarsh. NEST colonial or semi-colonial; scrape on ground; lined with down from ♀. ♀. EGGS 4–5, cream, 76mm. BROODS 1. INC 24–25, ♀. YOUNG fug, 40–45, ♂♀. IMM 0. AGE 3 (2), 23, 90–92%. FOOD grasses.

Breeding season p. 249.

■ **BRENT GOOSE** *Branta bernicia* 58cm. ♂ 1,400–1,600g, ♀ 1,300–1,500g. Local winter visitor (order 5). All-black head; white collar round front of throat (absent in immatures); two forms, dark-bellied breeds n. Asia, pale-bellied breeds Spitzbergen, Greenland. VOICE soft, growling 'rrott'; large flocks may be noisy. HAB SUM arctic tundra, close to sea; WIN shallow estuaries and saltmarshes, grassy fields near sea. NEST colonial; shallow scrape on ground, lined with vegetation and down from ♀. ♀. EGGS 3–5, cream, 70mm. BROODS 1. INC 24–26, ♀. YOUNG fug, 40, ♂♀. IMM 12. AGE 2–3, 13+, 86%. FOOD grass, especially eel-grass *Zostera*.

Breeding season p. 249.

●■ **CANADA GOOSE** *Branta canadensis* 95cm. ♂ 4,700–5,000g, ♀ 4,300–4,500g. Widespread resident (order 4–5 summer, 5 winter), introduced and increasing rapidly. The largest black goose and the only one which breeds south of arctic circle. VOICE loud, nasal 'a-honk'. HAB wide range of freshwater lakes and rivers and nearby farmland. NEST colonial; scrape on ground, lined with quantities of down from ♀. ♀. EGGS 5–6, cream, 86mm. BROODS 1. INC 28–30, ♀. YOUNG fug, 40–48, ♂♀. IMM 0. AGE 3, 24, 78%. FOOD plant material, mainly grass and spilt grain from fields, but also aquatic vegetation.

Interval between eggs p. 269; Introduction to Britain p. 312.

SHELDGEESE genera *Tadorna, Alopochen* and others 16 species in the world.
Largish, somewhat goose-like ducks. The sexes are fairly similar in appearance. The birds spend some of their time on land where they can run extremely swiftly. Some conceal their nests in holes.

Hatchling p. 218; Flightless in moult p. 222.

○□ **EGYPTIAN GOOSE** *Alopochen aegyptiacus* 70cm. ♂ 1,900–2,250g, ♀ 1,500–1,800g. Local resident (order 2–3 summer, 3 winter), introduced. Longer-necked and longer-legged than Shelduck, pink bill and legs. VOICE low-pitched 'kek-kek'. HAB mostly on lakes in Norfolk, but also on rivers. NEST in large holes in trees or deeply buried in thick vegetation; usually only a little lining. EGGS 8–9, cream, 70mm. BROODS 1. INC 28–30, ♀. YOUNG fug, 70–75, ♂♀. IMM 12. AGE 1–2, (6). FOOD grass, leaves.

Introduction to Britain p. 312.

●■ **SHELDUCK** *Tadorna tadorna* 61cm. ♂1,100–1,450g, ♀ 850–1,250g. Widespread resident (order 5). A largely white bird with glossy green head and chestnut breast-band. VOICE ♂ makes wide range of whistles, ♀ rapid quacking notes. HAB shallow coasts and estuaries. NEST usually in rabbit burrows, lined with down from ♀. ♀. EGGS 8–10, cream, 66mm. BROODS 1. INC 29–31, ♀. YOUNG fug, 45–50, ♂♀. IMM 12. AGE 2, 16, 80%. FOOD mainly invertebrates, especially small molluscs and crustaceans.

Moult migration p. 240; Food for egg formation p. 246.

□ **RUDDY SHELDUCK** *Tadorna ferruginea* 64cm. ♂ 1,200–1,500g, ♀ 900–1,250g. Rare vagrant, a few escapes may breed. Deep orange-brown or buff-brown, with paler head; large white wing patch in flight. VOICE nasal honks and more musical trumpetings. HAB fresh water, but often on bank away from water. NEST in holes in trees, among rocks, in burrows; little lining. EGGS 8–9, cream, 67mm. BROODS 1. INC 28–29, ♀. YOUNG fug, 55, ♂♀. IMM 0. AGE ?2, ?. FOOD omnivorous: leaves, seeds, crustaceans and other invertebrates, etc.

adult
juvenile
ad.

adult light-bellied
juv. light
adult dark-bellied
juvenile dark-bellied
ad. light

adult
juvenile
ad.

SHELDGEESE

The three species treated here are all fairly distinctive. Each is distinctively coloured and has a striking wing pattern including a large area of white on the forewing and dark, blackish tips to the wings.

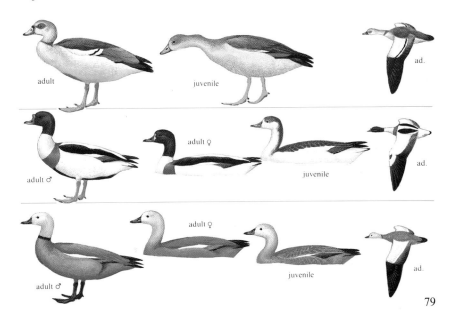

adult
juvenile
ad.

adult ♂
adult ♀
juvenile
ad.

adult ♂
adult ♀
juvenile
ad.

DUCKS genera *Anas, Aythya* among others 110 species in the world.

The ducks are the most numerous group of the Order; they are divided into several different tribes. The eiders (which together with the sawbills, Long-tailed Duck and scoters all belong to the same tribe) are mostly sea-ducks, feeding on animals such as molluscs; the 'sawbills' (genus *Mergus*) have saw-edged bills and are fish-eaters. The important tribes are dabbling ducks (e.g. genus *Anas*) which are primarily vegetarian, and diving ducks (e.g. genus *Aythya*) which are primarily animal feeders.

Flight muscles p. 15; Bills, p. 16–17; Grazing p. 19; Smell p. 26; Touch p. 27; Down p. 29; Swimming under water p. 44; Walking p. 46; Hybridisation p. 53, 57; Nest site p. 208, 264; Hatchling p. 218;

Seasonal plumages and moult p. 220, 222–3; Fat stores p. 229; Migration p. 237–8; Pairing and display p. 255, 259–60; Egg size p. 268; Habitat drainage p. 308, 311; New Habitat p. 311.

○□ **MANDARIN DUCK** *Aix galericulata* 43cm. ♂ 500–700g, ♀ 400–600g. Local resident (order 3–4). introduced. Drake unmistakeable, gaudy, with flowing crest and orange crescent 'sails' standing up on back (these are tertial feathers); ♀ small, grey, streaky sides, white eye ring and fine white line running back behind eye. VOICE high note, likened to Coot (p. 107). HAB wooded lakes and rivers. NEST in hole in tree, lined with down from ♀. EGGS 9–12, cream, 49mm. BROODS 1. INC 28–30, ♀. YOUNG fug, 40–45, ♀. IMM 3. AGE 1, ?. FOOD mainly leaves and seeds, also some insects.

Introduction to Britain p. 312.

○■ **WIGEON** *Anas penelope* 46cm. ♂ 700–900g, ♀ 500–850g. Breeds (order 3), but mainly winter visitor (order 6). Drake chestnut head with buff crown stripe, inner wing largely white in flight; ♀ smaller than Mallard with higher forehead, smaller bill, inner wing palish grey in flight. VOICE ♂ has almost disyllabic whistling 'whee-oo', ♀ a quiet growl. HAB SUM lakes and marshes; WIN estuaries and inland marshes, and nearby grassy fields. NEST on ground in cover near fresh water, often on islands, lined with down from ♀ and some vegetation, ♀. EGGS 8–9, cream, 54mm. BROODS 1. INC 24–25, ♀. YOUNG fug, 40–45, ♀. IMM 3. AGE 1, 18, 53%. FOOD leaves, grasses and roots.

Grazing p. 18–19.

○■ **GADWALL** *Anas strepera* 51cm. ♂ 700–900g, ♀ 650–850g. Widespread, but not common breeder (order 3); winter visitor (order 4). Drake grey with black rear end, shows white patch in speculum in flight and at rest; ♀ much like small Mallard, but also shows white patch in wing (not always easy to see at rest). VOICE ♂ a deep croak; ♀ quiet quacking, higher than Mallard. HAB wide range of freshwater habitats. NEST on ground in thick vegetation by water, lined with leaves and down from ♀, ♀. EGGS 8–12, cream, 54mm. BROODS 1. INC 24–26, ♀. YOUNG fug, 45–50, ♀. IMM 2. AGE 1, 13. FOOD mainly freshwater vegetation.

●■ **TEAL** *Anas crecca* 35cm. 250–400g. Local breeder (order 4), winter visitor (order 5). The smallest common duck: ♂ chestnut head with green stripe back from eye, cream undertail; ♀ like small ♀ Mallard, black and green speculum, pale belly. VOICE ♂ melodious double whistle; ♀ high-pitched harsh 'quack'. HAB wide range of streams and marshes, in winter shallow fresh waters and estuaries. NEST on ground in thick vegetation near water, lined with vegetation and down from ♀, ♀. EGGS 8–11, cream, 46mm. BROODS 1. INC 21–23, ♀. YOUNG fug, 25–30, ♀. IMM 3. AGE 1, 16, up to 61%. FOOD mainly vegetable, including seeds; some invertebrates.

Speculum and plumage p. 31; Copulation p. 261.

●■ **MALLARD** *Anas platyrhynchos* 58cm. 850–1,400g. Abundant resident (order 6). The largest inland duck, common almost everywhere; ♂ has bright green head, yellow bill; ♀ brown with purple speculum; many colour varieties in towns as a result of hybridisation with domestic ducks. VOICE familiar 'quack'. HAB almost all waters, mainly fresh, but some on sea in winter. NEST usually concealed on ground, sometimes up trees, on top of buildings; lined with wide range of materials and down from ♀, ♀. EGGS 9–13, creamy to greenish, 57mm. BROODS 1. INC 27–28, ♀. YOUNG fug, 50–60, ♀. IMM 3. AGE 1 (2), 29, 52%. FOOD wide range of vegetable matter and invertebrates.

Respiration p. 20; Feet and swimming p. 45; Nest site p. 208; Survival of young p. 214; Feeding rates p. 228; Clutch weight p. 245; Incubation p. 248; Breeding season p. 253; Territory p. 256; Copulation p. 261; New habitat p. 311.

DUCKS

It is useful to note whether ducks dive regularly or not, since this helps to narrow the possibilities; also, the diving ducks are very rarely seen on land except at the nest. Identification of drakes is for the most part easy, since each is distinctively coloured. Their mates, however, are often quite difficult to identify because they tend to look alike. Often the ducks can be identified by the drakes with whom they keep company.

Look for face marks, signs of crests, and details of wing bars.

After breeding, the males of many species of duck adopt a special, short-term 'eclipse' plumage of dull coloration, before moulting again into their winter plumage (see p. 222–3).

○ ■ **PINTAIL** *Anas acuta* ♂ 66cm, ♀ 56cm. ♂ 750–1,050g. ♀ 600–850g. Rare breeder (order 2); common winter visitor (order 5). Drake long, pointed tail, long neck with brown head; ♀ difficult, bit slimmer and longer necked than Wigeon or Gadwall. VOICE ♂ has quiet whistle; ♀ growling quacks. HAB SUM lakes and marshes; WIN mainly coastal, but widespread inland in small numbers. NEST concealed on ground; vegetation and down from ♀, ♀. EGGS 7–9, creamy to greenish, 54mm. BROODS 1. INC 22–24, ♀. YOUNG fug, 40–45, ♀. IMM 3. AGE 1 (2), 27, 52%. FOOD wide range of vegetable matter, including seeds, also some worms, crustaceans, etc.

Sense of touch in bill p. 27.

○ **GARGANEY** *Anas querquedula* 38cm. 300–440g. Uncommon summer visitor (order 2). Almost as small as Teal; ♂ striking whitish eyestripe and pale blue-grey inner wing in flight; ♀ like Teal, but paler, and whitish throat. VOICE ♂ has rattling notes; ♀ quacks. HAB shallow freshwater marshes, etc. NEST concealed in long grass on ground; plant material and down from ♀, ♀. EGGS 8–11, creamy, 45mm. BROODS 1. INC 21–23, ♀. YOUNG fug, 35–40, ♀. IMM 3. AGE 1, 20. FOOD plant and animal material.

○ ■ **SHOVELER** *Anas clypeata* 51cm. 500–700g. Breeder (order 3); winter visitor (order 4). Distinctive shovel-shaped bill; ♂ chestnut flanks and white breast, ♀ green speculum, pale blue-grey inner wing in flight. VOICE ♂ a quiet 'chook-chook', ♀ a quack. HAB SUM wet, marshy meadows; WIN more open marshes, mostly on fresh water. NEST concealed on ground near water; vegetation and down from ♀, ♀. EGGS 9–11, buffy-white to greenish, 52mm. BROODS 1. INC 22–23, ♀. YOUNG fug, 40–45. IMM 3. AGE 1, 21, 56%. FOOD mainly sieves tiny seeds and animals from water.

Bill p. 16.

MARBLED DUCK *Marmaronetta angustirostris* 41cm. ♂ 500–600g, ♀ 400–550g. Pale, mottled duck with dark patch through eye, sexes similar. VOICE quiet croaks and quacks. HAB fresh water, often close to cover. NEST on ground deep in vegetation; plant material and down from ♀, ♀. EGGS 7–14, cream to buffish, 46mm. BROODS 1. INC 25–27, ♀. YOUNG fug, ?, ♀. IMM 3. AGE 1, ?. FOOD probably chiefly vegetable, but some invertebrates.

□ **RED-CRESTED POCHARD** *Netta rufina* 56cm. 1,000–1,300g. Rare vagrant (order 2, but many likely to be escapes); rarely breeds. Drake has rich chestnut head, feathers slightly raised, pink bill; ♀ has pale cheeks below a dark crown. VOICE usually silent, but has a hoarse 'kat'. HAB vegetated freshwater lakes. NEST concealed on ground in vegetation; lined with vegetation and down from ♀, ♀. EGGS 8–11, creamy to pale green, 58mm. BROODS 1. INC 26–28, ♀. YOUNG fug, 45–50, ♀. IMM 3. AGE 1 (2), (7). FOOD mainly aquatic vegetation.

○ ■ **POCHARD** *Aythya ferina* 46cm. 700–1,100g. Widespread breeder (order 3), common winter visitor (order 5). Both sexes have large, pale, indistinct wing bar; ♂ black breast and rump, grey on back, pale grey on sides, head chestnut; ♀ lighter on back than Scaup or Tufted. VOICE occasional deep growls and wheezes. HAB SUM reedy freshwater lakes; WIN more open waters including reservoirs. NEST on ground near water or in reed bed; dense mat of vegetation and down from ♀, ♀. EGGS 8–10, pale greenish, 61mm. BROODS 1. INC 25, ♀. YOUNG fug, 50–55, ♀. IMM 3. AGE 1 (2), 10. FOOD aquatic plants; also small molluscs, crustaceans.

Hybridisation p. 53; Isolating mechanism p. 57; New habitat p. 311.

□ **FERRUGINOUS DUCK** *Aythya nyroca* 41cm. 650–800g. Rare vagrant (order 1). Drake deep chestnut-mahogany, ♀ similar to Tufted; both sexes have bright white under-tail coverts. VOICE ♂ a quiet 'chuck-chuck'; ♀ more drawn-out notes. HAB SUM vegetated freshwater lakes and marshes; WIN more open waters. NEST concealed on ground in vegetation by water's edge; vegetation, down from ♀, ♀. EGGS 8–10, pale buff, 52mm. BROODS 1. INC 25–27, ♀. YOUNG fug, 55–60, ♀. IMM 3. AGE 1, (8). FOOD mainly aquatic plants; some insects and other invertebrates.

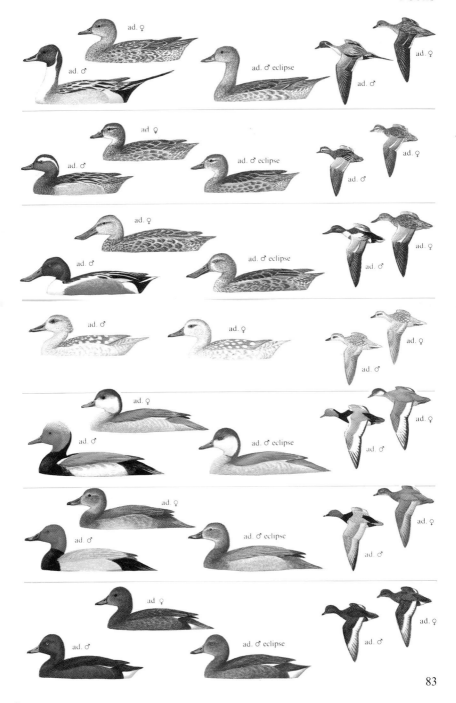

● ■ **TUFTED DUCK** *Aythya fuligula* 43cm. 550–900g. Widespread breeder (order 4), common winter visitor (order 5). Drake glossy black with white sides, crest; ♀ mainly brown with smaller crest; both have white wing bar. VOICE ♂ soft whistles, ♀ growls. HAB SUM mainly freshwater lakes and ponds; WIN many move onto larger open waters, including reservoirs. NEST well-hidden on ground near water; lined with vegetation and down from ♀, ♀. EGGS 8–11, palish, green tinge, 58mm. BROODS 1. INC 25, ♀. YOUNG fug, 45–50, ♀. IMM 3. AGE 1, 15, 54%. FOOD some aquatic vegetation, many small molluscs, other invertebrates.

Bill p. 17; Hybridisation p. 53; Isolating mechanism p. 57; Clutch weight p. 245; Breeding season p. 253; Territory p. 256; New habitat p. 311.

○ ■ **SCAUP** *Aythya marila* 48cm. 700–1,100g. Breeds sporadically Scotland (order 0–1); winter visitor (order 4). Almost always on sea; ♂ similar to Tufted, but grey back, green not purple gloss on head, no crest; ♀ like Tufted, but without crest and with white round base of bill (some Tufted have a trace). VOICE usually silent. ♂ has quiet croon, ♀ harsher 'kacks'. HAB SUM freshwater lakes; WIN almost exclusively marine. NEST concealed on ground; lined with vegetation and down from ♀, ♀. EGGS 8–11, greenish, pale, 63mm. INC 26–28, ♀. YOUNG fug, 40–45, ♀(♂). IMM 3. AGE 1–2, 13, 48%. FOOD invertebrates, esp. molluscs; some veg.

Hybridisation p. 53; Isolating mechanism p. 57.

● ■ **EIDER** *Somateria mollissima* 58cm. 1,200–2,800g. Common resident in north (order 5). Almost exclusively marine; ♂ striking black and white, ♀ uniform dark brown, heavily built with very flat head profile. VOICE ♂ has crooning song, ♀ a short 'gurr'. HAB coastal, into estuaries in some places. NEST sometimes colonial; hollow among rocks under driftwood, etc., usually within a few hundred metres of sea; lined with 'eider-down' from ♀, ♀. EGGS 4–6, pale greenish-grey. BROODS 1. INC 25–28, ♀. YOUNG fug, 65–75, ♀. IMM ♀ 3, ♂ up to 36. AGE 2–3, 18, 80%. FOOD animal, especially molluscs.

Bill p. 18; Breeding season p. 250; Display p. 259; Parental care and crèches p. 275.

□ **KING EIDER** *Somateria spectabilis* 56cm. 1,500–1,800g. Rare vagrant. Drake has white front, rest black, orange forehead and red bill; ♀ like Eider, but with smaller bill, steeper forehead. VOICE ♂ resonant crooning notes; ♀ similar to Eider. HAB SUM freshwater tundra pools; WIN coastal seas. NEST shallow hollow on ground; lined with down from ♀, ♀. EGGS 4–5, light olive. BROODS 1. INC 22–24, ♂. YOUNG fug, ?, ♀. IMM ♀ 3, ♂ longer. AGE 3, (6). FOOD animal, especially molluscs.

□ **STELLER'S EIDER** *Polysticta stelleri* 46cm. 700–950g. Rare vagrant. Drake has white head, black and white upperparts, chestnut underparts; ♀ like Eider, but smaller, darker, with white-edged blue speculum. VOICE similar crooning to Eider; ♀ has quiet growl. HAB SUM freshwater tundra pools; WIN coastal seas. NEST hollow on ground; lined with vegetation and down from ♀, ♀. EGGS 6–8, pale olive-green, 61mm. BROODS 1. INC ?, ♀. YOUNG fug, ?, ♀. IMM 3. AGE 3. ?. FOOD animal, especially molluscs and crustaceans.

□ **HARLEQUIN DUCK** *Histrionicus histrionicus* 43cm. 500–700g. Rare vagrant. Almost confined to Iceland in our area; ♂ unique in white, chestnut and blue; ♀ brown, lighter on flanks, with three pale spots on face. VOICE ♂ whistles quietly, ♀ croaks. HAB SUM fast-flowing streams and rivers; WIN coastal. NEST concealed on ground near to river; mainly lined with down from ♀, ♀. EGGS 5–7, cream to pale buff, 58mm. BROODS 1. INC 27–29, ♀. YOUNG fug, 60–70, ♀. IMM 3–9. AGE 1, ?. FOOD almost all animal: insects in summer, marine invertebrates in winter.

■ **LONG-TAILED DUCK** *Clangula hyemalis* ♂ 53cm, ♀ 41cm. 600–900g. Winter visitor, mainly to north (order 4–5). Drake is striking black and white duck (black front in breeding season); ♀ greyish white and brown with sooty cheek mark. VOICE ♂ has range of yodelling calls; ♀ deeper barks. HAB SUM arctic tundra pools; WIN mainly at sea. NEST concealed hollow on ground; lined with some vegetation and down from ♀, ♀. EGGS 6–9, creamy yellow, 54mm. BROODS 1. INC 24–29, ♀. YOUNG fug, 35–40, ♀. IMM 3. AGE 2, ?, 72%. FOOD mainly animal, especially crustaceans and molluscs; many insects in summer.

Swimming under water p. 44–5; Heat loss from legs p. 47.

ad. ♀

ad. ♂

ad. ♂ eclipse

ad. ♀

ad. ♂

ad. ♀

ad. ♂

ad. ♂ eclipse

ad. ♀

ad. ♂

ad. ♀

ad. ♂

ad. ♂ eclipse

ad. ♀

ad. ♂

ad. ♂

ad. ♀

ad. ♂ eclipse

ad. ♀

ad. ♂

ad. ♂

ad. ♀

ad. ♂ eclipse

ad. ♀

ad. ♂

ad. ♂

ad. ♀

ad. ♂ eclipse

ad. ♀

ad. ♂

ad. ♂ win.

ad. ♂ win.

ad. ♂ sum.

ad. ♂ sum.

ad. ♀ sum.

ad. ♀ win.

85

○■ **COMMON SCOTER** *Melanitta nigra* 48cm. ♂ 1,300–1,450g, ♀ 1,200–1,300g. Rare breeder (order 3), winter visitor (order 5). Drake is only all-black duck, has orange saddle on bill; ♀ dark brown with pale sides to face (see Red-crested Pochard). VOICE ♂ repeated, musical piping notes; ♀ growls. HAB SUM freshwater lakes on tundra or moorland; WIN almost exclusively marine. NEST concealed hollow on ground; lined mainly with down from ♀, ♀. EGGS 6–8, creamy to buff, 65mm. BROODS 1. INC 30–31, ♀. YOUNG fug, 45–50, ♀. IMM 3. AGE 2–3, 16, 77%. FOOD mainly insects in summer; mainly molluscs in winter.

Swimming under water p. 44–5; Heat loss from legs p. 47.

■ **VELVET SCOTER** *Melanitta fusca* 56cm. ♂ 1,200–2,000g, ♀ 1,100–1,250g. Winter visitor (order 4). White wing-bar present in both sexes; ♂ an otherwise all black duck; ♀ dark brown with pale patches on sides of face. VOICE ♂ whistles, ♀ growls. HAB SUM freshwater lakes or offshore islets; WIN almost exclusively marine. NEST concealed hollow on ground; lined with vegetation and down from ♀, ♀. EGGS 7–9, cream to buff, 71mm. BROODS 1. INC 27–28, ♀. YOUNG fug, 50–55, ♀. IMM 3. AGE 2 (3), 13. FOOD on freshwater, insects; otherwise marine invertebrates, especially molluscs.

Swimming under water p. 44–5; Heat loss from legs p. 47.

□ **BARROW'S GOLDENEYE** *Bucephala islandica* 53cm. ♂ 1,150–1,300g, ♀ 700–950g. In our area almost exclusively Icelandic; ♂ differs from Goldeneye in having glossy purple head, less white on wing and much larger white mark in front of eye; ♀ very difficult to tell from Goldeneye, but has shaggier head feathers and more peaked forehead. VOICE usually silent; ♂ has 'kaaa' when courting. HAB freshwater lakes and rivers. NEST in holes amongst rocks; lined with down from ♀, ♀. EGGS 8–11, bluish-green, 62mm. BROODS 1. INC 28–30, ♀. YOUNG fug, ?, ♀. IMM 3. AGE 2, ?. FOOD small aquatic invertebrates.

○■ **GOLDENEYE** *Bucephala clangula* 46cm. ♂ 820–1,150g, ♀ 600 900g. Rare breeder (order 2); winter visitor (order 4). Drake striking black and white with glossy green head; ♀ greyish with rich brown head, white collar and white wing patch. VOICE usually silent; ♂ has double note 'zeee-zeee', rather nasal; ♀ hoarser notes. HAB SUM freshwater lakes; WIN more on coastal waters. NEST in hole, usually in tree (uses nestboxes readily); lined with down from ♀, ♀. EGGS 8–11, bluish-green, 59mm. BROODS 1. INC 29–30, ♀. YOUNG fug, 57–66, ♀. IMM 3. AGE 2, 17, 63%. FOOD aquatic invertebrates, crustaceans, molluscs, insects.

Pairing and territory p. 255.

□ **SMEW** *Mergus albellus* 41cm. ♂ 600–800g, ♀ 500–650g. Winter visitor (order 2). Small; ♂ largely white with a few black markings; ♀ grey with chestnut cap, white cheeks. VOICE usually silent; low 'kurr-rick'; whistles. HAB SUM wooded, freshwater lakes; WIN more open waters, including reservoirs, sheltered sea bays, estuaries. NEST hole in tree; lined with down from ♀, ♀. EGGS 7–9, buffy cream, 52mm. BROODS 1. INC 26–28, ♀. YOUNG fug, ?, ♀. IMM 3. AGE ?2, ?. FOOD mainly small fish, more insects in summer.

Bill p. 16–17.

●■ **RED-BREASTED MERGANSER** *Mergus serrator* 55cm. 1,000–1,250g. Widespread breeder (order 4), winter visitor (order 4). Drake similar to Goosander, but with shaggy crest, brown breast band, grey flanks; ♀ browner on back, and neck colours merge. VOICE croaks and 'carr's. HAB SUM by lakes and rivers; WIN mainly marine. NEST deeply concealed in thick vegetation or rocks, rarely in tree-hole; lined with down from ♀, ♀. EGGS 8–11, greenish or buffish, 66mm. BROODS 1. INC 31–32, ♀. YOUNG fug, 60–65, ♀. IMM 3. AGE 2, 9. FOOD mainly fish.

Bill p. 17.

●■ **GOOSANDER** *Mergus merganser* 62cm. ♂ 1,550–1,650g, ♀ 1,050–1,250g. Widespread breeder (order 3–4); winter visitor (order 4). Larger than the Merganser; ♂ whiter than Merganser with slightly shaggy head feathers, but no crest; ♀ greyer on back, neck colours sharply distinct. VOICE usually silent, but in courtship ♂ has ringing double note, ♀ a variety of 'kerr's and 'karr's. HAB SUM freshwater lakes and rivers; WIN tends to stay on fresh water, unlike Merganser. NEST in hole, often in tree; lined with down, ♀. EGGS 7–12, creamy, 66mm. BROODS 1. INC 30–34, ♀. YOUNG fug, 60–70, ♀. IMM 3. AGE 2, 10, 60%. FOOD mainly fish.

Bill p. 17; Egg-tooth p. 205.

adult ♂   adult ♀   ad. ♂   ad. ♀

adult ♂   adult ♀   ad. ♂   ad. ♀

adult ♂   adult ♀   ad. ♂   ad. ♀

adult ♂   adult ♀   ad. ♂   ad. ♀

adult ♂   adult ♀   ad. ♂   ad. ♀

adult ♂   adult ♀   ad. ♂   ad. ♀

adult ♂   adult ♀   ad. ♂   ad. ♀

○□ **RUDDY DUCK** *Oxyura jamaicensis* 41cm. ♂ 550–800g. ♀ 350–650g. Introduced to Britain; now local resident (order 3). Drake rich chestnut with white face, blue bill, often swims with long tail cocked up; ♀ like White-headed, but less heavy bill; ranges do not overlap. VOICE mostly silent, quiet croaks and chuckles. HAB fresh water, especially lakes and reservoirs. NEST floating mass of vegetation, anchored to reeds, etc., ♀. EGGS 6–10, buff-white, 63mm. BROODS 1. INC 25–26, ♀. YOUNG fug, 50–55, ♀♂. IMM 3. AGE 2 (1), ?. FOOD wide range: plants, seeds, insects.

Introduction to Britain p. 312.

WHITE-HEADED DUCK *Oxyura leucocephala* 46cm. 700–900g. Swollen base to bill (which is blue in summer), long cocked tail; ♂ white face, chestnut breast; ♀ white line across face. VOICE usually silent, has ticks and purrs. HAB vegetated fresh or brackish lakes. NEST floating mat of vegetation anchored to reeds, etc., ♀. EGGS 5–10, white, 66mm. BROODS 1. INC 25–26, ♀. YOUNG fug, 60–70, ♀. IMM 3. AGE ?1, ?. FOOD primarily aquatic vegetation, some invertebrates.

Order Accipitriformes

VULTURES, EAGLES, BUZZARDS, etc. family *Accipitridae* 211 species in the world
This important Order contains all the birds of prey except the falcons and the New World vultures. However, they are all large, take several years to mature, and are very difficult to age.

Fossils p. 11; Moult p. 32–3; Soaring and wing shape p. 37–8, 41–2; Carrion feeding p. 230; Conservation p. 302–3.

VULTURES genera *Gypaetus, Neophron, Gyps* and *Aegypius* 14 species in the world
A group of mostly very large birds with unfeathered heads and necks. They are some of the most outstanding soaring birds, being able to stay aloft without flapping their wings for very long periods of time.

LAMMERGEIER *Gypaetus barbatus* 110cm. 5,000–7,000g. Very large; narrower wings than Griffon and Black Vultures, with a longer, tapering tail. VOICE usually silent; thin screams and whistles. HAB extensive mountain ranges. NEST sheltered ledge or cave; twigs and small branches, ♂♀. EGGS 1–2, whitish, blotched and stained brown and yellow, 86mm. BROODS 1. INC 55–60, ♀(♂). YOUNG col, 100–110, ♂♀. IMM 36+. AGE 5 or more, ?. FOOD meat scavenged from animal corpses, contents of bones (which it breaks by dropping them on rocks).

Incubation p. 248, 272; Breeding season p. 253.

EGYPTIAN VULTURE *Neophron percnopterus* 62cm. 1,600–2,200g. Adults yellowish-white, often looking grubby; wings longish with black flight feathers; yellow shaggy head. VOICE rarely vocal, has hisses and mews. HAB wide range from mountains to close to villages. NEST in small cleft or cave in rocks; twigs, ♂♀. EGGS 2, dirty white, mottled and stained. BROODS 1. INC 42, ♂♀. YOUNG col, 90–95, ♂♀. IMM 36+. AGE 4–5, ?. FOOD carrion; often feeds at rubbish dumps.

GRIFFON VULTURE *Gyps fulvus* 100cm. ♂ 7,500–10,500g, ♀ 8,000–11,000g. Very large, broad-winged; light brown body contrasts with very dark wing feathers, white head and ruff; often seen circling in groups. VOICE croaks, grunts and hisses. HAB mountainous areas, but comes down to plains especially to feed. NEST can be colonial, in rock ledges, caves; twigs, ♂♀. EGGS 1, whitish, sometimes speckled darker, 92mm. BROODS 1. INC 52, ♂♀. YOUNG col, 110–115, ♂♀. IMM 12. AGE 5–6, ?. FOOD carrion from large carcasses.

Moult p. 33; Flight p. 37; Clutch weight p. 245; Incubation p. 248, 272.

BLACK VULTURE *Aegypius monachus* 104cm. 7,000–12,500g. Very large, all-dark vulture with very broad wings. VOICE usually silent; can make hisses or grunts. HAB open woodland, forested hills. NEST often in tree; re-used regularly; twigs, ♂♀. EGGS 1, whitish, variably blotched with browns, 90mm. BROODS 1. INC 50–55, ♂♀. YOUNG col, 100–120, ♂♀. IMM 12–24. AGE ?5–6, (6). FOOD carrion from dead animals.

Declining population p. 302.

ad. ♀

ad. ♂ sum.

ad. ♂ eclipse

ad. ♀

ad. ♂ sum.

ad. ♀

ad. ♂ sum.

ad. ♂ eclipse

ad. ♀

ad. ♂ sum.

VULTURES

Vultures rely on thermals of warm air to glide so they are rarely on the wing until the day has warmed up. They often soar in circles for long periods. The commonest, the Griffon, is often seen in groups.

Look for wing and tail shape.

Flying birds are seen from below.

OSPREY family *Pandionidae* 1 species in the world.
The Osprey is specially adapted to catching fish, with bare legs and roughened feet for holding slippery prey. It has a wide distribution, being common throughout much of the Old World and North America. It is a migrant, leaving the cooler northern areas for warmer climates in the winter. Some lay eggs so heavily spotted that the ground colour is barely visible.

○ **OSPREY** *Pandion haliaetus* 55cm. ♂ 1,200–1,750g, ♀ 1,200–2,050g. Rare summer visitor (order 2). Usually close to water into which it dives spectacularly for food; long angled wings, white body, underwing and head, with dark band back from eye. VOICE loud yelps and whistling 'pew-pew-pew'. HAB near water, often with large trees. NEST on top of large tree; twigs, ♂♀. EGGS 2–3, white or creamy, heavily blotched with dark browns, 62mm. BROODS 1. INC 37, ♀(♂). YOUNG col, 44–59, ♂♀. IMM 6. AGE 2–3, 32, 81·5%. FOOD almost exclusively fish.

Breeding season p. 250.

EAGLES family *Accipitridae*: genera *Haliaeetus*, *Circaetus*, *Aquila* and others.
These are mostly medium-large or very large birds of prey with broad wings and shortish tails. Technically, they are not in a single taxonomic unit, since the White-tailed Eagle and the Short-toed Eagle are not thought to be closely related to each other, nor to the other eagles listed here. However, they are all large, and easily confused; so they are placed together here. The female of most species are larger than the males.

Vision p. 24; Pairing p. 261; Conservation p. 302–3.

○□ **WHITE-TAILED EAGLE** *Haliaeetus albicilla* 70–90cm. ♂ 3,100–5,500g, ♀ 4,100–7,000g. Re-introduced, now rare resident (order 1). Very large, heavily-built eagle with deep bill, wedge-shaped tail white in adults and not square-ended. VOICE wide range of yelps and yaps, loud and far-carrying. HAB rocky shore or inland waters. NEST in large tree or on cliff; twigs, ♂♀. EGGS 2, dull white, becoming stained, 76mm. BROODS 1. INC 36–42, ♀(♂). YOUNG col, 70–75, ♂♀. IMM 60+. AGE 5–6, 20, 70%. FOOD wide range, including fish, many seabirds, carrion.

Re-introduction to Britain p. 314.

SHORT-TOED EAGLE *Circaetus gallicus* 66cm. ♂ 1,100–2,000g. ♀ 1,300–2,300g. Osprey-size; the only large bird of prey to hover frequently; white underparts (black on some). VOICE high squealing, and musical fluty notes often descending in pitch. HAB wide range of open country from rocky hillsides to coastal plains. NEST usually in top of tree; twigs, ♂♀. EGGS 1, white, 73mm. BROODS 1. INC 45–47, ♀(♂). YOUNG col, 70–75, ♂♀. IMM 0. AGE 3–4, 18. FOOD mainly reptiles, especially snakes.

Territory p. 254; Declining population p. 302.

LESSER SPOTTED EAGLE *Aquila pomarina* 64cm. 1,200–1,750g. Very similar to Spotted, only slightly smaller; tail broadens more obviously from narrower base than Spotted. VOICE high-pitched 'kyeep' and barking notes. HAB mixed forest and open country, often near water. NEST high in large tree; twigs, ♂♀. EGGS 2, whitish, spotted brown, 63mm. BROODS 1. INC 38–41, ♀. YOUNG col, 50–58, ♂♀. IMM 48+. AGE 4–6, 17. FOOD mainly mammals.

SPOTTED EAGLE *Aquila clanga* 70cm. ♂ 1,650–1,950g, ♀ 1,750–2,500g. Very similar to Lesser Spotted, but has more spots, and looks slightly less uniform black; in flight wings are broader than Lesser Spotted. VOICE shrill barking calls, deeper than Lesser Spotted. HAB open forest, usually near water. NEST in large tree; twigs, ♂♀. EGGS 2, greyish-white, unmarked or with brown splotches, 67mm. BROODS 1. INC 42–44, ♀. YOUNG col, 63–77, ♂♀. IMM 48+. AGE 4–6, ?. FOOD wide range, medium to small mammals, birds, carrion.

OSPREY

The Osprey is usually found in the vicinity of water; often perched in a tree alongside a river or lake, or flying slowly over the water.
Look for the conspicuous 'kink' in the wings in flight.

Flying birds on this page are seen from below.

EAGLES

Eagles, like other birds of prey, are often seen soaring, and are difficult to identify. Particular note should be taken of any other bird in their vicinity (e.g. a crow mobbing them), since this may give a crucial clue to size. Most take years to reach fully adult plumage, and many are varied in colour even when they do. Hence plumage colour may vary markedly within a species.

Wing shape and flying behaviour provide important clues to identity.

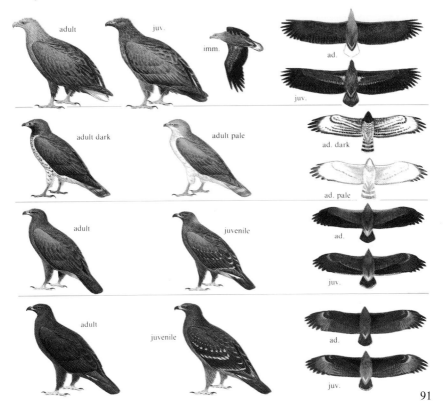

91

IMPERIAL EAGLE *Aquila heliaca* 80cm. ♂ 2,450–2,700, ♀ 3,150–4,000g. Large, similar to Golden; usually has a small amount of white on shoulder; head may look pale; in flight wings held straight out; tail smaller than Golden's. VOICE deep barking notes quickly repeated, high whistles. HAB open Mediterranean woodland. NEST in large, often isolated, tree; may be very large as used over many years; twigs, ♂♀. EGGS 2, whitish with a few brown markings, 73mm. BROODS 1. INC 43–45, ♀(♂). YOUNG col, 63–67, ♂♀. IMM 48–60. AGE 4 + , ?. FOOD mostly medium to small mammals, some birds.

○□ **GOLDEN EAGLE** *Aquila chrysaetos* 80cm, but variable. ♂ 2,850–4,500g, ♀ 3,850–6,700g. Widespread but rare resident (order 3). Large, glides with wings in shallow 'V'; young and immatures have white at base of tail. VOICE fairly quiet, but can produce loud nasal yelps and screams. HAB mountains, open plains. NEST on cliff or in large tree; may be large as used over many years; twigs, ♂♀. EGGS 2, whitish, usually blotched with brown, 77mm. BROODS 1. INC 43–45, ♀(♂). YOUNG col, 65–70, ♂♀. IMM 36 + . AGE 4–5, 26. FOOD wide range of birds and mammals, carrion.

Interval between eggs p. 35; Baby bird p. 208; Territory p. 254, 256; Conservation p. 302.

BOOTED EAGLE *Hieraaetus pennatus* 50cm. ♂ 500–800g, ♀ 850–1,250g. Buzzard-size; longish square-ended tail; colour very variable, light brown above and white underwing with black flight feathers, or almost uniformly dark except for pale tail. VOICE shrill repeated short whistles. HAB open Mediterranean woodland. NEST in tree; twigs. ♂♀. EGGS 2, white, marked with brown, 55mm. BROODS 1. INC 36–38, ♀(♂). YOUNG col, 50–55, ♂♀. IMM 0. AGE ?, ?. FOOD mainly small to medium-sized birds, some mammals.

BONELLI'S EAGLE *Hieraaetus fasciatus* 70cm. 1,600–2,500g. Larger than Booted Eagle and buzzards; adults have broad black band across underwing and at end of tail; young and immatures can be difficult. VOICE barks and shrill cries. HAB SUM low mountains; WIN moves to lower areas. NEST on rock ledge or in tree; twigs, ♂♀. EGGS 2, white with a few darker markings, 69mm. BROODS 1. INC 37–40, ♀(♂) YOUNG col, 60–65, ♂♀. IMM 0–12 + . AGE 4–5, ?. FOOD medium-sized mammals and birds.

BUZZARDS AND KITES genera *Buteo, Milvus, Pernis* and *Elanus* 35 species in the world.

Flight feathers p. 39; Carrion feeding p. 230.

Buzzards are small relatives of the *Aquila* eagles, and much the same shape; kites are distinctive with rather long wings and slightly to very forked tails (Black-shouldered has a square-ended tail). Buzzards are mainly predatory, but will eat carrion, whereas *Milvus* kites take a great deal of carrion. The females of most species are larger than the males. Many lay eggs so heavily spotted that the ground colour is barely visible.

○ **HONEY BUZZARD** *Pernis apivorus* 55cm. 600–1,100g. Rare summer visitor (order 1–2). Colour very variable; two dark bars near base of tail; in flight wings and tail thinner and longer than buzzards, and head looks much smaller than most birds of prey. VOICE usually quiet but has range of high disyllabic 'whee-oo' calls. HAB open woodland. NEST in tree; twigs, ♂♀. EGGS 2, white or pale buff, heavily marked, 51mm. BROODS 1. INC 30–35, ♀(♂). YOUNG col, 40–44, ♂♀. IMM 6–12. AGE ?2, 29. FOOD mainly larvae of wasps which it digs out of nest in ground, but also wide range of small birds and mammals; also frogs.

Habitat loss p. 308.

BLACK-SHOULDERED KITE *Elanus caeruleus* 33cm. 200–250g. A smart, small grey raptor with white underparts and black shoulders, bright red eye. VOICE quiet whistles. HAB open forests or cultivated land with trees. NEST in tree; twigs, ♀(♂). EGGS 3–4, cream with dark blotches, 39mm. BROODS 1. INC 30–32, ♀(♂). YOUNG col, 30–35, ♂♀. IMM 6. AGE ?1–2, ?. FOOD mainly small rodents.

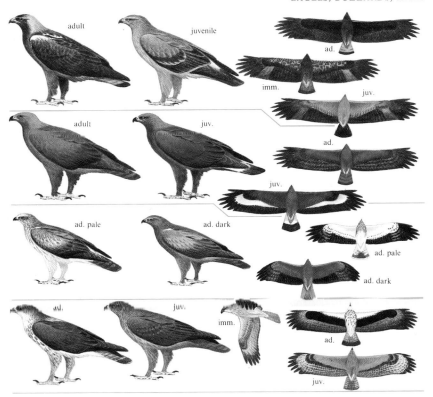

BUZZARDS AND KITES

Plumage is often of little help in identifying buzzards, as they vary
so much in colour.

*Look for underwing pattern, and particularly tail pattern. Kites
are usually identifiable by their angular wings and distinctive tail
shape.*

Flying birds on this page are seen from below.

☐ **BLACK KITE** *Milvus migrans* 56cm. 650–950g. Very rare vagrant. Dark bird which flies with wings slightly bent; tail has slight fork but often looks square-ended if spread. VOICE loud shrill trilling notes. HAB wide range of open country, may come to rubbish dumps, often near water. NEST usually in tree; twigs, ♂♀. EGGS 2–3, dirty white, usually spotted or blotched, 53mm. BROODS 1. INC 34–38, ♀. YOUNG col, 42–50, ♀. IMM 10–12. AGE 3–5, 24, 78%. FOOD wide range of prey; also scavenges for fish along shore, at rubbish dumps.

Speciation p. 55.

○☐ **RED KITE** *Milvus milvus* 61cm. ♂ 750–1,050g. ♀ 950–1,300g. Rare local resident (order 2). Long bent wings, long deeply-forked red tail. VOICE mewing notes reminiscent of Buzzard; longer first note, then rapidly repeated 2–3 times. HAB open country with woods and trees. NEST in tree; twigs, ♀(♂). EGGS 2–3, white, blotched reddish-brown, 57mm. BROODS 1. INC 31–32, ♀. YOUNG col, 50–60, ♂♀. IMM 10–12. AGE 2–4, 26, 82%. FOOD wide range of birds and mammals; also scavenges.

Speciation p. 55; Habitat history p. 309.

●■ **BUZZARD** *Buteo buteo* 54cm. ♂ 550–850g, ♀ 700–1,200g. Widespread resident (order 4–5 summer, 5 winter). Variable in plumage; broad wings, short broad tail with several fine bands across, and thicker terminal band; palish underwing, dark carpal joint. VOICE vocal, distinctive descending 'mew'. HAB wide range of open habitats, mountains, coasts, farmland with woods. NEST in tree or on rock ledge; twigs, ♂♀. EGGS 2–4, white, blotched with reddish-browns, 57mm. BROODS 1. INC 36–38, ♀(♂). YOUNG col, 50–55, ♂♀. IMM 0. AGE 2–3, 26, 81%. FOOD wide range: usually medium or small birds, mammals, esp. Rabbit; scavenges.

Vision p. 24; Migration p. 243; Food for young p. 275; Survival rate p. 285; Habitat history p. 309.

LONG-LEGGED BUZZARD *Buteo rufinus* 54cm. ♂ 600–1,200g, ♀ 950–1,750g. Very varied; typically more rufous than Buzzard, with pale (rufous above) tail, unbarred in adult; but eastern Buzzard can look similar. VOICE descending mew, similar to Buzzard. HAB dry, open country. NEST on rock ledge, rarely in tree; twigs, ?♂♀. EGGS 3–4, white, blotched with red-browns, 55mm. BROODS 1. INC 32–34, ?♀. YOUNG col, 40–42, ♂♀. IMM 0. AGE ?, ?. FOOD wide range of small mammals; also some reptiles.

☐ **ROUGH-LEGGED BUZZARD** *Buteo lagopus* 55cm. ♂ 600–950g, ♀ 950–1,300g. Rare winter visitor (order 1–2). Usually greyer-headed than Buzzard, with whitish underwing with very obvious dark carpal patch; usually dark belly; white tail without barring except for broad dark terminal band. VOICE Buzzard-like mews, louder and lower. HAB open country. NEST on rock ledge or tree in wooded area; twigs, ♂♀. EGGS 3–4, white, blotched with reddish-brown, 55mm. BROODS 1. INC 28–31, ♀(♂). YOUNG col, 39–43, ♂♀. IMM 10–14. AGE 2–3, 11. FOOD mainly small mammals, especially voles and lemmings, frequently located while hovering.

Population movements p. 291.

HARRIERS genus *Circus* 9 species in the world.
Medium-sized birds of prey with slender bodies; most have long thin wings and longish tail. Their flight is particularly light and buoyant; they fly low over moorland or reed-beds, dropping on small mammals and birds.

○☐ **MARSH HARRIER** *Circus aeruginosus* 52cm. ♂ 400–650g, ♀ 550–800g. Rare resident (order 2 summer, 1–2 winter). Largest harrier; no white on rump; ♂ browner than other species; ♀ very dark with pale crown and leading edge to wing. VOICE usually silent; display-call a shrill 'kee-eek' Lapwing-like; alarm-call a repeated 'kek'. HAB almost always reedy marshes. NEST (some polygamous) in reed-bed; a mound of reeds and twigs, ♀. EGGS 4–5, bluish-white, 50mm. BROODS 1. INC 31–38, ♀. YOUNG col, 40–42, ♂♀. IMM 0. AGE 2–3, 17, 74%. FOOD small to medium mammals and birds, especially water-birds

Habitat drainage p. 308–9.

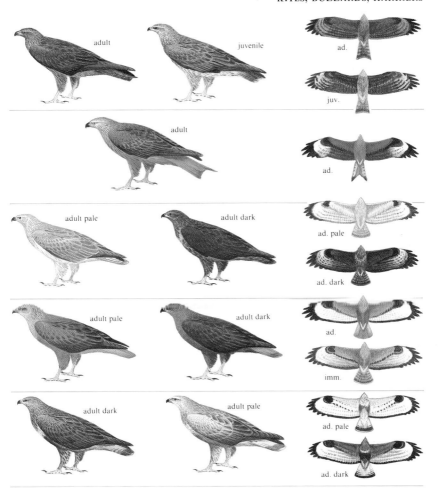

adult

juvenile

ad.

juv.

adult

ad.

adult pale

adult dark

ad. pale

ad. dark

adult pale

adult dark

ad.

imm.

adult dark

adult pale

ad. pale

ad. dark

Flying birds above are seen from below.

HARRIERS

The male Harriers are usually fairly easy to identify, though ♀ Marsh Harriers, the largest species, take two or more years to reach adult plumage, and are variable. The females of Pallid, Hen and Montagu's, called 'ringtails' from their banded tails, are much more difficult and require experience. They fly, with their wings held in a shallow 'V'.

Look for white rump and wing markings.

Flying birds below are seen from above.

adult ♂

adult ♀

ad. ♂

ad. ♀

○☐ **HEN HARRIER** *Circus cyaneus* 47cm. ♂ 300–400g, ♀ 400–700g. Resident (order 3); winter visitor (order 3). Grey ♂ has prominent white rump; ♀ larger, more streaked underneath than v. similar Montagu's. VOICE although usually silent away from nest, has a whistling flight call; at nest chatters and 'chuck's. HAB moorland, new conifer plantations, other open ground. NEST (often polygamous) on ground; sticks and grasses, ♀. EGGS 4–6, bluish-white, 46mm. BROODS 1. INC 29–31, ♀. YOUNG col, 35–42, ♀(♂). IMM 0. AGE 1–3, 17, 72%. FOOD mainly small birds and rodents.

Pair bond p. 283.

☐ **PALLID HARRIER** *Circus macrourus* 45cm. ♂ 300–350g, ♀ 400–450g. Very rare vagrant. Male like Hen, but paler with very pale head and breast; lacks whitish rump; ♂ like Montagu's, differs from Hen in being unstreaked underneath. VOICE silent except at nest, like Hen. HAB as Hen, but drier steppe country in east. NEST on ground; grasses, ?♀. EGGS 4–5, bluish-white, 45mm. BROODS 1. INC 29–30, ♀. YOUNG col, 34–35, ♂♀. IMM 0. AGE 2–3, ?. FOOD small mammals, birds, insects.

○ **MONTAGU'S HARRIER** *Circus pygargus* 44cm. ♂ 225–300g, ♀ 300–450g. Rare summer visitor (order 1). The smallest harrier; ♂ has black line on inner wing, streaks underneath; ♀ very difficult, but usually has less white on rump than Hen; immature has rufous underparts. VOICE like Hen, but rarely used. HAB open country with bushes and trees. NEST (sometimes bigamous) on ground; twigs and grasses, ♀(♂). EGGS 4–5, bluish-white, 42mm. BROODS 1. INC 28–29, ♀. YOUNG 35–40, ♂♀. IMM 10–14. AGE 2–3, 16. FOOD small mammals, reptiles and birds; also insects.

SPARROWHAWKS genus *Accipiter* 44 species in the world. An important group of woodland birds of prey, widely distributed. Almost all of them specialise in preying on birds, taking a wide range of sizes from the smallest up to Pheasant-size. The two sexes are often markedly different in size (especially in those species whose main prey is birds), the females being the larger. Their short, rounded wings and longish tails enable them to manoeuvre well inside woodland.

Flight feathers p. 39; Wing shape and turning p. 42–3.

○☐ **GOSHAWK** *Accipiter gentilis* ♂ 50cm, ♀ 60cm. ♂ 500–1,100g, ♀ 800–1,350g. Rare resident (order 2 summer, 3 winter); exterminated, now re-established by falconers' escaped birds. Broad, rounded wings, longish tail, white eyestripe and undertail coverts. VOICE 'kek-kek-kek' louder and harsher than Sparrowhawk. HAB forest, though may feed out over open country. NEST in tree; twigs, ♀(♂). EGGS 3–4, bluish-white, sometimes marked reddish-brown, 57mm. BROODS 1. INC 35–38, ♀. YOUNG col, 40–43, ♂♀. IMM 14–16. AGE 2–3, 19, 89%. FOOD mainly birds, thrush- to pigeon-size, also Pheasant.

Wing-loading and sizes of ♂ and ♀ p. 43, 298; Moult p. 222; Woodpigeon prey p. 231; Display flight p. 259; Habitat loss p. 308.

● ■ **SPARROWHAWK** *Accipiter nisus* ♂ 30cm, ♀ 38cm. ♂ 150g, ♀ 280–320g. Common resident (order 5). Broad-winged, long-tailed, ♀ rather similar to Goshawk but lacks eyestripe and white undertail coverts. VOICE loud high 'kek-kek-kek'. HAB woodland, but may hunt outside, especially along hedgerows. NEST in tree; twigs, ♂♀. EGGS 3–5, bluish-white with red-brown blotches, 40mm. BROODS 1. INC 33–35, ♀. YOUNG col, 24–30, ♀(♂). IMM 12 +. AGE 1–2, 16, 60%. FOOD small birds, mostly up to thrush-size.

Wing-loading and sizes of ♂ and ♀ p. 43, 298; Parental care p. 213; Age of first breeding p. 217; Moult p. 222; Great Tit prey p. 246–7; Breeding season p. 252–3; Display flight p. 259; Poisons p. 304, 313.

LEVANT SPARROWHAWK *Accipiter brevipes* 33–38cm, less difference in size between sexes than in Sparrowhawk. 150–275g. Similar to Sparrowhawk but both sexes show much whiter under-wing in flight, with black tips to flight feathers; ♂ has greyer cheeks, paler grey ♀ like Sparrowhawk but greyer above; migrates in flocks. VOICE shrill double note 'kee-vick'. HAB woodland and surroundings. NEST in tree; twigs, ?♀. EGGS 3–5, bluish-white, lightly marked, 41mm. BROODS 1. INC 32–35, ♀. YOUNG col, 40–45, ♂♀. IMM 12. AGE 1–2, ?. FOOD many large insects, lizards; also birds.

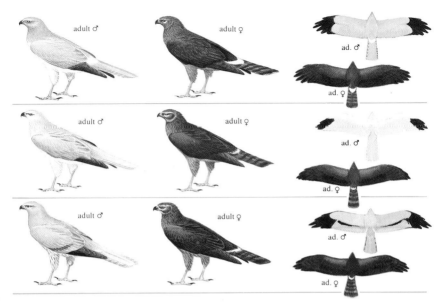

Flying birds above are seen from above.

SPARROWHAWKS

Typically sparrowhawks sit on a perch and then chase prey they see, or hunt low over the ground or along hedges, hoping to catch prey unawares. Often difficult to identify because of their secretiveness and speed; but few species in Europe.

Look for size, white undertail, eyestripe.

Flying birds below are seen from below.

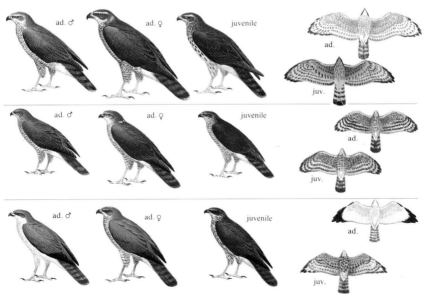

97

Order Falconiformes

FALCONS family Falconidae 61 species in the world.
The facons of the genus *Falco* (38 species in the world) are characterised by their long, pointed wings and rapid flight. Females are usually larger than males. They nest in holes in cliffs or on ledges, or in old tree-nests of other birds such as crows; most do not carry in nesting material of their own. Their eggs are so heavily spotted as to appear wholly reddish-brown.

Wing shape p. 42–3.

LESSER KESTREL *Falco naumanni* 30cm. ♂ 90–170g, ♀ 140–210g. Often gregarious; like Kestrel but ♂ lacks spotting on back so looks richer chestnut, has grey area on wings, lacks moustachial streak; ♀ difficult from Kestrel; light, horn-coloured claws (Kestrel has black claws). VOICE shrill chatters. HAB hunts over open country. NEST often colonial, in rock crevices, walls of buildings; no material. EGGS 3–5, buff-white, speckled or blotched with reddish-brown, 35mm. BROODS 1. INC 28–29, ♀. YOUNG col, 28–29, ♂♀. IMM 0. AGE 1–2, (6). FOOD mainly insects, some small mammals, a few birds.

● ■ **KESTREL** *Falco tinnunculus* 34cm. ♂ 190–240g, ♀ 220–300g. Common resident (order 5). Over most of Europe, only small birds of prey which regularly hovers; often along road-, railsides; ♂ reddish-brown with grey tail and paler underparts; ♀ streaky brown all over. VOICE loud 'kee-kee-kee'. HAB open country. NEST in large hole in tree, cliff or building, or may use old crow's nest; no material. EGGS 3–6, basically whitish but heavily marked with reddish-brown, blotched darker still, 40mm. BROODS 1. INC 27–29, ♀. YOUNG col, 27–32, ♂♀. IMM 0. AGE 1–2, 17, 66%. FOOD mainly small mammals, some large insects.

Moult p. 222; Clutch weight p. 245; Incubation p. 248; Breeding season p. 252–3; Nest hole p. 265; Survival rate p. 285; Habitat history p. 309.

□ **RED-FOOTED FALCON** *Falco vespertinus* 30cm. 130–200g. Rare vagrant. Often gregarious; ♂ striking dark grey with chestnut thighs and undertail; ♀ sandy-rufous crown and underparts. VOICE shrill 'kee-kee-kee'. HAB open country round woods. NEST colonial, in old bird's nests, esp. Rook; no material. EGGS 3–4, off-white, variably marked with reddish-browns, 37mm. BROODS 1. INC 22–23, ♂♀. YOUNG col, 27–30, ♂♀. IMM 12, 12–24. AGE 5, 2, ?, ?. FOOD mostly insects, though small vertebrates brought to young.

Bill p. 16; Young as food for man p. 210; Breeding season p. 252.

○ □ **MERLIN** *Falco columbarius* 30cm. ♂ 140–180g, ♀ 190–230g. Resident and summer visitor (order 3), passage migrant (order 4). Smallest falcon; ♂ grey above, streaky rufous beneath, with grey tail and black terminal band, no moustachial streak; ♀ dark brown above, pale and streaked below. VOICE shrill chatters, resembling Kestrel. HAB wide range of open country, especially hilly moorland; also along coast in winter. NEST on ground (or in old crow's-nest in tree), bare hollow; no material. EGGS 3–5, buffish, heavily overlaid with reds and browns, 40mm. BROODS 1. INC 28–32, ♀. YOUNG col, 28–32, ♂♀. IMM 0. AGE 1, 11. FOOD mainly small birds.

Hatchling p. 218.

○ **HOBBY** *Falco subbuteo* 34cm. ♂ 130–230g, ♀ 140–340g. Summer visitor (order 3). Silhouette similar to Red-footed, but longer wings, shorter tail than most falcons (reminiscent of giant Swift, p. 143); chestnut thighs and undertail; rest of underparts whitish, heavily streaked; sexes similar. VOICE shrill 'ker' and 'kee-kee-kee'. HAB open country close to woodland. NEST in old nest of other species such as crow; no material. EGGS 2–3, pale, speckled and blotched with reddish-browns, 42mm. BROODS 1. INC 28–31, ♀. YOUNG col, 28–34, ♂♀. IMM 12+. AGE 2 (1), 13. FOOD large insects and small birds, especially swallows and martins.

Wing shape p. 43; Breeding season p. 252–3.

ELEONORA'S FALCON *Falco eleonorae* 38cm. 350–450g. Sexes similar, plumage variable but mainly two forms: paler birds like very dark Hobby, darker birds like Red-footed but lack chestnut thighs and undertail. VOICE harsh 'kee-air' often repeated rapidly. HAB rocky islets in Mediterranean. NEST colonial, cliff ledges; no material. EGGS 2–3, off-white, blotched with browns, 42mm. BROODS 1. INC 28, ♀. YOUNG col, 35–40, ♂♀. IMM 0. AGE 2 (1), (6). FOOD mainly small birds, also insects.

Development of young p. 210; Migration p. 239–41; Breeding season p. 252–3.

FALCONS

Falcons are usually recognisable by the rapid, direct flight and great speed; often they 'stoop' on prey in the open. The fleeting glimpses offered, and the diversity of species, make them hard to identify at times; but only the two kestrels regularly hover, and many of the others are conspicuously coloured.

Look for head pattern, colour of crown, size of moustachial streaks, and shape in flight (broadness of wings, length of tail, etc.).

Flying birds are seen from above.

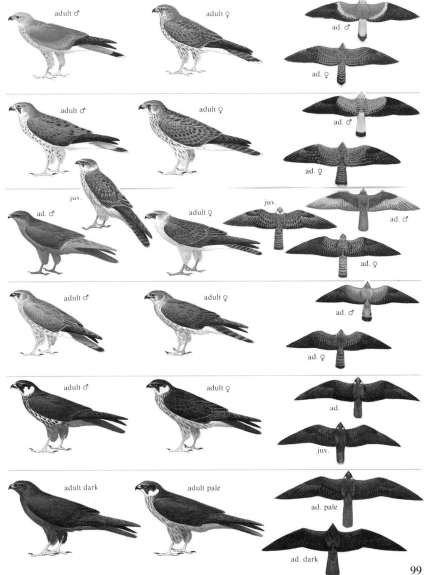

99

LANNER *Falco biarmicus* ♂ 37cm, ♀ 47cm. ♂ 500–600g, ♀ 700–900g. Similar to Peregrine but browner above with conspicuous buff crown and nape. VOICE shrill 'kree-kree' calls similar to Peregrine but more drawn-out. HAB low rocky mountains to semi-desert. NEST rock ledge, rarely old bird's nest in tree; no material. EGGS 3–4, white base heavily overlaid with brownish blotching, 52mm. BROODS 1. INC 32–35, ♂♀. YOUNG col, 44–46, ♂♀. IMM 10–12. AGE ?, ?. FOOD chiefly small to medium-sized birds.

SAKER *Falco cherrug* ♂ 45cm, ♀ 55cm. ♂ 750–1,000g, ♀ 1,000–1,300g. Browner than Peregrine, with pale head, moustachial streak at best faint. VOICE similar to Peregrine and Lanner; also a gull-like squeal. HAB open country, semi-desert. NEST in tree, using old nest of another bird, or on cliff; no material. EGGS 3–5, off-white, heavily spotted reddish-browns, 54mm. BROODS 1. INC 28–30, ♂♀. YOUNG col, 40–45, ♂♀. IMM 0. AGE 2–3, ?. FOOD mainly small mammals.

□ **GYRFALCON** *Falco rusticolus* ♂ 53cm, ♀ 56cm. ♂ 800–1,300g, ♀ 1,400–2,100g. Rare vagrant. The largest falcon; varies from almost white to dark grey, some immatures browner; almost no moustachial streak. VOICE similar to Peregrine but deeper and harsher 'kack-kack-kack'. HAB open country, often along sea-coast. NEST usually on cliff; no material. EGGS 3–4, buff-white, spotted with reddish-brown, 59mm. BROODS 1. INC 35, ♀(♂). YOUNG col, 46–49, ♂♀. IMM 0. AGE 2–4, ?. FOOD medium-sized birds, seabirds, duck, Ptarmigan.

Food for young
p. 275–6.

○□ **PEREGRINE** *Falco peregrinus* ♂ 40cm, ♀ 46cm. ♂ 600–750g, ♀ 900–1,300g. Widespread but uncommon resident (order 3 summer, 4 winter). Large, heavily-built falcon; variable in plumage, often dark grey above and streaky pale below; may be browner; marked moustachial streak. VOICE range of 'kee-kee-kee' to harsher 'kek-kek-kek'. HAB mountains, sea-cliffs. NEST usually cliff ledge; no material. EGGS 3–4, whitish, heavily overlaid with reddish-browns, 52mm. BROODS 1. INC 29–32, ♀(♂). YOUNG col, 35–42, ♂♀. IMM 8–20. AGE 2–3, 17. FOOD mainly medium-sized birds, e.g. duck, seabirds, grouse, pigeons: species depend on area.

Air speed p. 43; Predation of Black Grouse lek p. 216; Territory p. 259; Nest site p. 263; Poisons p. 313.

Order Galliformes

GAMEBIRDS 265 species in the world.
Game-birds are unusual in that the chicks can fly well before they are fully grown. Most members of the order are primarily vegetarian, but their young usually take many insects which provide the protein for rapid growth. Once they are fully grown, the young are indistinguishable from adult females.
GROUSE family *Tetraonidae* 16 species in the world.

Flight muscles p. 15; Leaves as food p. 19; Excretion p. 19; Vision p. 24; Down p. 29; Wing shape p. 42; Baby bird p. 208; Development of young p. 211; Migration p. 236; Nest concealment and material p. 263, 265; Egg size p. 268; Prey of Gyrfalcon p. 275; Pair bond p. 283; Population cycles p. 290; Hunting p. 295.

/ ● ■ **WILLOW/RED GROUSE** *Lagopus lagopus* 40cm. 650–750g. Common resident (order 6 summer, 6–7 winter). Variable plumage. Willow Grouse: in winter, white with black tail; in summer, rich brown though still with white wings and underparts. Red Grouse (Britain): rich brown all over throughout the year. VOICE loud, harsh 'go-back, go-back'. HAB heather moorland and arctic willow bogs. NEST shallow scrape, barely lined with grasses, ♀. EGGS 6–9, yellowish base, heavily overlaid with very dark brown blotching, 46mm. BROODS 1. INC 19–25, ♀. YOUNG fug, 30–35, ♂♀. IMM 0. AGE 1, 8, 35%. FOOD vegetation, esp. heather shoots.

Subspeciation p. 52–3; Spring moult p. 219–220; Food choice p. 230; Copulation p. 261; Food for young p. 276; Pair bond p. 283; Population cycles p. 290, 293; Habitat history p. 309.

● ■ **PTARMIGAN** *Lagopus mutus* 35cm. 400–600g. Local resident (order 4–5 summer, 5 winter). In winter v. similar to Willow Grouse but ♂ has small black mark between bill and eye; in summer, grey above with white wings and underparts. VOICE low, harsh grating noise. HAB open rocky mountainsides, at higher altitude than Willow/Red Grouse. NEST shallow scrape, barely lined with grasses, ♀. EGGS 5–8, pale with many dark blotches, 44mm. BROODS 1. INC 21–23, ♀. YOUNG col, 70–84, ♂♀. IMM 2–12. AGE 1, ?. FOOD vegetarian: leaves, buds, berries.

Spring moult p. 219–220; Heat loss, survival in cold p. 225, 229; Prey of Gyrfalcon p. 275; Population cycles p. 290; Habitat history p. 309.

Flying birds are seen from above.

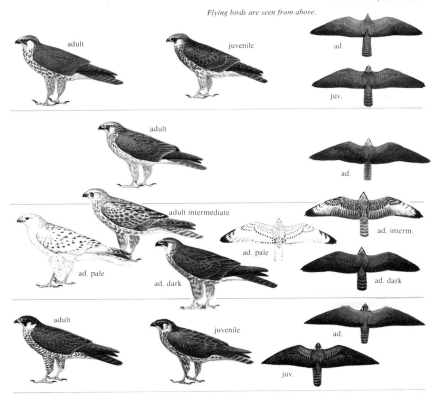

adult
juvenile
ad.
juv.

adult
ad.

adult intermediate
ad. interm.

ad. pale
ad. dark
ad. pale
ad. dark

adult
juvenile
ad.
juv.

GROUSE

Solidly built birds with short, rounded wings and feathered legs. Usually grouse 'explode' from cover at close range and fly off with fast whirring wing-beats interspersed with glides; they seldom fly long distances. Most live in woodland, though the Willow Grouse and Ptarmigan live on open moorland or rocky hillsides. The European ones are easy to distinguish, except some females.

Look for tail shape, since female Black Grouse has slightly forked tail.

WILLOW GROUSE

ad. ♂ win
ad. ♂ sum.
ad. ♀ sum.
ad. ♂ aut.
ad. ♂ win.
ad. ♂ sum.

RED GROUSE

ad. ♂
ad. ♀
ad. ♂
ad. ♀

ad. ♂ sum.
ad. aut.
ad. ♀ sum.
ad. ♂ win.
ad. ♀ sum.
ad. ♀ win.
ad. ♂ win.
ad. ♂ sum.

BLACK GROUSE *Tetrao tetrix* ♂ 35cm, ♀ 41cm. ♂ 1,000–1,400g, ♀ 750–1,100g. Fairly common resident (order 5). Sexes very different: ♂ glossy, blue black with lyre-shaped tail; ♀ smaller, greyer, slightly forked tail. VOICE ♂ at lek, bubbling 'rookoo', ♀ scolding cackles. HAB wooded moorland, rough agricultural land. NEST (polygamous: ♂s display at lek, ♀s come for mating); scrape on ground, sparse lining of grasses, ♀. EGGS 6–11, creamy, blotched with browns, 51mm. BROODS 1. INC 25–27, ♀. YOUNG fug, 40–50, independent *c.* 90, ♀. IMM 5. AGE ♂ 2–3, ♀ 1, 6, 40–60%. FOOD vegetarian: buds, shoots, berries.

Age of first breeding p. 216–17; Heat loss p. 225; Lek p. 256, 261; Pair bond p. 282–283; Habitat loss p. 308.

CAPERCAILLIE *Tetrao urogallus* ♂ 86cm, ♀ 62cm. ♂ 3,400–4,400g, ♀ 1,500–2,000g. Re-introduced, fairly common resident (order 4). ♂ huge, mainly dark grey; ♀ like Black Grouse but browner, with rufous breast, rounded tail. VOICE ♂ varied, including noises like popping corks, drum rolls; ♀ brays and cackles. HAB mainly forest, especially conifer. NEST on ground, lined with vegetation, ♀. EGGS 7–11, pale yellowish, speckled with browns, 57mm. BROODS 1. INC 24–26, ♀. YOUNG fug, fully-grown and independent *c.* 70–90, ♀. IMM 0. AGE ♀ 1, ♂ 2–3, 10, 54–59%. FOOD vegetarian: buds, shoots, berries, in winter many conifer needles.

Leaves as food p. 19; Age of first breeding p. 217; Heat loss p. 225; Seasonal movements p. 239–40; Lek p. 261; Egg size p. 268; Food for young p. 276; Pair bond p. 283; Habitat loss p. 308; Status in Britain p. 314.

HAZEL GROUSE *Bonasa bonasia* 35cm. 300–450g. Small greyish woodland grouse, often perches in trees; black band at end of grey tail; ♂ has black throat, edged white, inconspicuous crest. VOICE v. high-pitched whistle. HAB woodland. NEST shallow, on ground, little lining. EGGS 7–11, yellowish-buff, spotted with reddish-browns, 41mm. BROODS 1. INC 25, ♀. YOUNG fug, 30–40, independent *c.* 90, ♀. IMM 0. AGE 1, 7. FOOD buds, leaves, berries.

PHEASANTS, PARTRIDGES AND QUAIL family *Phasianidae* 183 species in the world.

By far the largest of the gamebird families. The pheasants are long-tailed birds of medium size; the partridges are smaller, similar in size to Red Grouse; the Quail is very small and rather secretive. All except the Quail (which migrates to Africa for the winter) have relatively short, rounded wings and fly powerfully in shorts bursts, but only for short distances.

Fossils p. 11; Flight muscles, feathers, wing shape p. 15, 39, 42; Vision p. 24; Down p. 29; Development of young p. 211; Migration p. 236; Nest concealment and material p. 263, 265; Egg size and colour p. 268–9; Incubation p. 272–3; Pair bond p. 283; Population cycles p. 290; Hunting p. 295.

PHEASANT *Phasianus colchicus* ♂ up to 89cm, ♀ up to 63cm. ♂ 1,050–1,400g, ♀ 900–1,050g. Common resident (order 6 summer, 7 winter); introduced. Varied in size and plumage, but typical ♂ is long-tailed, bronzy, with green head; ♀ pale, greyish brown. VOICE strident double-note 'kaark-kok'. HAB primarily wooded country, but commonly leaves woodland to feed. NEST (polygamous); shallow depression in ground, usually unlined. EGGS 8–15, light buffy-cream to pale greenish, 36mm. BROODS 1. INC 23–28, ♀. YOUNG fug, independent *c.* 70–80, ♀. IMM 0. AGE 1, 8, 42%. FOOD wide range: green shoots, berries, grain, insects.

Wing shape and taking off p. 42; Plumage p. 49; Breeding season p. 253; Pairing p. 261; Nest concealment p. 263; Incubation p. 269; Harem p. 283; Populations p. 288; Shooting p. 295; Introduction p. 311.

○□ **GOLDEN PHEASANT** *Chrysolophus pictus* ♂ up to 110cm, ♀ 67cm. 800–900g. Introduced, now feral in Britain, local resident (order 3). Male unmistakeable with scarlet underparts, golden crown and hood; ♀ like lightly built Pheasant, but longer, strongly banded tail. VOICE harsh, loud 'chack's. HAB thick woodland. NEST a shallow depression, usually unlined. EGGS 5–12, pale buff to cream, 44mm. BROODS 1. INC 22–23, ♀. YOUNG fug, ?, ♀. IMM 0. AGE 1, ?. FOOD largely vegetarian, some insects.

Incubation p. 272; Introduction to Britain p. 311.

○□ **LADY AMHERST'S PHEASANT** *Chrysolophus amherstiae* ♂ up to 170cm, ♀ up to 70cm. 600–700g. Introduced, now feral in Britain, local resident (order 3). Male black wings and back, white underparts, tail of up to 115cm in length, white with black bars; ♀ very like Golden. May hybridise with Golden. VOICE as Golden, but has 'su-kik' call starting off with a hiss. HAB thickets in parkland. NEST (polygamous); shallow depression. barely lined. EGGS 6–11, buff to creamy, 50mm. BROODS 1. INC 22–23, ♀. YOUNG fug, ?, ♀. IMM 0. AGE 1, ?. FOOD vegetable and animal matter.

Introduction to Britain p. 311.

PHEASANTS, PARTRIDGES AND QUAIL

Pheasants are woodland birds and more easily heard than seen. Partridges are birds of open country and more easily seen, but they too are noisy and often best located by call. The Quail, by reason of its size, is very difficult to see and is usually located by its distinctive call. The Rock Partridges (Genus *Alectoris*) can usually be identified by range.

103

○ **QUAIL** *Coturnix coturnix* 18cm. ♂ 70–100g, ♀ 85–135g. Summer visitor (order 3–4). Very small, secretive game-bird, whose presence usually only established by call; in Mediterranean region migrates low over sea in large numbers. VOICE distinctive trisyllabic whistle, on same note, often characterised as 'wet-my-lips'. HAB grassy meadows, corn-fields, etc. NEST shallow hollow in ground, lightly lined with grass, ♀. EGGS 8–13, creamy or yellow, heavily blotched with very dark brown, 30mm. BROODS 1 (but see p. 253). INC 17–20, ♀. YOUNG fug, independent at 30–50, ♀. IMM 0. AGE 1, 8. FOOD mainly seeds and invertebrates.

Hatchling p. 205; Migration p. 236; Breeding season and migration between broods p. 253; Egg size p. 268; Habitat history p. 309.

○□ **CHUKAR** *Alectoris chukar* 33cm. ♂ 500–600g, ♀ 450–550g. (See Red-legged Partridge for status.) One of a group of exceedingly similar species, best identified by area or call. VOICE a decelerating chucking, rather like domestic hen. HAB stony open ground. NEST shallow depression, sparsely lined, ♀. EGGS 8–11, palish cream with fine reddish speckles, 43mm. BROODS sometimes 2 (simultaneous, see p. 283). INC 22–24, ♂ on one, ♀ on other. YOUNG fug, full size by 50, ♂♀. IMM 2–4. AGE 1, ?. FOOD mainly seeds and grasses.

Niche p. 296–7; Captive breeding and release p. 312.

ROCK PARTRIDGE *Alectoris graeca* 33cm. ♂ 650–750g, ♀ 500–650g. Similar to Chukar except for small black mark on lores. VOICE like Chukar, but deeper and repetitive. HAB open stony hillsides. NEST on ground, concealed by plants or rocks, sparsely lined. EGGS 8–14, palish cream with fine red speckles, 42mm. BROODS sometimes 2 (simultaneous, see p. 283). INC 24–26, ♂ on one, ♀ on other. YOUNG fug, full size 50–60, ♂♀. IMM 2–4. AGE 1, ?. FOOD mainly leaves, seeds, some insects.

Niche p. 296–7.

●■ **RED-LEGGED PARTRIDGE** *Alectoris rufa* 34cm. ♂ 500–550g, ♀ 400–500g. Introduced, now widespread resident (order 6); many bred and released each year, some Chukar amongst them. Most easily separated from Chukar and Rock by black speckling below white throat. VOICE 'chuk, chuker'. HAB open ground including agricultural. NEST on ground, concealed amongst vegetation; slight lining of grass. EGGS 8–11, palish cream with fine reddish speckles, 42mm. BROODS sometimes 2 (simultaneous, see p. 283). INC 23–24, ♂ on one, ♀ on other. YOUNG fug, full size 50–60, ♂♀. IMM 2–4. AGE 1, 6. FOOD mainly seeds and shoots.

Clutch size p. 244; Second clutch p. 283; Niche p. 296–7; Introduction to Britain p. 311–12.

BARBARY PARTRIDGE *Alectoris barbara* 33cm. In Europe only found in Gibraltar and Sardinia; differs from relatives mainly in lacking black line through eye and below white throat. VOICE harsh, disyllabic 'kutchuk'. HAB rocky hillsides with scrub. NEST shallow scrape on ground with little lining. EGGS 8–11, palish cream with fine reddish speckles, 42mm. BROODS probably sometimes 2 (see p. 283). INC probably 23–24, ♂ on one, ♀ on other. YOUNG fug, fully grown at 50–60, ♂♀. IMM 2–4. AGE 1, ?. FOOD mainly vegetable, some insects.

Niche p. 296–7.

●■ **GREY PARTRIDGE** *Perdix perdix* 30cm. 350–450g. Common resident (order 6). In many parts of Europe the commonest Partridge; orange face, less striking barring on flanks than the other partridges, dark brown horseshoe-shaped mark on upper belly, dark grey legs. VOICE loud 'kerr-r-r-rick' likened to swinging rusty gate. HAB wide range of open country including farmland. NEST on ground, concealed amongst vegetation. EGGS 10–20, buff-orange-brown, unmarked, 37mm. BROODS 1. INC 23–25, ♀. YOUNG fug, fully grown *c*. 90–100, ♂♀. IMM 2–4. AGE 1, 7. FOOD mainly vegetable.

Clutch size and weight p. 244–5; Pair bond p. 283; Habitat history p. 309.

Order Gruiformes

CRANES, RAILS, etc. 189 species in the world.
A large order containing 12 families of birds that do not, at first sight, seem closely-related.

BUTTON-QUAILS family *Turnicidae* 15 species in the world.

ANDALUSIAN HEMIPODE *Turnix sylvatica* 15cm. ♂ ?*c*. 60g, ♀ ?*c*. 70g. A tiny quail-like bird, rarely seen, usually heard, orange breast, bold black spots on flanks. VOICE quiet crooning or mooing noises. HAB wide range of open country with thick scrub. NEST shallow scrape, little lining. ♂♀. EGGS 4, buff with reddish speckles, 21mm. BROODS sometimes several (♀ lays series of clutches for different ♂'s – see p. 283). INC 12–14, ♂. YOUNG fug, fully grown 30, ♂. IMM 0. AGE ?1, ?. FOOD seeds and insects.

adult ♂   adult ♀   juv.   ad. ♂

adult   juvenile   ad.   ad.

adult   juvenile   ad.   ad.

adult   juvenile   ad.   ad.

adult   juvenile   ad.   ad.

adult   juvenile   ad.   ad.

ad. ♂   ad. ♀   juv.   ad. ♂

RAILS, CRAKES AND GALLINULES family *Rallidae*
124 species in the world.
This is the largest family in the order. It includes many very
secretive birds which live in thick beds of reeds and other aquatic
vegetation and are rarely seen. In addition, they are nidifugous
(p. 206) and therefore difficult to study. As a result, many of the
species are poorly known; even the ranges of the European species
are not well-known. They can be identified by call, but are often
silent outside the breeding season.

Fossils p. 11; Skeleton
p. 13; Feet and swim-
ming p. 44–5; Baby
bird p. 207; Flightless
in moult p. 222;
Migration p. 236–7;
Egg size p. 268;
Parental care and
asynchronous hatching
p. 274.

●■ **WATER RAIL** *Rallus aquaticus* 28cm. ♂ 100–190g, ♀
85–135g. Widespread resident, very difficult to census (order 4);
also passage migrant, winter visitor. Rarely seen in the open; the
only crake or rail with a long bill (red with darker tip); white
undertail tinged buff. VOICE range of grunts, squeals and screams.
HAB wet marshy ground with thick vegetation. NEST in thick vegetation; reeds, aquatic plants, ♂♀. EGGS 6–11, creamy-brown overlaid with reddish-brown spots, 36mm. BROODS 2. INC 19–22, ♂♀.
YOUNG fug, 20–30, ♂♀. IMM 0–3. AGE 1, 6. FOOD wide range of
aquatic invertebrates, molluscs, insects, some vegetable matter.

Feet p. 45; Baby bird
p. 207; Migration
p. 237.

○ **SPOTTED CRAKE** *Porzana porzana* 23cm. 60–115g. Rare
summer visitor (order 1). A little smaller than Water Rail, but has
much shorter bill (yellow-green with red base); breast spotted.
VOICE short high-pitched monosyllabic whistle, repeated regularly.
HAB thick vegetation in marshes; very secretive and hard to see.
NEST well concealed in vegetation; reeds, sedges, etc., ♂♀. EGGS
10–12, olive-brown, blotched with reddish-brown and grey, 34mm.
BROODS 2. INC 18–19, ♂♀. YOUNG fug, 25, ♂♀. IMM 0–3. AGE 1, 7.
FOOD aquatic invertebrates and plants.

Migration p. 236–7;
Parental care and
asynchronous hatching
p. 274.

□ **LITTLE CRAKE** *Porzana parva* 19cm. 35–60g. Rare vagrant.
Very secretive; very small, red base to bill. green legs; ♂ grey
underparts, faintly barred posteriorly; ♀ buff underparts. VOICE
sharp 'kwek-kwek', accelerating into a descending trill. HAB thick
marshy vegetation, especially reeds. NEST in thick growth; small
cup of sedges, etc., ?♂♀. EGGS 7–9, buff, spotted and streaked
brown, 29mm. BROODS ?2. INC 21–23, ♂♀. YOUNG fug, 45–50, ♂♀.
IMM 3–4. AGE 1, (6). FOOD aquatic invertebrates, seeds, vegetation.

Migration p. 236–7;
Parental care and
asynchronous hatching
p. 274.

□ **BAILLON'S CRAKE** *Porzana pusilla* 18cm. 40–50g. Rare
vagrant. Very secretive; often confused with Little, but olive legs
and no red on bill; ♂ strongly barred flanks; ♀ grey underparts
fairly well-barred. VOICE even, low trill, frog-like or like finger
being drawn along comb. HAB thick vegetation in marshes, ponds.
NEST small cup of leaves from water plants, ?♂♀. EGGS 6–8, yellow-
buff, streaked and spotted with browns, 29mm. BROODS ?2. INC
17–20, ♂♀. YOUNG fug, 35, ♂♀. IMM 3–4. AGE 1, ?. FOOD mainly
aquatic insects, some plants, seeds.

Migration p. 236–7;
Parental care and
asynchronous hatching
p. 274.

● **CORNCRAKE** *Crex crex* 27cm. 135–200g. Summer visitor
(order 4). Distinctive call (rarely seen anyway); the only crake in
meadows rather than marshes; in flight very distinctive chestnut
wings (flight feathers darker). VOICE loud rasping 'crex-crex' often
at night; also mewing note. HAB rich meadows. NEST small.
flattish; grasses, ♀. EGGS 8–12, pale greenish or brownish, blotched
with reddish-browns and greys, 37mm. BROODS ?2. INC 16–19, ♀.
YOUNG fug, fully-grown *c.* 60, ♀ or ♂♀. IMM 0. AGE 1, 6. FOOD mainly
invertebrates, some plant material.

Migration p. 237;
Breeding season p. 253.

PURPLE GALLINULE *Porphyrio porphyrio* 48cm. ♂ 750–1,000g.
♀ 500–900g. Large, bulky, Moorhen-like, bluish-purple; red bill.
frontal shield and legs. VOICE loud and varied including trumpetings and hootings, sometimes at night. HAB swamps, reedy edges
to lakes. NEST platform of aquatic plants, ♂♀. EGGS 3–5, pale buff.
spotted and blotched with reddish-browns or greys, 55mm. BROODS
1 (2). INC 23–25, ♀(♂). YOUNG fug, fully grown *c.* 60, ♂♀. IMM 4–9.
AGE ?, ?. FOOD mainly aquatic plants.

RAILS, CRAKES AND GALLINULES

Rails and crakes usually skulk in thick vegetation, permitting only brief views; by far the commonest in most areas is the Water Rail which can be speedily identified by bill length or undertail coverts as it retreats.

Look for flank, bill and leg coloration.

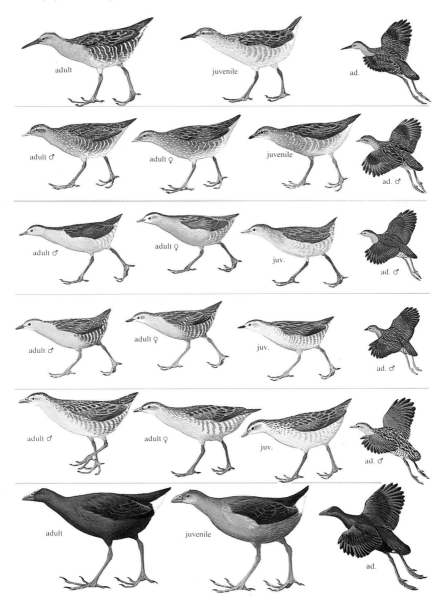

● ■ **MOORHEN** *Gallinula chloropus* 35cm. ♂ 250–420g. ♀ 260–373g. Common resident (order 6 summer, 6–7 winter). Very common and widespread; white line along flank and white undertail; adult has red bill, tipped yellow. VOICE loud, resonant 'kirrick'. HAB fresh water with fringing vegetation; often comes out into fields to feed. NEST in thick waterside cover; rushes, etc., ♂♀. EGGS 5–9, light brown, blotched with dark reddish-brown and grey, 45mm. BROODS 2 (3). INC 21–22, ♂♀. YOUNG fug, 40–50, ♂♀ plus some siblings from earlier brood. IMM 4–9. AGE 1, 15. FOOD wide range of plant and animal material.

Moult p. 32–3, 222; Feet p. 45; Migration p. 237; Multiple broods, brood parasitism, co-op. breeding p. 250, 278, 280; breeding season p. 245, 248, 253; Parental care, hatching p. 274.

● ■ **COOT** *Fulica atra* 38cm. ♂ 650–900g, ♀ 575–800g. Common resident (order 5), winter visitor (order 6). Greyish-black bird with white bill and frontal shield; unlike Moorhen white trailing edge of wing visible in flight. VOICE short, sharp 'peu'; some screaming notes. HAB SUM vegetation-fringed lakes and rivers; WIN some on more open water when may form large flocks. NEST cup of dead waterside vegetation hidden in reeds, etc., ♂♀. EGGS 6–10, light brown finely spotted with dark brown, 53. BROODS 1 (2). INC 21–24, ♂♀. YOUNG fug, fully grown 55–60, ♂♀. IMM 4–9. AGE 1, 18, 75%. FOOD mainly aquatic plants, some animal matter.

Migration p. 237; Multiple broods, brood parasitism p. 250, 278; Breeding season p. 253; Parental care and asynchronous hatching p. 274.

CRESTED COOT *Fulica cristata* 41cm. ♂ 750–900g, ♀ 500–800g. Differs from Coot in having two tiny red knobs at top of white frontal shield (need exceptional view to see); lacks white wing bar in flight. VOICE varied, differs from Coot mainly in more hooting 'hoo-hoo-hoo'. HAB vegetated marsh and lake edges. NEST cup of dead waterside vegetation hidden in reeds, etc., ♂♀. EGGS 5–7, pale buff with fine reddish speckling, 52mm. BROODS ?1. INC 18–20, ♂♀. YOUNG fug, fully-grown 55–60, ♂♀. IMM 4–9. AGE ?1, (6). FOOD omnivorous, but mainly plants.

CRANES family *Gruidae* 14 species in the world.
Very tall heron-like birds which often migrate in flocks of considerable size; they tend to fly in 'V' formation.

☐ **CRANE** *Grus grus* 115cm. 4,000–7,000g. Rare vagrant. A large heron-like bird that flies with neck outstretched; grey with black wings, neck and head black and white with small red cap. VOICE varied, but far-carrying bugling most striking. HAB SUM swamps, often amongst woodland; WIN large lakes and open fields. NEST on dryish area in marsh; large mound of vegetation, ♂♀. EGGS 2, varied, greenish-buff, blotched and streaked with reddish-browns, 96mm. BROODS 1. INC 30, ♂♀. YOUNG fug, 65–70, ♂♀. IMM 12–18. AGE ?4–6, ?. FOOD mainly plants, but some animal including fish and even small birds.

Feathers p. 29; Air speed p. 43; Legs p. 47; Flightless in moult p. 222; Breeding season p. 250; Parental care and asynchronous hatching p. 274; Habitat drainage p. 308.

BUSTARDS family *Otidae* 21 species in the world.
Large, solidly-built birds reminiscent of rather long-legged gamebirds. They live in open country, taking a wide variety of food. They lay small clutches, and the female incubates and looks after the young on her own. The young are nidifugous and the fledging periods hard to define.

Running p. 46.

☐ **LITTLE BUSTARD** *Tetrax tetrax* 44cm. 600–950g. Rare vagrant. Looks like slightly long-legged gamebird; speckled brown except for black and white neck of breeding ♂; in flight, striking white wings (marked with black). VOICE male has a snorting display call; a short 'prrett', rather frog-like. HAB large grassy areas, cornfields, etc. NEST shallow unlined hollow. EGGS 3–5, green-olive or olive-brown, streaked and blotched brown, 52mm. BROODS 1. INC 20–22, ♀. YOUNG fug, 50–55, ♀. IMM 0. AGE 1–2, ?. FOOD vegetable shoots, etc.; also insects.

☐ **GREAT BUSTARD** *Otis tarda* ♂ 90cm, ♀ 74cm. ♂ 7,000–18,000g, ♀ 3,500, 4,100g. Rare vagrant. In flight wings white with black tips; ♀ brown above, white below, grey neck; ♂ enormous, similar to ♀ except brown breast band, long white moustaches. VOICE gruff barking notes. HAB wide open spaces inc. agricultural land. NEST (♂'s loose leks) shallow hollow in herbage. EGGS 2–3, olive-green, streaked and blotched with reddish-brown, 79mm. BROODS 1. INC 21–28, ♀. YOUNG fug, independent at c. 35, ♀. IMM ♀ c. 24, ♂ up to 72; takes up to 3 years to full size. AGE ♂ 5–6, ♀ 3–4, ?. FOOD wide range, much vegetable, also animals, e.g. mice.

Re-introduction to Britain p. 314.

adult

juvenile

ad.

adult

juvenile

ad.

adult

juvenile

ad.

CRANES

adult

juvenile

ad.

In flight they are most easily separated from herons by their outstretched necks.

BUSTARDS

Bustards are surprisingly difficult to see, considering their size; often they crouch with their heads down if danger threatens. Flight is strong and the wing-beats surprisingly leisurely and un-hurried.

Look for striking white wing pattern.

ad. ♂   juv.   ad. ♀   ad. ♀   ad. ♂

ad. ♂   juv.   ad. ♀   ad. ♂   ad. ♀

Order Charadriiformes

WADERS, GULLS, TERNS AND AUKS 316 species in the world.
A very large order of 16 families, many associated with the sea or shore. Most lay clutches of 3–4 very well-camouflaged eggs in open situations.

OYSTERCATCHERS family *Haematopodidae* 6 species in the world.

●■ **OYSTERCATCHER** *Haematopus ostralegus* 43cm. 400–700g. Common resident (order 5 summer, 6 winter). Black and white with long orange-red bill and pink legs. VOICE a piping trill and loud 'chip's. HAB mainly seashore, but also inland on fields. NEST on shingle beach, rocky outcrop or more hidden in vegetation; shallow scrape with little lining, ♂♀. EGGS 2–4, yellowish or greyish-buff with dark spots and streaks, 57mm. BROODS 1. INC 24–27, ♂♀. YOUNG fug, 35–42, ♂♀. IMM 12. AGE 2, 36. FOOD wide range of marine animals: limpets, cockles, crabs; also leatherjackets, earthworms.

Bills and touch p. 16–17, 27; Vision p. 24; Down p. 29; Legs, wading, heat loss, running p. 46–7; Classification p. 59; Hatchling p. 218; Seasonal plumages p. 220; Moult p. 223; Heat loss in incubation

p. 226–7; Learning to feed p. 230; Migration p. 237; Breeding season p. 250; Nest p. 263, 265; Egg shape and colour p. 268–9; Pair bonds p. 283; Conservation p. 304–5; Tundra p. 306.

Baby bird p. 207; Clutch weight p. 245; Incubation p. 248; Nest material p. 265; Parental care p. 274; Pair fidelity p. 283; Conservation p. 304–5.

STILTS AND AVOCETS family *Recurvirostridae* 7 species in the world.
A small family of very distinctive black-and-white waders. They often nest in small groups or colonies on islands in shallow marshes. They search for food in the water or thin mud at the bottom.

Bills and touch p. 16–17, 27; Vision p. 24; Wading, legs, heat loss p. 46–7; Hatchling p. 218; Moult p. 223; Heat loss in incubation p. 226–7; Learning to feed p. 230; Migration

p. 237; Breeding season p. 250; Nest site, concealment and material p. 263, 265; Egg shape and colour p. 268–9; Pair bonds p. 283; Conservation p. 304–5.

☐ **BLACK-WINGED STILT** *Himantopus himantopus* 38cm. 160–200g. Rare vagrant, has nested. Unmistakeable; black back and wings, white underparts, very long bright pink legs which trail far behind tail in flight. VOICE sharp 'ky-air' or 'kek', latter repeated rapidly. HAB shallow marshes. NEST shallow hollow often in exposed site on mud. EGGS 4, pale buff with blackish blotches. 44mm. BROODS 1. INC 22–25, ♂♀. YOUNG fug, 28–32, ♂♀. IMM 9. AGE 2, 12. FOOD small aquatic invertebrates, especially insects.

New habitat p. 311.

○☐ **AVOCET** *Recurvirostra avosetta* 43cm. 250–400g. Very local breeder (order 3), many leave for winter (but still order 3). Unmistakeable; black-and-white with markedly up-turned bill. VOICE fluty, almost disyllabic 'klooit'. HAB shallow waters, usually brackish or saline. NEST colonial, shallow hollow on mudflats, often on small island. EGGS 4, pale buff, spotted with black, 51mm. BROODS 1. INC 23–25, ♂♀. YOUNG fug, 35–42, ♂♀. IMM 3. AGE 2 (3), 25, 78%. FOOD small invertebrates, picked from out of water or fine mud.

Bill and sense of touch p. 17, 27; Feet p. 45; Habitat drainage p. 308–9; New habitat p. 311.

STONE CURLEWS family *Burhinidae* 9 species in the world. Brownish, well-camouflaged birds, several of which live in dry country away from water. They have very large eyes and are active at dawn and dusk. The European species is migratory, going to southern Europe and Africa for the winter.

○ **STONE CURLEW** *Burhinus oedicnemus* 41cm. 370–450g. Rare summer visitor (order 3). Often active at night; stocky brownish bird with double white wing-bar and yellowish legs, striking large yellow eye. VOICE wide range including 'curlee' (hence name) and shrill 'kikiwick'. HAB open stony fields and heaths. NEST shallow scrape on bare ground (vegetation may grow up later round it). EGGS 2, pale buff, spotted with dark browns. 54mm. BROODS 1 (2). INC 24–26, ♂♀. YOUNG fug, 36–42, ♂♀. IMM 2. AGE 3 (2), 16. FOOD mainly invertebrates.

Running p. 46.

OYSTERCATCHERS

Only one species of Oystercatcher occurs in Europe, and the combination of black and white plumage and straight orange-red bill distinguish it from all other waders. It often lives in flocks in estuaries in winter. Its piping and trilling cries are audible at great distance.

adult summer   adult winter   juvenile   ad. sum.

STILTS AND AVOCETS

Stilts and avocets are striking black-and-white birds; only two species occur in Europe and these are easily distinguished on the basis of leg colour and bill shape. The Black-winged Stilt is more often found in freshwater marshes than the Avocet.

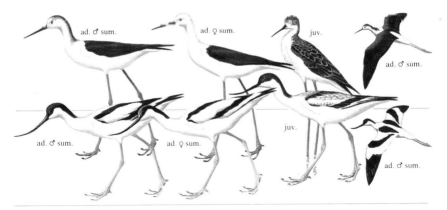

ad. ♂ sum.   ad. ♀ sum.   juv.   ad. ♂ sum.

ad. ♂ sum.   ad. ♀ sum.   juv.   ad. ♂ sum.

STONE CURLEWS

The Stone Curlew is distinguished from other waders by its brown plumage and short neck and bill. It usually occurs on heathland, chalk downland or other dryish open country. Although occasionally in largish groups, it is more usually seen in ones and twos. Its distinctive calls, heard particularly at dusk and into the night, are a good clue to its presence.

adult   juvenile   ad.

111

PRATINCOLES AND COURSERS family *Glareolidae* 17 species in the world.
Pratincoles are long-winged, rather short-legged waders with short necks. They run jerkily and not very fast; unusually for waders, most of their prey is caught on the wing.

☐ **COLLARED PRATINCOLE** *Glareola pratincola* 25cm. 70–90g. Rare vagrant. Very short-legged, looks like enormous swallow in flight; brown with black-edged creamy throat. VOICE shrill, dry twitters and chatters, likened to terns; also shriller 'ky-ick'. HAB dried mud-flats on edge of marshes. NEST colonial, on mud; almost no material. EGGS 3, creamy-buff, blotched and speckled with dark browns or blacks, 32mm. BROODS 1. INC 17–19, ♂♀. YOUNG fug, 25–30, ♂♀. IMM 3. AGE ?1, ?. FOOD mainly insects caught in flight.

PLOVERS family *Charadriidae* 62 species in the world.
This is a large group of waders, several of which breed in Europe. They are stocky and short-billed, with shortish necks. Typically they run a few paces, pause and look, then run on again. Some such as the Golden and Grey Plovers acquire bright summer plumages; in the others there is little change.

Vision p. 24; Down p. 29; Running p. 47; Hatchling p. 218; Heat loss in incubation p. 226–7; Learning to feed p. 230; Migration p. 237; Breeding season p. 250; Nest site, concealment and material p. 263, 265; Egg shape and colour p. 268–9; Pair bonds p. 283; Tundra p. 306.

○ **LITTLE RINGED PLOVER** *Charadrius dubius* 15cm. 30–50g. Local summer visitor (order 3); first bred in Britain in 1938. Like Ringed, but lacks orange beak and legs, has thin white line above black forehead, yellow eye-ring, no wing bar. VOICE disyllabic 'pee-u', falling in pitch. HAB SUM primarily beside freshwater pools, especially gravel pits; WIN more coastal. NEST on shingle bank, shallow scrape. EGGS 4, pale brownish or buffish, spotted with dark browns, 30mm. BROODS 2. INC 24–25, ♂♀. YOUNG fug, 24–27, ♂♀. IMM 3. AGE 1, 10, 65%. FOOD invertebrates, especially insects.

Seasonal plumages p. 220.

● ■ **RINGED PLOVER** *Charadrius hiaticula* 19cm. 55–75g. Widespread breeder (order 4), common winter visitor and passage migrant (order 4–5). Orange legs and bill (latter duller in winter), black breast band; more heavily built than Little Ringed, white wing-bar. VOICE disyllabic 'tulee'; more fluty than Lit. R., rising pitch. HAB SUM mainly coastal, shingle shores or river-banks; WIN many on coastal mud-flats. NEST shallow scrape, usually on shingle. EGGS 4, greyish- or brownish-buff, speckled blackish, 36mm. BROODS 1–3, depending on area. INC 23–25, ♂♀. YOUNG fug, 24, ♂♀. IMM 3. AGE 1, 10, 60%. FOOD invertebrates, esp. small worms.

Bill p. 16–17; Seasonal plumages p. 220; Heat loss in incubation p. 227; Number of broods p. 250; Nest material and heat loss p. 265; Egg size p. 268.

☐ **KENTISH PLOVER** *Charadrius alexandrinus* 16cm. 40–60g. Rare vagrant; used to breed (still order 0–1). Differs from Ringed and Little Ringed by blackish legs, lack of complete breast-band (but beware juveniles of the other species); has whiter forehead and, in males, often a conspicuously sandy orange crown and nape; has white wing bar. VOICE more monosyllabic 'pit' or 'huit'. HAB mainly coastal, but inland along sandy streams, lagoons. NEST shallow scrape in open. EGGS 3, buffish with fine black spots, 33mm. BROODS 1–2. INC 24–27, ♂♀. YOUNG fug, 26–31, ♂♀. IMM 3. AGE 1–2, 10, 60%. FOOD small invertebrates.

Seasonal plumages p. 220; New habitat p. 311.

○ **DOTTEREL** *Charadius morinellus* 22cm. 90–145g. Local summer visitor (order 3), passage migrant. ♀ in summer larger and brighter than ♂; white stripes over eye and on breast at all seasons. VOICE usually silent; soft 'titi' often runs into trill. HAB SUM stony mountainous areas or tundra; WIN (and on migration) open ground, not usually close to water. NEST shallow hollow on open ground. EGGS 3, yellowish to buffish with large dark spots and blotches, 44mm. BROODS 1 (2). ♀ sometimes lays two clutches for different ♂s. INC 24–28, ♂(♀). YOUNG fug, 25–30, ♂(♀). IMM 5. AGE 1, ?. FOOD mainly small invertebrates.

PRATINCOLES AND COURSERS
The very long-winged, swallow-like appearance immediately distinguishes pratincoles from other waders. The Collared Pratincole, the only species to breed in Europe, has a chestnut lining to the underwing which distinguishes it from the Black-winged (black lining) which occurs in Europe on rare occasions. Coursers do not nest in Europe but one species, Cream-coloured is a rare vagrant from North Africa.
Look for colour of underwing.

PLOVERS
The short bill, white underparts with breast bands or head markings help to identify the plovers.
Look also for presence of a wing-bar in the small plovers, colour of 'armpit' in larger plovers.

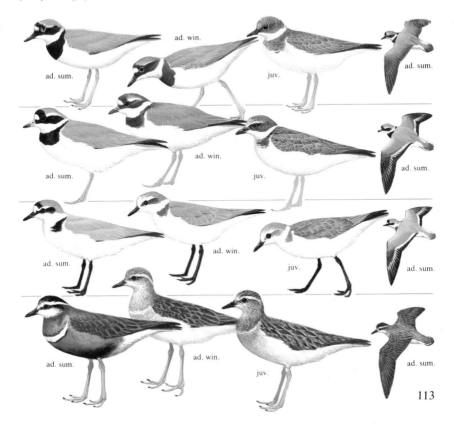

113

●■ **GOLDEN PLOVER** *Pluvialis apricaria* 28cm. 140–210g.
Common breeder (order 5), winter visitor and passage migrant
(order 6). In summer speckled golden back, black underparts; in
winter paler, often in mixed flocks with Lapwings. VOICE plaintive
musical 'tooee'. HAB SUM moorland; WIN fields, estuaries. NEST
shallow scrape on open ground, often slightly concealed by vegetation. EGGS 4, buff to yellowish, heavily spotted blackish, 52mm.
BROODS 1. INC 28–31, ♂♀. YOUNG fug 25–33, ♂♀. IMM 3. AGE 1, 12.
FOOD wide range invertebrates, especially worms; also some
vegetable matter.

Seasonal plumages
p. 220; Feeding flocks
p. 230–1.

■ **GREY PLOVER** *Pluvialis squatarola* 28cm. 170–240g. Common passage migrant and winter visitor (order 4). Similar to
Golden, but distinguished at all seasons by black axillaries ('armpit'), white rump, white tail and more white in upper wing. VOICE
similar to Golden but higher-pitched and usually trisyllabic 'tlee-
oo-ee'. HAB SUM tundra; WIN coastal, mudflats, etc. NEST shallow
scrape, little lining. EGGS 4, pale buff, blotched with dark browns
often mainly around widest part, 52mm. BROODS 1. INC 26–27,
♂♀. YOUNG fug, 35–45, ♂♀. IMM 3. AGE 2–3, 14. FOOD invertebrates:
insects in summer; largely marine worms in winter.

Seasonal plumages and
moult p. 220, 223.

SPUR-WINGED PLOVER *Vanellus spinosus* 27cm. 125–160g.
Striking black-and-white plumage, longer legged than Lapwing.
and lacks crest. VOICE most often heard making harsh ticking or
chacking notes, often run together 'zic-zac-zac'. HAB open ground
by marshes, often saltmarshes. NEST shallow hollow, some plant
lining. EGGS 4, whitish to yellowish, heavily blotched black. 40mm.
BROODS 1 (2). INC 22–24, ♂♀. YOUNG fug, ?, ♂♀. AGE ?1, ?.
FOOD mainly invertebrates.

●■ **LAPWING** *Vanellus vanellus* 30cm. 150–310g. Common
resident (order 6), winter visitor, arriving from Continent as early
as June. Very familiar bird with tall plume on head; common over
much of Europe, noisy and conspicuous, often in large flocks.
VOICE loud 'pee-wit' (which is one of its alternative names). HAB
commonest on farmland and short grassy areas, also saltmarshes.
NEST shallow scrape often in open, sometimes extensively lined
with vegetation. EGGS 4, pale buff to warm brown, heavily blotched
with blackish, 47mm. BROODS 1. INC 26–28, ♀(♂). YOUNG fug,
35–40, ♂♀. IMM 3. AGE 1, 23, 68%. FOOD mainly invertebrates.

Feeding flocks p. 230–
231; Migration p. 237;
Breeding season
p. 253; Egg size and
shape p. 268; Defence
against predators
p. 263; Nest material
p. 265; Pair bond
p. 283; Habitat history
p. 309.

SANDPIPERS AND SNIPE family *Scolopacidae* 81 species
in the world.
A large and varied family, ranging from the small, short-billed
waders to the large, long-billed curlews and godwits, and the
secretive snipes. Basically, this family includes all the familiar
waders except the minor families and the plovers. It is difficult to
give any distinguishing feature, but most have dark, blackish back
feathers strongly edged with brown so that they have a markedly
mottled, spotted or streaked appearance. Almost all lay four well-
camouflaged eggs and many are strongly migratory.

Bills and touch p. 16–
17, 27; Vision p. 24;
Down p. 29; Wading,
legs, heat loss, running
p. 46–7; Classification
p. 58–9; Hatching
p. 218; Seasonal
plumages p. 220;
Moult p. 223; Heat
loss in incubation

p. 226–7; Learning to
feed p. 230; Migration
p. 237; Breeding
season p. 250; Nest
p. 263, 265; Egg shape
and colour p. 268–9;
Pair bonds p. 283;
Conservation p. 304–5;
Tundra p. 306.

■ **KNOT** *Calidris canutus* 25cm. 125–215g. Common winter
visitor and passage migrant (order 6). A chunky medium-sized
wader, with a medium-short bill; in winter grey above, pale to
white below, has pale rump and tail and white wing-bar; may be
in very large flocks. VOICE a disyllabic 'twit-twit' in flight; more
musical double-note in summer. HAB SUM tundra; WIN seashore.
estuaries. NEST a hollow scrape lined with lichens. EGGS 4, pale
olive-green with blackish spots, 43mm. BROODS 1. INC 21–22,
♂(♀). YOUNG fug, 18–20, ♂(♀). IMM 5. AGE 2–3, 16, 68%. FOOD
mainly insects in summer; marine invertebrates in winter.

Seasonal plumages and
moult p. 220, 223;
Migration p. 242;
Nest material p. 265.

■ **SANDERLING** *Calidris alba* 20cm. 45–85g. Common winter
visitor and passage migrant (order 4). A smallish wader which
keeps close to the edge of the sea, running quickly in and out with
the waves; in winter pale grey above and white below, broad white
wing bar, white rump with black line down middle. VOICE a disyllabic 'twick-twick'. HAB SUM arctic tundra; WIN sandy shores.
NEST small hollow in stony ground, lined with leaves, ♀. EGGS 4,
olive-green with dark blotches, 35mm. BROODS 1 (2); if 2, each
parent takes care of one. INC 24–27, YOUNG fug, 23–24, IMM 5.
AGE ?2, 13. FOOD insects in summer; marine invertebrates in winter.

Seasonal plumages
p. 220; Migration
p. 242; Conservation
p. 305.

ad. sum.
northern

ad. sum.
southern

ad. win.

juv.

ad. win.

ad. win.

ad. sum.

ad. win.

juv.

ad. win.

ad. win.

adult

juvenile

ad.

ad. ♂ sum.

ad. win.

ad. ♀ sum.

juv.

ad.

SMALLER SANDPIPERS

Except for the stints, most sandpipers have relatively longer bills than plovers. There are a number of American and Asiatic species which are rare visitors. This is one of the *very* difficult groups, and even experts are sometimes unable to identify a wader with certainty.

Look for rump pattern (including whether or not there is a black band down the centre of the white rump), details of wing bar and back pattern.

ad. sum.

ad. win.

juv.

ad. win.

ad. sum.

ad. win.

juv.

ad. win.

☐ **LITTLE STINT** *Calidris minuta* 13cm. 20–40g. Uncommon passage migrant (order 2). Very small, straight bill shorter than Dunlin, black legs; in summer and autumn warm brown above with two white 'V's on back, brown breast, white underparts; in winter plainer and greyer. VOICE short 'tit', sometimes run into a trill. HAB SUM northern marshes, tundra; WIN mudflats, saltmarshes, etc. NEST small hollow, lined with leaves. EGGS 4, pale greenish or buffish with dark brown spots, 29mm. BROODS 1 or 2; if 2, each parent looks after one. INC 20–21. YOUNG fug, ?. IMM 5. AGE 1, 9. FOOD invertebrates: insects summer: more marine winter.

Seasonal plumages
p. 220; Conservation
p. 304–5.

○☐ **TEMMINCK'S STINT** *Calidris temminckii* 14cm. 17–32g. Breeds intermittently Scotland (order 1); scarce passage migrant (order 2–3). Similar to Little, but greyer back without 'V', grey breast, white outer tail feathers (Little has grey) and brownish or greenish legs. VOICE rapid trills and titters. HAB SUM tundra and open country; WIN less coastal than Little. NEST in short grass, often near water; cup lined with grass, ?♀. EGGS 3–4, pale greenish to buffish with dark red-brown spots, 28mm. BROODS 1 (2); if 2, each parent looks after one. INC 21–22. YOUNG fug, 15–18. IMM 3. AGE ♀ 1, ♂ ?longer, 81%. FOOD small invertebrates, esp. insects.

Seasonal plumages
p. 220; Second and
third clutches p. 283.

○■ **PURPLE SANDPIPER** *Calidris maritima* 21cm. 60–75g. Very rare breeder (order 1), common winter visitor (order 4); many here most of year. Often fairly tame; a rather dark wader, almost purplish-brown in summer plumage, yellow legs, yellow base to bill. VOICE a 'twit', sometimes run together as a trill. HAB SUM tundra; WIN (and a few throughout the year) on rocky, sea-weedy shores. NEST on ground; a hollow lined with grass, ♂. EGGS 4, pale buff-grey, spotted with dark browns, 37mm. BROODS 1. INC 21–22 ♂(♀). YOUNG fug, c. 28, ♂. IMM 3. AGE 1, 8. FOOD invertebrates: mainly insects in summer; small molluscs in winter.

Egg-bound ♀ p. 245;
Conservation p. 304–5.

☐ **CURLEW SANDPIPER** *Calidris ferruginea* 19cm. 45–90g. Uncommon passage migrant (order 3). Like Dunlin but with longer, more decurved beak; in winter plumage white rump without central black line; in summer plumage white rump often not visible, but bright reddish underparts distinctive. VOICE disyllabic 'chirrip'. HAB SUM Siberian arctic tundra; WIN marshes, mudflats. NEST shallow hollow lined with grasses, lichens. EGGS 4, olive to greenish with dark brown spots, 36mm. BROODS 1. INC ?, ♂♀. YOUNG fug, ?, ♂♀. IMM 5. AGE ?1, (6). FOOD mainly invertebrates.

Seasonal plumages
p. 220.

●■ **DUNLIN** *Calidris alpina* 18cm. 40–50g. Widespread breeder (order 4), common winter visitor and passage migrant (order 6). The commonest small wader in winter; variable in size; in some, bill decurved; in summer black belly distinctive. VOICE slightly grating 'zee', often repeated until a trill. HAB SUM moorland, saltmarshes; WIN mudflats, saltmarshes, sometimes large flocks. NEST in grass tussock or heather; shallow cup. ?♀. EGGS 4, cream, buffish or greenish, spotted and blotched with dark browns, 35mm. BROODS 1. INC 21–22, ♂♀. YOUNG fug, 19–21, ♂(♀). IMM 4. AGE 1–2, 20, 75%. FOOD mainly invertebrates.

Seasonal plumages and
moult p. 220, 223;
Clutch weight p. 245;
Food for egg
formation p. 245;
Conservation p. 304–5.

☐ **BROAD-BILLED SANDPIPER** *Limicola falcinellus* 16cm. 30–45g. Rare vagrant. Smaller than Dunlin, with shortish legs; bill longish with distinct downwardly-kinked tip; belly never black; forked supercilium. VOICE low trilling 'chr-reek'. HAB SUM arctic bogs; WIN marshes, mudflats. NEST usually in grass tussock, cup lined with vegetation, ♂. EGGS 4, pale buff, speckled or blotched dark browns, 32mm. BROODS 1. INC 21, ♂♀. YOUNG fug. ?, ♂♀. IMM (3). AGE ?, ?. FOOD mainly invertebrates, some seeds.

○■ **RUFF** *Philomachus pugnax* ♂ 29cm, ♀ 23cm. ♂ 130–230g, ♀ 70–150g. Rare breeder (order 2), regular passage migrant and winter visitor (order 3). Male much larger than ♀; legs yellowish to reddish, white rump with black centre; in summer ♂ unmistakeable with showy ruff of wide variety of colours. VOICE usually silent, but has range of quiet noises, including grunts. HAB SUM marshlands or wet meadows; WIN mainly inland marshes. NEST (♂s gather at leks), scrape on ground lined with grass. EGGS 4, 44. BROODS ♂ several, ♀ 1. INC 20–23, ♀. YOUNG fug, 25–28, ♀. IMM 5. AGE 1–2, 11. FOOD mainly invertebrates, some plant material.

Seasonal plumages
p. 220; Migration
p. 240–1; Lek p. 256,
260; Pair bond p. 282;
Habitat drainage
p. 308; Habitat history
p. 309.

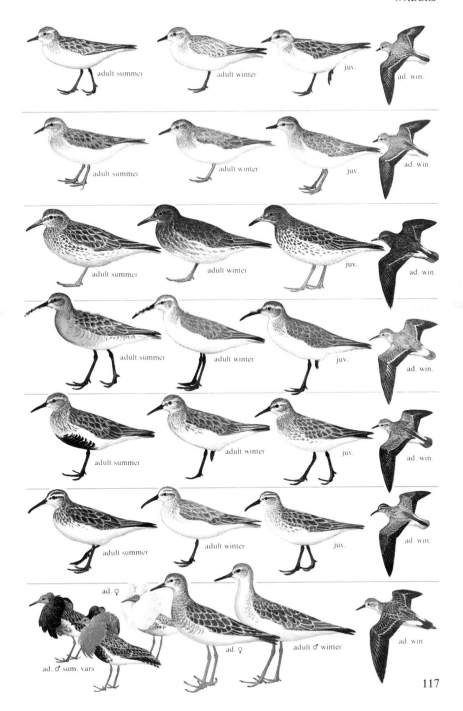

adult summer — adult winter — juv. — ad. win.

adult summer — adult winter — juv. — ad. win.

adult summer — adult winter — juv. — ad. win.

adult summer — adult winter — juv. — ad. win.

adult summer — adult winter — juv. — ad. win.

adult summer — adult winter — juv. — ad. win.

ad. ♀ — ad. ♀ — adult ♂ winter — ad. win.

ad. ♂ sum. vars

SNIPE AND WOODCOCK genera *Gallinago, Scolopax,* etc. 22 species in the world.
Secretive, longish-billed birds which usually stay in cover or close to it. The snipes are mostly birds of freshwater swamps, marshes and wet meadows, while the woodcocks live in woodland

Bills and touch p. 16–17, 27; Vision p. 24; Classification p. 59; Hatchling p. 218;

Moult p. 223; Learning to feed p. 230; Breeding season p. 250; Nest site.

■ **JACK SNIPE** *Lymnocryptes minimus* 19cm. 35–70g. Winter visitor (order 5). The smallest snipe, difficult to see, usually drops back into cover after flying a short distance; short bill, uniform dark tail, no pale central crown stripe. VOICE usually silent in winter, unlike Snipe; muffled thudding sounds in summer. HAB wet, marshy ground, bogs. NEST on ground; cup, lined with grass or leaves. EGGS 4, olive-green, blotched and speckled with dark browns, 39mm. BROODS 2. INC 24? or more ♀. YOUNG fug, ?, ?♀. IMM 2. AGE 1, (5). FOOD invertebrates, mainly insects, worms; also some seeds.

Bill p. 17; Polygamy and display p. 283.

●■ **SNIPE** *Gallinago gallinago* 27cm. 80–120g. Widespread breeder (order 4), common winter visitor (order 6). The commonest snipe; long bill, white on sides of rufous tail, pale central crown stripe; when flushed rises in towering zig-zag with harsh 'creech'. VOICE in summer a 'drumming' noise (produced by the tail feathers), also a regular, repeated 'chi-per'. HAB wide range of wet ground. NEST hollow in clump of herbage, ?♀. EGGS 4, olive-brown, heavily blotched with dark browns, 39mm. BROODS 1 (2). INC 18–20, ♀. YOUNG fug, 19–20, ♂♀. IMM 2, 12–24. AGE 12, 48%. FOOD invertebrates, especially worms, insects.

Bill and sense of touch p. 17, 27; Territory and drumming p. 258; Habitat history p. 309.

□ **GREAT SNIPE** *Gallinago media* 28cm. 160–190g. Scarce winter visitor, passage migrant (order 2). Heavily-built, shorter-billed than Snipe with more white in sides of tail; flight heavier, less twisting, usually silent. VOICE high-pitched bubbling noises at lek; usually croaking noise when flushed. HAB SUM marshes, wet ground; WIN same but also drier ground. NEST (♂s gather in leks in late evening, night, ♀s come for mating); hollow in a grass tussock, lined with grass. EGGS 4, pale buff, blotched dark brown, 45mm. BROODS ♂ several, ♀ ?1. INC 22–24, ♀. YOUNG fug, 21–28, ♀. IMM 3. AGE ?, ?. FOOD mainly earthworms, insects.

Bill p. 17.

●■ **WOODCOCK** *Scolopax rusticola* 34cm. 250–420g. Widespread breeder (order 5), common winter visitor (order 6) Heavily-built, brown snipe-like bird usually seen in woodland, flying low, calling, on early summer evenings. VOICE mainly silent; in display-flight ♂ gives croaking or growling noises and wheezy 'tsiwick'. HAB large woodlands, esp. with ground cover. NEST (♂ mates with series of ♀s) shallow hollow on woodland floor, lined with dead leaves. EGGS 4, camouflaged, buff to brownish, spotted darker, 44mm. BROODS ♂ several, ♀ 1. INC 22, ♀. YOUNG fug, 15–20, ♀. IMM 2. AGE ♀ 1, ♂ 2, 21, 61%. FOOD invertebrates, esp. worms.

Vision p. 24–5; Polygamy and roding p. 283.

GODWITS AND CURLEWS general *Limosa* and *Numenius* 12 species in the world.
Tall, long-legged, long-necked birds with long bills. They probe deep into soft soil and mud to collect prey, often largish worms. In godwits, the females are larger and have longer bills.

Bills and touch p. 16–17, 27; Wading, legs, heat loss, running p. 46–7; Classification p. 59; Nest site, conceal-

ment and material p. 263, 265; Egg shape and colour p. 268–9; Pair bonds p. 283; Conservation p. 304–5.

○■ **BLACK-TAILED GODWIT** *Limosa limosa* 41cm. ♂ 280–400g, ♀ 300–500g. Rare breeder (order 2), passage migrant and winter visitor (order 4). Long-legged, long-billed wader, conspicuous white wing-bar and white tail with broad black terminal band; more uniform upperparts than Bar-tailed in winter. VOICE 'pee-wit' like Lapwing (p. 113), also loud 'wicka wicka'. HAB SUM damp meadows; WIN usually coastal, estuaries. NEST grassy meadows; scrape lined with grass, ♀. EGGS 4, olive-brown, heavily blotched darker, 55mm. BROODS 1. INC 22–24, ♂♀. YOUNG fug, 25–30, ♂♀. IMM 3. AGE 2 (1), 16, 63%. FOOD invertebrates.

Bill p. 17, 298; Evolutionary change p. 50; Habitat drainage p. 308; Habitat history p. 309.

■ **BAR-TAILED GODWIT** *Limosa lapponica* 38cm. ♂ 280–380g, ♀ 400–450g. Passage migrant and winter visitor (order 5). Slightly smaller than Black-tailed; no white on wing and barred, not black-and-white, tail; upperparts more 'textured' than Black-tailed in winter. VOICE usually silent; has trilling song; alarm call 'keewick'. HAB SUM marshy tundra; WIN mainly coastal and estuaries. NEST hollow on ground, lined with grasses. EGGS 4, olive to greenish, spotted with drak brown, 53mm. BROODS 1. INC 20–21, ♂(♀). YOUNG fug, ?, ♂♀. IMM 3. AGE 2, 18, 71%. FOOD invertebrates.

Bill p. 16–17, 298; Copulation p. 261.

concealment and
material p. 263, 265;
Egg shape and colour
p. 268–9.

SNIPE AND WOODCOCK
In snipes, *look for white in tail, bill size, flight behaviour.*

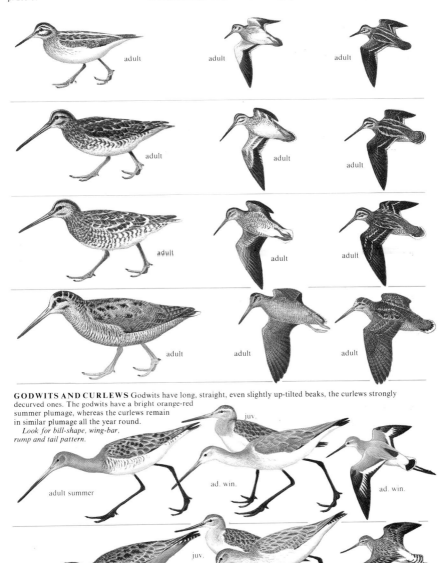

adult   adult   adult

adult   adult   adult

adult   adult   adult

adult   adult   adult

GODWITS AND CURLEWS Godwits have long, straight, even slightly up-tilted beaks, the curlews strongly
decurved ones. The godwits have a bright orange-red
summer plumage, whereas the curlews remain
in similar plumage all the year round.
    *Look for bill-shape, wing-bar,
rump and tail pattern.*

juv.

adult summer   ad. win.   ad. win.

juv.

adult summer   ad. win.   ad. win.

119

○□ **WHIMBREL** *Numenius phaeopus* 41cm. 270–450g. Scarce summer visitor (order 3), passage migrant (order 2). Like a small Curlew, shorter bill, black stripes on head; in flight slightly darker inner wing does not contrast with outer as in Curlew. VOICE loud whistling trill, often given in flight. HAB SUM moorland, often fairly wet; WIN many coastal. NEST shallow hollow on ground, sparsely lined, ♀ (?♂). EGGS 3–4, greenish to olive-brown, blotched darker, 58mm. BROODS 1. INC 27–28, ♂♀. YOUNG fug, 35–40, ♂♀. IMM 2. AGE 2, 12, 69%. FOOD invertebrates.

Bill p. 17.

●■ **CURLEW** *Numenius arquata* 55cm. ♂ 575–800g, ♀ 675–950g. Widespread breeder (order 5), common winter visitor (order 5–6). Large, brown, with very long, decurved bill; in flight, palish brown back contrasts with dark wingtips. VOICE familiar 'curlee'; song a long, accelerating, bubbling trill. HAB SUM moorland, marshes, occas. water-meadows; WIN mainly coastal mudflats, estuaries. NEST shallow hollow on ground, often well-concealed in heather, lined plant material, ♀(?♂). EGGS 4, greenish to brownish, spotted darker, 68mm. BROODS 1. INC 27–29, ♂♀. YOUNG fug, 32–38, ♂♀. IMM 2. AGE 2, 32, 74%. FOOD wide range of invertebrates.

Bill p. 17; Pair bond p. 283; Habitat history p. 309.

'SHANKS' AND LARGER SANDPIPERS genera *Tringa* and *Actitis* 16 species in the world.
A widespread group of smallish to medium-sized waders; most of the larger ones have long legs. Most vary rather little between summer and winter plumages, but the Spotted Redshank has a very different summer plumage from its winter one. Most nest on marshy bogs in the north, often close to forests, in forest clearings or along stream-edges.

Bills and touch p. 16–17, 27; Vision p. 24; Down p. 29; Wading, legs, heat loss, running p. 46–7; Classification p. 58–9; Hatchling p. 218; Seasonal plumages and moult p. 220, 223; Learning to feed p. 230;

Migration p. 237; Breeding season p. 250; Nest site, concealment and material p. 263, 265; Egg shape and colour p. 268–9; Pair bonds p. 283; Conservation p. 304–5; Tundra p. 306.

□ **SPOTTED REDSHANK** *Tringa erythropus* 30cm. ♂ 135–170g, ♀ 160–205g. Uncommon passage migrant (order 2). In summer unmistakeable white-spotted black plumage; in winter orange-red legs, white rump and lower back. VOICE commonest call is loud 'chu-it'; rising, drawn out 'tchwee'. HAB SUM bogs and heaths, in forest; WIN marshes, mudflats, estuaries. NEST shallow hollow lined with grass, etc. EGGS 4, greenish or olive, blotched blackish-brown, 47mm. BROODS 1. INC ?, ♂. YOUNG fug, ?, ♂(♀) but some ♀s leave before eggs hatch. IMM 3. AGE ?1, 6. FOOD invertebrates.

Preening p. 30; Seasonal plumages p. 220; Role reversal p. 283.

●■ **REDSHANK** *Tringa totanus* 28cm. ♂ 85–140g, ♀ 110–155g. Widespread breeder (order 5), common passage migrant and winter visitor (order 5). Common, noisy, orange-red-legged wader, with very broad white trailing edge to wing. VOICE very vocal, a drawn out 'tyu-yu-yu-yu', or 'tyuk-tyuk'. HAB SUM wet meadows, salt-marshes, etc; WIN more on coast. NEST shallow hollow, often in tussock, lined with grass, ♀. EGGS 4, cream to buff, spotted and blotched dark brown, 45mm. BROODS 1. INC 24, ♂♀. YOUNG fug. 25–35, ♂♀ but ♀ often leaves before young fledged. IMM 3. AGE 1–2, 17, 69%. FOOD invertebrates.

Seasonal plumages p. 220; Habitat history p. 309.

□ **MARSH SANDPIPER** *Tringa stagnatilis* 23cm. 55–90g. Rare vagrant. Reminiscent of small Greenshank, with fine straight bill, often pale forehead; longer legs (in flight feet project further beyond tail). VOICE 'teu' and high twittering notes. HAB edges of lakes and marshes, almost always by fresh water. NEST shallow hollow, lined with grass. EGGS 4, pale to mid-buff, spotted and blotched with reddish and blackish browns, 39mm. BROODS 1. INC ?, ♂♀. YOUNG fug, ?, ♂♀. IMM 3. AGE ?1, ?. FOOD invertebrates.

○□ **GREENSHANK** *Tringa nebularia* 31cm. 140–270g. Uncommon summer visitor (order 3), regular passage migrant (order 3), some overwinter. The largest 'shank'; long bill, very slightly up-turned; green legs; white rump and wedge up back. VOICE a loud 'teu-teu-teu', usually trisyllabic and usually in flight; song a ringing 'tew-i' repeated regularly. HAB SUM moorland and heaths, near forest; WIN marshes and estuaries. NEST shallow scrape on ground, lined with vegetation, ♀. EGGS 4, cream to buff, lightly marked with reddish-brown, 51mm. BROODS 1. INC 24, ♂♀. YOUNG fug, 25–31, ♂♀. IMM 3. AGE 2, 12. FOOD invertebrates.

Legs p. 47.

adult   adult   adult

adult   adult   adult

'SHANKS' AND LARGER SANDPIPERS

Most 'shanks' and sandpipers can be recognised by their darkish
plumage and streaked underparts and elongated, fine straight bill.
Look for wing-bars, tail pattern and leg colour.

adult summer   adult winter   juv.   ad. win.

adult summer   adult winter   juv.   ad. win.

adult summer   adult winter   juv.   ad. win.

adult summer   adult winter   juv.   ad. win.

121

■ **GREEN SANDPIPER** *Tringa ochropus* 23cm. 70–90g. Regular passage migrant and winter visitor (order 3). Similar to Wood, but green legs; much darker back makes more striking contrast with white rump; dark underwing. VOICE 'tit-loo-eet', and 'weet-weet' usually 4–5 times, much louder than Wood; song a trill of variable pitch. HAB SUM forest bogs; WIN marshes, mainly fresh water. NEST usually up tree in old nest of pigeon, thrush, etc. EGGS 4, creamish, small speckles of reddish and dark browns, 39mm. BROODS 1. INC 20–23, ♀(♂). YOUNG fug (drop from tree), 28, ♂(♀). IMM 3. AGE 1, 10. FOOD invertebrates.

○□ **WOOD SANDPIPER** *Tringa glareola* 20cm. 50–90g. Rare, irregular breeder (order 1–2), regular passage migrant (order 3). Slightly smaller than Green, paler (esp. under-wing), more mottled; yellowish legs extend further behind tail in flight. VOICE high 'chiff-iff-iff'; song a descending trill. HAB SUM northern bogs and marshes; WIN wide range of fresh waters, lakes, streams, etc. NEST sometimes in old bird's nest in tree; usually hollow on ground, lined vegetation. EGGS 4, pale greenish or buff, blotched and spotted dark browns, 38mm. BROODS 1. INC 22–23, ♂♀. YOUNG fug, 30, ♂(♀). IMM 3. AGE 1, 9. FOOD invertebrates, esp. insects.

Moult p. 223.

TEREK SANDPIPER *Tringa cinerea* 23cm. 60–90g. Often flies low over water like Common; greyish, short legs yellow to orange, long, slightly upturned bill; in flight white trailing edge to wing, not as extensive as Redshank. VOICE musical 'du-du-du', usually 3–5 syllables. HAB SUM streams and marshes near woodland; WIN wide range of waters mainly coastal, some fresh. NEST shallow cup on ground, lined with vegetation. EGGS 4, cream or buff, spotted with dark browns, 39mm. BROODS 1. INC 21–23, ♂♀. YOUNG fug. ?, ♂♀. IMM 3. AGE ?1, (5). FOOD invertebrates, some seeds.

●□ **COMMON SANDPIPER** *Actitis hypoleucos* 20cm. 40–60g. Common summer visitor (order 5); a few winter (order 2), olive-brown upperparts, white below; bobs vigorously, flies low over water with shallow wing-beats and glides, broad white wing-bar. VOICE shrill, piping 'twee-wee-wee'; song a high, rapid trill. HAB SUM swift streams, lakes; WIN marshes, estuaries, coasts, etc., very small pools. NEST scrape on ground, often in thick vegetation, lined with vegetation, ♀. EGGS 4, whitish to yellowish, spotted reddish-brown, 36mm. BROODS 1. INC 21–22, ♂♀. YOUNG fug, 26–28, ♂♀. IMM 4. AGE 1, 10. FOOD invertebrates, esp. insects.

□ **SPOTTED SANDPIPER** *Actitis macularia* 20cm. 35–50g. Rare vagrant, has bred in Scotland. Very similar to Common, but in summer strikingly spotted underneath, and bright pinkish base to bill; juvenile paler and greyer than Common, with patch of barring on wing. VOICE harsher than Common, 'chwit'. HAB SUM swift streams, lakes; WIN marshes, estuaries, coasts, etc., often on very small pools. NEST scrape on ground, often in thick vegetation (p. 283). EGGS 4, buff, spotted reddish-brown, 36mm. BROODS ♂1, ♀ up to 4. INC 21–22, often only ♂. YOUNG fug, 18–21, often only ♂. IMM 4. AGE 1–2, ?. FOOD mainly invertebrates.

Energy for breeding p. 226; Feeding rates p. 228; Multiple clutches p. 283.

TURNSTONES genus *Arenaria* 2 species in the world.
Fairly small, solidly built waders with short beaks. Live on rocky shores, obtaining their food by probing under seaweed and stones which they flick aside with a quick movement of their head, hence their name.

Only one turnstone species occurs in Europe. Although this breeds in the far north, many non-breeding birds stay behind in the wintering areas; so it can be seen in many areas all the year round.

Vision p. 24; Down p. 29; Running p. 47; Classification p. 59; Hatchling p. 218; Seasonal plumages and moult p. 220, 223; Learning to feed p. 230; Breeding seasons p. 250; Nest site, concealment and material p. 263, 265; Egg shape and colour p. 268–9; Pair bonds p. 283; Conservation p. 304–5; Tundra p. 306.

■ **TURNSTONE** *Arenaria interpres* 23cm. 80–110g. Common winter visitor (order 5), some present almost all year; very rare breeder (order 0–?1). Orange legs, short bill; black-and-white pattern in flight, rich chestnut back in summer plumage. VOICE slightly metallic twittering. HAB breeds arctic tundra; in Britain, rocky coasts and estuaries. NEST shallow hollow on open ground, sometimes lined, ♀. EGGS 4, olive or palish-green, blotched blackish-brown, 40mm. BROODS 1. INC 22–24, ♀(♂). YOUNG fug, 19–21, ♂(♀). IMM 3. AGE 2, 20, 78%. FOOD invertebrates, usually insects in summer, marine in winter.

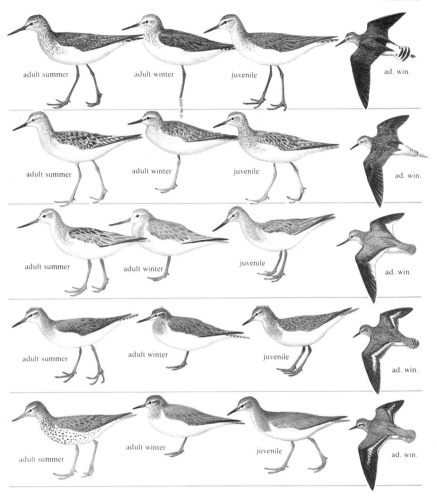

adult summer   adult winter   juvenile   ad. win.

adult summer   adult winter   juvenile   ad. win.

adult summer   adult winter   juvenile   ad. win.

adult summer   adult winter   juvenile   ad. win.

adult summer   adult winter   juvenile   ad. win.

TURNSTONES

The stocky build and orange legs, together with the *variable, chequered pattern in flight*, are distinctive.

ad. ♂ sum.   ad. win.   juv.

ad. ♀ sum.   ad. win.

123

PHALAROPES family *Phalaropodidae* 3 species in the world. Small, very tame waders that spend most of their time swimming; European species spend the winter at sea. Their summer plumage is brighter than the greyish winter plumage. The females are slightly larger and brighter than the males.

Vision p. 24; Feet and heat loss p. 45, 47; Hatchling p. 218; Seasonal plumages and moult p. 220, 223; Heat loss in incubation p. 226–7; Migration p. 237; Breeding season p. 250; Nest site, concealment and material p. 263, 265; Egg shape and colour p. 268–9; Brood patch p. 283; Tundra p. 306.

○□ **RED-NECKED PHALAROPE** *Phalaropus lobatus* 18cm. 25–50g. Rare breeder (order 2), uncommon passage migrant. Darker and more speckled than Grey in winter, bill finer, all black; Dunlin-like (p. 115) in flight. VOICE 'twit' or 'twit-twit'. HAB SUM freshwater marshes, pools; WIN mostly at sea. NEST side of grass tussock close to water, small hollow lined with vegetation. ♂♀. EGGS 4, pale greenish to buff, heavily blotched darker, 30mm. BROODS ♀ 2, ♂ 1. INC 17–21, ♂. YOUNG fug, 16–18, ♂. IMM 4. AGE 1, 5. FOOD small invertebrates: insects in summer, marine in winter.

□ **GREY PHALAROPE** *Phalaropus fulicarius* 20cm. 50–75g. Uncommon passage migrant. Broad bill with yellow base in summer, traces of yellow in some in winter; slightly more heavily built than Red-necked, more powerful in flight; in winter more uniform grey above. VOICE shrill 'twit'. HAB SUM arctic tundra; WIN at sea. NEST at side of tussock, shallow hollow lined with grass, etc. EGGS 4, greenish to buff, heavily blotched darker, 30mm. BROODS ♂ 1, ♀ 2. INC 18–20, ♂. YOUNG fug, 16–18, ♂. IMM 4. AGE 1. ?. FOOD invertebrates.

SKUAS family *Stercorariidae* 5 species in the world.
Medium to large relatives of the gulls, skuas are gull-like in appearance except for the dark plumage. They spend most of the winter offshore, sometimes far out at sea. Their feeding habits include piracy in which they harry other seabirds, forcing them to drop the food they have caught for themselves.

□ **POMARINE SKUA** *Stercorarius pomarinus* 51cm. 550–900g. Scarce passage migrant. Very similar to Arctic, but heavier; in full plumage elongated tail feathers are blunt and twisted. VOICE harsh, barking 'grek' and rolling 'yeew' or 'yeew-eee', likened to a forced laugh. HAB SUM breeds arctic tundra; WIN at sea, but occasionally seen inshore. NEST shallow scrape on ground, no material. EGGS 2 (3), buff to light brown, blotched dark brown, 65mm. BROODS 1. INC 25–27, ♂♀. YOUNG semifug, 31–32, ♂♀. IMM 24–36. AGE ?, ?. FOOD mainly lemmings in summer, fish in winter; scavenges, steals fish from other seabirds.

●□ **ARCTIC SKUA** *Stercorarius parasiticus* 46cm. 380–600g. Widespread summer visitor (order 4), passage migrant, some offshore in winter. Commonest small skua; elongated tail feathers straight and pointed. VOICE yelping notes and rising 'ka-aaow'. HAB SUM tundra, moorland, usually near sea; WIN at sea, commoner along coasts on migration than other skuas. NEST small colonies; shallow scrape on ground, ♂♀. EGGS 2, greenish to brown with darker blotches, 57mm. BROODS 1. INC 25–28, ♂♀. YOUNG semifug, 25–30, ♂♀. IMM 24–36. AGE 4–5, 18. FOOD mammals, birds, insects, fruits; at sea, fish; robs other seabirds.

Egg-tooth p. 205.

□ **LONG-TAILED SKUA** *Stercorarius longicaudus* 50cm (inc. tail feathers). 250–450g. Scarce passage migrant. By far the smallest skua with light, almost tern-like flight, tail feathers very long in adult. VOICE shriller, sharper than the others, 'kree'. HAB nests arctic tundra; otherwise pelagic, uncommon inshore. NEST small colonies; shallow hollow on ground, usually unlined. EGGS 2, pale buff, brown or green, blotched darker, 55mm. BROODS 1. INC 23–25, ♂♀. YOUNG semifug, 24–26, ♂♀. IMM 12. AGE ?, ?. FOOD on breeding ground, mammals, insects, berries; at sea presumably fish.

Clutch size p. 271; Population movements p. 291.

●□ **GREAT SKUA** *Stercorarius skua* 58cm. 1,200–1,650g. Widespread summer visitor (order 4), passage migrant, some offshore in winter. Much heavier and stockier than the other skuas, with shorter, broader wings; always dark underneath, conspicuous white wing flashes. VOICE harsh barking 'uk-uk-uk'. HAB breeds moorland, usually near sea; rest of year at sea. NEST shallow scrape on ground. EGGS 2, olive, blotched or spotted dark browns, 71mm. BROODS 1. INC 29, ♀(♂). YOUNG semifug, 42–49, ♂♀. IMM 12. AGE 7–8, 16, 93%. FOOD wide range, fish; also robs other birds of fish; kills birds, mammals up to rabbit size; scavenges.

PHALAROPES

Persistent swimming distinguishes phalaropes from all other waders.

To separate the two, *look for bill shape and the tone and texture of the upperparts.*

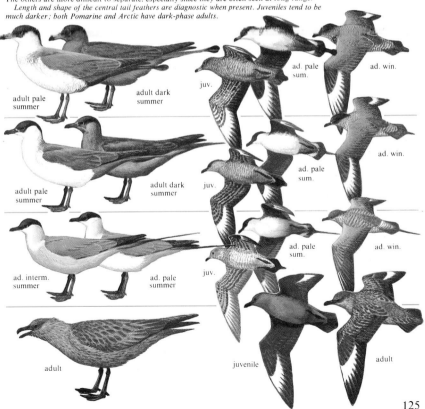

adult ♀ summer

juvenile

ad. ♂ sum.

adult winter

ad. win.

adult ♀ summer

juvenile

ad. ♂ sum.

adult winter

ad. win.

SKUAS

Great Skua is much larger and more heavily built than the others with conspicuous white wing-flashes. The others are more difficult to separate, especially since they are often seen at long-range.

Length and shape of the central tail feathers are diagnostic when present. Juveniles tend to be much darker; both Pomarine and Arctic have dark-phase adults.

adult pale summer

adult dark summer

juv.

ad. pale sum.

ad. win.

adult pale summer

adult dark summer

juv.

ad. pale sum.

ad. win.

ad. interm. summer

ad. pale summer

juv.

ad. pale sum.

ad. win.

adult

juvenile

adult

GULLS family *Laridae* 45 species in the world.
Gulls are a familiar group; all European species are predominantly white underneath (white birds are more difficult for fish under water to see). Although many are marine, some live largely in freshwater habitats, at least during the breeding season.

○ □ **MEDITERRANEAN GULL** *Larus melanocephalus* 39cm. 200–350g. Very rare breeder (order 1); rare vagrant (order 2). Like Blackheaded, but lacks white leading edge to wing and black wingtips; heavy bill; black hood goes well down back of neck. VOICE harsh, nasal 'kraar'; short yaps. HAB mainly coastal, lagoons, estuaries, etc. NEST colonial, on ground; seaweed, etc., ♂♀. EGGS 3, pale yellowish or buff, spotted with dark browns, 54mm. BROODS 1. INC 23–25, ♂♀. YOUNG semifug, 35–40, ♂♀. IMM 12. AGE 2–3, 15. FOOD terrestrial and aquatic insects, fish, molluscs.

□ **LITTLE GULL** *Larus minutus* 28cm. 90–150g. Rare vagrant (order 3), v. rare breeder (order 0–1). Small; summer adult has black head, wings all-grey above, dark below; juveniles have black line on wings, square tail, dark cap. VOICE quiet 'kek-kek-kek'. HAB SUM inland marshes; WIN more widespread, incl. coastal. NEST colonial; on ground; hollow lined vegetation, ♂♀. EGGS 3, olive-brown to buff, blotched dark brown, 42mm. BROODS 1. INC 23–25, ♂♀. YOUNG semifug, 21–24, ♂♀. IMM 12. AGE 2–3, 6. FOOD mainly insects in summer; otherwise fish, marine invertebrates.

□ **SABINE'S GULL** *Larus sabini* 33cm. 150–210g. Vagrant (order 2–3) off western Europe in autumn. In breeding plumage (rarely seen Europe) a grey hood; forked tail, striking black, grey and white wing pattern, rather tern-like flight. VOICE grating and tern-like. HAB nests northern tundra, otherwise mainly at sea. NEST colonial, often with Arctic Tern; shallow cup lined with vegetation. EGGS 2(3), buff-olive, blotched dark browns, 44mm. BROODS 1. INC 23–25, ♂♀. YOUNG semifug, ?, ♂♀. IMM 12. AGE ?, ?. FOOD insects in breeding season, otherwise fish.

● ■ **BLACK-HEADED GULL** *Larus ridibundus* 36cm. 225–350g. Common resident (order 6 summer, 7 winter). The commonest gull; white leading edge to outer wing; in summer brown hood does not go down back of neck. VOICE rather harsh, nasal 'kraah', varied. HAB SUM marshes, inland and coastal; WIN widespread, common inland. NEST colonial; on ground; wide range of plant material, ♂♀. EGGS 3, pale greenish to brownish, blotched dark browns, 52mm. BROODS 1. INC 23–26, ♂♀. YOUNG semifug, 35, ♂♀.IMM 12. AGE 2–3, 32. FOOD varied, insects, marine invertebrates, fish; follows plough.

□ **SLENDER-BILLED GULL** *Larus genei* 43cm. 250–350g. Rare vagrant. Like stocky Black-headed with longer bill; in summer has faint pink wash on body; immature has yellow legs. less brownish on wing than Black-headed, Mediterranean. VOICE like Black-headed, but has higher yelping notes. HAB SUM fresh and brackish lakes; WIN coastal, estuaries. NEST hollow on ground, lined with plant material. EGGS 2–3, creamy-white, blotched dark browns, 56mm. BROODS 1. INC 22, ♂♀. YOUNG semifug, ?, ♂♀. IMM 12. AGE ?, 23. FOOD mainly fish, invertebrates; also scavenges. .

● ■ **COMMON GULL** *Larus canus* 41cm. 300–500g. Common resident (order 5), winter visitor (order 6). Smaller than Herring, greenish-yellow legs, bill. VOICE shrill 'kee-ya', first syllable sometimes drawn out. HAB SUM often inland, moorland, lochs; WIN widespread, coasts, farmland. NEST colonial; on ground, from simple scrape to well-built nest of vegetation, ♂♀. EGGS 2–3, greenish to dark olive, blotched dark browns, 58mm. BROODS 1. INC 22–28, ♂♀. YOUNG semifug, 35–40, ♂♀. IMM 12. AGE 2–4, 24. FOOD fish, also invertebrates; many moths in summer, earthworms in winter.

● ■ **KITTIWAKE** *Rissa tridactyla* 41cm. 300–500g. Common summer visitor (order 6), offshore in winter (order ?4). Like Common Gull but black legs, solid black wing tips; first-year young has dark 'W' pattern across wings, black nape mark. VOICE loud 'kitti-wake'; also quieter 'ock-ock-ock'. HAB nests on cliffs, occasionally on buildings, otherwise at sea. NEST colonial; tiny cliff ledge; bulky, of seaweed, mud, ♂♀. EGGS 2–3, bluish-grey to pale brown, blotched dark browns, 55mm. BROODS 1. INC 25–32, ♂♀. YOUNG col, 33–54, ♂♀. IMM 12. AGE 4–5, 21, 86%. FOOD small fish, marine invertebrates.

Feather wear p. 32;
Feet and swimming
p. 45; Baby bird
p. 206; Hatchling

Moult p. 220.

Nest density and
colonial nesting p. 49,
262; Moult p. 220;
Feeding flocks p. 230–231; Change of habits
p. 310.

Feather wear p. 32;
Change of habits
p. 310.

Juvenile plumage
p. 219; Migration
p. 238, 240–1; Pairing
and pair bond p. 261–262.

p. 218; Feeding on
rubbish-tips p. 230;
Pairing p. 260; Nest
predation p. 262:

Brood patches p. 272;
Change of habits
p. 310; New habitat
p. 311.

GULLS Most gulls are easy to identify in adult summer plumage, but at other ages and times can be difficult.

Look for leg colour, size and colour of the bill and the details of the black and white patterning of the wingtip.

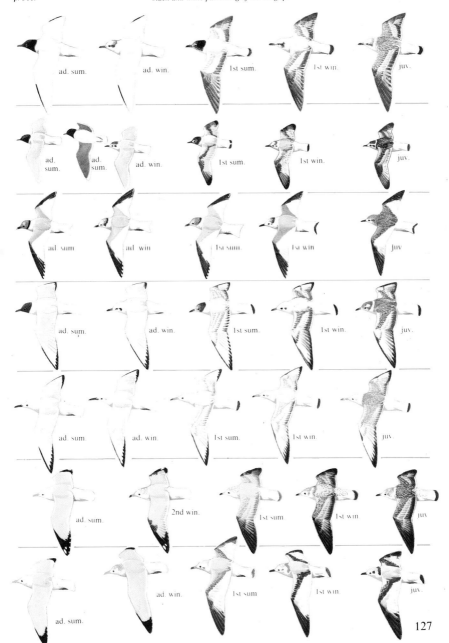

127

AUDOUIN'S GULL *Larus audouinii* 50cm. ?550–800g. Rare Mediterranean species; resembles small Herring Gull, but with dark green legs, red bill with black band, yellow tip; wing tips have fewer white 'mirrors' than other species so look blacker; immature has browner back, yellower bill than adult. VOICE varied, but most calls short and hoarse. HAB Mediterranean rocky shores; at sea. NEST colonial; shallow scrape on ground, lined with seaweed, ♂♀. EGGS 2–3, olive-buff with dark blotches, 64mm. BROODS 1. INC 28–29, ♂♀. YOUNG semifug, 35–40, ♂♀. AGE ?, ?. FOOD mainly fish.

●■ **LESSER BLACK-BACKED GULL** *Larus fuscus* 55cm. 659–1,000g. Common summer visitor (order 6), winter visitor (order 5: many British leave for winter, replaced by Scandinavian birds). Very dark grey back (blacker in Scand.); yellow legs, smaller than Great B.-b. VOICE 'kyow' and others. HAB SUM usually coastal, some moorland; WIN coastal and inland. NEST colonial, on ground; scrape or nest, vegetation, ♂♀. EGGS 3, olive to green-blue to dark brown, heavily blotched darker brown, 68mm. BROODS 1. INC 24–27, ♂♀. YOUNG semifug, 30–40, ♂♀. IMM 36–48. AGE 4, 26, 90%. FOOD mainly natural food, e.g. fish; also scavenges.

Subspecies p. 60; Post-fledging moult p. 219; Breeding season p. 253; Display p. 258; Pair bond and parental care p. 282.

●■ **HERRING GULL** *Larus argentatus* 60cm. 750–1,250g. Common resident (order 6). Largest gull with grey upperparts and black wingtips; yellow bill with red spot; legs pink (yellow in Mediterranean race). VOICE familiar 'kee-yow', but wide range of other calls. HAB SUM mainly coastal, also nests in towns on roof-tops; WIN almost ubiquitous, coastal, inland in towns. NEST on ground or cliff ledge, increasingly on roof-top; vegetation, ♂♀. EGGS 3, pale greenish to light-brown, blotched with dark browns, 70mm. BROODS 1. INC 28–30, ♂♀. YOUNG semifug, 35–40, ♂♀. IMM 48. AGE 3–5, 32, 93.5%. FOOD wide range, especially scavenging.

Flight p. 38, 43; Plumage succession p. 219; Energy for breeding p. 226–7; Breeding p. 245, 248, 253; Display p. 258; Nest predation p. 262; Survival rate p. 285, 287; Change of habits p. 310.

□ **ICELAND GULL** *Larus glaucoides* 60cm. ?750–1,000g. Scarce winter visitor (order 2). Very pale grey above, white below, no black in wing tips, yellow bill with red spot; young (more often seen further south in Europe than adults) uniform pale brown above with pinkish, black-tipped bill. VOICE similar to Herring. HAB coastal. NEST colonial; on cliff ledges, rocky coasts; vegetation. EGGS 2–3, pale buff with dark blotches, 76mm. BROODS 1. INC ?, ♂♀. YOUNG semifug, ?, ♂♀. IMM 48. AGE ?, ?. FOOD mainly fish, also carrion.

Heat loss from legs p. 47.

□ **GLAUCOUS GULL** *Larus hyperboreus* 70cm (but very variable in size). 1,000–2,200g. Scarce winter visitor (order 2–3). Like very large Iceland with heavier beak, size of Great Black-backed; relatively shorter wings than Iceland, at rest wings only just project beyond tail; has yellow eye-ring (Iceland red). VOICE as Herring. HAB rocky cliffs and shores. NEST on cliff ledge or flat ground; vegetation, may be substantial, ♂♀. EGGS 3, pale grey to brown, blotched dark browns, 77mm. BROODS 1. INC 27–28, ♂♀. YOUNG semifug, 45–50, ♂♀. IMM 48. AGE ?, 21. FOOD varied; scavenges, kills many birds, robs others of their prey.

Heat loss from legs p. 47; Moult p. 221.

●■ **GREAT BLACK-BACKED GULL** *Larus marinus* 70cm. 1,150–2,150g. Common resident (order 5). Very large gull, black back, pink legs. VOICE deep 'owk-owk'. HAB SUM mainly rocky coasts and islands; WIN widespread, some inland. NEST some single, some colonial; on cliffs or rocky outcrop with good all-round view; vegetation, may be bulky, ♂♀. EGGS 3, pale buff to olive-brown, blotched dark browns, 77mm. BROODS 1. INC 27–28, ♂♀. YOUNG semifug, 49–56, ♂♀. IMM 36–48. AGE 4–5, 20. FOOD very varied; scavenges, but also predatory, killing birds and mammals to size of Shag (p. 67) and Rabbit.

Territory and predation on terns p. 255.

□ **IVORY GULL** *Pagophila eburnea* 44cm. ♂ 580–640g, ♀ 480–540g. Rare vagrant. The only pure white gull; juvenile has blackish mask, dark spots, esp. on tips of coverts and flight feathers; these are visible but paler on immature. VOICE a shrill 'krii-krii', and harsher 'karr'. HAB usually offshore. NEST on cliff or flat ground; cup of seaweed, sometimes scanty, ♂♀. EGGS 1–2, olive or buff, spotted browns and greys, 61mm. BROODS 1. INC c.25, ♂♀. YOUNG col, 35 (?+), ♂♀. IMM 2 (?3), ?. AGE ?. FOOD marine invertebrates, small fish; also scavenges.

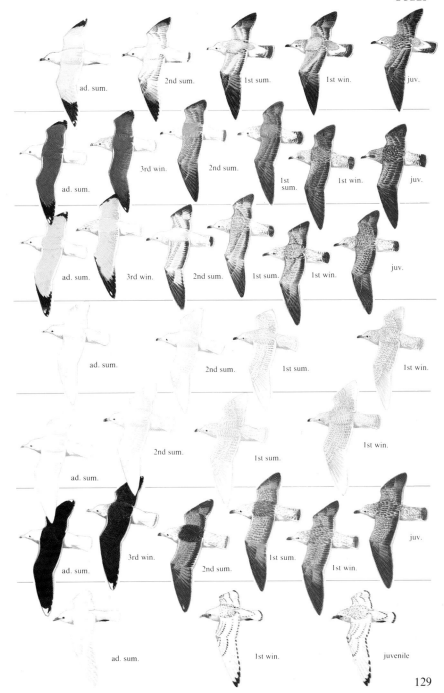

ad. sum.

2nd sum.

1st sum.

1st win.

juv.

ad. sum.

3rd win.

2nd sum.

1st sum.

1st win.

juv.

ad. sum.

3rd win.

2nd sum.

1st sum.

1st win.

juv.

ad. sum.

2nd sum.

1st sum.

1st win.

ad. sum.

2nd sum.

1st sum.

1st win.

ad. sum.

3rd win.

2nd sum.

1st sum.

1st win.

juv.

ad. sum.

1st win.

juvenile

129

TERNS

TERNS family *Sternidae* 41 species in the world.
Small relatives of the gulls (put in the same family by some). The majority are primarily marine birds; in Europe these 'sea terns' are largely white with black caps, these being lost in winter plumage. The small 'marsh' terns of the genus *Chlidonias* live mainly on fresh water during the breeding season. Young terns leave the nest soon after hatching, and it is difficult to establish the exact age at fledging.

Feet p. 45; Baby bird p. 206; Hatchling p. 218; Moult p. 220; Colonial nesting and defence against predators p. 255, 262.

☐ **GULL-BILLED TERN** *Gelochelidon nilotica* 38cm. 200–300g. Rare vagrant. Black legs, very similar to Sandwich, but bill shorter, much stouter, all black, tail grey, less forked. VOICE 'ge-rek', much harsher than Sandwich; also a 'cac-cac-cac'. HAB saltmarshes and freshwater habitats; sometimes hunts insects over land. NEST colonial, close together on small islands; shallow scrape on ground, little or no lining. EGGS 2–3, palish, blotched with dark browns and greys, 49mm. BROODS 1. INC 22–23, ♂♀. YOUNG semifug, 28–35, ♂♀. IMM 3. AGE ?3, 16. FOOD very largely insectivorous, rarely plunges into water.

☐ **CASPIAN TERN** *Sterna caspia* 53cm. 550–750g. Rare vagrant. A very large tern, almost as large as Herring Gull; bright orange-red bill, dark underside of wing tips. VOICE deep 'kaark', slightly crow-like. HAB usually coastal, sometimes inland. NEST colonial, on shingle; unlined shallow scrape. EGGS 2–3, palish cream, finely marked with browns and greys, 64mm. BROODS 1. INC 20–22, ♂♀. YOUNG semifug, 26–30, ♂♀. IMM 3. AGE 3–4, 26. FOOD mainly fish.

● **SANDWICH TERN** *Sterna sandvicensis* 41cm. 210–260g. Summer visitor (order 5). Black legs, similar to Gull-billed, but bill finer, longer with small yellow tip, tail more forked, white. VOICE harsh 'kir-rick', higher than Gull-billed. HAB mostly marine, coastal, not inland. NEST colonial, close together; on sand or shingle bar, shallow scrape, usually unlined. EGGS 1–2, whitish to light brown, spotted and blotched dark brown and grey, 52mm. BROODS 1. INC 21–24, ♂♀. YOUNG semifug, c. 35, ♂♀. IMM 3. AGE 3–4, 24. FOOD fish.

Hunting efficiency p. 217.

○**ROSEATE TERN** *Sterna dougallii* 38cm. 90–130g. Summer visitor (order 3). Medium-sized tern, red legs, black bill (base reddish in summer); tail longer than Arctic or Common (much longer than folded wings when at rest); pinkish flush on body in summer. VOICE 'aark' harsher and lower than Arctic or Common. HAB marine, coastal. NEST colonial, often with Common and Arctic, often on small island; scrape on sand or shingle, often concealed under plant, usually no lining. EGGS 1–2, cream to buff, speckled with reddish-brown and grey, 44mm. BROODS 1. INC c. 22, ♂♀. YOUNG semifug, 21–28, ♂♀. IMM 3. AGE 2–3, 16. FOOD fish.

Hatchling p. 218.

●**COMMON TERN** *Sterna hirundo* 35cm. 90–150g. Summer visitor (order 5). Very similar to Arctic; juveniles very difficult to separate; in summer usually has black tip to red bill (all blackish in winter); legs longer than Arctic; see also dark/light wing pattern. VOICE high, slightly grating 'kik-kik-kik' with emphasis on first note, and scolding screams. HAB mainly coastal, but some inland. NEST colonial, including in mixed colonies with Arctic; shallow scrape on shingle, often among plants. EGGS 2–3, cream to brown, blotched dark browns, 41mm. BROODS 1. INC 22–26, ♂♀. YOUNG semifug, 21–26, ♂♀. IMM 3. AGE 1–2, 25. FOOD fish.

Food for egg formation p. 245–6; Niche p. 296.

●**ARCTIC TERN** *Sterna paradisaea* 35cm. 80–120g. Summer visitor (order 5). See Common; legs shorter; in summer bill deeper red, lacks black tip; wing pattern; more likely to dive and strike observer if nest is closely approached. VOICE as Common, but notes higher and harsher with emphasis on second and third notes, more screaming. HAB coastal, inland in arctic. NEST colonial, often mixed in with Common; shallow scrape on shingle, sand. EGGS 1–3, cream to brown, blotched dark browns, 40mm. BROODS 1. INC 21–22, ♂♀. YOUNG semifug, 21–26, ♂♀. IMM 3. AGE 2, 34. FOOD fish.

Migration p. 238–41; Colonial nesting and defence against predators p. 255, 262; Niche p. 296.

130

TERNS

Terns have deeply forked tails and longer, thinner wings than the gulls, and a light, buoyant flight. Most hover over water and plunge dive for small fish.

Look for bill and leg colour, and pattern of dark and light in wing.

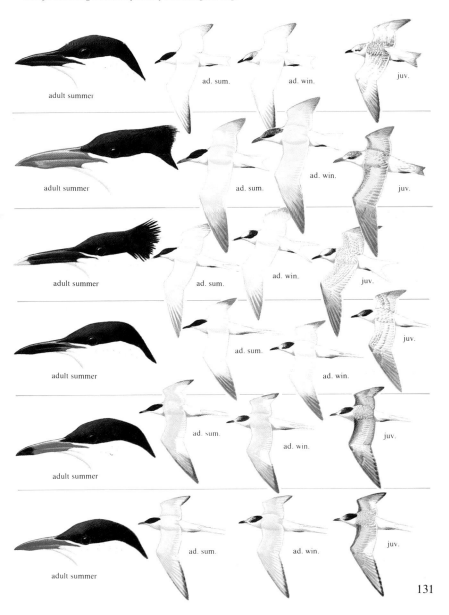

131

○**LITTLE TERN** *Sterna albifrons* 24cm. 50–65g. Summer visitor (order 4). The smallest tern; white forehead, yellowish bill with black tip; orange legs. VOICE 'kree-ick'; rapid trilling chatter. HAB mainly coastal, shingle and sandy beaches. NEST small colonies, nests not very close; usually bare scrape in shingle or field. EGGS 2–3, off-white to greenish, spotted and blotched dark browns. 33mm. BROODS 1. INC 19–22, ♂♀. YOUNG semifug, 15–17, ♂♀. IMM 3. AGE 1–2, 21. FOOD small fish.

Diving p. 44.

□ **WHISKERED TERN** *Chlidonias hybrida* 24cm. 80–95g. Rare vagrant. In summer, dark grey body, but white cheeks, black cap; red bill and legs; winter adults and immatures difficult, from White-winged by grey rump. VOICE high, rasping note, often double. HAB inland waters, may be coastal on migration. NEST colonial; floating nest of aquatic vegetation, anchored to water plants, ♂♀. EGGS 3, olive to greenish, spotted blackish-brown, 39mm. BROODS 1. INC 18–20, ♀(♂). YOUNG semifug, 23, ♂♀. IMM 3. AGE ?, ?. FOOD mainly insects; also small fish.

Nest design and material p. 266.

○□ **BLACK TERN** *Chlidonias niger* 24cm. 50–75g. Has bred in recent years (order 0–1), passage migrant. Less forked tail than 'sea-terns'; fairly uniform black in summer but with whitish underwing; in winter has blacker cap than Whiskered, and usually a small black mark at shoulder. VOICE squeaky 'kreek'. HAB normally fresh water, but some coastal or offshore on migration. NEST colonial; floating nest of vegetation, anchored to water plants, ♂♀. EGGS 3, light brown or green, heavily blotched blackish-brown, 35mm. BROODS 1. INC 14–17, ♂♀. YOUNG semifug, 21–28. ♂♀. IMM 3. AGE ?2, 17. FOOD mainly insects, also small fish.

Nest design and material p. 266; Habitat drainage p. 308.

□ **WHITE-WINGED BLACK TERN** *Chlidonias leucopterus* 24cm. 50–75g. Rare vagrant. Much rarer in W. Europe than Black; has white rump and tail; in summer has white forewing, black underwing; in winter very similar to Black, but lacks mark on shoulder. VOICE similar to Black, but less squeaky. HAB freshwater marshes, some coastal on migration. NEST colonial; floating nest of vegetation, anchored to water plants, ♂♀. EGGS (2)3, light brown or green, heavily blotched blackish-brown, 35mm. BROODS 1. INC 18–22, ♂♀. YOUNG semifug, 24–25, ♂♀. IMM 3. AGE ?2, ?. FOOD mainly insects, some small fish.

Nest design and material p. 266.

AUKS family *Alcidae* 21 species in the world.
Small to medium-sized sea birds which have small, stubby wings which they also use as paddles under water. Because of the small size of their wings, they fly with rapid, rather whirring wing-beats and may have difficulty in taking off.

Skeleton for diving, swimming under water p. 13, 44; Wing loading p. 42; Feet p. 45; Baby bird p. 208; Development of young p. 210–11; Copulation p. 261.

●□ **GUILLEMOT** *Uria aalge* 42cm. 850–1,130g. Common breeder (order 6), offshore in winter (order ?5). Very dark brown to blackish above (races differ), white below, longish, pointed blackish bill; bridled form has white 'spectacles'. VOICE usually silent at sea; noisy at colony, long rolling 'arrrrh'. HAB maritime. NEST colonial, in very dense groups on cliff ledges, flat tops of stacks, no nest. EGGS 1, very varied, white to blue, variously spotted and blotched with dark marks, 81mm. BROODS 1. INC 28–34, ♂♀. YOUNG semifug, fed ♂♀ until leaves colony 14–21 before fully grown, taken to sea by ♂. IMM 24. AGE 4, 32, 90–95%. FOOD fish.

Diving p. 13; Landing, taking off p. 40–1; Flightless in moult p. 44, 221–2; Development of young p. 204, 211; Migration p. 238, 240–1; Clutch, nesting and egg p. 245, 262, 269; Territory p. 254, 256.

□ **BRÜNNICH'S GUILLEMOT** *Uria lomvia* 42cm. 750–1,050g. Rare vagrant. Very similar to Guillemot but has stouter, shorter beak with whitish line along base of upper mandible; in winter has more black on cheek. VOICE similar to Guillemot, but harsher and lower. HAB maritime, more northerly than Guillemot. NEST colonial, in very dense groups on cliff-ledges, flat tops of stacks, no nest. EGGS very varied, white to blue, variously spotted and blotched with dark marks, 80mm. BROODS 1. INC 28–35, ♂♀. YOUNG semifug, fed ♂♀ until leaves colony 15–25 before fully grown, taken to sea by ♀. IMM ?24. AGE ?4, 23, 91%. FOOD fish.

Territory p. 254; Most references for Guillemot also apply.

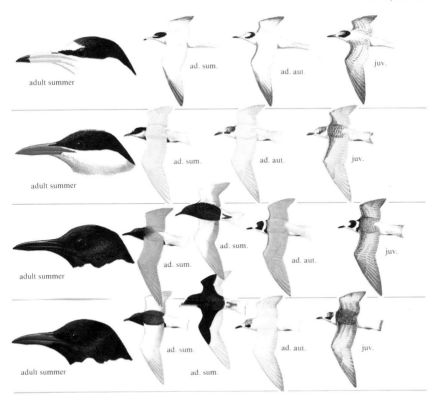

adult summer

ad. sum.

ad. aut.

juv.

adult summer

ad. sum.

ad. aut.

juv.

adult summer

ad. sum.

ad. sum.

ad. aut.

juv.

adult summer

ad. sum.

ad. sum.

ad. aut.

juv.

AUKS

Most European auks are fairly easy to identify when seen closely. At sea in winter most look black above and white below and are less easy.

Look for length and shape of the bill, amount of white on face.

ad. sum. bridled

ad. sum.

ad. win.

juv.

ad. win.

ad. sum.

ad. win.

juv.

ad. win.

133

●□ **RAZORBILL** *Alca torda* 41cm. 500–750g. Common breeder (order 6) offshore in winter (order ?4). Blacker than southern Guillemots, much deeper beak with white line near tip; in winter darker cheeks than Guillemot. VOICE long, deep growling notes. HAB maritime. NEST colonial; site varies, some on ledges like Guillemot but more dispersed, some in boulders or down burrows, no nest. EGGS 1, varied, whitish to bluish or brownish, blotched blackish-brown, 73mm. BROODS 1. INC 26–32, ♂♀. YOUNG semifug, fed ♂♀ till leave colony 14–21 when taken to sea by ♂ where they complete growth. IMM 24. AGE 4–5, 20, 90–95%. FOOD fish.

Diving p. 13; Flight, flightlessness in moult p. 44; Swimming under water p. 44; Development of young p. 211; Migration p. 238, 240–1.

●■ **BLACK GUILLEMOT** *Cepphus grylle* 34cm. 340–490g. Common resident (order 5). In summer black with large white wing patch; in winter piebald with much whiter head than Razorbill or Guillemot. VOICE high whistling cries, rapidly repeated until almost a trill. HAB coastal, rocky shores. NEST usually in small colonies; in holes in cliff or deep under boulder, no nest. EGGS 1(2), whitish to buff or pale blue-green, spotted dark browns and black, 58mm. BROODS 1. INC 21–24, ♂♀. YOUNG col, 35, ♂♀. IMM 12. AGE 2, 20. FOOD fish, some small crabs.

Diving p. 13; Subdivision of range p. 56; Development of young p. 211.

□ **LITTLE AUK** *Alle alle* 20cm. 130–180g. Winter visitor (order ?3). Much the smallest Atlantic auk, short stubby bill; throat and breast black in summer, white in winter. VOICE silent at sea, shrill chatter at colony. HAB maritime. NEST colonial; in crevices under boulders, no nest. EGGS 1, v. light blue, usually unmarked, 48mm. BROODS 1. INC 24, ♂♀. YOUNG col, 21–28, ♂♀. IMM ?12. AGE ?2, ?. FOOD crustaceans.

●□ **PUFFIN** *Fratercula arctica* 30cm. 320–550g. Common summer visitor (order 6), very few inshore in winter (order ?4). In summer adult unmistakeable, huge triangular red and yellow bill, the plates of which are moulted in winter when bill is dark and much smaller. VOICE silent at sea, growling 'arr'. HAB maritime; pelagic in winter. NEST colonial; in earth burrow, rock crack, under boulders; some plant material. EGGS 1, white, usually unmarked, 61mm. BROODS 1. INC 39–43, ♂♀. YOUNG col. 38–44. ♂♀. IMM 24. AGE 4, 22, 95%. FOOD fish, crustaceans.

Diving p. 13; Bill moult p. 33; Subdivision of range p. 56; Development of young p. 210–12, 230; Migration p. 238, 240–1; Breeding p. 264–5, 269–70, 276, 296, 303; Survival rate p. 285–7; Fish p. 313.

Order Columbiformes

PIGEONS AND DOVES family *Columbidae* 280 species in the world.
A large family with an almost worldwide distribution. They are vegetarian, feeding on leaves, seeds and fruits. All species lay either one or two white eggs and feed their small young on 'cropmilk', a substance formed from the cells of the crop. Feral, fancy and racing pigeons are all descendants of the Rock Dove.

Skeleton p. 12; Crop milk p. 18, 276–7; Vision p. 24–5; Short legs p. 46; Feeding flocks p. 230; Migration p. 236; Multiple broods p. 250; Poisons p. 313.

●■ **COLLARED DOVE** *Streptopelia decaocto* 32cm. 150–225g. Common resident (order 5 summer, 5–6 winter). A smallish pigeon, lighter and more uniform above than Turtle and with more white in the tail; narrow black band round back of neck. VOICE cooing 'oo-oooo-oo' with emphasis on second syllable; also a complaining 'mair'. HAB mainly suburban or at good feeding in town or country, e.g. grain-stores, chicken-farms. NEST in building or tree; flimsy of twigs, ♂♀. EGGS 2, white, 31mm. BROODS 2–3, or more. INC 14–16, ♂♀. YOUNG col, 17+ (often not fullgrown), ♂♀. IMM 2–3. AGE 1, 14, 71%. FOOD leaves, seeds, etc.

Populations and recruitment p. 289, 292, 294; Change of habits p. 310.

● **TURTLE DOVE** *Streptopelia turtur* 27cm. 100–500g. Common summer visitor (order 6). More slender than the larger pigeons, also more rufous; black tail with white tip, black-and-white patch on side of neck. VOICE soft musical purring. HAB thick hedges, woodland edge, scrub. NEST in thick bush; flimsy, twigs, ♂♀. EGGS 2, white, 31mm. BROODS 2(3). INC 13–14, ♂♀. YOUNG col, *c.* 20, ♂♀. IMM 2–3. AGE 1, 13. FOOD leaves and seeds.

Short legs p. 46; Moult p. 223; Energy for breeding p. 237; Migration p. 236; Egg colour p. 269.

PIGEONS AND DOVES
European pigeons and doves are either grey or brown.
  *Look for the amount of white in the tail or on the rump and wings
and, if close enough, marks on the neck.*

135

○□ **ROCK DOVE** *Columba livia* 33cm. 240–300g. Resident (order ?5): true Rock Dove now restricted to Ireland and western Scotland; elsewhere they intrebreed with feral forms. White rump most distinctive feature, wing tips greyer than Stock Dove. VOICE 'coo-roo-coo' as in town pigeons. HAB true Rock Doves occur almost exclusively on rocky coasts. NEST ledge in cave; stems, seaweed, et., ♂♀. EGGS 2, white, 39mm. BROODS 3, sometimes more. INC 16–19, ♂♀. YOUNG col, 35–37, ♂♀. IMM 0. AGE 1, (6). FOOD seeds and leaves.

Energy for breeding p. 226.

●■ **STOCK DOVE** *Columba oenas* 33cm. 250–340g. Common resident (order 6 summer, 5 winter). Large and grey, without any white markings. VOICE cooing 'oooo-oo' with emphasis on first syllable, repeated in sometimes accelerating crescendo. HAB wide range of open country, especially agricultural near woodland. NEST in hole, usually in tree, in buildings, etc. but in rabbit-burrow in dunes; poor nest of sticks, leaves, etc., ♂♀. EGGS 2, white, 38mm. BROODS 2–3 (sometimes more). INC 16–18, ♂♀. YOUNG col, 20–30 (but not full grown when leave), ♂♀. IMM 0. AGE 1, 13. FOOD leaves and seeds.

Hole nesting p. 209, 265.

●■ **WOODPIGEON** *Columba palumbus* 41cm. 450–520g. Common resident (order 7). The largest pigeon; white patches on sides of neck; in flight conspicuous white bands on wings. VOICE cooing 'oo-oooo-oooo-oo-oo' with emphasis on 2nd and 3rd syllables, repeated 3 or 4 times and followed by single concluding 'oo'. HAB wide range, primarily farmland near woods, but also towns, islands, etc. NEST usually above ground in thick vegetation; flimsy; twigs, ♂♀. EGGS 2, white, 41mm. BROODS 2–3. INC 17, ♂♀. YOUNG col, 33–34, ♂♀. IMM 2–5. AGE 1, 16, 64%. FOOD leaves, seeds.

Air speed p. 43; Pre-roost feeding p. 229; Safety in flocks p. 231; Breeding p. 245, 248, 253, 266, 269; Survival rate p. 285; Population control p. 295; Habitat gain p. 309.

SANDGROUSE family *Pteroclididae* 16 species in the world. Birds of open country, often semi-desert. They live on the ground where their pale, predominantly sandy coloration makes them hard to see. At dusk and dawn many fly considerable distances to water, gathering in large flocks to drink; in the breeding season the males soak up water in their specially-adapted belly feathers and carry it back for the chicks.

Short legs p. 46; Irruptions p. 291.

BLACK-BELLIED SANDGROUSE *Pterocles orientalis* 34cm. 400–550g. The largest European species and the only one without elongated tail feathers; completely black belly (even in juvenile) also characteristic. VOICE rattling churr, reminiscent of Black Grouse (p. 101). HAB open, stony semi-desert. NEST shallow scrape on ground, no material. EGGS 2–3, variable, usually cream or buff, spotted and streaked with wide range of colours, 47mm. BROODS 1–2. INC 21–22, ♂♀. YOUNG fug, ?, ♂♀. IMM 0. AGE 1, ?. FOOD mainly small seeds.

PIN-TAILED SANDGROUSE *Pterocles alchata* 37cm. 200–280g. Elongated central tail feathers (not in juvenile); the only European species with a completely white belly. VOICE disyllabic croaking notes, mostly given in flight. HAB dry, open country from rocky hills to saltmarsh edge. NEST scrape on ground, no material. EGGS 2–3, cream to buff, variably spotted and streaked dark, 46mm. BROODS 1 (?2). INC 19–20, ♂♀. YOUNG fug, ? (can fly at 28), ♂♀. IMM 2–3, AGE ?, ?. FOOD mainly small seeds.

□ **PALLAS'S SANDGROUSE** *Syrrhaptes paradoxus* 40cm. 230–300g. Rare (now very rare) irruptive to western Europe; the only species in Europe north of Spain. Elongated central tail feathers (except in juvenile), black band across belly. VOICE 'chack's and 'chuck's. HAB in main breeding area, steppe, elsewhere wide range of open areas. NEST scrape on ground, usually no material. EGGS 2–3, cream to buff, spotted and streaked with various darker colours. BROODS 2(3). INC 28, ♂♀. YOUNG fug, ?, ♂♀. IMM 3. AGE ?1, ?. FOOD mainly small seeds.

Irruptions p. 291.

SANDGROUSE
Close to, the different sandgrouse are distinctively patterned, but
they are often seen in rapid flight.
*Look for the pattern on the underside and the presence/absence of
tail streamers. Voices are clearly different.*

Order Psittaciformes

PARROTS family *Psittacidae* 328 species in the world.
A very large family of distinctive birds. They occur mainly in
tropical or other warm areas. Most nest in holes in trees and lay
white eggs.

Perching p. 46.

○□ **RING-NECKED PARAKEET** *Psittacula krameri* 41cm (including long tail). 100–150g. Local resident (order 3). Bright
green bird with red parrot-shaped bill and very long tail; ♂ has
ring round neck. VOICE distinctive high-pitched screech. HAB
mostly suburban areas, parks and gardens; comes to bird-tables.
NEST in tree-hole, no material. EGGS 3–5, white, 31. BROODS 1.
INC 22–28, ♀. YOUNG col, *c.* 55, ♂♀. IMM 0. AGE 2(3), ?. FOOD seeds,
berries, etc.

Introduction to
Britain p. 312.

Order Cuculiformes

CUCKOOS family *Cuculidae* 127 species in the world.
A largish family of birds famed for their habit of laying eggs in the
nests of other birds and leaving the hosts to incubate the eggs and
raise the young.

Brood parasites
p. 278–80.

□ **GREAT SPOTTED CUCKOO** *Clamator glandarius* 39ccm.
140–170g. Rare vagrant. Heavily spotted back, white edges to tail,
dark cap with crest (not always easily seen); in flight juvenile
shows striking chestnut patch in wing. VOICE tern-like chatter and
crow-like 'ark'. HAB open woodland. NEST none; lays eggs in nests
of members of crow family, especially Magpie (p. 189). EGGS may
lay up to *c.* 18 in a season, greenish-blue, spotted dark, 32mm. INC
12–14. YOUNG col, 16–24. IMM 8–20. AGE ?1, ?. FOOD mainly insects,
especially hairy caterpillars.

Brood parasite
p. 278–80.

● **CUCKOO** *Cuculus canorus* 33cm. 105–130g. Common summer
visitor (order 5). Resembles pointed-winged hawk; most are grey
with white spots in tail; a rare ♀ form is brown; juvenile is brown
or grey with white spot on nape. VOICE gives well-known 'cuck-oo'
and variants; ♀ has bubbling call. HAB wide range: reed-beds,
woodland, moorland. NEST none; lays eggs in nests of other
species. EGGS lays up to 25 per season, each in a different nest,
variable in colour, matching host's, 23mm. INC *c.* 12. YOUNG col,
20–23 but often not fully grown. IMM 6–9. AGE 1, 13. FOOD mainly
insects, especially hairy caterpillars.

Bristles p. 29; Egg
colour p. 269; Brood
parasite p. 278–80.

Order Strigiformes

OWLS family *Tytonidae* 10 species in the world.
family *Strigidae* 126 species in the world.
Two families of mainly nocturnal birds of prey with wide distribution. Several European species have both brown and grey forms.

Bills p. 17; Vision
p. 24–5; Hole nesting
p. 209; Hatchling
p. 218; Migration
p. 236; Nest site
p. 265; Egg shape and

colour p. 268–9;
Clutch size p. 271;
Brood reduction
strategy p. 273; Pair
bonds p. 283.

●■ **BARN OWL** *Tyto alba* 34cm. ♂ 290–340g, ♀ 330–460g.
Widespread resident (order 4 summer, 4–5 winter). Sandy-coloured
above, white below, eyes black. VOICE drawn-out screech; at nest
hisses and snores. HAB mostly open agricultural land. NEST in barn,
church tower, large tree-hole; no material. EGGS 4–7, white, 40mm.
BROODS 1–2. INC 30–32, ♀. YOUNG col, 55–65, ♂♀. IMM 0. AGE 1 (2),
18. FOOD mainly small mammals.

Second brood p. 251;
Breeding season
p. 253; Incubation and
asynchronous hatching
p. 273; Brood reduc-
tion strategy p. 273.

□ **SCOPS OWL** *Otus scops* 19cm. ♂ 75–80g, ♀ 90–95g. Rare
vagrant. A small owl with usually conspicuous ear-tufts; pale
yellow eye. VOICE quiet, but far-carrying 'pew', repeated continuously for long periods. HAB wooded open country, including
towns. NEST in tree-hole, building, old bird's-nest; no material.
EGGS 4–5, white, 31mm. BROODS 1. INC 24–25, ♀. YOUNG col, 21–29,
♂♀. IMM 0. AGE ?1, ?. FOOD mainly insects, a few small vertebrates.

Migration p. 236.

PARROTS

Only the one parrot occurs in Europe, originally as an escape, but now small feral populations are established and seem to be maintaining themselves. The brilliant green plumage and long tail are distinctive.

adult ♂   juvenile   adult ♀

CUCKOOS

Two fairly distinctive cuckoo species, slender with long tails (Azure-winged Magpie is roughly the same build). Great Spotted has dark cap, a white-edged tail and white underparts; Cuckoo is heavily barred beneath.

adult   immature   adult ♂   large nestling   ad. ♀ rufous   immature

OWLS

Almost all owls are predominantly brown or grey and often difficult to get good views of as they slip away in forest.
Look for pattern in facial disc, presence/absence of 'ear'-tufts; eye colour can be useful.

adult light   adult dark   adult light   adult grey   adult brown   adult brown

139

□ **EAGLE OWL** *Bubo bubo* 65–70cm. ♂ 1,500–2,000g, ♀ 2,300–3,000g. Rare vagrant. Very large owl with large ear-tufts and deep orange eyes. VOICE deep 'oo-hoo'; also barks and chuckles. HAB wild country, especially areas with rocky outcrops. NEST in small cave, large tree-hole; no material. EGGS 2–4, white, 60mm. BROODS 1. INC 34–36, ♀. YOUNG col, 50–60, ♂♀. IMM 2–3. AGE 0, 21. FOOD birds up to size of Eider (p. 83), but mainly mammal up to fox; even hedgehogs.

□ **HAWK OWL** *Surnia ulula* 35–40cm. ♂ 250–375g, ♀ 325–380g. Rare vagrant. Hawk-like in flight because of longish tail and pointed wings; strongly barred underparts, white facial disc with black border, eyes pale yellow; juvenile has brown crown. VOICE noisy and variable, including rolling 'ooo-ooo-ooo' of up to 60 notes, lasting 10 seconds or more. HAB northern conifer and birch forests. NEST tree-hole or old bird's-nest; no material. EGGS 6–10, white, 40mm. BROODS 1. INC 25–30, ♀. YOUNG col, 25–35, ♂♀. IMM 2–4. AGE 1, ?. FOOD mostly small mammals.

○□ **SNOWY OWL** *Nyctaea scandiaca* 55–65cm. ♂ 1,500–2,000g, ♀ 1,900–2,400g. Rare vagrant, has bred Shetland (order 0–1). Male often pure white, ♀ larger with more grey-brown speckling; eyes yellow. VOICE deep barking notes, repeated up to 4 times; variety of clicks. HAB very open country, mountains or tundra. NEST scrape on ground; little or no material. EGGS 4–8 but sometimes more, white, 57mm. BROODS 1. INC 30–33, ♀. YOUNG col, 43–50, ♂♀. IMM 0. AGE ?, ?. FOOD mainly small mammals.

Population movements p. 291.

PYGMY OWL *Glaucidium passerinum* 16cm. 50–80g. A tiny owl, no ear-tufts, facial disc not strikingly patterned, yellow eyes with white eyebrows; juvenile less barred, darker facial disc. VOICE repetitive 'wee'. HAB forest, usually conifer. NEST in tree hole, often that of woodpecker, no material. EGGS 4–7, white, 29mm. BROODS 1. INC 28–30, ♀. YOUNG col, 27–34, ♂♀. IMM 2–14. AGE 1, ?. FOOD small mammals, birds, insects.

●■ **TAWNY OWL** *Strix aluco* 38cm. ♂330–440g, ♀ 420–590g. Common resident (order 5 summer, 5–6 winter). Solidly built, dark both above and below, no ear-tufts, black eyes; fledged young often very downy. VOICE very variable, but usually ♂ which hoots the familiar 'tu-whit-tu-whoo', and ♀ who answers 'ke-wick'; fledged young have a scratchy persistent 'ti-sweep'. HAB woodland especially deciduous), parks, towns. NEST usually in tree hole; no material. EGGS 2–3, white, 47mm. BROODS 1. INC 28–30, ♀. YOUNG col, 32–37, ♂♀. IMM 2. AGE 1 (2), 18, 74%. FOOD mostly small mammals; also birds, frogs, worms.

Vision p. 25; Parental care p. 213; Clutch weight and size p. 245, 271; Breeding season and number of broods p. 251–3; Bigamy p. 283; Populations p. 286; Missing from Ireland p. 298; Habitat gain p. 309.

URAL OWL *Strix uralensis* 60cm. ♂ 680–750g, ♀ 820–970g. A large owl with unmarked facial disc and black eyes, tail longer than Tawny; fledged young very downy. VOICE has hooting and 'ke-wick' types of call, both deeper and more barking than Tawny; young has wheezy notes. HAB woodland, especially conifer. NEST tree-hole, old bird's-nest, etc.; no material. EGGS 2–4, white, 46mm. BROODS 1. INC 27–29, ♀. YOUNG col, 30–40, ♂♀. IMM 2. AGE 3–4, 14, 90%. FOOD mainly small mammals, some birds, etc.

Clutch size p. 271.

GREAT GREY OWL *Strix nebulosa* 70cm. ♂ 550–1,100g, ♀ 700–1,250g. A very large owl, no ear-tufts, facial disc covered with concentric dark grey rings, yellow eyes. VOICE ♂ regular, deep growling or booming hoots and 'ke-wick' calls, similar to Tawny, but deeper. HAB northern conifer forests. NEST old bird's-nest, top of broken tree stump; no material. EGGS 3–5, white, 54. BROODS 1. INC 28–30, ♀. YOUNG col, 60–65, ♂♀. IMM 2. AGE 2 (1), (7). FOOD mostly small mammals.

adult EAGLE

adult EAGLE

adult HAWK

adult HAWK

ad. ♀

ad. ♂

ad. ♂

ad. ♀

adult

adult

adult

adult

adult
URAL

adult
URAL

adult
GREAT GREY

adult
GREAT GREY

● ■ **LONG-EARED OWL** *Asio otus* 36cm. ♂ 210–270g, ♀ 240–330g. Widespread resident (order 4 summer, 4–5 winter). The only medium-sized owl with large ear-tufts; deep orange eyes; more slender than Tawny, in flight much less dark on top of underwing than Short-eared. VOICE soft, rather regular, moaning 'oo-oo-oo'; 'kwick'; fledged juvenile has far-carrying 'peeu'. HAB woodland, mainly conifer. NEST usually in old bird's-nest, e.g. crow; no material. EGGS 3–5, white, 41mm. BROODS 1. INC 25–30, ♀. YOUNG col, 30+, ♂♀. IMM 0. AGE 1, 28, 70%. FOOD wide range of small mammals, birds.

Energy for breeding p. 227.

● ■ **SHORT-EARED OWL** *Asio flammeus* 38cm. ♂ 260–310g, ♀ 290–350g. Widespread resident (order 3 summer, 4–5 winter). A day-hunting owl, usually seen quartering open country at a relatively low level, frequently glides; ear-tufts small, rarely visible, eyes pale yellow. VOICE high nasal yelp; repeated resonant 'hoo-hoo-hoo'; fledged young has series of wheezy notes, persistent. HAB open country, moorland, reed-beds, young conifer plantations. NEST scrape on ground, no material. EGGS 4–8, white, 40mm. BROODS 1 (sometimes 2 in vole plagues). INC 24–29, ♀. YOUNG col, 24–27, ♂♀. IMM 0. AGE 1, 13. FOOD mainly mammals, esp. voles.

Second brood p. 251; Scarcity in Ireland p. 299.

● ■ **LITTLE OWL** *Athene noctua* 22cm. ♂ 140–180g, ♀ 150–200g. Fairly common resident (order 4–5 summer, 5 winter); introduced. Small, rather dumpy owl, often seen in daylight; fierce expression, no ear-tufts, pale yellow eyes. VOICE plaintive, rather shrill 'kiu'; barks and yelps. HAB open areas with trees, parkland, woodland edge, rocky areas. NEST hole in tree or rock crevice, rabbit burrow; no material. EGGS 2–5, white, 36mm. BROODS 1. INC 27–28, ♀. YOUNG col, 30–36, ♂♀. IMM 0. AGE 1, 16, 65%. FOOD mainly insects, worms, some small vertebrates.

Vision p. 25; Evolutionary change p. 50; Introduction to Britain p. 312.

☐ **TENGMALM'S OWL** *Aegolius funereus* 25cm. ♂ 90–120g, ♀ 120–210g. Rare vagrant. Similar to Little, but strictly nocturnal; browner than Little with quite un-fierce facial pattern, much-deeper discs with black upper edge, yellow eyes. VOICE rapid 'poo-poo-poo' usually 5–6 notes, soft but far-carrying. HAB forest, mainly conifer. NEST tree-holes; no material. EGGS 3–7, white, 33mm. BROODS 1. INC 25–32, ♀. YOUNG col, 28–36, ♂♀. IMM 0. AGE 1 (8). FOOD mainly small mammals.

Order Caprimulgiformes

NIGHTJARS family *Caprimulgidae* 72 species in the world. A family of insectivorous birds which feed mainly around dusk and dawn. They lay one or two well-camouflaged eggs on the bare ground. Most are tropical, but two species come to Europe for the summer. They tend to rest on ground, though sometimes along tree branch.

Bill p. 18; Egg colour p. 269.

● **NIGHTJAR** *Caprimulgus europaeus* 27cm. 75–100g. Local breeder (order 4). The only nightjar over most of Europe; usually located by call; greyish with small white slash across throat; ♂ has white in wing and small amount in outer tail feathers; ♀ lacks white in wings and tail. VOICE nasal 'chuck', usually in flight; song distinctive, a rising and falling churr, can be very prolonged. HAB commons bordering on woods, large woodland glades. NEST on ground, no material. EGGS 2, well-camouflaged, marbled pattern of grey and dark, 32mm. BROODS 1–2. INC 17–18, ♀(♂). YOUNG semifug, can fly at 16–17, ♂♀. IMM 0. AGE 1, (8). FOOD flying insects.

Baby bird p. 206; Hatchling p. 218; Clutch weight p. 245; Second brood p. 250; Breeding season p. 253.

☐ **RED-NECKED NIGHTJAR** *Caprimulgus ruficollis* 31cm.? Rare vagrant. Sandier than Nightjar, with larger, flatter head, more white on throat and in tail; juveniles paler. VOICE like tapping on hollow wood; song prolonged 'cerchuck-cerchuck-cerchuck'. HAB dry wooded or shrubby areas. NEST on ground, no material. EGGS 2, well-camouflaged, marbled patterns of grey and dark, 31mm. BROODS ?2. INC ?. YOUNG semifug, ?, ♂♀. IMM 3. AGE ?1, ?. FOOD large flying insects.

adult

adult

adult

ad.

adult

adult

ad.

adult

adult

adult

adult

adult

NIGHTJARS
Red-necked Nightjar is larger and paler.
Look especially for amount of white on throat and in tail. Calls distinctive.

adult ♂

adult ♂

adult ♀

adult

adult

Order Apodiformes

SWIFTS family *Apodidae* 71 species in the world.
Perhaps the most aerial of all birds, feeding entirely on insects caught on the wing. Non-breeding Swifts are known to spend the night on the wing in Europe, and all birds may do so in their winter quarters in Africa. Most European birds now nest in buildings; they lay white eggs. Juveniles have pale edgings to feathers, giving them a scaly appearance, and are whitish around bill.

Bill p. 18; Short legs p. 46–7; Hole nesting p. 209; Migration p. 237; Egg colour p. 269; Incubation and egg chilling p. 272; Brood reduction strategy p. 273; Habitat history p. 310.

● **SWIFT** *Apus apus* 16cm. 36–50g. Common summer visitor (order 6). The only swift over much of Europe and the only black-bellied one outside Mediterranean; an all-black bird often screaming noisily in small parties. VOICE noisy; shrill screams. HAB almost ubiquitous, often high in the sky. NEST usually in roof of building, rarely (though presumably once normally) in tree-hole; leaves, feathers, etc. gathered on the wing, glued with saliva, ♂♀. EGGS 2–3, white, 25mm. BROODS 1. INC 18–25, ♂♀. YOUNG col. 37–56, ♂♀. IMM 6–8. AGE 4, 21, 85%. FOOD aerial insects.

Flight p. 15, 43; Bill p. 18; Young p. 209, 212, 218, 230, 276; Moult p. 223; Migration p. 243; Breeding p. 245, 248, 253, 261, 269–71; Survival rate p. 285; Habitat history p. 309–10.

□ **PALLID SWIFT** *Apus pallidus* 16cm. 38–45g. Very rare vagrant. Very difficult to tell from Swift, but browner and some with more white on throat; patchier coloration of wings and upperparts only usually a distinction if looking *down* on the bird. VOICE noisy; shrill screams. HAB common in many Mediterranean areas. NEST usually in roof of building, rarely (though presumably once normally) in tree-hole; leaves, feathers, etc. gathered on the wing, glued with saliva, ♂♀. EGGS 2–3, white, 26mm. BROODS 1–2. INC 20–23, ♂♀. YOUNG col, 44–49, ♂♀. IMM 6–8. AGE ?, ?, 75%. FOOD aerial insects.

□ **ALPINE SWIFT** *Apus melba* 22cm. 80–120g. Rare vagrant. A very large swift, in coloration similar to gigantic Sand Martin (p. 151); brown above, white below with brown throat band; forked tail. VOICE loud chittering trill. HAB mountainous areas, coastal cliffs. NEST in cave, crevice, large building, bracket of material collected on wing fixed to wall with saliva, ♂♀. EGGS 3, white, 31mm. BROODS 1. INC 17–23, ♂♀. YOUNG col, 45–55, ♂♀. IMM 6–8. AGE 2–3, 26, 79%. FOOD aerial insects.

Moult p. 223.

WHITE-RUMPED SWIFT *Apus caffer* 14cm. 18–28g. The only European swift with a white band on rump (North African Little Swift which sometimes occurs in Europe also has white rump, but is smaller with square-ended tail). VOICE quieter, more twittering than Swift. HAB has bred southern Spain since 1960s, found in areas used by swallows. NEST takes over nests of swallows, especially Red-rumped, lines with feathers, ♂♀. EGGS 2, white, 23mm. BROODS ?2. INC 19–22, ♂♀. YOUNG col, 41 53, ♂♀. IMM 6–8. AGE ?, (10). FOOD aerial insects.

Order Coraciiformes

BEE-EATERS family *Meropidae* 23 species in the world.
ROLLERS family *Coraciidae* 16 species in the world.
HOOPOE family *Upupidae* 1 species in the world.
All belong to Old-World, largely tropical families of which one species of Bee-eater, one of Roller, and the Hoopoe are common summer visitors to temperate areas. Most are very brightly coloured. Most bee-eaters have slightly de-curved beaks; many have elongated tail feathers.

Hole nesting p. 209; Brood reduction strategy p. 273.

□ **BEE-EATER** *Merops apiaster* 28cm. Rare vagrant (has bred on three occasions). Mostly blue-green below, chestnut and yellow above; long, slightly de-curved bill and elongated central tail feathers; often in small groups, fairly noisy. VOICE far-carrying, rather musical 'prrupp', almost di-syllabic. HAB open country with perches such as bushes, telephone-wires, etc. NEST colonial; usually in burrows in sand banks, but also digs down in level ground; no lining, ♂♀. EGGS 6–7, white, 26mm. BROODS 1. INC 20, ♂♀. YOUNG col, 20–25, ♂♀. IMM 4–8. AGE 1–2, ?. FOOD largish insects, e.g. bees, dragonflies, caught on wing.

Leaving nest p. 212; Nest hole p. 264–5; Egg colour p. 269; Brood reduction strategy p. 273; Food for young p. 276; Co-operative breeding p. 280.

SWIFTS

Swifts are longer-winged than swallows and martins, and all except the very large Alpine Swift have dark bellies; *all* swallows are white or pale underneath.

Look for white on rump and tail shape.

BEE-EATERS, ROLLERS AND HOOPOE

The European Bee-eater is not easily mistaken for any other species; it has brilliant colouration and elongated central tail-feathers.

The Roller is equally brightly-coloured, but is a more solidly-built bird, less often seen in groups.

The Hoopoe is unmistakeable and butterfly-like with its salmon-pink body plumage, large crest and black-and-white wings.

145

☐ **ROLLER** *Coracias garrulus* 31cm. 110–155g. Rare vagrant. Size of small crow, strong bill, undulating flight showing brilliant blue wing patches; juvenile has browner head and neck. VOICE crow-like chatter. HAB open woodland or open country with trees. NEST usually in hole in tree, usually no lining. EGGS 3–5, white, 35. BROODS 1. INC 17–19, ♂♀. YOUNG col, 26–28, ♂♀. IMM 3–6. AGE 1–2. (9). FOOD pounces from perch onto large insects, small lizards, etc. etc.

Nest hole p. 264–5; Egg colour p. 269.

☐ **HOOPOE** *Upupa epops* 28cm. 55–80g. Vagrant, has bred (order 0–1). Unmistakeable, striking; rounded black-and-white wings, salmon-pink body and large crest. VOICE a resonant 'pooop-pooop-pooop', sounds rather like dog barking in far distance. HAB open ground with trees, spends much of time on ground. NEST hole in tree or among rocks, no lining. EGGS 5–8, dirty-looking, grey, green or yellow, 26mm. BROODS 1 (2). INC 16–18, ♀. YOUNG col, 26–29, ♂♀. IMM 0. AGE 1, ?. FOOD large insects, small lizards, etc.

Nest hole p. 265; British records p. 298.

KINGFISHERS family *Alcedinidae* 90 species in the world. A family with a very wide distribution. Many are strikingly or brilliantly coloured. Although most live close to water and eat fish, some live in forests away from water and are primarily insectivorous. Most excavate burrows in banks and lay white eggs.

Short legs p. 46; Hole nesting p. 209; Egg shape p. 268; Brood reduction strategy p. 273.

●■ **KINGFISHER** *Alcedo atthis* 16cm. 40–45g. Widespread resident (order 4). Unmistakeable; almost always near water, usually sitting on projection or flying rapidly close to water surface; chestnut-orange below and brilliant blue above. VOICE shrill, drawn-out whistle; shrill piping notes. HAB close to water, preferring still or slow-flowing in some areas coastal. NEST in burrow in bank, no material, ♂♀. EGGS 5–7, white, 23mm. BROODS 2. INC 19–21, ♂♀. YOUNG col, 23–27, ♂♀. IMM 0. AGE 1, 15. FOOD small fish.

Vision p. 25; Migration p. 237; Clutch weight p. 245; Incubation p. 248; Multiple broods p. 250; Breeding season p. 253; Nest hole p. 264–5; Egg colour p. 269.

Order Piciformes

WOODPECKERS family *Picidae* 206 species in the world. Widely distributed (not Australasia). Most are strong-legged species with stiffened tail feathers; they work their way up tree-trunks in their search for food.

Bill and tongue p. 16–17; Climbing p. 46; Hole nesting and competition p. 209, 265. 296; Hatchling p. 218; Post-fledging moult p. 219; Migration p. 236; Egg colour p. 269; Missing from Ireland p. 298.

○ **WRYNECK** *Jynx torquilla* 16cm. 30–45g. Very rare summer visitor (order 0–1), passage migrant. Does not look like a woodpecker; rather greyish and nondescript unless good view obtained, when detailed patterning distinctive; flies with slightly undulating flight, often low down in cover. VOICE repetitive 'keeu', likened to Nuthatch, but also reminiscent of distant falcon. HAB open woodlands, orchards, etc. NEST in hole in tree, will use nest-boxes; no lining. EGGS 7–10, white, 21mm. BROODS 1 (2). INC 12–14, ♂♀. YOUNG col, 18–22, ♂♀. IMM 0. AGE 1, 10. FOOD insects, esp. ants.

Tongue p. 17; Migration p. 236–7.

GREY-HEADED WOODPECKER *Picus canus* 25cm. 125–165g. Like a small Green Woodpecker, but less (or no) red on head, greyer head and grey underparts, lacks yellow-green rump. VOICE a laugh, similar to Green, but clearer, and pitch falls more rapidly, becoming slower towards the end. HAB open woodland, especially deciduous; sometimes high in montane forest. NEST hole drilled in tree; no lining, ♂♀. EGGS 7–9, white, 28mm. BROODS 1. INC 14–15, ♂♀. YOUNG col, 24–28, ♂♀. IMM 0. AGE 1, (6). FOOD wide range of insects, much collected on ground.

●■ **GREEN WOODPECKER** *Picus viridis* 32cm. 180–220g. Common resident (order 5). Largish woodpecker, green with red cap, bright yellow-green rump and lower back. (Spanish race greyer, but still has red cap and yellow-green rump). VOICE distinctive maniacal ringing laugh. HAB open woodland, parks. NEST hole drilled in tree; no lining, ♂♀. EGGS 5–7, white, 32mm. BROODS 1. INC 17–19, ♂♀. YOUNG col, 23–27, ♂♀. IMM 3. AGE 1, 7. FOOD mainly insects, especially ants; feeds mainly on the ground.

Tongue p. 17; Hatchling p. 218.

KINGFISHERS

Only one species of kingfisher occurs in Europe and it is familiar to most people. It is resident over much of the range, but migrates from those areas where the water regularly freezes over in winter, so preventing it from fishing.

WOODPECKERS

Note head colouration in the two green species, but the black-and-white ones are more difficult, especially since the amount of red on the head varies with sex and age within each species; most are strongly resident, and range is a useful guide.

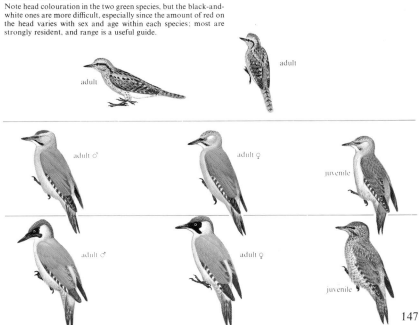

BLACK WOODPECKER *Dryocopus martius* 45cm. 300–350g. A black, crow-sized woodpecker, far larger than any other European woodpecker; pale ivory bill and yellow eye. VOICE loud whistles and yelps; loud ringing laugh 'kree-kree-kree-kree . . .' more liquid than Green's. HAB mature forest, usually conifer. NEST hole drilled in tree; no lining, ♂♀. EGGS 4–6, white, 34mm. BROODS 1. INC 12–14, ♂♀. YOUNG col, 24–28, ♂♀. IMM 3. AGE ?, 7. FOOD mainly insects.

Missing from Britain p. 299.

THREE-TOED WOODPECKER *Picoides tridactylus* 22cm. 60–75g. Unlike other European black-and-white woodpeckers has no red and has white all way down back; black moustachial streak and eyestripe give side of head a striking barred appearance; ♂ has yellow crown. VOICE rather quiet, but similar to much-slowed call of Great Spotted; drums slowly. HAB northern or montane forests, usually conifer. NEST hole drilled in tree; no lining, ♂♀. EGGS 3–5, white, 23mm. BROODS 1. INC 12–14, ♂♀. YOUNG col, 22–23, ♂♀. IMM 0. AGE ?, ?. FOOD mainly insects, but sometimes drills series of holes and drinks sap which runs from them.

Niches of ♂ and ♀ p. 298.

●■ **GREAT SPOTTED WOODPECKER** *Dendrocopos major* 23cm. 70–90g. Common resident (order 5). The most widespread of the black-and-white group; only juvenile has red crown (moulted by end-November); large white patch on inner wing, no white on rump; continuous black line from base of bill to nape. VOICE sharp 'chick' or 'keck', occasionally rapidly repeated; drums rapidly. HAB woodland, parks, gardens. NEST hole drilled in tree; no lining, ♂♀. EGGS 4–7, white, 26mm. BROODS 1. INC 15–16, ♂♀. YOUNG col, 20–24, ♂♀. IMM 3–4. AGE (1), 11. FOOD in summer mostly insects; many seeds in winter.

Bill and tongue p. 16–17; Baby bird p. 206–207; Incubation p. 248; Population movements p. 291; Niche p. 297; Habitat gain p. 309.

SYRIAN WOODPECKER *Dendrocopos syriacus* 23cm. 70–90g. Spreading steadily north-westwards across Europe. Similar to Great Spotted, but lacks black band from moustachial streak to nape. VOICE quieter, more clucking than Great Spotted. HAB overlaps with Great Spotted, but more common in gardens, orchards, less in forest. NEST hole drilled in tree; no lining, ♂♀. EGGS 4–7, white, 26mm. BROODS 1. INC 12–14, ♂♀. YOUNG col, 17–25, ♂♀. IMM 3–4. AGE 1, ?. FOOD primarily fruits and seeds in winter; insects in summer.

MIDDLE SPOTTED WOODPECKER *Dendrocopos medius* 22cm. 50–80g. Like Great Spotted and Syrian, has large white wing patch, but unlike these both adults (both sexes) have red crown; black mark on lower cheek not connected to nape or bill. VOICE similar to Great Spotted, but lower; rarely drums. HAB primarily in deciduous forests, especially hornbeam-oak. NEST hole drilled in tree; no lining, ♂♀. EGGS 4–7, white, 24. BROODS 1. INC 12–14, ♂♀. YOUNG col, 22–23, ♂♀. IMM 0. AGE ?1, 8. FOOD mainly insects.

Habitat loss p. 306–7.

WHITE-BACKED WOODPECKER *Dendrocopos leucotos* 25cm. 100–115g. Differs from preceding three in lacking white wing patch and having large white patch on lower back; ♂ has red crown. VOICE like Great Spotted, but rarely drums. HAB mainly in montane deciduous woodland, prefers areas with many dead trees. NEST hole drilled in tree; no lining, ♂♀. EGGS 3–5, white, 28mm. BROODS 1. INC 12–14, ♂♀. YOUNG col, 24–28, ♂♀. IMM 0. AGE 1, ?. FOOD mainly insects, also seeds.

Niches of ♂ and ♀ p. 298.

●■ **LESSER SPOTTED WOODPECKER** *Dendrocopos minor* 15cm. 18–22g. Widespread resident (order 4). A sparrow-sized black-and-white woodpecker; lacks large white patch on inner wing and red under tail; ♀ is only European woodpecker to have front half of crown white. VOICE shrill 'kee-kee-kee' like Nuthatch, but shriller; drums rapidly. HAB open woodland, often moist or riverine, large gardens. NEST hole drilled in tree, often on underside of branch; no lining, ♂♀. EGGS 4–6, white, 19mm. BROODS 1. INC 12–14, ♂♀. YOUNG col, 18–20, ♂♀. IMM 0. AGE ?1, 7. FOOD mainly insects.

Climbing p. 47; Non-migrant p. 237; Niche p. 297.

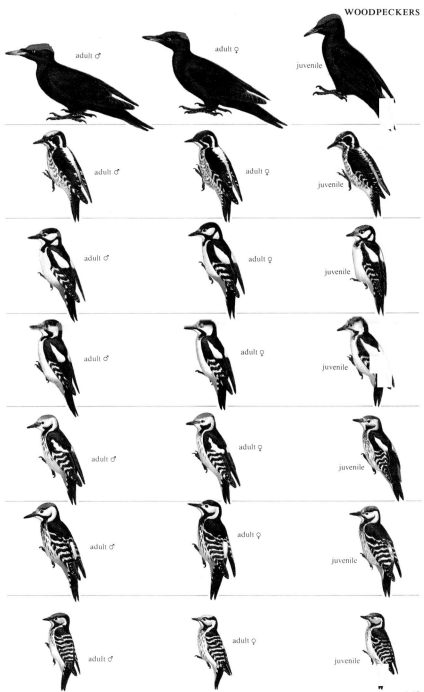

adult ♂   adult ♀   juvenile

adult ♂   adult ♀   juvenile

adult ♂   adult ♀   juvenile

adult ♂   adult ♀   juvenile

adult ♂   adult ♀   juvenile

adult ♂   adult ♀   juvenile

adult ♂   adult ♀   juvenile

Order Passeriformes

LARKS family *Alaudidae* 76 species in the world.
Birds of open, often treeless country; most are brown; sexes are
similar. Most have moderately pointed bills for dealing with the
small seeds and insects which are their diet. Most sing on the
wing, and many are very fine songsters. Many young larks scatter
from the next several days before they can fly properly. Most are
not long-distance migrants, but the Skylark and Shorelark leave
the colder parts of Europe for the winter.

Running p. 47; Nest
design p. 267.

☐ **CALANDRA LARK** *Melanocorypha calandra* 19cm. 53–70g.
Rare vagrant. The largest European lark, with a stout yellow bill
and black patches on either side of the neck. VOICE wheezy 'chirrup'; song rather Skylark-like, but contains trills and copies of
other species' songs. HAB open, stony ground, dry agricultural
land, etc. NEST on ground in the shelter of plants; cup lined with
grasses, ♀. EGGS 4–5, pale, finely spotted dark browns and greys.
24mm. BROODS 2. INC ?, ♀. YOUNG col, ?, ♂♀. IMM 3. AGE ?1, ?.
FOOD insects and seeds.

☐ **SHORT-TOED LARK** *Calandrella brachydactyla* 14cm. 19–
25g. Vagrant. Smaller and paler than Skylark, very pale underneath with little streaking; sooty patch at shoulders; often gives
appearance of slightly sandy cap. VOICE sparrow-like 'chirrup';
song 6–8 twittery notes, repeated. HAB dry open country, saltmarshes edged with *Salicornia*. NEST on ground; a deep cup of
grasses lined with hair, ♀. EGGS 3–5, whitish or buff, speckled
with greys and dark browns, 20mm. BROODS 2. INC 13, ♀(♂).
YOUNG col, 12, ♂♀. IMM 3. AGE ?1, ?. FOOD insects and small seeds.

☐ **LESSER SHORT-TOED LARK** *Calandrella rufescens* 14cm.
22–28g. Rare vagrant. Very similar to Short-toed, slightly greyer,
lacks shoulder marks, has neat streaking down breast. VOICE
'prrit'; song starts with same note, more musical than Short-toed,
but still twittery. HAB dry, open country, saltmarshes edged with
Salicornia. NEST, EGGS, BROODS, INC, YOUNG poorly known, but
seem very similar to Short-toed. IMM 3. AGE ?1, ?. FOOD insects and
small seeds.

DUPONT'S LARK *Chersophilus duponti* 16cm. ?g. The only
European lark (or pipit) with a long, slightly decurved bill; heavily
streaked breast, conspicuous pale eye-stripe; very skulking. VOICE
whistling 'wheet'; striking song flight, mixture of musical phrases
and more rasping notes. HAB dry, near-desert with small bushes.
NEST on ground beside plant tussock; cup of grass, ?. EGGS 3–4,
white, heavily spotted dark, 24mm. BROODS ?2. INC ?, ?. YOUNG
col, ?, ♂♀. IMM 0. AGE ?1, ?. FOOD small seeds, insects.

☐ **CRESTED LARK** *Galerida cristata* 17cm. 35–45g. Vagrant.
Similar in size to Skylark, but conspicuous long upright crest,
buff-edged tail shorter than Skylark's. VOICE very distinctive,
loud, musical 'whee-whee-ooo', trisyllabic; song repeated phrases,
short, less musical than Skylark. HAB dry open ground, often on
fields, near towns. NEST on ground in shelter of plant or stone; cup
of grass, lined hair, ♀. EGGS 3–5, grey to buff, finely spotted greys
and browns, 23mm. BROODS 2 (3). INC 12–13, ♀. YOUNG col, *c.*
13–15, ♂♀. IMM 3. AGE ?1, ?. FOOD insects, small seeds.

THEKLA LARK *Galerida thecklae* 17cm. 34–41g. Almost indistinguishable from Crested; has slightly shorter bill and is
greyer (not buff) on underwing. VOICE very distinctive, loud,
musical 'whee-whee-ooo', trisyllabic; song more like Skylark's
than is Crested, often from top of bush. HAB more common on
hillsides than Crested, also on more bushy ground. NEST on
ground in shelter of plant or stone; cup of grass, lined hair, ♀.
EGGS 3–5, grey to buff, finely spotted greys and browns, 23mm.
BROODS 2. INC 12–13, ♀. YOUNG col, *c.* 13–15, ♂♀. IMM 3. AGE ?1, ?.
FOOD insects and seeds.

LARKS

LARKS can be difficult to identify; songs are particularly important.

Look for bill shape, the presence or absence of a crest and the patterning of the underparts, especially around the breast and shoulders.

151

○ □ **WOODLARK** *Lullula arborea* 15cm. 24–36g. Local resident (order 3 summer, 2 winter). Slightly smaller than Skylark; shorter tail without white edges; broad eye-stripes meet at back of head; black-and-white alula. voice 'tit-loo-eee'; song shorter, sweeter, less powerful than Skylark's, and on descending scale, interspersed with trills. HAB SUM usually in areas with at least a few trees; WIN more open areas, fields, etc. NEST small hollow on ground, often in cover of bush; cup of grasses, lined hair, ♂♀. EGGS 3–4, pale, with brown and red-brown speckles, 22mm. BROODS 2. INC 14, ♀. YOUNG col, 11–13, ♂♀. IMM 3. AGE 1, ?. FOOD insects, small seeds.

Baby bird p. 209; Post-fledging moult p. 219.

● ■ **SKYLARK** *Alauda arvensis* 18cm. 33–45g. Common resident (order 7) and winter visitor (order 7). Largish lark with vestige of crest, streaked breast, white underparts and edges to tail. voice liquid 'chirrup'; famous powerful, prolonged song-flight, often to a considerable height. HAB open ground, fields, meadows, etc. NEST on ground, often built into side of grass tussock; cup of grass, lined with fine grass or hair, ♀. EGGS 3–5, whitish, heavily marked with fine speckles of greys and browns, 24mm. BROODS 2 (3). INC 11–12, ♀. YOUNG col, 18–20, ♂♀. IMM 3. AGE 1, 12. FOOD insects and small seeds.

Walking and hopping p. 47; Post-fledging moult p. 219; Incubation p. 248; Song flight p. 259; Habitat history p. 309.

□ **SHORE LARK** *Eremophila alpestris* 16cm. 33–45g. Rare winter visitor (order 3); very rare breeder (order 0–1). Yellow face with black mark, black breast-band and small black 'horns'; marks less conspicuous in winter adults and juveniles. voice 'tsee-ee', rather pipit-like; song a tinkling version of Skylark's, often from the ground. HAB SUM dry tundra or mountains; WIN often on shingle beaches, saltmarshes. NEST on ground in shelter of grass; cup of grass, lined fine grass or hair, ?. EGGS 4, pale, speckled and lined with blacks and browns, 23mm. BROODS 1–2. INC 10–14, ♀. YOUNG col, 12, ♂♀. IMM 2–3. AGE 1, ?. FOOD insects and small seeds.

Post-fledging moult p. 219.

SWALLOWS AND MARTINS family *Hirundinidae* 74 species in the world.
A group of mostly small, often distinctively patterned birds which spend much of their time on the wing hawking insects. Most nest colonially on or in man-made structures. Except for the Crag Martin, the European species are long-distance migrants, going to Africa for the winter.

Bill p. 18; Turning in flight p. 40; Leaving nest p. 212; Post-fledging moult p. 219; Migration p. 236–7; Breeding season and predators p. 252; Food for young p. 276; Habitat history p. 310.

● **SAND MARTIN** *Riparia riparia* 12cm. 12–18g. Common summer visitor (order 6). The smallest swallow, with a barely forked tail; drab brown upperparts with white underside and brownish breast band. voice 'cirrrip'; song a quiet twitter. HAB usually feeds over water, gravel pits, rivers, etc. NEST colonial; burrow in a sandy bank, may be up to 1 metre deep; lined feathers, ♂♀. EGGS 4–5, pure white, 18mm. BROODS 2. INC 14, ♂♀. YOUNG col, 19, ♂♀. IMM 6. AGE 1, 8. FOOD insects caught on the wing.

Recognition of parents p. 213; Energy for breeding p. 226; Migration p. 239–41, 243; Nest hole p. 265; Incubation p. 272; Habitat history p. 310.

● **SWALLOW** *Hirundo rustica* 19cm, inc. long tail. 16–25g. Common summer visitor (order 6). Widespread and familiar; steel blue back with long tail streamers; white spots in tail; reddish-chestnut throat; even juveniles (which have short tails) have a faint red throat and dark breast-band. voice 'sweet', or 'swiit'; song a dry warbling twitter. HAB widespread, most common on farms and edges of villages, towns. NEST in barn, garage; open cup of mud attached to side of rafter, lined feathers, ♂♀. EGGS 4–6, white, spotted with red, 20mm. BROODS 2 (3). INC 14–16, ♀. YOUNG col, 17–24, ♂♀. IMM 6–8. AGE 1, 16. FOOD insects caught on wing.

Feathers p. 30; Migration p. 232–3, 235, 243; Breeding season p. 253; Incubation p. 272; Habitat history p. 309–10.

□ **RED-RUMPED SWALLOW** *Hirundo daurica* 18cm, inc. long tail. 18–21g. Rare vagrant. Similar to Swallow, but shorter tail; lacks white spots in tail, and breast band; has buffer underparts, rufous collar, pale buff rump. voice harsher than Swallow, 'tee-wit'; song a warbling twitter, less musical than Swallow. HAB wide range of open country, coast; especially streams with bridges. NEST under bridge, in culvert, etc; mud, completely enclosed with spout entrance, lined feathers, ♂♀. EGGS 3–5, white with fine red spots, 20mm. BROODS 2. INC 14–15, ♂♀. YOUNG col, 23–25, ♂♀. IMM 6–8. AGE 1, 8. FOOD insects caught on wing.

Nest design and material p. 267; Incubation p. 272.

adult

adult

adult

adult

adult summer

adult winter

ad. win.

SWALLOWS AND MARTINS

In martins look for tail shape: even in silhouette at long distance this is a useful guide. The swallows have long, deeply forked tails; the House Martin's is clearly, but not deeply forked; the Sand and Crag Martins' are barely forked or straight-ended. Colour of underparts, presence or absence of breast bands and rump patterns are also useful. See also Swifts, p. 143).

adult

adult

adult ♂

juvenile

adult

juvenile

153

CRAG MARTIN *Ptyonoprogne rupestris* 14cm. 20–22g. The only swallow to over-winter in Europe; tail square-ended; brown like Sand Martin above, but underparts dusky without contrasting breast-band; on close view has speckled throat, whitish marks in tail. VOICE weak 'chirrip' and longer twitterings. HAB rocky cliffs, in mountains inland and on coast. NEST loosely colonial, under overhanging rock; a half-cup of mud, lined feathers, ♂♀. EGGS 3–5, white, some with fine reddish-brown speckling, 21mm. BROODS 1–2. INC 14, ♀. YOUNG col, 25–26, ?♂♀. IMM 3. AGE 1, ?. FOOD insects.

Non-migrant p. 236;
Incubation p. 272;
Habitat history p. 310.

● **HOUSE MARTIN** *Delichon urbica* 12cm. 15–21g. Common summer visitor (order 6). Short, slightly forked tail; glossy bluish-black on back, white underneath, conspicuous white rump. VOICE a quiet 'chirrip'; song a rather monotonous squeaky twitter. HAB often feeds over water, but also common over open country, especially round towns. NEST often in small colonies, usually on house wall, sometimes in cliffs; mud, almost completely enclosed except for small entrance, lined grass, feathers, ♂♀. EGGS 4–5, pure white, 19mm. BROODS 2–3. INC 14, ♂♀. YOUNG col, 19–22, ♂♀. IMM 0. AGE 1, 15. FOOD insects caught on wing.

Energy for breeding p. 227; Migration p. 243; Breeding season p. 253; Nest, egg, incubation, food for young p. 267, 269, 272, 276; Cooperative breeding p. 280; Habitat history p. 309–10.

PIPITS AND WAGTAILS family *Motacillidae* 54 species in the world.
Both groups are of long-legged birds which spend much of their time running on the ground. Pipits are brownish, streaky and usually have white outer tail feathers. Their young often leave the nest before they can fly. Wagtails are more strikingly coloured or patterned, and are larger and longer-tailed than pipits. They usually nest off the ground. Some members of both groups are long-distance migrants.

Running p. 47;
Migration p. 236; Nest design p. 267.

☐ **RICHARD'S PIPIT** *Anthus novaeseelandiae* 18cm. 27–37g. Vagrant. Usually only seen in w. Europe in autumn; a very large pipit with long tail and legs; breast buff, strongly streaked, conspicuous eye-stripe; frequently perches on bushes, wires, etc. VOICE loud, rather harsh 'shreep'; song an irregular pattern of grating and chirping notes. HAB damp meadows, edges of marshes, etc. NEST on ground, usually in side of grass tussock; cup of dead grass, some other veg., ♀(?♂). EGGS 4–6, greyish to pinkish, spotted dark red or grey, 21mm. BROODS usually 2. INC ?14, ♀. YOUNG col, ?16, ♂♀. IMM 0. AGE 1, 5. FOOD insects, small seeds.

Breeds in eastern Asia; frequent vagrant to Europe; especially in autumn.

●■/☐ **ROCK/WATER PIPIT** *Anthus spinoletta* 17cm. 21–30g. Rock common resident (order 5). Water rare passage migrant. Both large, long-billed and with dark legs: Rock has grey outer tail feathers; Water's are white, and in summer is largely unstreaked beneath. VOICE 'tseep'; song rather like Meadow, but more regular, less tuneful. HAB Rock mainly rocky coasts; Water mountainous areas, winter in lowlands. NEST in a crevice among rocks; grass, lined with hair, ♀. EGGS 4–5, whitish, spotted with greys and browns, 21mm. BROODS 2. INC 14, ♀. YOUNG col, 16, ♂♀. IMM 0. AGE 1, 9. FOOD insects and small seeds; Rock also marine food from shore.

Moult p. 32–3.

● **TREE PIPIT** *Anthus trivialis* 15cm. 20–25g. Common summer visitor (order 5–6). Like Meadow Pipit, but browner above, yellower breast, pinkish legs. VOICE slightly grating 'teez'; song loud and usually in flight, long trills ending in drawn out 'chew' notes. HAB open ground near trees, e.g. heaths, grassy edges of woods; more widespread on migration. NEST well-hidden on ground, in bank or grass tussock; cup of grass, some hair in lining, ♀(♂). EGGS 4–6 variable, bluish, pinkish, brownish, overlaid with darker spots and blotches, 21mm. BROODS 1 (2). INC 13–14, ♀. YOUNG col, 12–13, ♂♀. IMM 0. AGE 1, 8. FOOD insects, small seeds.

Migration p. 236, 243;
Song flight p. 259;
Cuckoo host p. 278–9.

●■ **MEADOW PIPIT** *Anthus pratensis* 14cm. 16–25g. Common resident (order 7), winter visitor (order 6–7). Present all the year round, the commonest pipit; like Tree, but more olive upperparts, less yellow underparts; legs darker (juveniles can be more like Tree). VOICE best for separating from Tree, a 'tseep' usually repeated 2–3 times; song rather quiet usually in flight, increasing in speed into trill. HAB SUM mainly moorland, rough meadows; WIN wide range of open country. NEST well-hidden on ground, in grass tussock; cup of grass, ♀. EGGS 4–5, white, heavily spotted with greyish-browns, 20mm. BROODS 2. INC 13–14, ♀. YOUNG col, 13–14, ♂♀. IMM 0. AGE 1, 8. FOOD insects, small seeds.

Clutch weight p. 245;
Nest site p. 263;
Cuckoo host p. 278–9;
Habitat history p. 309.

PIPITS AND WAGTAILS

Pipits, especially juveniles, are difficult to identify, and call-notes are a valuable guide.

Look for amount of streaking on upperparts and underparts, and leg-colour. Wagtails wag their tails conspicuously. *Colour of the upperparts distinguishes the two wagtails that have yellow underparts.*

☐ **TAWNY PIPIT** *Anthus campestris* 16cm. 20–28g. Vagrant. A large pipit, but very slim and pale; sandy above, pale and un-streaked beneath; pale creamy eyestripe; juvenile has spotted breast. VOICE variable and rather sparrow-like, but less harsh than Richard's; song 'suivee' repeated, usually given in flight. HAB rather open country, dunes, sandy heaths, etc. NEST well-hidden on ground; small grass cup, lined with hair. ?. EGGS 4–5, whitish, blotched brown, 22mm. BROODS ?2. INC 13–14, ♀(♂). YOUNG col. ?, ♂♀. IMM 2–8. AGE 1, ?. FOOD mainly insects in summer, small seeds in winter.

Nest orientation p. 267; British records p. 298.

☐ **RED-THROATED PIPIT** *Anthus cervinus* 14cm. 16–23g. Rare vagrant. More strongly streaked than Meadow on upper-parts, esp. rump; variable red on throat and upper breast in sum-mer; in winter underparts heavily streaked. VOICE 'tsee' rather like Tree, also a 'chup'; song more twittering than Meadow, often in flight. HAB usually on damp ground, often with small bushes, often near coast. NEST on ground; concealed cup of grass, lined with hair. EGGS 5–6, variable, olive or buffish, spotted with greys and browns, 19mm. BROODS 1. INC 12–14, ♀. YOUNG col, 11–13, ♂♀. IMM 0. AGE 1, ?. FOOD insects, small seeds.

Migration p. 235–6.

●/☐ **YELLOW/BLUE-HEADED WAGTAIL** *Motacilla flava* 17cm. 16–22g. Yellow common summer visitor (order 6); Blue-headed (w. Europe) vagrant. Greenish above, yellow below; juveniles look much more like Pied/White; head colour very vari-able depending on geographical location. VOICE a loud 'sweep'; song a short, trilling 'chip-chip-chip'. HAB damp meadows, edges of lakes and rivers. NEST on ground, often in shelter of plant; cup of grass, lined with hair etc., ♀. EGGS 5–6, pale buff, speckled with darker marks, 19mm. BROODS 2. INC 13, ♀. YOUNG col, 13, ♂♀. IMM 3. AGE 1, 8. FOOD mainly insects, small seeds.

Seasonal plumages p. 220; Migration p. 234–6, 243; Breeding seasons of subspecies p. 251; Nest site p. 263; Irish records p. 298.

●■ **GREY WAGTAIL** *Motacilla cinerea* 18cm. 15–23g. Com-mon resident (order 5 summer, 4–5 winter). Long-tailed, bluer-grey on back than Yellow, adults more intense yellow underneath, juveniles may only be yellow under tail. VOICE sharp 'tsik', also 'tsee'; song 'tsee-tsee-tsee' usually 3 or 4 notes. HAB usually along-side swiftly-flowing streams and rivers. NEST on ledge, in hole or crevice in rocks or under bridge; moss, grass and roots, lined with hairs, ♀. EGGS 4–6, buffish, spotted with greyish-browns, 19mm. BROODS 2. INC 13–14, ♀. YOUNG col, 12, ♂♀. IMM 9. AGE 1 (6). FOOD insects, small aquatic invertebrates.

Nictitating membrane p. 25.

●■/☐ **PIED/WHITE WAGTAIL** *Motacilla alba* 18cm. 19–27g. Common resident (order 6), winter visitor (order 6–7); larger winter roosts on buildings, in trees, etc. Plumage varies consider-ably with sex and age as well as race, but Pied (UK) has black rump, White (vagrant from Europe) has grey. VOICE 'chizzick'; song a quiet twitter. HAB usually near water; also farms, large gardens. NEST in a crevice in bank, ivy-covered wall; bulky cup of grass, moss, lined hair, feathers, ♀. EGGS 5–6, pale grey speckled dark, 21mm. BROODS 2. INC 13–14, ♀. YOUNG col, 14–16, ♂♀. IMM 3. AGE 1, 10. FOOD insects, small seeds.

Cuckoo host p. 279.

WAXWINGS family *Bombycillidae* 8 species in the world. Only one of this family occurs in Europe; they are dependent on northern fruit crops and when these fail sometimes move south-wards and westwards in great numbers, when they can be seen feeding on berries in parks and gardens.

☐–■ **WAXWING** *Bombycilla garrulus* 18cm. 40–68g. Winter visitor in very variable numbers (order 2–4). Dumpy brown bird with marked crest, red tips to inner wing feathers, red under tail, yellow tail-tip; usually very silent. VOICE usually silent, has high trilling 'shreee'; song quiet twitters of varying pitch but mainly high. HAB SUM northern forests; WIN often in gardens, orchards. NEST in small tree; cup of twigs, moss, lined hair, ?. EGGS 4–6, pale blue, some faint spotting, 25mm. BROODS 1. INC 13–14, ♀. YOUNG col, 15–17, ♂♀. IMM 3. AGE ?1, 13. FOOD in winter quarters mainly berries, fruits.

Irruptions p. 291.

adult

juvenile

adult

juvenile

ad. ♀ sum.

juv.

ad. ♀ sum.

ad. ♂ sum.

BLUE-HEADED

ad. ♂ sum.

YELLOW

ad. ♂ sum.

ad. ♀ sum.

ad. ♂ win.

juvenile

ad. ♀ sum.

juv.

ad. ♀ win.

ad. ♂ sum.

ad. ♀ sum.

WHITE

ad. ♂ win.

ad. ♂ sum.

PIED

WAXWINGS

Waxwings are unmistakeable; although they have a rather starling-like flight and often move around in flocks, their colouration is distinctive, as is their rather dumpy, crested silhouette.

adult

juvenile

157

DIPPERS family *Cinclidae* 4 species in the world.
The most aquatic passerines, and the only ones that regularly sub-merge themselves in water in search of prey. They can dive and walk along the bottom of the stream-bed to catch aquatic insects.

●■ **DIPPER** *Cinclus cinclus* 18cm. 55–75g. Common resident (order 5). Unmistakeable, stout, brown bird with dazzling white throat and breast. VOICE loud 'clink'; song warbling notes mixed with louder single notes. HAB fast-flowing streams. NEST in crevice in overhanging bank, under bridge; bulky, domed; moss, grass, lined leaves, ♂♀. EGGS 4–6, white, 26mm. BROODS 2. INC 16, ♀. YOUNG col, 19–25, ♂♀. IMM 3. AGE 1, 8. FOOD aquatic invertebrates.

Moult p. 222; Egg colour p. 269.

WRENS family *Troglodytidae* 59 species in the world.
All but the one species occur only in the New World. The male builds a series of nests ('cock's nests') and invites potential mates to visit them; when a female accepts one she lines it, and lays in it; when she starts to incubate the clutch, the male will sing to try to encourage another female into another of his nests.

●■ **WREN** *Troglodytes troglodytes* 12cm. 8–13g. Common resident (order 7). Very small, short-tailed, cocks tail frequently; barred brown, paler underside. VOICE harsh 'tic' or scolding churr; song loud, prolonged and musical, with rapid trills; can be heard throughout year. HAB needs thick cover, woods, hedges, gardens, cliffs, etc. NEST (♂ polygamous); in thick vegetation, e.g. brambles, against tree trunk, on bank; domed; leaves, moss, ♂; lined feathers, ♀. EGGS 5–6, white, spotted reddish-brown, 17mm. BROODS ♂ up to 4, ♀ 1–2. INC 14–15, ♀. YOUNG col, 16–17, ♀(♂). IMM 0. AGE 1, 6. FOOD mainly insects.

Juvenile plumage p. 218; Size, energy and heat loss p. 224–5, 227; Nest design and material p. 267; Bigamy p. 282–3; Populations p. 295.

ACCENTORS family *Prunellidae* 13 species in the world.
Rather secretive birds which tend to shuffle along on the ground. They have complex mating systems in which two to four birds may live in a single territory. Mainly resident, except in the most northerly areas.

●■ **DUNNOCK (HEDGE SPARROW)** *Prunella modularis* 14cm. 19–24g. Common resident (order 7). Quiet brown bird with greyish head, breast; usually hopping along ground in or near to cover, flicks wings frequently. VOICE penetrating high 'tseep'; song fairly complex, thin high steady warbling. HAB bushy ground, woods, hedges, gardens. NEST (odd pairing patterns); usually deep inside bush; twigs, moss, leaves, lined hair, feathers, ♀. EGGS 4–5, blue, 20mm. BROODS 2(3). INC 12, ♀. YOUNG col, 12, ♂♀. IMM 0. AGE 1, 9. FOOD mainly insects, small seeds.

Spring moult p. 219; Cuckoo host p. 279; Polygamy p. 280–1; Diffuse competition p. 298.

ALPINE ACCENTOR *Prunella collaris* 18cm. 25–35g. Like large version of Dunnock, but smarter; greyish with rufous flanks, neat black-spotted white throat. VOICE 'chirrip', lark-like; song rapid, varied, prolonged warbling. HAB rocky mountain slopes, often at high altitudes, comes down lower in winter. NEST in crevice in rocks; grass, lined moss, hair, ?. EGGS 3–4, light blue, 23mm. BROODS 2. INC 15, ♂♀. YOUNG col, 16, ♂♀. IMM 0. AGE 1, ?. FOOD insects, small seeds.

Migration p. 238.

DIPPERS

Dippers' low, whirring, direct flight and rapid bobbing when perched on a rock, immediately distinguish dippers from all other birds. The British and central European races have a rufous belly; other races are dark brown, and have sometimes been considered to be separate species.

ad. chestnut-bellied (Brit.)

ad. black-bellied (Eur.)

juvenile

WRENS

The small size, direct flight and tendency to cock the tiny tail, together with the noisy chattering, make the Wren easy to identify.

adult

juvenile

ACCENTORS

The two accentors which occur in Europe live in separate habitats. They can be recognised by their fine, pointed bills and quiet plumage.

fresh adult

worn adult

juvenile

adult

juvenile

159

CHATS AND ROBINS part of family *Turdidae* 304 species in the world.

This enormous family includes several important groups, including the chats, the smaller relations of the true thrushes (pp. 162–165). In summer, they mostly feed on insect prey, often catching it on the ground, either by hopping or running rapidly after it, or by dropping down from a vantage point; in winter they also take berries.

Hopping p. 47;
Migration p. 237.

☐ **RUFOUS BUSH-CHAT** *Cercotrichas galactotes* 15cm. 20–27g. Rare vagrant. A brownish bird with very conspicuous long, graduated, rufous tail with black and white marks at tip; frequently raises and fans tail; bounds along ground, perches on bushes. VOICE 'check-check'; song musical, short, rather lark-like phrases, but slower, sometimes given in flight. HAB dry ground with cover, scrub, open woodland. NEST in shrub, prickly pear; untidy cup of grass, lined feathers, ♂♀. EGGS 4–5, whitish, finely spotted reds and browns, 22mm. BROODS 1–2. INC ?, ♀. YOUNG col. ?, ♂♀. IMM 3. AGE ?1, ?. FOOD insects, small fruits.

● ■ **ROBIN** *Erithacus rubecula* 14cm. 16–22g. Common resident (order 7), winter visitor (order 7). Very well-known; small brown bird with orange-red breast; scaly golden-brown juvenile. VOICE sharp 'tic', often repeated; song rather clear jingling warble, spring different from autumn; sings most of year, even at night under street-lights. HAB woodland, parks, gardens, scrub. NEST well-hidden in ivy-covered bank, at base of tree, in garden shed; domed; leaves, lined roots, hairs, ♀. EGGS 4–6, whitish, finely spotted light red, 20mm. BROODS 2 (3). INC 13–14, ♀. YOUNG col, 12–15, ♂♀. IMM 3. AGE 1, 13. FOOD insects, small seeds.

Baby and juvenile p. 208, 219; Migration p. 235–6; Clutch, incubation, breeding season p. 245, 248, 252, 271; Territory p. 256; Survival, populations, competition p. 284–6, 288, 298; Habitat gain p. 309.

☐ **THRUSH NIGHTINGALE (SPROSSER)** *Luscinia luscinia* 16cm. 22–32g. Rare vagrant. Virtually indistinguishable from Nightingale unless exceptional views obtained; is darker, has less red tail, faint grey spotting on breast. VOICE 'wheet' or 'tac'; song as Nightingale, but trills more metallic. HAB woodland with thick undergrowth, often damp. NEST well-concealed on ground, often against fallen branch; cup of leaves, lined grass, rootlets, ♀. EGGS 4–6, usually darkish olive-brown, but variable, 22mm. BROODS 1. INC 13, ♀. YOUNG col, 12, but may leave before can fly, ♂♀. IMM 2. AGE 1, 9. FOOD insects, berries.

Habitat loss p. 306–7.

● **NIGHTINGALE** *Luscinia megarhyncha* 16cm. 18–27g. Common summer visitor (order 4). Very like Thrush Nightingale, but slightly browner on back, tail is more rufous. VOICE sharp 'tac's and 'wheet's; song similar to Thrush Nightingale, very rich, varied and loud, includes slow 'piu-piu-piu' sections; sings at night as well as in day. HAB deciduous woodland with thick undergrowth, especially coppice. NEST in thick cover, on or near ground, often beside fallen branch; leaves, often lined with fine grasses, hair, ♀. EGGS 4–5, olive-brown, 21mm. BROODS 1. INC 13–14, ♀. YOUNG col, 12–13, ♂♀. IMM 2. AGE 1, 8. FOOD mainly insects, small berries.

Migration p. 238; Missing from Ireland p. 298.

☐ **BLUETHROAT** *Luscinia svecica* 14cm. 15–23g. Scarce passage migrant (order 2). Summer ♂ has bright blue throat (with red or white spot); ♀ duller throat; many in Britain are juvs or winter ads lack blue; rufous panels in tail distinctive. VOICE 'tac', 'wheet', or several run together; song musical, varied, metallic notes; mimics. HAB marshy areas, edges of reed-beds, often thick undergrowth. NEST on ground, in bank or vegetation; cup of moss and grasses, lined fine grass, hair, ♀. EGGS 5–6, pale greenish, speckled reddish, 19mm. BROODS 1–2. INC 14–15, ♀. YOUNG col, 14, but may leave before can fly, ♂♀. IMM 2. AGE 1, ?. FOOD insects, small seeds.

Intermingling of forms p. 54–5.

☐ **RED-FLANKED BLUETAIL** *Tarsiger cyanurus* 14cm. 13–19g. Rare vagrant. Orange flanks, white throat; ♂ bright blue above, ♀ and juvenile blue only on upper tail, rump. VOICE Robin-like ticking; song quiet, rather monotonous, thrush-like with repetitive short phrases (sometimes at night). HAB dense conifer forest. NEST on ground beside fallen branch, in bank; moss and grass, lined hair, ?. EGGS 3–5, whitish, usually spotted reddish-browns, 18mm. BROODS 1–2. INC ?, ♀. YOUNG col, c. 15, ♂♀. IMM 3. AGE 1, ?. FOOD mainly insects.

CHATS AND ROBINS
Most chats and robins tend to be distinctively marked.
  Look for features such as face and breast pattern, tail pattern and colour.

ad. rufous

adult brown

juvenile

adult

juvenile

adult

juvenile

adult

juvenile

ad. ♂ sum.

ad. ♂ sum.
white-spotted

ad. ♂ sum.

ad. win.

juvenile

ad. ♂ sum.

ad. ♀ sum.

1st win. ♂

juvenile

161

○□ **BLACK REDSTART** *Phoenicurus ochrurus* 14cm. 14–20g. Scarce summer visitor (order 2–3), a few over-winter (order 3). Striking rufous tail; ♀ dusky all over; ♂s vary markedly in brightness, black with white wing patch. VOICE shrill 'tsip'; song short musical snatches, simpler than Redstart. HAB rock-faces, cliffs, but also commonly in gardens and on buildings over much of Europe; in Britain usually associated with very large buildings. NEST on ledge, in cavity; moss, leaves, etc., lined hair, ♀. EGGS 4–6, white, 19mm. BROODS 2. INC 12–13, ♀. YOUNG col, 16–18. ♂♀. IMM 2. AGE 1, 8. FOOD mainly insects, some berries in autumn.

Intermingling of forms p. 54–5; Egg colour p. 269.

● **REDSTART** *Phoenicurus phoenicurus* 14cm. 12–20g. Common but local summer visitor (order 6). Distinctive reddish tail; in almost all plumages markedly paler below than Black Redstart. VOICE loud, plaintive 'hweet'; song short burst of musical notes followed by short, fading trill. HAB woodland, including open areas with large trees. NEST usually in tree-hole, but also ledges in buildings, etc; moss, grass, lined hair and few feathers, ♀. EGGS 5–7, light blue, 19mm. BROODS 1 (2). INC 13–14, ♀. YOUNG col, 14–16, ♂♀. IMM 2. AGE 1, 9. FOOD mainly insects.

Migration p. 243; Breeding season p. 252; Nest hole p. 264–5; Egg colour p. 269; Diffuse competition p. 298; Irish records p. 298.

● **WHINCHAT** *Saxicola rubetra* 12·5cm. 16–24g. Common but local summer visitor (order 5). White or pale eye-stripe, and in flight white patches on tail distinguish from Stonechat. VOICE ticking notes; song short bursts of rather quiet warbling interspersed with long gaps. HAB heaths, rough agricultural land, etc. NEST on ground, by tussock or bush; cup of grass, sometimes lined hair, ♂. EGGS 5–7, greenish-blue. often speckled reddish. 19mm. BROODS 1–2. INC 13, ♀. YOUNG col, 13, ♂♀. IMM 2. AGE 1, 5. FOOD mainly insects.

Preening p. 30; Migration p. 243; Habitat history p. 309.

●■ **STONECHAT** *Saxicola torquata* 12·5cm. 14–17g. Common resident (order 5). Perches conspicuously on low bushes, etc; orange breast, ♂ has blackish head. VOICE harsh 'tchack' like two stones being struck together, hence name; song variable, repeated short phrases, rather like Dunnock (p. 156). HAB wide range of open land, especially heaths, moors. NEST low, in thick vegetation, especially thick gorse, heather, often v. deep into bush with 'tunnel' to reach it; cup of grass and moss, ♀. EGGS 5–6, light blue, speckled reddish-brown, 19mm. BROODS 2 (3). INC 14–15, ♀. YOUNG col. 14–16, ♂♀. IMM 2. AGE 1, 5. FOOD mainly insects.

Juvenile plumage p. 218; Habitat history p. 309.

□ **ISABELLINE WHEATEAR** *Oenanthe isabellina* 16cm. 22–35g. Rare vagrant. Both sexes similar to ♀ Wheatear but wings same colour as back (much darker in ♀ Wheatear); large, pale and long-legged (leg is visible above ankle-joint); more black in tail than ♀ Wheatear. VOICE loud cheeps and chacks; song lark-like, different from other wheatears, with much mimicry and whistling. HAB bare ground in steppes, plains. NEST in crevice or hole; grass, lined hair, ♀. EGGS 4–6, pale blue, 22mm. BROODS 1–2. INC 14, ♀. YOUNG col, ?, ♂♀. IMM 2. AGE 1, ?. FOOD mainly insects.

● **WHEATEAR** *Oenanthe oenanthe* 15cm. 17–30g. Common summer visitor (order 5). Striking black-and-white tail pattern; in summer ♂ has grey back; ♀ richer buff underparts than most wheatears. VOICE sharp 'tchack', also 'hweet'; song varied melodious warble, interspersed with harsher notes. HAB wide variety of open land, needs short turf. NEST in crevice or burrow; grass, lined hair, ♀. EGGS 5–6, pale blue, 21mm. BROODS 1–2. INC 14, ♀. YOUNG col, 15, ♂♀. IMM 2. AGE 1, 7. FOOD mainly insects.

Greenland subspecies p. 60; Migration p. 234–5, 240–3; Nest hole p. 265; Egg colour p. 269.

□ **BLACK WHEATEAR** *Oenanthe leucura* 18cm. 35–40g. Rare vagrant. Distinctive black in all plumages, inc. juvenile. VOICE 'pee-pee'; song a short thrush-like warble preceded by 1–2 short, separate notes. HAB rocky areas, inc. cliffs, mountains, etc. NEST in crevice among rocks, old walls, etc., edged by 'rampart' of small stones; grass, lined hair, ♀. EGGS 4–6, very pale blue, 22mm. BROODS 2. INC 15–17, ♀. YOUNG col, 14–15, ♂♀. IMM 0. AGE ?1, ?. FOOD mainly insects.

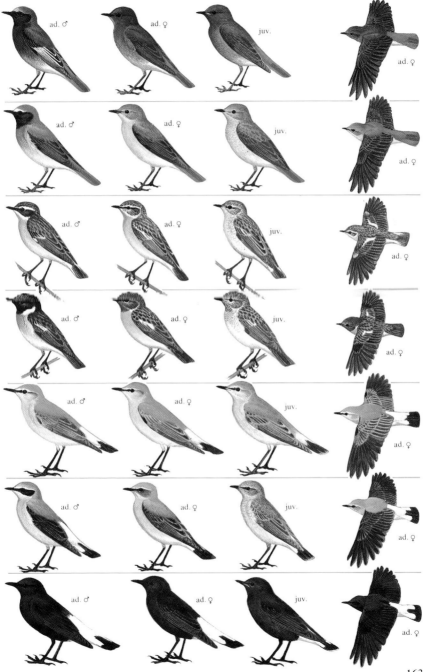

ad. ♂   ad. ♀   juv.   ad. ♀

ad. ♂   ad. ♀   juv.   ad. ♀

ad. ♂   ad. ♀   juv.   ad. ♀

ad. ♂   ad. ♀   juv.   ad. ♀

ad. ♂   ad. ♀   juv.   ad. ♀

ad. ♂   ad. ♀   juv.   ad. ♀

ad. ♂   ad. ♀   juv.   ad. ♀

☐ **PIED WHEATEAR** *Oenanthe pleschanka* (But some authors treat this and Black-eared as the same species.) 14cm. 15–22g. Rare vagrant. Male distinctive black-and-white pattern; ♀ very similar to other species. VOICE sharp 'tchack'; song short varied warble. HAB rocky hillsides, rock-strewn desert. NEST in crevice; grass cup lined hair, ♀. EGGS 4–5, light blue, 20mm. BROODS 2. INC ?. ♀. YOUNG col, ?, ♂♀. IMM 2. AGE 1, ?. FOOD mainly insects.

☐ **BLACK-EARED WHEATEAR** *Oenanthe hispanica* (See also Pied Wheatear.) 14cm. 15–22g. Rare vagrant. Blacker wings more white on tail than Wheatear; two forms of ♂'s, white-throated has black cheeks, black-throated has black throat too; ♀ duskier cheeks than Wheatear. VOICE grating notes and whistles; song variable, incl. rapid phrases such as 'schwer-schwer-schwee-oo'. HAB open ground in wide variety of habitats, usually with bushes and trees. NEST well-hidden in rocky crevice or under vegetation, grass cup lined hair, ♀. EGGS 4–5, pale blue, some speckled reddish, 20mm. BROODS 2. INC ?, ♀. YOUNG col, ?, ♂♀. IMM 2. AGE 1, ?. FOOD insects.

☐ **ROCK THRUSH** *Monticola saxatilis* 19cm. 42–65g. Rare vagrant. Male very distinctive, ♀ speckly, rather like very large baby Wheatear, much paler and more scaly than ♀ Blue Rock Thrush, and has rufous tail. VOICE scolding 'tchack'; song flute-like warble, sometimes in flight. HAB rocky areas from low mountains to sea-level. NEST in crevice or hole; cup of grass, lined fine grass, ♀. EGGS 4–5, pale blue, 26mm. BROODS 1. INC 14–15, ♀. YOUNG col, 14–16, ♂♀. IMM 3. AGE ?1, ?. FOOD wide range of insects, berries.

BLUE ROCK THRUSH *Monticola solitarius* 20cm. 37–54g. Male distinctive dark blue (can look black in some lights); ♀ dark grey-brown, speckled, but can have bluish tinge. VOICE Blackbird-like 'tchuck'; song loud and musical, reminiscent of Blackbird. HAB wide range of rocky habitats, especially cliffs. NEST in crevice among rocks; large cup of grass and moss, lined fine grass, ♀. EGGS 4–5. pale blue. 27mm. BROODS 1 (2). INC 12–13. ♀. YOUNG col. 16–17, ♂♀. IMM 3. AGE ?1, ?. FOOD insects, berries.

TRUE THRUSHES part of family *Turdidae* 64 species in the world.

The true thrushes (genus *Turdus*) are larger than the chats. Although many will take insects when available, they also tend to take larger prey such as worms, and rely to a considerable extent on berries in winter.

Bills p. 16–17; Taking off p. 40; Hopping p. 47; Spring moult p. 219; Nest design and materials p. 266–7; Pair bond and parental care p. 282.

● **RING OUZEL** *Turdus torquatus* 24cm. 90–130g. Common summer visitor (order 4–5). White band across breast is diagnostic: (but beware Blackbirds with white markings); Ring Ouzels are markedly greyer, not black, above. VOICE harsh 'tchack-tchack' like Blackbird; song a short series of rich di- or trisyllabic notes. HAB rough moorland with bushes, shrubs; rare at sea-level. NEST usually near ground in vegetation overhanging bank or in heather, etc.; cup of grass, lined fine grasses, ♂♀. EGGS 4–5, bluish-green, blotched reddish-brown, 30mm. BROODS 2. INC 14, ♂♀. YOUNG col. 14, ♂♀. IMM 3. AGE 1, (8). FOOD wide range of invertebrates, berries.

●■ **BLACKBIRD** *Turdus merula* 25cm. 80–110g. Common resident (order 7), winter visitor (order 7). Male orange bll, all-black (but ♂ up to 1 year have browner wings); ♀ dark brown. VOICE wide range of 'pink' and 'chook' often run together to make angry chatter; song loud, rich, tuneful, slow warbling, each phrase falling away. HAB wide range of areas with trees, inc. bushy moorland. NEST in thick bush, up trees, in sheds, etc.; untidy cup of moss, grass, mud, lined fine grass, ♀. EGGS 3–5, greenish-blue, spotted red-brown, 29mm. BROODS 2–3. INC 13–15, ♀. YOUNG col, 12–15, ♂♀. IMM 3. AGE 1, 16. FOOD mainly worms; also berries; insects at certain times.

Evolutionary change p. 50; Baby p. 209; Breeding p. 213, 245, 248, 250–2, 270–1, 292; Survival p. 215, 285; Migration p. 236–7; Territory p. 256–7; Populations p. 286, 288; Habitat gain p. 309.

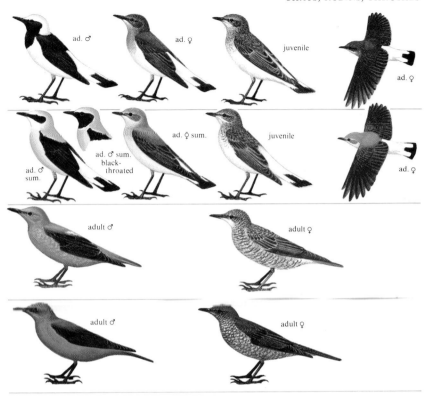

TRUE THRUSHES

The thrushes tend to be similar in size, but different in coloration.
The more difficult ones are the females and the brown thrushes,
such as Song Thrush and Redwing.
   Look for pattern on the head, colour of flanks and underwing.

FIELDFARE *Turdus pilaris* 26cm. 80–140g. Scarce breeder (order 1–2), common winter visitor (order 6). Grey head and rump, dark slightly reddish-brown back, black tail, white underwing. VOICE loud harsh chuckle, and 'chack-chack-chack'; song a rather uninspiring series of squeaks and chuckles. HAB SUM usually in woodland edges; WIN often in open country, fields, etc. NEST often colonial; in tree; grass and mud, lined fine grass, ♀. EGGS 4–6, similar to Blackbird but often brighter blue, 29mm. BROODS 1 (2). INC 13–14, ♀. YOUNG col, *c.* 14, ♂♀. IMM 3. AGE 1, 18. FOOD insects, worms, berries.

Legs p. 47; Colonial nesting p. 263.

SONG THRUSH *Turdus philomelos* 23cm. 65–90g. Common resident (order 7), winter visitor (order 7). Uniform brown above, heavily spotted below; light orange underwing in flight; see Redwing. VOICE 'tsip', scolding chuckles; song loud and musical, differs from Blackbird by regularly repeating each phrase. HAB wide range of habitats with trees, woodland, agricultural, gardens. NEST in bush or tree; large cup of moss and grass, lined mud, ♀. EGGS 3–5, light blue with small black speckles and spots, 28mm. BROODS 2 (3). INC 12–14, ♀. YOUNG col, 12–15, ♂♀. IMM 3. AGE 1, 14. FOOD worms, insects, berries; also snails.

Bill p. 16–17; Survival of young p. 214–15; Territory p. 256; Nest material p. 267; Habitat gain p. 309.

REDWING *Turdus iliacus* 21cm. 55–75g. Scarce breeder (order 2–3), common winter visitor (order 6) Like Song Thrush, but darker on back (beware dark Song Ts from Europe in winter), conspicuous cream eye-stripe; deep red-orange on flank and underwing. VOICE thin high 'tseep'; song 4–6 musical notes, often descending, followed by quieter, harsher warble. HAB SUM usually woodland; WIN often open fields, hedges. NEST in tree, shrub; like Song T. but has lining of fine grass, ♀. EGGS 5–6, bluish-green, spotted red-brown, 26mm. BROODS 2. INC 12–14, ♀. YOUNG col, 12–14, ♂♀. IMM 3. AGE 1, 19. FOOD worms, insects, berries.

Flight p. 38.

MISTLE THRUSH *Turdus viscivorus* 27cm. 110–140g. Common resident (order 6). The largest thrush, pale greyish-brown, white underwing and white tips to outer tail feathers (only visible in flight as a rule). VOICE harsh scolding rattle or chatter; song can be confused with Blackbird, but more repetitive and less musical. HAB open woodland, parks, etc. NEST usually in fork of tree, often higher than other thrushes; grass and moss, lined fine grass, ♀. EGGS 3–5, bluish-green with reddish-brown blotches and spots, 31mm. BROODS 2. INC 13–14, ♀. YOUNG col, 14–16, ♂♀. IMM 3. AGE 1, 11. FOOD worms, insects, berries.

Breeding season p. 253; Habitat gain p. 309.

WARBLERS family *Sylviidae* 339 species in the world.
A large family of small, primarily insectivorous birds with small thin bills. Within Europe the main subdivisions are the grasshopper warblers (genus *Locustella*), the reed warblers (*Acrocephalus*), the 'hippolaids' (*Hippolais*), the 'typical' and scrub warblers (*Sylvia*), and the leaf warblers (*Phylloscopus*). Sexes and ages are similar in most, except for many *Sylvia* warblers. Most are migratory, leaving Europe for the winter; but some, especially in the Mediterranean area, remain behind. See also 'Crests' (p. 177).

Bills p. 16–17; Song p. 23; Seasonal plumages p. 220; Learning to feed p. 230; Migration p. 236–8, 241; Nest design and material p. 266; Conservation p. 305.

CETTI'S WARBLER *Cettia cetti* 14cm. 12–18g. Scarce resident (order 3). Presence mainly noted by song, since extremely skulking; dark rufous-brown, greyish underneath, with rather rounded tail. VOICE 'tic', 'tsee'; song explosive and very loud series of 'chew-eee-ooo' notes from thick cover. HAB dense low vegetation, usually near water. NEST (♂ often polygamous); in thick bush usually just above ground; cup of leaves, grass, lined fine grass, hair, etc. EGGS 4–5, distinctive brick-red, 18mm. BROODS 1. INC 16, ♀. YOUNG col, ♂♀. IMM 0. AGE 1, (5). FOOD mainly insects.

FAN-TAILED WARBLER *Cisticola juncidis* 10cm. 7–9g. Rare vagrant. Tiny, with short tail with black-and-white tips; most easily recognised by jerky flight and distinctive call. VOICE 'zit-zit-zit' given almost non-stop in flight; also 'tew'. HAB short vegetation, often damp, but also on dry hillsides. NEST in long grass, rushes; a frail purse of grass and plant down, bound together with spiders' webs, ♂♀. EGGS 4–6, whitish, finely speckled and blotched with dark browns, 15mm. BROODS 2 (3). INC *c.* 12, ♂♀. YOUNG col, ?, ♂♀. IMM ♀. AGE 1, ?. FOOD insects.

Size and energy p. 224; Non-migrant p. 236; Protection p. 300–1.

WARBLERS

Experience is required to separate the warblers; reed and hippo-laid warblers tend to have longish bills and rather flat foreheads (without a sharp angle at the base of the bill).

The presence of streaking on the back, and wing-bars, help to separate some species; and in adult Sylvia warblers eye and eye-ring colour can be useful.

● **GRASSHOPPER WARBLER** *Locustella naevia* 13cm. 11–15g. Common summer visitor (order 5). Very secretive, more often seen than heard; olive-chestnut upperparts with dark streaks, rounded tail. VOICE 'pit'; song distinctive grasshopper reel from thick cover, usually very prolonged. HAB dense grassy areas, wet or dry, often in *young* conifer plantations. NEST on ground, well-hidden in edge of grass tussock; leaves and grass, ♂♀. EGGS 5–6, pinkish-white, speckled reddish, 18mm. BROODS 2. INC 13–15, ♂♀. YOUNG col. 10–12. ♂♀. IMM 0. AGE 1, 5. FOOD mainly insects.

□ **RIVER WARBLER** *Locustella fluviatilis* 13cm. 16–22g. Rare vagrant. Similar to Grasshopper, but darker above, browner, unstreaked; paler below, streaked on breast. VOICE harsh 'swee'; song slower reel than Grasshopper, rhythmic notes sounding paired; often sings from exposed position. HAB thick herbage, inc. brambles; also woodland glades. NEST on ground at base of tall herbage; cup of grass and leaves, lined fine grass, hair. EGGS 5–6, whitish, speckled dark reds and browns, 19mm. BROODS 1. INC 13, ?. YOUNG col. ?, ♂♀. IMM 0. AGE 1, ?. FOOD mainly insects.

○ **SAVI'S WARBLER** *Locustella luscinioides* 14cm. 13–16g. Rare summer visitor (order 2). From Grasshopper by unstreaked, more rufous, plumage; less skulking; see also Reed Warbler. VOICE 'twit' and scolding chatter; song similar to Grasshopper, lower and faster, often much shorter bursts; may start with ticking notes; often from exposed position. HAB marshes, especially reed-beds. NEST well-hidden in dense mat of vegetation near water-level; vegetation, lined fine grasses, etc., ♀. EGGS 4–6, whitish, speckled browns and greys, 20mm. BROODS 2. INC 12, ♀. YOUNG col. 12–14, ♀(♂). IMM 0. AGE 1, ?. FOOD insects.

Habitat drainage
p. 308–9.

□ **MOUSTACHED WARBLER** *Acrocephalus melanopogon* 13cm. 10–13g. Rare vagrant. Like Sedge, but darker cheeks, much darker crown. VOICE chucks and churrs; song similar to Reed with musical Nightingale-like notes. HAB marshes, especially reed-beds. NEST over water, attached to plant stems; deep cup of reed or other plant, lined reed-flowers, feathers, ?. EGGS 3–4, whitish, almost covered fine olive-green speckles, 18mm. BROODS 2. INC ?, ?. YOUNG col. ?, ♂♀. IMM 0. AGE 1, ?. FOOD insects.

□ **AQUATIC WARBLER** *Acrocephalus paludicola* 13cm. 10–14g. Vagrant. Like pale Sedge, but broad buff central crown-stripe, streaked orange rump and pale, pinkish legs. VOICE chucks and loud churrs; •ong like Sedge but shorter bursts, less variable, and without mimicry. HAB marshes and damp surroundings. NEST (♂ often polygamous) near ground; cup of grasses, plant flowers, spider's-web, lined feathers, ?. EGGS 5–6, whitish, well-covered with fine olive-buff speckles, 18mm. BROODS 1. INC ?, ♀. YOUNG col, 13–14, ♀. IMM 0. AGE 1, ?. FOOD insects.

● **SEDGE WARBLER** *Acrocephalus schoenobaenus* 13cm. 10–13g. Common summer visitor (order 6). The most widespread of the 'sedge-type' warblers, conspicuous eye-stripe, unstreaked orangish rump, dark legs. VOICE loud chucks and churrs; song long varied, some clear trills, mimics other species. HAB damp ground, often near water, ditches, etc. NEST a little above ground in herbage; deep cup of grasses, spider's-web, finer lining inc. feathers, ?. EGGS 5–6, pale, blotched yellow-brown and with thin black marks, 18mm. BROODS 1–2. INC 13–14, ♀. YOUNG col. 12–14, ♂♀. IMM 0. AGE 1, 7. FOOD insects.

Song and pairing p. 23, 259; Moult p. 223; Migration p. 242; Breeding season p. 253.

□ **BLYTH'S REED WARBLER** *Acrocephalus dumetorum* 12·5cm. 10–14g. Rare vagrant. Almost indistinguishable from Reed and Marsh except by song; shorter wings, slightly greyer, but races of all species differ. VOICE 'chack'; song rich and mellow, slowish, mimics other species; long bursts of repetitive song; sings at night also. HAB thick vegetation, less confined to water than Reed. NEST suspended from tall herbage; deep cup of grasses and spider's-web, lined finer grasses, ?. EGGS 4–5, whitish, spotted and blotched dark greens, grey-browns, 18mm. BROODS 1. INC ?, ?. YOUNG col, 11, ♂♀. IMM 0. AGE 1, ?. FOOD insects.

adult

adult

adult

adult

adult   immature

adult   immature

adult

169

○ **MARSH WARBLER** *Acrocephalus palustris* 12·5cm. 11–15g.
Scarce summer visitor (order 2); declined markedly in recent years.
Distinguished from Reed and Blyth's Reed by song, and by paler
legs and pale alula (Reed's is darker than rest of wing), and longer
wings. VOICE wide variety of chucks; song variable, long, complex,
much mimicry. HAB thick vegetation, usually near water, but also
drier hedgerows, osier-beds, etc. NEST suspended in tall herbage;
grass, lined fine grass, hair, ♀. EGGS 4–5, whitish spotted olive-
green, clearer markings than Reed's, 19mm. BROODS 1. INC 12, ♂♀.
YOUNG col, 10–14, ♂♀. IMM 0. AGE 1, 8. FOOD insects.

Song p. 23, 258;
Speciation p. 55;
Moult p. 222; Migra-
tion p. 238, 242;
Breeding season
p. 253; Territory
p. 256; Nest building
p. 267.

● **REED WARBLER** *Acrocephalus scirpaceus* 12·5cm. 10–15g.
Common summer visitor (order 5). See Marsh and Blyth's Reed:
the most widespread of these. VOICE chacks and churrs; song loud,
sharp, prolonged at even pace (*cf* Sedge); 'jug-jug-jug' notes nearly
always included. HAB mainly *Phragmites* reed-beds, but also away
from water in some places. NEST sometimes almost colonial,
suspended from reed-stems; grass, reed-flowers, etc., with finer
lining, ♀. EGGS 3–5, whitish, blotched olive-greens and grey, 18mm.
BROODS 2. INC 11–12, ♂♀. YOUNG col, 10–14 but often leave nest
earlier, ♂♀. IMM 0. AGE 1, 12. FOOD insects.

Speciation p. 55; Baby
bird p. 209; Migration
p. 242; Incubation
p. 248; Pairing and
song p. 258–9; Cuckoo
host p. 279; Missing
from Ireland p. 298.

□ **GREAT REED WARBLER** *Acrocephalus arundinaceus* 19cm.
25–37g. Rare vagrant. A gigantic Reed Warbler, but otherwise the
same, though stouter bill. VOICE harsh deep notes; song rasping,
repetitive, with almost frog-like croaks. HAB mainly reed-beds.
NEST sometimes colonial, large nest suspended from reeds; grass,
reed-flowers, etc., with finer lining, ?. EGGS 4–6, off-white, blotched
dark browns, olive-greens, etc., 23mm. BROODS 1. INC 14–15, ♂♀.
YOUNG col, 12, ♂♀. IMM 0. AGE 1, 9. FOOD insects.

Moult p. 223;
Migration p. 242;
Cuckoo host p. 279.

□ **OLIVACEOUS WARBLER** *Hippolais pallida* 13·5cm. 10–13g.
Rare vagrant. Similar to Melodious, but lacks yellow below and is
greyer above; wings very short, scarcely reaching beyond base of
tail. VOICE quiet ticking notes; song loud babbling phrases,
repeated and prolonged. HAB open areas with trees and bushes,
often cultivated land. NEST in low bushes; twigs, grasses, lined fine
grass, ?. EGGS 3–4, whitish with black speckles, 17mm. BROODS 2.
INC 12–13, ♀. YOUNG col, 11–13, ♂♀. IMM 0. AGE 1, ?. FOOD insects,
some berries.

OLIVE-TREE WARBLER *Hippolais olivetorum* 15cm. 15–21g.
Secretive; a very large *Hippolais* warbler with very long bill, pale
edges to feathers on inner wing. VOICE quiet chucks; song louder,
less harsh, deeper than relatives. HAB scrub and small
trees. NEST in fork of branch in bush; cup of grasses and other
vegetation, ?. EGGS 3–4, pinkish-white, speckled black, 22mm.
BROODS ?. INC ?. YOUNG col, ?, ?. IMM 0. AGE ?1, ?. FOOD probably
mainly insects.

□ **ICTERINE WARBLER** *Hippolais icterina* 13·5cm. 12–16g.
Vagrant. Flatter head, longer beak than leaf warblers *Phylloscopus*;
like Melodious, but longer wings, usually pale patch on wing
feathers; bluer legs. VOICE tecks and ticks; song forceful, prolonged,
repetitive, harsh jangle, inc. mimicked notes. HAB wooded open
spaces, parks, gardens, wood edges, etc. NEST in fork of shrub,
1–4m above ground; cup of plant material, etc., bound with
spider's-web and plant fibres, lined finer material, ♂♀. EGGS 4–5,
pinkish-white, fine black spots, 18mm. BROODS 1. INC 13, ♂♀.
YOUNG col, 13, ♂♀. IMM 0. AGE 1, 6. FOOD mainly insects.

Bill p. 16; Niche
p. 297; British records
p. 298.

□ **MELODIOUS WARBLER** *Hippolais polyglotta* 13cm. 9–15g.
Vagrant. See Icterine; similar in build to Olivaceous with very
short wings, but greener above, yellow below. VOICE 'hweet' and
sparrow-like notes; song a twittering babble, but more musical
and less repetitive than Icterine. HAB open ground with trees and
bushes, often near water. NEST usually in twig fork of low shrub
rather than tree; deep cup of fine plant material and spider's-web.
♀. EGGS 3–5, pinkish, speckled black, 18mm. BROODS 1–2. INC 12–
13, ♀. YOUNG col, 12–13, ♂♀. IMM 0. AGE 1, ?. FOOD mainly insects.

Niche p. 297.

adult

adult

adult

adult

adult

adult spring

adult autumn

adult spring

adult autumn

171

MARMORA'S WARBLER *Sylvia sarda* 12cm. 8–12g. Red eye and eye-ring, long tail; ♂ dusky grey all over, ♀ paler below. VOICE distinctive 'tsig', notes sometimes run together; song similar to Dartford but less grating. HAB low scrubby vegetation. NEST in low bush; cup of twigs, leaves, etc., lined grass, hair, ?. EGGS 3–4, whitish, speckled with red-browns and greys, 18mm. BROODS ?2. INC ?, ?. YOUNG col, ?, ♂♀. IMM 3. AGE ?1, ?. FOOD insects.

○□ **DARTFORD WARBLER** *Sylvia undata* 12·5cm. 9–12g. Local resident (order 3). Build as Marmora's, red eye and eye-ring, long tail, but lighter grey above; ♂ purplish-brown below (throat spotted white); ♀ paler and browner. VOICE scolding chucks and churrs; song short musical chatter, often in flight. HAB low shrubby country; in UK heather and gorse; in s. Europe *Cistus maquis*. NEST usually near ground, often in thick bush; plants material, lined fine grasses, ♂♀. EGGS 3–5, whitish, finely spotted red-browns and greys, 18mm. BROODS 2. INC 12–13, ♀(♂). YOUNG col, 13–15, ♂♀. IMM 0. AGE 1, ?. FOOD insects.

Non-migrant p. 236; Protection p. 300–1; Habitat history p. 309.

□ **SPECTACLED WARBLER** *Sylvia conspicillata* 12·5cm. 8–10g. Rare vagrant. Similar to small Whitethroat, ♂ with pinker breast, darker cheek, brighter wing-patch; ♀ duller. VOICE sharp 'tac', Wren-like rattle, and churrs; song Whitethroat-like but less scratchy. HAB open country with short, small bushes, especially *Salicornia* on coastal mudflats. NEST near ground in thick cover; cup of grass, lined finer grasses, ♂♀. EGGS 4–5, whitish. finely speckled olive-green, 17mm. BROODS 2. INC 12–14, ♂♀. YOUNG col. 12–13, ♂♀. IMM 0. AGE ?1, ?. FOOD insects.

Niche p. 297.

□ **SUBALPINE WARBLER** *Sylvia cantillans* 12cm. 9–13g. Vagrant. Male reminds of Dartford, but shorter tail with white edges, paler back and conspicuous white moustachial streaks; ♀ like dull Whitethroat, similar to Spectacled but has red eye. VOICE 'tec-tec'; song like Sardinian but more musical. HAB edges of woods, bushy areas with a few trees. NEST in small bush; cup of dry grasses, etc., lined finer, ?. EGGS 3–4, whitish, spotted browns and greys, 17mm. BROODS 2. INC 11–12, ♂♀. YOUNG col, 11–12, ♂♀. IMM 0. AGE 1, ?. FOOD insects.

Niche p. 297.

□ **SARDINIAN WARBLER** *Sylvia melanocephala* 13·5cm. 10–12g. Rare vagrant, but often very common within range. Rounded tail shows white outer feathers; ♂ conspicuous, black head, white chin, red eye and eye-ring; ♀ much duller, though still has red eye and eye-ring. VOICE sharp chatter; song rather muddled and fast. series of musical notes interspersed with harsher ones. HAB low undergrowth and scrub. NEST usually near ground, in bush; plant material, lined finer, ♂♀. EGGS 3–4, whitish with fine brown and grey markings, 17mm. BROODS 2. INC 11–12, ♀(♂). YOUNG col, 11–12, ♂♀. IMM 0. AGE 1, ?. FOOD insects, berries, sometimes nectar.

Niche p. 297.

CYPRUS WARBLER *Sylvia melanothorax* 13·5cm. ?g. Cyprus only (where Sardinian absent). Similar to Sardinian (regarded as race of that species by some); ♂ distinctively marked with black underneath; ♀ clearly speckled on breast. VOICE sharp chatter; song rather muddled and fast, series of musical notes interspersed with harsher ones. HAB scrubby countryside. NEST low in bush; cup of plant material lined with fine grasses, ♀. EGGS 4–5, whitish. inclined greenish, covered with fine reddish-brown speckles. 17mm. BROODS ?2. INC ?, ?. YOUNG col, ?, ?. IMM 0. AGE 1, ?. FOOD insects, some berries.

Restricted range p. 301.

RÜPPELL'S WARBLER *Sylvia rüppelli* 14cm. ?g. Male differs from Sardinian by having black throat with clear white moustachial streak between it and dark head; ♀ more similar to Sardinian, but usually shows faint signs of moustachial streak; both sexes have orange-brown legs. VOICE sharp chatter; song rather muddled and fast, series of musical notes interspersed with harsher ones; shorter phrases than Sardinian. HAB open, bushy country. NEST in thick bush; cup of grass and other plant material, lined finer, ?. EGGS 4–5, whitish to greenish, covered with fine reddish-brown speckles, 18mm. BROODS ?2. INC 13, ♂♀. YOUNG col. ?, ♂♀. IMM 0. AGE 1, ?. FOOD insects, some berries.

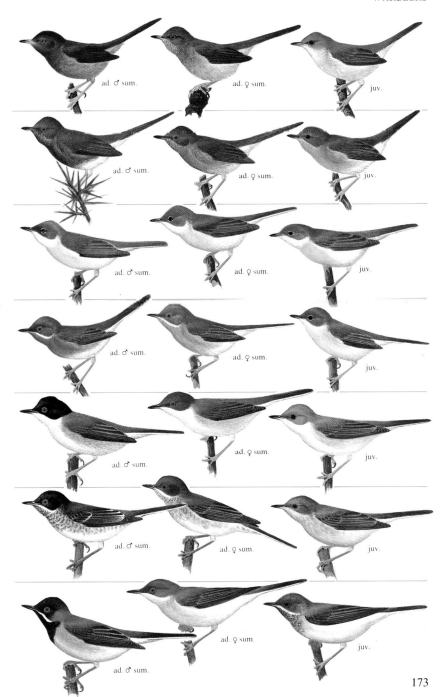

ad. ♂ sum.

ad. ♀ sum.

juv.

ad. ♂ sum.

ad. ♀ sum.

juv.

ad. ♂ sum.

ad. ♀ sum.

juv.

ad. ♂ sum.

ad. ♀ sum.

juv.

ad. ♂ sum.

ad. ♀ sum.

juv.

ad. ♂ sum.

ad. ♀ sum.

juv.

ad. ♂ sum.

ad. ♀ sum.

juv.

☐ **ORPHEAN WARBLER** *Sylvia hortensis* 15cm. 18–25g. Rare vagrant. A large warbler with striking white eye (juvenile's is dark) contrasting with blackish cheeks and crown; distinctive white outer tail feathers. VOICE 'tack's and rattles; song loud, clear, musical, thrush-like in repetition. HAB areas with large trees, orchards, parkland. NEST in branches of small trees; cup of small twigs, grass, etc., lined fine roots, hair, ?. EGGS 4–5, whitish, boldly marked with small spots of brown and grey, 20mm. BROODS ?2. INC 12, ♂♀. YOUNG col, 13, ♂♀. IMM 5–8. AGE 1, ?. FOOD insects and fruits.

☐ **BARRED WARBLER** *Sylvia nisoria* 15cm. 21–35g. Scarce passage migrant. A large greyish warbler with two palish wing-bars and some white in outer tail; adults have yellowish eye and, in spring, clearly barred underparts; juveniles greyer than Garden Warbler. VOICE harsh 'chack's and churrs; song musical Blackcap-like but with harsh notes. HAB woodland edge, clearings, hedges, etc. NEST often in thorny bush, in fork of branch; deep cup of grass, lined roots, hair, etc., ?. EGGS 4–6, whitish, finely speckled light greys, 21mm. BROODS 1 (2). INC 12–15, ♂♀. YOUNG col, 12–15, ♂♀. IMM 5–8. AGE ?1, 10. FOOD insects, berries.

● **LESSER WHITETHROAT** *Sylvia curruca* 13·5cm. 10–16g. Common summer visitor (order 5). Whitethroat-like but duller, lacks rich chestnut wing patch, has greyer upperparts, darker cheeks. VOICE 'chack's and churrs; song a rattle reminiscent of Chaffinch 'chikka-chikka-chikka . . .' preceded by short quiet warble. HAB usually in thicker scrub than Whitethroat, tall haw-thorns, etc. NEST low in bush; cup of fine twigs and grass, lined hair, etc., ♂♀. EGGS 4–6, cream, blotched greyish-browns, 17mm. BROODS 1–2. INC 11, ♂♀. YOUNG col, 11, ♂♀. IMM 0. AGE 1, 7. FOOD mostly insects.

Migration p. 238–9, 242–3; Niche p. 297.

● **WHITETHROAT** *Sylvia communis* 14cm. 12–18g. Common summer visitor (order 6). White throat, rufous wing patch; ♂ has greyer head than ♀, and pinkish wash on breast. VOICE scolding 'chack's and churrs, quieter 'wheet's; song rather short scratchy chatter often given in flight. HAB open areas with small bushes, brambles, etc., hedgerows. NEST low in brambles, etc.; cup of grasses, lined fine grass, hair, ♂♀. EGGS 4–5, pale buff, spotted dark browns and greens, 19mm. BROODS 1–2. INC 11–13, ♂♀. YOUNG col, 10–12, ♂♀. IMM 0. AGE 1, 9. FOOD insects, small fruits.

Calls and song flight p. 23, 259; Migration p. 243; Clutch weight p. 245; Populations p. 289; Niche p. 297.

● **GARDEN WARBLER** *Sylvia borin* 14cm. 16–23g. Common summer visitor (order 6). A solidly-built warbler with no distinctive features at all! heavyish, rounded head with stoutish bill, bluish tinge to legs, faint eye-ring. VOICE 'check's; song beautiful, like Blackcap's but more flowing and prolonged, mellow. HAB woodland (trees may be quite small) with thick undergrowth. NEST usually in low cover such as brambles; cup of grasses, lined fine grass, hair, ♂♀. EGGS 4–5, pale buff, spotted dark browns and greys, 20mm. BROODS 1–2. INC 12, ♂♀. YOUNG col, 10–12, ♂♀. IMM 0. AGE 1, 7. FOOD insects and small fruits.

Moult p. 223; Migration p. 238–9, 243; Territory p. 256.

●☐ **BLACKCAP** *Sylvia atricapilla* 14cm. 14–20g. Common summer visitor (order 6), small numbers overwinter (order 3–4: immigrants from n. Europe). Greyish-brown, undistinguished except for black cap in ♂ (not below eye-level, cf other *Sylvia* species), chestnut in ♀ and juvenile. VOICE sharp 'chack's and churrs; song rich clear warble, usually shorter and less flowing than Garden Warbler. HAB wooded country with plentiful under-growth. NEST wide ranges of low sites, nettles, brambles, etc.; cup of plant stems, lined fine grasses, etc., ♀. EGGS 4–5, pale buff, spotted dark browns, 20mm. BROODS 1–2. INC 10–12, ♂♀. YOUNG col, 10–13, ♂♀. IMM 0. AGE 1, 7. FOOD insects, small fruits.

Moult p. 223; Migration p. 238–9, 243; Territory p. 256.

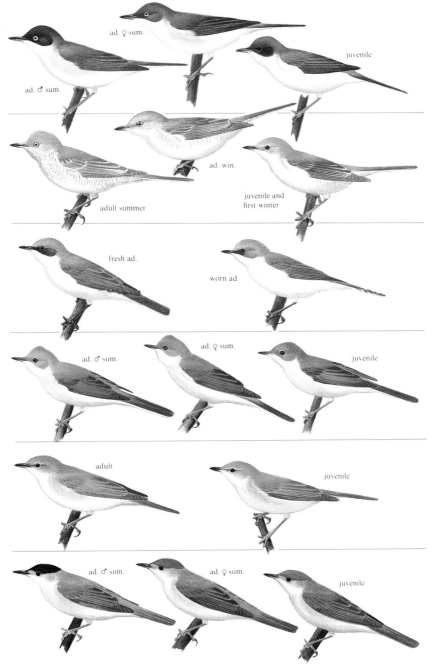

ad. ♀ sum.

ad. ♂ sum.

juvenile

ad. win.

adult summer

juvenile and
first winter

fresh ad.

worn ad.

ad. ♂ sum.

ad. ♀ sum.

juvenile

adult

juvenile

ad. ♂ sum.

ad. ♀ sum.

juvenile

175

☐ **GREENISH WARBLER** *Phylloscopus trochiloides* 11cm. 7–9g. Rare vagrant. Very like Chiffchaff; a small greenish or even greyish warbler whose main feature is a single pale (and not always very distinct) waing bar; conspicuous eyestripe. VOICE 'twee-wee'; song distinctive, a few 'chip's followed by a Wren-like trill. HAB wide range of open woodlands inc. some with quite small trees. NEST on ground among herbage, domed; grass and leaves, lined hair, ♀. EGGS 4–6, white, 15mm. BROODS 1. INC ?, ♀. YOUNG col, ?, ♂♀. IMM 0. AGE 1, ?. FOOD insects.

Song p. 23; Moult p. 223; Migration p. 237.

☐ **ARCTIC WARBLER** *Phylloscopus borealis* 12cm. 9–12g. Rare vagrant. Very similar to Greenish but larger, whiter throat, darker line through eye, long upturned supercilium, one wing-bar (a second visible on some). VOICE 'tsip'; song short rather buzzy trill on one note. HAB wide range of woodland habitats, often near water. NEST on ground; grass, lined finer, ♀. EGGS 5–6. white, finely spotted red-browns, 16mm. BROODS 1. INC ?, ♀. YOUNG col, ?, ♂♀. IMM 0. AGE 1, ?. FOOD insects.

Migration p. 235, 237.

☐ **YELLOW-BROWED WARBLER** *Phylloscopus inornatus* 10cm. 5–8g. Scarce passage migrant. Very small; two conspicuous wing-bars, marked creamy eyestripe. VOICE 'swee'; song a series of double call-notes run into trill. HAB wide range of woodland, scrub. NEST on ground, domed; grass, etc., lined fine grass, hair, ?. EGGS 5–6, white, finely speckled red-browns, 14mm. BROODS 1. INC ?, ?. YOUNG col, ?, ?. IMM 0. AGE 1, ?. FOOD insects.

Breeds in Siberia and eastern Asia; frequent vagrant to Europe, especially in autumn.

☐ **BONELLI'S WARBLER** *Phylloscopus bonelli* 11·5cm. 7–9g. Rare vagrant. Similar in size to Willow, but much greyer above. whiter below; yellowish rump (not always easy to see). VOICE quiet 'whee-eet'; song a slowish trill on one note. HAB variety of woodlands. NEST on ground, domed; grass, lined finer grass, hair. ♀. EGGS 4–6, white, speckled dark browns, 16mm. BROODS 1. INC ?, ♀. YOUNG col, ?, ♂♀. IMM 0. AGE 1, ?. FOOD insects.

Song p. 23.

● **WOOD WARBLER** *Phylloscopus sibilatrix* 12·5cm. 7–12g. Common summer visitor (order 5). A large leaf warbler, yellow breast and eyestripe, white underparts. VOICE 'whit' and 'pee-ou'; two songs, one a distinctive 'pip-pip-pip . . .' notes speeding up into a trill, the other a laboured repetition of the 'pee-ou' call. HAB woodland with rather little ground cover. NEST built into ground, often on slope, domed; grass, leaves, lined fine grass, ♀. EGGS 5–7, white, speckled purplish-brown, 16mm. BROODS 1. INC 13, ♀. YOUNG col, 11–12, ♂♀. IMM 0. AGE 1, ?. FOOD insects.

Song and territory p. 23, 257; Bigamy p. 282.

●☐ **CHIFFCHAFF** *Phylloscopus collybita* 11cm. 6–9g. Common summer visitor (order 6), a very few overwinter (order 3). A rather dull version of Willow, but legs usually blackish; northern races greyer. VOICE 'hweet'; song distinctive 'chiff-chaff' notes repeated in any order. HAB wide range of open woodland, scrub. NEST usually a little above ground, e.g. in bramble bush, domed; leaves and grass, lined feathers, ♀. EGGS 5–6, white, spotted purplish-brown. 15mm. BROODS 1–2. INC 13, ♀. YOUNG col, 13–14, ♂♀. IMM 0. AGE 1, 6. FOOD insects.

Song p. 23; Wing shape and migration p. 42; Isolating mechanism p. 57; Territory p. 256.

● **WILLOW WARBLER** *Phylloscopus trochilus* 11cm. 6–10g. Common summer visitor (order 7). Very widespread and common; greenish above, yellowish below; yellowish eyestripe and no wing-bars, similar to Chiffchaff but usually rather brighter and with paler legs. VOICE 'hooeet'; song distinctive musical series of descending notes, ending with a flourish. HAB wide range of open woodland and bushy habitats. NEST on or almost buried in ground, domed; grass and leaves, lined feathers, ♀. EGGS 6–7, white, spotted reddish, 15mm. BROODS 1. INC 13, ♀. YOUNG col, 13–14, ♂♀. IMM 0. AGE 1, 7. FOOD insects.

Song p. 23; Wing shape and migration p. 42; Isolating mechanism p. 57; Moult p. 220; Migration p. 235, 243.

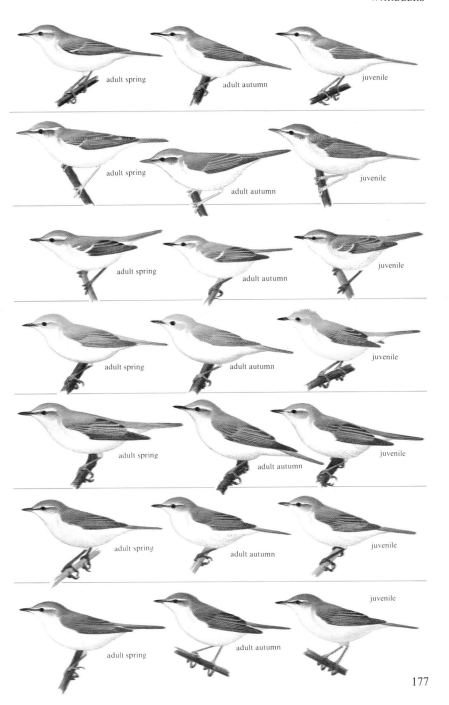

adult spring

adult autumn

juvenile

adult spring

adult autumn

juvenile

adult spring

adult autumn

juvenile

adult spring

adult autumn

juvenile

adult spring

adult autumn

juvenile

adult spring

adult autumn

juvenile

juvenile

adult spring

adult autumn

177

'CRESTS' genus *Regulus* 3 species in the world.
These are also members of the warbler family, with coloured crown feathers which they can spread to emphasise the colour (different in the sexes) in display. Although there is some movement, both Goldcrest and Firecrest remain within Europe for the winter.

Leaving nest p. 212; Size and energy p. 224.

●■ **GOLDCREST** *Regulus regulus* 9cm. 5–7g. Common resident (order 6 summer, 7 winter). Tiny; black-edged yellow crown; ♂ has orange centre to crown, often covered by the yellow feathers. VOICE high 'see' repeated; song 'seeter-seeter-seeter . . .' ending in flourish. HAB widespread, but commonest in conifer woodland. NEST usually in twigs at tip of conifer branch; in deciduous woods may be in ivy; tiny deep cup of moss and spider's-web, lined feathers, ♂♀. EGGS 7–8, white, finely spotted red-brown, 14mm. BROODS 2. INC 16, ♀. YOUNG col, 18–20, ♂♀. IMM 2–3. AGE 1, 7. FOOD insects.

Nest site and design p. 264, 267; Diffuse competition p. 298; Coniferous habitat p. 310.

○□ **FIRECREST** *Regulus ignicapillus* 9cm. 5–7g. Scarce breeder (order 2) increasing; uncommon passage migrant (order 3). Different from Goldcrest in stripy head-pattern, bronzy blush at breast-sides, deeper green back. VOICE 'zit-zit' sharper than Goldcrest; song like Goldcrest's but of *mono*syllabic notes, accelerating at end. HAB woodland, especially conifer. NEST usually in twigs at tip of conifer branch; tiny deep cup of moss and spider's-web, lined feathers, ♂♀. EGGS 7–9, whitish, pinker than Goldcrest's, with faint overlay of brownish, 13mm. BROODS 2. INC 14–15, ♀. YOUNG col, 19–20, ♂♀. IMM 2–3. AGE 1, (4). FOOD insects.

Nest site and design p. 264, 267; Coniferous habitat p. 310.

FLYCATCHERS family *Muscicapidae* 134 species in the world. A large family of primarily insectivorous, typically short-legged birds which perch on twigs and sally out after flying insects, or drop on the ground to catch them. They have small, broad, rather flattened bills with large gapes.

Bill p. 18; Hatchling p. 218; Migration p. 237; Breeding season p. 252; Food for young p. 276; Conservation p. 305.

● **SPOTTED FLYCATCHER** *Muscicapa striata* 14cm. 13–19g. Common summer visitor (order 6). Widespread; sits on prominent perch and flies out to snap up insects; greyish-brown above, whitish below, dark streaks on breast. VOICE thin 'tsee' sometimes followed by quiet 'chuck'; song a series of about six thin squeaky notes. HAB woodland clearings, gardens, parks. NEST in ivy, hole in wall, on ledge, etc., sometimes in old nest of other species; cup of moss and other vegetation, lined finer, inc. feathers, ♀. EGGS 4–5, washy greenish-blue, blotched dark reds, 19mm. BROODS 2. INC 12–14, ♂♀. YOUNG col, 12–15, ♂♀. IMM 2. AGE 1, 9. FOOD flying insects.

Bill and bristles p. 18, 29; Moult p. 32–3; Migration p. 238, 243; Food for young p. 276; Parental care p. 277.

□ **RED-BREASTED FLYCATCHER** *Ficedula parva* 11·5cm. 8–13g. Scarce passage migrant. Often drops to ground to pick up insects; birds on passage in w. Europe seldom have much red; whitish eye-ring and distinctive white sides to base of tail. VOICE quiet chatter and 'zeek'; song musical descending notes, starting slow, may end with trill. HAB mainly deciduous forest, often rather clear of ground cover. NEST either in hole or against tree-trunk; moss, spider's-web, lined hair, ♀. EGGS 5–6, whitish or pale bluish, overlaid with fine brown speckling, 17mm. BROODS 1. INC ?, ♀. YOUNG col, 11–15, ♂♀. IMM 2. AGE 1, ?. FOOD insects.

Bill p. 18; Migration p. 235, 237.

● **PIED FLYCATCHER** *Ficedula hypoleuca* 13cm. 9–15g. Common but local summer visitor (order 5). Apart from Collared, ♂ unmistakeable black-and-white; ♀ grey-brown above, grey-buff below, white edges to flight feathers most distinctive feature. VOICE 'whit' and 'wheet'; song series of mellow disyllabic notes, occasionally ending with short trill. HAB woodland, mainly deciduous in UK, but also in conifer elsewhere. NEST (♂ sometimes bigamous); hole in tree; leaves, plant fibres, lined finer materials, ♀. EGGS 5–8, light blue, 18mm. BROODS 1. INC 12–13, ♀. YOUNG col, 16, ♀ or ♂♀. IMM 2. AGE 1, 9. FOOD insects.

Seasonal plumage p. 220; Migration p. 242–3; Territory p. 254; Egg colour p. 269; Bigamy p. 282.

□ **COLLARED FLYCATCHER** *Ficedula albicollis* 13cm. 10–14g. Rare vagrant. Male as Pied but with conspicuous white collar; (eastern race, Semi-collared, a separate species according to some, lacks all or most of collar); ♀, juvenile and winter ♂ doubtfully distinguished from Pied. VOICE high-pitched 'wheet-wheet' notes; song as Pied but shorter and interspersed with 'ee' notes. HAB forests, primarily deciduous, but also conifer. NEST in hole; leaves, plant fibres, lined finer fibres, hair, ♀. EGGS 5–8, light blue. 18mm. BROODS 1. INC 12–13, ♀. YOUNG col, 13–16, ♂♀. IMM 2. AGE 1. ?. FOOD insects.

'CRESTS'

'Crests' can be recognised by their crown colours, and separated from each other by the black and white eyestripes in Firecrest, which are lacking in Goldcrest; and by voice.

FLYCATCHERS

European flycatchers are fairly easy to recognise and separate, except for female Pied and Collared, and even the males in winter.

Look for white collars (Pied and Collared), white in the base of the tail, or spotted breast.

179

PARROTBILLS family *Paradoxornithidae* 19 species in the world.
Only one species occurs in Europe, and it is distinctive. Parrotbills are related to the babblers (*Timaliidae*), not to the tits.

○□ **BEARDED TIT** *Panurus biarmicus* 11cm. 12–18g. Local resident (order 3 summer, 3–4 winter), suffers badly in severe winters. Long, graduated, brown tail; rufous above; ♂ grey head and black moustaches. VOICE main call a distinctive loud ringing 'ping' or 'ching'; also warbling twitters and 'tuu' notes. HAB almost exclusively confined to *Phragmites* reed-beds. NEST low down in marsh in thick vegetation, often where reeds have fallen over; cup of reed-leaves, lined reed-flowers, ♂♀. EGGS 5–7, white, spotted and streaked grey-browns, 17mm. BROODS 2. INC 12–13, ♂♀. YOUNG col, 9–12, ♂♀. IMM 0. AGE 1, 6. FOOD insects, small seeds.

Habitat drainage p. 308–9.

TITS family *Paridae* 46 species in the world.
A family of agile, arboreal, insectivorous birds with strong, small beaks which they use for hammering open seeds. Long-tailed (family *Aegithalidae*, 7 species in the world) and Penduline (family *Remizidae*, 9 species in the world) are not true tits.

Bills p. 16–17; Prey of woodpeckers p. 17; Feathers and spring moult p. 30, 219; Interval between eggs and clutch size p. 35, 270–1; Perching and hopping p. 46–7; Parental care and pair bond p. 212, 282;

●■ **MARSH TIT** *Parus palustris* 11·5cm. 9–12g. Common resident (order 6). Similar to Willow Tit; brownish above, whitish below; black cap and bib (*cf* Blackcap, p. 173). VOICE explosive 'pitchou', also nasal 'chay' and 'chikka-dee-dee-dee'; song ringing 'ship-ship-ship . . .' or 'shippi-shippi-shippi . . .' HAB deciduous woodland, sometimes hedges and gardens, seldom marshes. NEST in hole, usually low down; moss, lined hair or fur, ♀. EGGS 6–8, white, spotted reddish, 16mm. BROODS 1. INC 13, ♀. YOUNG col. 16–18, ♂♀. IMM 0. AGE 1, 10. FOOD insects in summer; mainly seeds in winter.

Bill p. 16; Subdivision of range p. 55; Isolating mechanism p. 57; Territory p. 256; Niche p. 297, 299; Missing from Ireland p. 298; Deciduous habitat p. 310.

SOMBRE TIT *Parus lugubris* 14cm. 16–17g. Like large Marsh or Willow Tit, but richer brown above, more extensive black bib, whiter cheeks and underparts. VOICE distinctive churrs; song repeated disyllabic first high, second lower. HAB wide range of woodlands. NEST hole in tree; moss and other plant material, lined feathers, ♀. EGGS 5–7, white with reddish spots, 17mm. BROODS 1–2. INC ?, ♀. YOUNG col, ?, ♂♀. IMM 0. AGE 1, ?. FOOD insects and seeds.

●■ **WILLOW TIT** *Parus montanus* 11·5cm. 9–12g. Common resident (order 5). Different races vary, British brownest and most like Marsh, but has bigger head, duller and untidier cap and bib, usually pale edges to flight feathers at rest. VOICE wheezy 'eez-eez'; high 'zee-zee' followed by 'tchair'; song rare, quiet variable silvery warbling. HAB wooded country (more in conifer than Marsh), often near water. NEST in hole in rotten wood, excavated by ♀; wood chips, plant fibres, hair, etc., ♀. EGGS 6–9, white with reddish-brown spots, 16mm. BROODS 1. INC 13, ♀. YOUNG col, 18, ♂♀. IMM 0. AGE 1, 9. FOOD insects, seeds.

Isolating mechanism p. 57; Food storing p. 229; Nest hole p. 264–5; Population movements p. 291; Missing from Ireland p. 298; Niche p. 299.

SIBERIAN TIT *Parus cinctus* 13·5cm. 12–16g. Resembles large Willow/Marsh Tit, but browner crown, back and flanks. VOICE drawn-out 'eeez' notes repeated; song a quiet high-pitched warble. HAB northern conifer and birch forests. NEST in hole in tree, may partly excavate; moss, lined hair, feathers, ♀. EGGS 6–9, white with reddish spots, 16mm. BROODS 1. INC 14, ♀. YOUNG col, ?, ♂♀. IMM 0. AGE 1, ?. FOOD insects and seeds.

Heat loss and survival in cold p. 225, 229.

○□ **CRESTED TIT** *Parus cristatus* 11·5cm. 10–13g. Local resident (order 4). Easily recognised by speckled black-and-white crest which sometimes short and not too conspicuous; black C-shaped mark on face; browner on back than other UK tits. VOICE quiet 'si-si-si' and a soft churr; song high tinkly trills of two notes. HAB conifer forests. NEST hole in rotten stump of tree. excavated by ♀; moss, lined fur, etc., ♀. EGGS 5–8, white with reddish spots, 16mm. BROODS 1. INC 13–15, ♀. YOUNG col, 16–20, ♂♀. IMM 3. AGE 1, (5). FOOD insects and seeds.

Food storing p. 229; Nest hole p. 265; Niche p. 297, 299; Coniferous habitat p. 310–1.

PARROTBILLS

The Bearded Tit is fairly easily identified by its rather direct flight in reed-beds, and by its loud pinging call, which often betrays its presence.

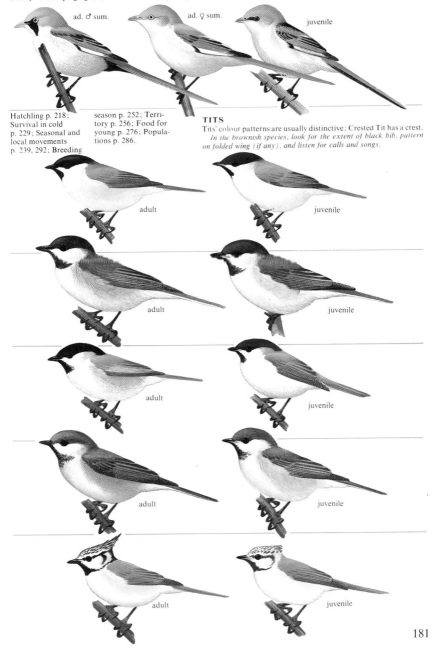

ad. ♂ sum.   ad. ♀ sum.   juvenile

Hatchling p. 218; Survival in cold p. 229; Seasonal and local movements p. 239, 292; Breeding season p. 252; Territory p. 256; Food for young p. 276; Populations p. 286.

TITS

Tits' colour patterns are usually distinctive; Crested Tit has a crest. *In the brownish species, look for the extent of black bib, pattern on folded wing (if any), and listen for calls and songs.*

adult   juvenile

adult   juvenile

adult   juvenile

adult   juvenile

adult   juvenile

181

●■ **COAL TIT** *Parus ater* 11·5cm. 8–10g. Common resident (order 6). A small tit with a black crown and bib, white cheeks and nape patch, two white wing bars. VOICE high 'fwee-twee', and high repeated 'tsee'; song repeated 'p'tee-p'tee-p'tee . . .' with emphasis on second syllable (*cf* Great Tit). HAB woodland, especially conifer, gardens, etc. NEST in hole, sometimes in ground or bank; moss, lined hair, ♀. EGGS 7–11, white with reddish spots, 15mm. BROODS 1 (2). INC 14, ♀. YOUNG col, 16–19, ♂♀. IMM 2–3. AGE 1, 7. FOOD insects, seeds.

Size, energy, feeding rates and storing p. 224, 228, 229; Hunting parties and peck-order p. 230–1; Population movements p. 291; Niche p. 297, 299; Coniferous habitat p. 310–1.

●■ **BLUE TIT** *Parus caeruleus* 11·5cm. 9–12g. Common resident (order 7). Widespread and common: the only blue tit in w. Europe; underparts yellow, sometimes with thin black line down centre. VOICE rapid 'tsee-tsee' and 'tsit', scolding churrs; song 'tsee-tsee' followed by 'tu-tu-tu' in rapid trill. HAB wide range of wooded areas inc. gardens; usually prefers deciduous. NEST hole in tree, wall, etc.; moss, strips of plant fibre, grass, lined feathers, ♀. EGGS 6–12, white, speckled with reddish, 15mm. BROODS 1. INC 13–14, ♀. YOUNG col, 18–20, ♂♀. IMM 2–3. AGE 1, 14, 30%. FOOD insects, seeds.

Breeding p. 35, 227, 245, 247; Air speed p. 43; Speciation p. 55; Feeding and young p. 228, 230–1, 275; Territory, survival, movements, habitat p. 256–7, 285–7, 292, 297, 309–10.

●■ **GREAT TIT** *Parus major* 14cm. 16–21g. Common resident (order 7). Widespread and common: looks like large and colourful version of Coal Tit. VOICE loud 'pink', churrs, and a multitude of other different calls; song loud 'teacher-teacher-teacher . . .' with emphasis on first syllable (*cf* Coal Tit), very occasionally tri-syllabic. HAB wide range of wooded areas, gardens, etc. NEST hole, usually in tree or wall; mainly moss, lined hair, wool, etc., not feathers, ♀. EGGS 5–11, white with reddish spots, 18mm. BROODS 1–2. INC 12–14, ♀. YOUNG col, 19–21, ♂♀. IMM 2–3. AGE 1, 5, 50%. FOOD insects, seeds.

Bill and feeding p. 17, 228, 230–1; Speciation p. 51; Pairing, territory, song, breeding p. 23, 246–7, 249, 256–9; Survival, populations, movements and habitat p. 288–9, 291–2, 309.

●■ **LONG-TAILED TIT** *Aegithalos caudatus* 14cm. 7–9g. Common resident (order 6), suffers badly in severe winters. Tiny bird with long tail; in winter usually in flocks of 5–15; black, white and pink; northern race has white head. VOICE 'tssrrrp' constantly in flock; also 'tsee-tsee'; song a trilling warble. HAB woodland, hedges, etc. NEST site varied; in thick herbage of gorse, hawthorn, etc., or high in tree against trunk; domed structure of feathers, spider's-web, covered with lichens, ♂♀. EGGS 7–12, white, some with fine reddish speckles, 14mm. BROODS 1. INC 13–14, ♀. YOUNG col, 15–16, ♂♀. IMM 1–2. AGE 1, 8. FOOD small insects.

Post-fledging moult p. 219; Size, energy and heat loss p. 225; Hunting parties p. 230; Nest site, design and material p. 264, 267; Co-operative breeding and group subdivision p. 281.

□ **PENDULINE TIT** *Remiz pendulinus* 11cm. 8–11g. Rare vagrant. Distinctive with grey head, black mask and chestnut 'saddle'; juveniles much paler, look rather warbler-like. VOICE soft falling 'see'; song 'wheet-choo-choo'. HAB thick vegetation along marsh edges. NEST suspended from thin twigs of tree branch, purse-like; plant fibres, ♂♀. EGGS 6–8, white 16mm. BROODS 1. INC 13–14, ♀. YOUNG col, 16–18, ♂♀. IMM 3–9. AGE 1, ?. FOOD insects, small seeds, especially of reed-mace; drifting down of reed-mace on a still day often indicates presence of this bird.

Nest design and material p. 267.

NUTHATCHES family *Sittidae* 21 species in the world.
CREEPERS family *Certhiidae* 6 species in the world.
These are two families of primarily tree-climbing birds which feed largely on insects or, in the case of nuthatches in winter, seeds. Nuthatches are short-tailed birds which, uniquely, climb up *and down* trees. Treecreepers are long-tailed and climb only up trees, using their tail as a prop. The Wallcreeper is an aberrant nuthatch which lives on rock-faces. All European species are residents.

Climbing p. 46.

WALLCREEPER *Tichodroma muraria* 16·5cm. 15–20g. Rare vagrant. A striking grey, black and white bird with broad red wings and conspicuous butterfly-like flight. VOICE plaintive slow 'pee-pee-pee' sometimes ending with short twitter. HAB rock-faces of mountains. NEST in deep rock crevice; moss and grass, lined hair, feathers, ♀. EGGS 4, white with a few black speckles, 21mm. BROODS 1. INC 18–19, ♀. YOUNG col, 21–26, ♂♀. IMM 0. AGE ?1, ?. FOOD insects.

adult

juvenile

adult

juvenile

adult

juvenile

adult
Britain
and
western
Europe

juv.

adult
northern Europe

adult

juvenile

NUTHATCHES AND CREEPERS

Nuthatches and creepers are separated by beak-shape, tail-length and tree-climbing behaviour. In nuthatches, *look for colour of flanks and head pattern*. The two creepers are virtually indistinguishable except *by range, and by call*.

ad. ♂ sum.

ad. ♀ sum.

ad. ♂ win.

183

CORSICAN NUTHATCH *Sitta whiteheadi* 12cm. 11–14g. Corsica only. Small; ♂ has black cap and eye-stripe highlighting white stripe over eye. VOICE single, rather Jay-like note; song level weak trills and nasal sounds, quieter than Nuthatch. HAB montane forests (especially of *Pinus laricio*) above c. 1,000m. NEST in tree-hole, apparently does not use mud to reduce hole-size; bark flakes, moss, lined hair, ?. EGGS 5–6, white with reddish-brown spots, 17mm. BROODS ?1. INC ?. ♀. YOUNG col, 22–25, ♂♀. IMM 0. AGE ?1, ?. FOOD insects, seeds.

Restricted range
p. 301.

NUTHATCH *Sitta europaea* 14cm. 19–24g. Common resident (order 5). Distinctive squat bird with dagger-shaped bill; grey above, rufous or buff beneath; white pattern in tail. VOICE loud liquid 'quipp' often repeated; song loud prolonged level trilling. HAB woodland, especially with large deciduous trees; also gardens, etc. NEST in tree-hole, plasters hole with mud which sets hard to leave just enough space for the adults to squeeze through; bark flakes (especially of conifer), ♂♀. EGGS 5–8, white with reddish spots, 19mm. BROODS 1. INC 14–15, ♀. YOUNG col, 23–25, ♂♀. IMM 0. AGE 1, 9. FOOD insects and seeds.

Intermingling of forms
p. 55; Nest hole
p. 264–5; Missing from
Ireland p. 298.

ROCK NUTHATCH *Sitta neumayer* 14cm. 25–35g. Very similar to Nuthatch but paler below, no white in tail. VOICE reminiscent of Nuthatch but more varied trills, descending in pitch. HAB rocky mountainous areas, preferring rocks to trees. NEST in crack in rocks, front plastered over with mud, and small tube built out from entrance; lined moss, hair, etc., ?. EGGS 6–10, white with reddish-brown spots, 21mm. BROODS ?1. INC ?. ♀. YOUNG col, ?. ♂♀. IMM 0. AGE ?1, ?. FOOD mainly insects.

●■ **TREECREEPER** *Certhia familiaris* 12·5cm. 8–12g. Common resident (order 6). Indistinguishable from Short-toed in appearance; small brown bird, vivid white underparts, decurved beak; pale stripes in wing. VOICE thin insistent 'tsee'; song weak, high-pitched set of 'tsee' notes run together and falling to finish in flourish. HAB woodland, especially with large trees; sometimes hedgerow trees. NEST behind split in bark on tree-trunk; small twigs, moss, lined finer materials, ♂♀. EGGS 5–6, white with reddish-brown spots, 16mm. BROODS 1–2. INC 14–15, ♀. YOUNG col, 14–15, ♂♀. IMM 0. AGE 1, 9. FOOD insects probed from bark.

Feathers p. 30;
Speciation p. 55.

?**SHORT-TOED TREECREEPER** *Certhia brachydactyla* 12·5cm. 8–12g. Status uncertain: may breed in one or two coastal sites. As Treecreeper: only separable in hand or by voice. VOICE sharper, shorter, more piping than Treecreeper; song richer and less thin than Treecreeper. HAB woodland, especially with large trees; in s. Europe Treecreeper tends to be at higher altitudes, Short-toed in the lowlands. NEST behind split in bark on tree-trunk; small twigs, moss, lined finer materials, ♂♀. EGGS 6–7, white with reddish-brown spots, 16mm. BROODS 1–2. INC 15, ♀. YOUNG col, 16–17, ♂♀. IMM 0. AGE 1, 6. FOOD insects.

Speciation p. 55.

ORIOLES family *Oriolidae* 28 species in the world.
Thrush-sized birds which are usually brilliantly coloured. Orioles live in trees, and eat insects and fruit. Only the Golden Oriole occurs in Europe; it is strongly migratory.

○ **GOLDEN ORIOLE** *Oriolus oriolus* 24cm. 65–67g. Rare summer visitor (order 2). Almost size of Mistle Thrush, with undulating flight; ♂ unmistakeable; ♀ duller, green and dark brown, but also longish red bill. VOICE range of chacks and churrs; song distinctive, far-carrying fluty notes, e.g. 'weela-weeoo'. HAB broad-leaved woods, parks, etc., hard to spot among foliage. NEST slung between two twigs on outermost part of tree branch; cup woven from grass, strips of bark, etc., lined finer materials, ♀. EGGS 3–4, white with small blackish spots, 31mm. BROODS 1. INC 14–15, ♀(♂). YOUNG col, 14–15, ♂♀. IMM 0. AGE 1, ?. FOOD insects, fruits.

Breeding in Britain
p. 298.

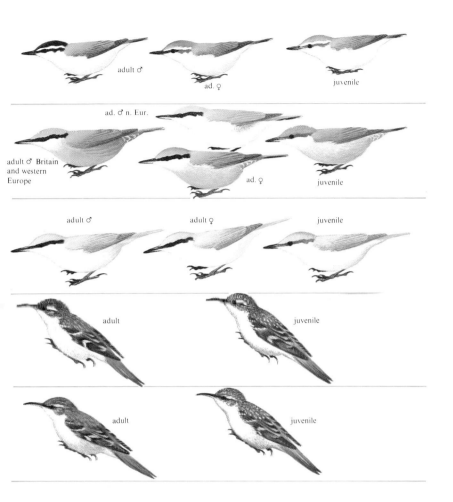

adult ♂

ad. ♀

juvenile

ad. ♂ n. Eur.

adult ♂ Britain
and western
Europe

ad. ♀

juvenile

adult ♂

adult ♀

juvenile

adult

juvenile

adult

juvenile

ORIOLES

Male Golden Orioles are easily recognised by colour; they also
have a strongly undulating flight. In spite of their bright colours,
they are secretive birds often only detected by their calls.

adult ♂

juvenile

adult ♀

SHRIKES family *Laniidae* 70 species in the world.
Shrikes have strong, sharply-hooked bills; they catch large insects, small lizards, mammals and birds. They store prey surplus to immediate requirements by impaling it on a thorn in a bush; such 'larders' may contain several prey.

○ **RED-BACKED SHRIKE** *Lanius collurio* 17cm. 22–47g. Rare summer visitor (order 2), marked decrease in recent years. Only European shrike with chestnut back, no white in wing; ♂ has grey head, black mask; ♀ and juvenile less bright, with crescentic marks on underparts. VOICE sharp grating 'chack' notes; song soft warble with buzzing notes. HAB bushy, open areas. NEST in thick, usually thorny, bush; small twigs, grass, etc., lined finer materials, ♀(♂). EGGS 5–6, very varied, buffish, cream, greenish, with dark spots usually at blunt end, 23mm. BROODS 1. INC 13–16, ♀. YOUNG col, 14, ♂♀. IMM 3–9. AGE 1, 7. FOOD insects, small birds, etc.

Migration p. 235.

□ **LESSER GREY SHRIKE** *Lanius minor* 20cm. 40–65g. Scarce passage migrant. Like Great Grey but smaller, shorter tail; black mask goes over top of bill, no white between it and grey crown. VOICE 'check' may be rapidly repeated; song quiet mixture of musical notes and grating sounds. HAB open country with trees and bushes. NEST may be within a metre or two from ground, or high in tree; cup of twigs, plant stems, etc., lined finer material inc. feathers, ?. EGGS 5–6, greenish or cream, blotched greenish, browns, 25mm. BROODS 1. INC 15, ♀(♂). YOUNG col, 14, ♂♀. IMM 3. AGE 1, ?. FOOD large insects, small reptiles, birds, etc.

□ **GREAT GREY SHRIKE** *Lanius excubitor* 24cm. 55–80g. Scarce winter visitor (order 2). Similar to Lesser Grey but shows more white on scapulars, bill is less deep, has white between black mask and grey crown. VOICE harsh 'check' repeated; song a mixture of musical and harsher notes. HAB open country with trees, bushes, forest edge. NEST commonly in thorny bushes; cup of twigs, stems, etc., lined fine grass, feathers, ?. EGGS 5–7, whitish or pale greenish, heavily marked dark browns, 26mm. BROODS 1. INC 15, ♀. YOUNG col, 19–20, ♂♀. IMM 0. AGE 1, ?. FOOD large insects, small lizards, birds, etc.

□ **WOODCHAT SHRIKE** *Lanius senator* 17cm. 25–35g. Rare vagrant. Rich chestnut crown and nape, striking white pattern in wing; juvenile brownish like Red-backed, but more scaly, with pale patch in wing. VOICE harsh 'chip' and chatters; song more musical, inc. mimicked phrases. HAB open country with bushes and trees. NEST in outer branches of tree; cup of fine twigs, other plant material, lined feathers, hair, ?. EGGS 5–6, cream to pale green, blotched browns and greys, 23mm. BROODS 1. INC 16, ♀. YOUNG col, 19–20, ♂♀. IMM 3–9. AGE 1, ?. FOOD large insects, small lizards, birds, etc.

Pairing and territory p. 255.

MASKED SHRIKE *Lanius nubicus* 17cm. 17–28g. Black above except for white forehead, eye-stripe, scapulars, wing patch and outer tail; pale below with orange-brown flanks. VOICE harsh 'keer'; song a string of scratchy notes, slightly reminiscent of Reed Warbler. HAB open country with trees and shrubs. NEST may be high in tree; cup of roots, other plant material, lined feathers, hair, ?. EGGS 4–6, cream to buff, heavily spotted dark brown and grey, 21mm. BROODS 2. INC ?, ♀. YOUNG col, ?, ♂♀. IMM 3–9. AGE ?1, ?. FOOD mainly large insects.

CROWS family *Corvidae* 103 species in the world.
A widespread family which includes the largest passerines. Conspicuous, often noisy, crows have powerful legs, feet and beaks, and take a wide range of foods. European species are mainly resident, though some northern populations may move south for the winter.

Walking and hopping p. 263; Nest design
p. 47; Carrion feeding and material p. 266;
p. 230; Single brooded Great Spotted Cuckoo
p. 250; Nest predation hosts p. 280.

□ **NUTCRACKER** *Nucifraga caryocatactes* 32cm. 130–190g. Rare vagrant. Reminiscent of small Rook; body plumage brown spotted whitish; white undertail and tip of tail. VOICE harsh cries, some rather Jay-like; also a churring alarm-call like harsh Trimphone. HAB SUM conifer forests mostly at highish altitudes; WIN comes down lower into deciduous woods. NEST in tree; large untidy cup of twigs, moss, etc., lined grasses, ♂♀. EGGS 3–4, pale greenish, very finely spotted with dark browns, 34mm. BROODS 1. INC 17–19, ♀. YOUNG col, 21–28, ♂♀. IMM 0. AGE ?1, 8. FOOD primarily nuts and seeds, some insects.

Population movements p. 291.

SHRIKES

Adult shrikes are easily separated by colour, except for the two grey species.

In the grey species, *look for details of the black face pattern and whether or not there is white above it*; the colour of the breast is also important.

Juvenile Red-backed and Woodchat are most easily separated by *the presence or absence of a pale wing-bar*.

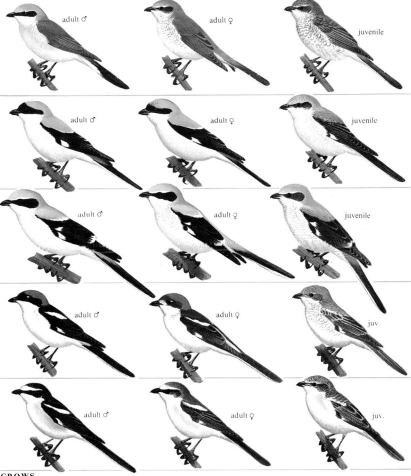

adult ♂   adult ♀   juvenile

adult ♂   adult ♀   juvenile

adult ♂   adult ♀   juvenile

adult ♂   adult ♀   juv.

adult ♂   adult ♀   juv.

CROWS

The jays, Nutcracker and magpies are all distinctively plumaged and easily recognisable.

The black crows are more difficult: *look for colour of bill* (choughs), *white face at base of bill* (Rook), *grey in plumage* (Jackdaw and Hooded Crow). *Tail shape or call* can distinguish the others.

adult   juvenile   adult

187

JAY *Garrulus glandarius* 34cm. 140–190g. Common resident (order 6). Races vary, but black tail and flight feathers, white rump common to all; brown to pinkish body, blue patch in wing, streaks or dark feathers on crown which can be erected. VOICE harsh shrieking far-carrying yells, also 'kraak-kraak'; song rare, varied musical carolling noises. HAB any woodland, parks, gardens. NEST usually not very high in tree; cup of twigs, lined roots, ♂♀. EGGS 5–6, greenish with very fine browning speckling, 32mm. BROODS 1. INC 16, ♂♀. YOUNG 20, ♂♀. IMM 0. AGE 1, 18. FOOD wide range: seeds. insects. nestling birds. etc.

Anting p. 30; Hopping p. 47; Population movements p. 291.

SIBERIAN JAY *Perisoreus infaustus* 31cm. 75–95g. Medium-brown bird with darker crown and wings, orangish, patches in wings, tail and wings. VOICE varied, 'whisk-ee', harsher 'kair', and others; some mimicry. HAB northern conifer and birch woodlands. NEST in conifer at varied height near trunk; cup of twigs, lined feathers, etc., ♀(♂). EGGS 4, whitish to very pale blue, spotted with olive-greys, 30mm. BROODS 1. INC 18–20, ♀. YOUNG 21–24, ♂♀. IMM 0. AGE 1, 9. FOOD mostly seeds, some insects.

AZURE-WINGED MAGPIE *Cyanopica cyanus* 34cm. 65–85g. Often in conspicuous, noisy parties; light brownish body with black crown, blue wings and tail. VOICE rather cat-like cries, and harsher 'kaah'. HAB mixed vegetation, trees, bushes, often along water. NEST in small loose colonies, in small tree, cup of twigs, lined hair, fur, ♂♀. EGGS 5–7, cream, spotted browns, 28mm. BROODS 1. INC 15, ♀. YOUNG col, ?, ♂♀. IMM 0. AGE ?1, ?. FOOD wide variety of insects, seeds.

Discrete populations p. 54.

MAGPIE *Pica pica* 46cm inc. long tail. 200–250g. Common resident (order 6). Unmistakeable long-tailed black-and-white bird. VOICE harsh, cackling chatters 'cak-cak-cak . . .'. HAB wood-land edge, open country with trees. NEST in top of tree, often haw-thorn; domed or with detached roof; twigs, lined mud, fine roots, ♂♀. EGGS 5–7, pale greenish, spotted dark browns and greys, 34mm. BROODS 1. INC 17–18, ♀. YOUNG col, 22–27, ♂♀. IMM 0. AGE 1, 15. FOOD omnivorous: seeds, insects, small birds, etc.

Walking and hopping p. 47; Nest design p. 266; Clutch size p. 271; Great Spotted Cuckoo host p. 280.

ALPINE CHOUGH *Pyrrhocorax graculus* 38cm. 170–330g. Like Chough but bill shorter, yellow and less decurved. VOICE rather whistling 'chirrip', quieter 'chup', and some more crow-like notes. HAB mountainous regions; comes lower in winter, but not to low-lands. NEST in crevice or small cave in rock-face; cup of small sticks, lined roots, grasses, ♂♀. EGGS 4, creamy, spotted olive-greens and greys, 39mm. BROODS 1. INC 17–21, ♀. YOUNG 25–30, ♂♀. IMM 0. AGE ?1, 11. FOOD mainly insects, worms.

Flight p. 38; Migration p. 238.

CHOUGH *Pyrrhocorax pyrrhocorax* 40cm. 280–360g. Local resident (order 4). The only European crow with a strongly decurved, bright red beak; also red legs. VOICE distinctive 'cheeow', longer and higher than Jackdaw, far-carrying. HAB mountains, sea-cliffs. NEST in deep crevice in rock-face or in small cave; cup of twigs, lined hair, wool, etc., ♂♀. EGGS 3–5, buffish, blotched browns and greys, 30mm. BROODS 1. INC 17–18, ♀. YOUNG col, 38, ♂♀. IMM 0. AGE 1, 17. FOOD mainly insects, worms, etc. obtained by probing in short turf.

Habitat history p. 309.

JACKDAW *Corvus monedula* 33cm. 220–270g. Common resident (order 6). Smallish crow with grey head and pale grey eye (in adults). VOICE distinctive 'chack' often repeated, shorter and less ringing than Chough. HAB wide range: farmland, parks, cliffs. NEST often semi-colonial; in hole in tree or building, cliff, rabbit-burrow on cliff top; twigs, lined wool, etc., ♂♀. EGGS 4–6, pale bluish-green with dark brown or blackish spots, 36mm. BROODS 1. INC 18–19, ♀. YOUNG col, 30–35, ♂♀. IMM 3–4. AGE 1, 14. FOOD wide range: insects, worms, steals sea-birds' eggs.

Feeding flocks p. 230; Breeding season p. 253; Nest hole p. 265.

adult juvenile ad.

adult juvenile ad.

adult juvenile ad.

adult juvenile ad.

adult juvenile ad.

adult juvenile ad.

adult juvenile ad.

189

● ■ **ROOK** *Corvus frugilegus* 46cm. 460–520g. Common resident (order 6–7 summer, 7 winter). Usually in flocks; bare whitish face and bill-base (not in juveniles); otherwise like Carrion Crow but bill finer, more dagger-shaped, and feathers above legs form shaggy 'leggings' when walking. VOICE wide range of 'caw' and 'kah' notes. HAB mainly on agricultural land. NEST colonial; in tops of tall trees (even pylons); large cup of twigs, lined grass, leaves, etc., ♀(♂). EGGS 4–6, light bluish-green with dark spots, 40mm. BROODS 1. INC 16–19, ♀. YOUNG col, 29–30, ♂♀. IMM 6–8. AGE ?1. 20. FOOD insects in soil, worms, spilled grain, etc.

Feeding flocks p. 230; Peck-order p. 231; Breeding season p. 253; Colonial nesting p. 262; Habitat history p. 309.

● ■ **CARRION/HOODED CROW** *Corvus corone* 47cm. 540–600g. Common resident (order 7). Usually not in flocks; heavier beak than Rook, no 'leggings'; Hooded has black head, wings, tail, otherwise grey; Carrion glossy black all over; gradation of these in hybrids. VOICE harsh 'kraah' usually three or more times. HAB almost everywhere, esp. where large trees. NEST solitary; top of large tree (sometimes cliff, building); cup of twigs, lined wool, etc., ♂♀. EGGS 4–6, pale bluish-green, spotted dark browns and greys, 43mm. BROODS 1. INC 19, ♀. YOUNG col, 26–35, ♂♀. IMM 0. AGE 1–2, 15. FOOD wide range: grain, insects, small birds, carrion.

Air speed p. 43; Predator on gull colony p. 49; Hybridisation p. 52; Migration p. 236; Nest predation p. 262–3; Nest site p. 263.

● ■ **RAVEN** *Corvus corax* 64cm. 800–1,500g. Resident (order 4). Very large crow with massive deep beak; in flight long tail tapers wedge-shaped towards tip (other crows are more or less square-ended). VOICE very deep throaty croaking 'prrrk'. HAB mountains, sea-cliffs, etc. NEST in large tree, on cliff; large cup of twigs, lined wool, etc., ♂♀. EGGS 4–6, pale bluish-green, spotted drak browns and greys, 50mm. BROODS 1. INC 21, ♀. YOUNG col, 35–40, ♂♀. IMM 0. AGE 2–3, 16. FOOD wide range: kills rabbits and birds; eats grain, carrion, etc.

Flight p. 38; Walking and hopping p. 47; Incubation p. 248; Nest site p. 263.

STARLINGS family *Sturnidae* 106 species in the world.
A large family of which only three species occur in Europe. Noisy, often highly sociable birds, they mostly nest in holes. The Starling migrates in large numbers within Europe, and the Rose-coloured Starling invades western Europe in some numbers in some years.

Iridescence p. 31.

● ■ **STARLING** *Sturnus vulgaris* 21cm. 75–90g. Common resident (order 7), winter visitor. Often in flocks, roost in enormous numbers; blackish with purple and green sheens, spotted with buffy-white markings; yellow bill (with bluish base in ♂) in breeding season; underside more spotted in winter. VOICE wide range, bubbly chatters, whistles and mimicry. HAB mainly near man: agricultural, towns, gardens, cliffs. NEST in hole in tree, building, cliff; cup of twigs, finer lining sometimes inc. feathers, ♂♀. EGGS 4–6, pale blue, 30mm. BROODS 1–2. INC 12–13, ♂♀. YOUNG col, 20–22, ♂♀. IMM 3–4. AGE 1 (2), 20. FOOD insects, invertebrates.

Bill p. 17; Air speed p. 43; Age of first breeding p. 217; Post-fledging moult p. 219; Energy for breeding p. 226–7; Migration p. 237; Clutch weight p. 245; Nest hole and competition p. 265, 296; Egg colour p. 269; Brood parasite p. 278; Populations p. 288; Habitat history p. 309; Urbanisation p. 312–13.

SPOTLESS STARLING *Sturnus unicolor* 21cm. ?g. Similar to Starling but in breeding season adults lack pale spots in plumage, appearing pure black. VOICE similar to Starling but with more whistling notes. HAB similar to Starling. NEST hole in tree, building or rock; cup of plant material, lined feathers, hair, etc., ?. EGGS 4, pale blue, 29mm. BROODS ?. INC 12–13, ♀. YOUNG col, 21–23, ♂♀. IMM 3–4. AGE 1, ?. FOOD wide range: primarily invertebrates.

□ **ROSE-COLOURED STARLING (ROSY PASTOR)** *Sturnus roseus* 21cm. 55–75g. Rare vagrant. Adults unmistakeable with shaggy black head and pink body; juveniles like Starling but paler, with paler rump and yellowish bill. VOICE high-pitched chatter, less varied and mimetic than Starling. HAB fairly open agricultural land, cliffs, etc. NEST colonial; in rocks or in ground; cup of grass and other plant material, lined roots, feathers, etc., ?. EGGS 4, pale blue, 29mm. BROODS ?1. INC 12–14, ♀. YOUNG col, 21–23, ♂♀. IMM 4–12. AGE ?1, 11. FOOD mainly insects, inc. locusts.

Irruptions p. 291.

STARLINGS

The Starling is so well-known as to barely need describing; but many bird-watchers are at first confused by the juveniles, though these soon begin, patchily, to take on the speckled plumage of the adults. Their sociable habits are a useful clue (enormous flocks fly to roost at dusk in winter), and they run, rather than hop, on the ground.

Juvenile Spotless Starling and Starling are indistinguishable; juvenile Rose-coloured Starling is paler.

SPARROWS family *Ploceidae* 141 species in the world.
A large family including the weavers and the Snow Finch; most
are tropical. Sparrows have heavy finch-like beaks, and short tails.
(The tails of most finches are slightly forked; those of sparrows are
not.) Most build rather untidy domed nests of grass.

Respiration p. 21;
Taking off p. 40;
Classification p. 58–9;
Hatchling p. 218;
Post-fledging moult
p. 219.

Evolutionary change
p. 50; Classification
and 'Italian Sparrow'
p. 58–9; Daily weight
cycles p. 228–9;
Incubation p. 248;
Multiple broods
p. 250; Breeding
season p. 253; Brood
parasite p. 278;
Survival rate p. 285;
Populations p. 288;
Habitat history p. 309;
Urbanisation p. 312–
313.

●■ **HOUSE SPARROW** *Passer domesticus* 14·5cm. 22–32g.
Common resident (order 7). Abundant and well-known: ♂ has
greyish crown, black throat; ♀ very nondescript, a faint wing-bar
near shoulder, stout bill. VOICE twittering and varied 'cheep's and
'chirrup's. HAB mainly urban, suburban and agricultural areas,
always near man. NEST in small colonies; may be in thick bush or
ivy, but usually in hole in building; untidy, domed; grass, lined
feathers, ♂♀. EGGS 3–6, whitish, speckled dark browns and greys,
22mm. BROODS 2–3. INC 12–14, ♀. YOUNG 14–16, ♂♀. IMM 0. AGE 1,
12. FOOD mainly grain, some insects.

SPANISH SPARROW *Passer hispaniolensis* 14·5cm. 22–32g.
Male differs from House in all-chestnut crown, larger black bib,
black running down flanks; ♀s and juveniles have whiter cheeks,
more streaked flanks than House. VOICE as House but some
notes slightly deeper 'wup-wup'. HAB includes more rural habitats,
e.g. wood edge, than House. NEST in small colonies; may be in
thick bush or ivy, but usually in hole in building; untidy, domed;
grass, lined feathers, ♂♀. EGGS 5–6, whitish, more lightly marked
than House's, 23mm. BROODS 2–3. INC 12, ♀. YOUNG col, 12–15,
♂♀. IMM 0. AGE 1, 9. FOOD mainly grain, some insects.

Classification p. 58–9.

●■ **TREE SPARROW** *Passer montanus* 14cm. 19–25g. Common resident (order 6). Slightly smaller than House; chestnut
crown, black mark on white cheek, neater black bib. VOICE similar
to House, but higher-pitched flight-call 'chip-chip'. HAB overlaps
with House in agricultural land, hedgerows; absent from urbs and
suburbs. NEST some semi-colonial; hole in tree, wall, farm-build-
ing, sometimes in thick ivy; domed; grass, lined feathers, ♂♀. EGGS
4–6, varied, cream or buff, spotted dark browns and grey, 19mm.
BROODS 2–3. INC 12–14, ♂♀. YOUNG col, 12–14, ♂♀. IMM 0. AGE 1,
10. FOOD grain and other vegetable matter, insects.

Classification p. 59.

ROCK SPARROW *Petronia petronia* 14cm. 25–36g. Striped head,
small yellow spot on throat; when flies shows white spots in tail.
VOICE notes like House, and more tuneful double note 'see-see'.
HAB dry mountain areas, rocky gorges. NEST in hole in wall, rock-
face, tree; domed; plant material, lined feathers, ?. EGGS 5–6.
whitish, spotted dark browns and greys, 22mm. BROODS 2. INC ?,
?. YOUNG col, 21, ♂♀. IMM 0. AGE 1, ?. FOOD mainly seeds, some
insects.

SNOW FINCH *Montifringilla nivalis* 18cm. 32–40g. Grey head,
black throat, finer bill than other sparrows; most conspicuous feature (in flight) is white wings with black tips, black-and-white tail;
may be in flocks of some size. VOICE harsh metallic 'tsweek'; song
highpitched 'sitticher-sitticher' followed by lower, liquid trill. HAB
SUM high bare mountainous areas; WIN comes lower. NEST in hole
or crevice in rock; cup of grass, moss, lined feathers, ?. EGGS 4–5,
white, 23mm. BROODS 1–2. INC 13–14, ♂♀. YOUNG col, 21, ♂♀.
IMM 3. AGE 1, ?. FOOD mainly seeds, some insects.

Migration p. 238.

SPARROWS

The Snow Finch is distinctive. In the other sparrows *look for white spots in the tail, or yellow on the throat, or a black mark on the cheek.*

ad. ♂ Italian

ad. ♂ winter

ad. ♂ sum.

ad. ♀

juv.

ad. ♂ sum.

ad. ♀

ad. ♂ win.

juv.

adult

juvenile

adult

juvenile

ad.

adult ♂

juvenile

ad. ♀

193

FINCHES family *Fringillidae* 125 species in the world.
A large family of primarily seed-eating birds. Finches have conical beaks with special grooves for shelling seeds, and some of them are very powerful. The crossbills are unique in having crossed mandibles; they eat the seeds from conifer cones, using the hooked bill-tip for extracting the seeds. Many finches feed their young on insects.

Bills, crop, gizzard
p. 16–18; Feathers,
plumage abrasion
p. 30, 221; Perching,
hopping p. 46–7;
Pre-roost feeding,
flocks p. 229–30;
Seasonal and between-

brood movements
p. 239, 253; Breeding
season p. 252; Nest
design and material
p. 266; Food for
young p. 276; Niches
p. 297; Poisons p. 304,
313.

● ■ **CHAFFINCH** *Fringilla coelebs* 15cm. 19–24g. Common resident (order 7), winter visitor. Male bluish-grey head, pinkish-brown underparts; ♀ drabber, but double white wing-bar and white in tail distinguish. VOICE loud 'pink'; flight-call 'cheup'; song a series of about a dozen notes, speeding up and ending in flourish. HAB almost anywhere with trees or bushes. NEST in tree or bush; neatly woven cup of grass, fibres, surfaced with lichens, lined hair, feathers, ♀. EGGS 4–5, pale blue or brown with spots and streaks of dark browns, 20mm. BROODS 1. INC 12–13, ♀. YOUNG col, 13–14, ♂♀. IMM 0. AGE 1, 14. FOOD seeds, insects in summer.

Song p. 22–3; Energy
for moult p. 32, 227;
Air speed p. 43;
Migration p. 236;
Clutch weight p. 245;
Breeding season
p. 248–9, 252, 253;
Territory p. 254; Nest
site p. 264; Habitat
gain p. 309.

○ ■ **BRAMBLING** *Fringilla montifringilla* 14·5cm. 23–29g. Rare breeder (order 0–1), winter visitor in variable numbers (order 5–7). Like Chaffinch, but striking white rump distinguishes; strong tinge of orange-buff. VOICE nasal 'tweerk', flight-call 'chip'; song monotonous 'dzeeeee' like Greenfinch. HAB SUM mainly northern birch woods; WIN wider range, esp. beech woods. NEST in tree or bush; neatly woven cup of grass, fibres, surfaced with lichens and strips of bark, lined hair, feathers. ♀. EGGS 5–7, greenish or brownish, spotted with dark browns, 20mm. BROODS 1. INC 13–14, ♀. YOUNG col, 14, ♂♀. IMM 0. AGE 1, 9. FOOD seeds, insects in summer.

Plumage abrasion
p. 220–1; Breeding
season p. 252; Nest
building p. 267;
Population movements
p. 291.

○ **SERIN** *Serinus serinus* 11·5cm. 9–14g. Rare breeder (order 1). Small, chunky finch with relatively stout bill; yellow rump in all plumages; otherwise ♀ and juvenile rather drab; ♂ brighter with yellow head and breast. VOICE flight-call fast trill 'twi-twi-twi . . .'; song loud, musical, like Canary, to which related. HAB open woodland, parks, gardens. NEST well-hidden in tree (often conifer); simple cup of grass, lined finer materials, hair, ♀. EGGS 3–5, pale blue, spotted dark browns, 16mm. BROODS 2. INC 13, ♀. YOUNG col, 13–17, ♂♀. IMM 2–3. AGE 1, 9. FOOD seeds, insects.

British records p. 298.

□ **CITRIL FINCH** *Serinus citrinella* 12cm. 11–15g. Rare vagrant. Small, yellowish-green with grey on head and back; in flight shows yellow bar in dark wing; juvenile has browner head. VOICE quiet, plaintive, metallic note; song rather Siskin-like musical twittering, often in flight. HAB open conifer areas on mountainsides; descends lower in winter. NEST in tree; small cup of grasses, lined hair, feathers, ?. EGGS 4–5, greyish-white, finely spotted dark browns and purples, 17mm. BROODS ?2. INC 13–14, ♀. YOUNG col, 17–18, ♂♀. IMM 3. AGE ?1, ?. FOOD small seeds, some insects.

● ■ **GREENFINCH** *Chloris chloris* 14·5cm. 25–34g. Common resident (order 6–7 summer, 7 winter). Bright yellow patches in wing and at base of tail; ♂ much brighter, bright yellow-green beneath. VOICE flight-call musical 'chi-chi-chi . . .' trilled; song monotonous, wheezy 'dzeeee' sometimes with twittering notes, often in flight. HAB open areas with trees, wood-edge, gardens, hedgerows, etc. NEST in shrub or low tree; cup of moss and twigs, lined finer grass, etc., ♀. EGGS 4–6, whitish or pale bluish, with dark marks, 21mm. BROODS 2 (3). INC 13–14. ♀. YOUNG col, 13–16, ♂♀. IMM 3. AGE 1, 13. FOOD mainly seeds; peanuts at bird-tables.

Coloration p. 31;
Breeding season p. 252;
Niche p. 297; Habitat
gain p. 309.

● ■ **GOLDFINCH** *Carduelis carduelis* 12cm. 14–18g. Common resident (order 6 summer, 5–6 winter). Bright red face and brilliant yellow wing patch juvenile lacks patterned head. VOICE 'teeze'; song musical series of liquid silvery 'switt-witt' notes which also used as flight-call. HAB open country with bushes and trees, gardens, waste ground, etc. NEST in thick bush or outermost twigs of tree branch; neatly built cup of grass, wool, etc., lined down or hair, ♀. EGGS 5–6, bluish-white, spotted and streaked dark brown, 17mm. BROODS 2 (3). INC 12–13, ♀. YOUNG col, 13–15, ♂♀. IMM 3. AGE 1, 8. FOOD mainly seeds, particularly fond of teasel and thistles.

Breeding season and
movement between
broods p. 252–3; Nest
design and material
p. 266; Niche p. 297;
Bill shape p. 298.

FINCHES

Most finches are brightly-coloured and easy to identify when settled. *Look for colour of head, size of bill, presence or absence of wing-patches, white in tail or rump.*

With the more difficult Linnet, Twite and redpolls, *look for the position of red markings, colour of throat and bill.*

Most finches look the same when silhouetted in flight overhead; in these circumstances, *calls are vital and usually diagnostic.*

● ■ **SISKIN** *Carduelis spinus* 12cm. 10–14g. Common resident (order 5 and winter visitor (order 6) has black cap and chin; undersides streaky; yellow patches in wings and tail. VOICE clear metallic single notes 'tsu'; zizzing twitter; flight-call 'fweet'; song rapid warbling twitter ending rather like Greenfinch. HAB SUM woodland, esp. conifer and birch; WIN often (with Redpolls) in riverside alders. NEST often high in conifer; small cup of moss and twigs, lined down and feathers, ♀. EGGS 4–5, pale blue, spotted red-brown, 16mm. BROODS 2. INC 12, ♀. YOUNG col, 15, ♂♀. IMM 3. AGE 1. 11. FOOD mainly seeds; peanuts at bird-tables.

Niche p. 297.

● ■ **LINNET** *Carduelis cannabina* 13·5cm. 15–20g. Common resident (order 6–7 summer, 7 winter). Breeding ♂ greyish head, red breast and crown; ♀ and juvenile dull streaky brown; silver-white edges to wing and tail feathers. VOICE 'tsweet'; flight-call a chipping twitter; song pleasant nasal, musical twitter. HAB open country with bushes, hedges, gorse, etc.; in winter many flocks on agricultural land. NEST some semi-colonial; in bush, esp. gorse; cup of grass and other vegetation, lined hair, wool, etc., ♀. EGGS 4–6, pale bluish, spotted darker, 18mm. BROODS 2 (3). INC 12–13, ♀. YOUNG col, 11–13, ♂♀. IMM 0. AGE 1, 9. FOOD mainly small seeds.

Breeding season and movement between broods p. 252–3; Niche p. 297.

● ■ **TWITE** *Carduelis flavirostris* 13·5cm. 13–18g. Common resident (order 5). Like Linnet but lacks red on head and breast, has less white in wing and tail; ♂ has pink rump; both sexes have yellow bill in winter. VOICE similar to Linnet in flight; has more nasal, harsher 'twa-it'; song a slow, dry twitter. HAB Twite is the northern and upland counterpart of Linnet; moorland, open country. NEST some semi-colonial; in small bush, heather; cup of grass, lined wool, ♀. EGGS 5–6, light blue, spotted darker, 17mm. BROODS 2. INC 12–13, ♀. YOUNG col, 14–15, ♂♀. IMM 0. AGE 1, 6. FOOD small seeds.

● ■ **REDPOLL** *Carduelis flammea* 13·5cm. 10–14g. Common resident (order 6), winter visitor. Small; two buff wing-bars; small red patch on forehead, black throat, yellow bill; ♂ has pinkish breast and rump; northern races paler, greyer. VOICE plaintive 'tweet'; flight-call buzzing 'zzzz-chee-chee-chee'; song like flight-call, brief, level, fast trills and twitters. HAB light woodland, birch, alder, etc.; in winter often in alders along rivers. NEST in small tree; tiny cup of vegetation, often neatly surfaced with lichens, ♀. EGGS 4–6, pale blue, spotted darker, 16mm. BROODS 1–2. INC 12, ♀. YOUNG col, 12, ♂♀. IMM 3. AGE 1, 8. FOOD small seeds.

Perching p. 47; Migration between broods p. 253; Nest design and material p. 267; Niche p. 297.

□ **ARCTIC REDPOLL** *Carduelis hornemanni* 13·5cm. 11–16g. Rare vagrant. Some v. similar to northern Redpoll, but white underneath, with unstreaked rump and whiter wing-bars. VOICE as Redpoll, but slower twitter. HAB rather open tundra with small bushes. NEST in bush or on ground, tiny cup of vegetation, often neatly surfaced with lichens, ♀. EGGS 5, pale blue, spotted darker, 17mm. BROODS 1. INC 11–12, ♀. YOUNG col, 11–12, ♂♀. IMM 3. AGE 1, ?. FOOD small seeds.

Heat loss p. 225.

TRUMPETER FINCH *Rhodopechys githaginea* 12·5cm. 20–24g. Small, greyish or brownish finch with dark wings and tail, pale legs, stubby yellow bill; breeding ♂ has pinkish hue, bright red bill. VOICE distinctive nasal buzzing (trumpeting) and zizzing notes. HAB dry open country, desert edge, barren hills. NEST in rock crevice; cup of grass and plant stems, lined hair, wool, ?. EGGS pale blue, speckled darker, 18mm. BROODS ?1. INC 13–14, ?♀. YOUNG col, 14, ?♂♀. IMM 3. AGE 1, ?. FOOD ?seeds.

□ **SCARLET ROSEFINCH (SCARLET GROSBEAK)** *Carpodacus erythrinus* 14·5cm. 19–26g. Rare vagrant, has bred. Male distinctive with red head, breast and rump; ♀ and juvenile difficult, sparrow-like but plain, with heavily spotted throat and breast, two pale wing-bars; black eye. VOICE quiet piping 'tew-it'; song clear piping series of 4–6 notes, emphasis on 2nd and 4th. HAB shrubby areas, often near water. NEST lowish in bush; cup of plant stems, grass, lined hair, etc., ♀. EGGS 5, pale blue, spotted darker, 20mm. BROODS 1. INC 12–14, ♀. YOUNG col, 12–16, ♂♀. IMM 0. AGE 1, ?. FOOD small seeds.

197

☐ **WHITE-WINGED CROSSBILL** *Loxia leucoptera* 14·5cm. 29–33g. Rare vagrant. Smaller than other crossbills, with lighter beak, two distinctive white wing-bars, and white-tipped tertials. VOICE 'chif-chir' less ringing than Common Crossbill. HAB conifer forests, especially larch. NEST in tree canopy; small cup of twigs, lined grass, hair, etc., ?. EGGS 3–4, pale bluish-white, spotted darker, 21mm. BROODS 1. INC ?, ?. YOUNG col, ?, ?. IMM ?. AGE 1, ?. FOOD conifer seeds, especially larch.

Bill p. 16–17; Breeding season p. 252–3; Nest site p. 264; Coniferous habitat p. 310.

○☐ **COMMON CROSSBILL** *Loxia curvirostra* 16·5cm. 28–40g. Fairly common resident (order 4), occasional visitor in large numbers. The most widespread crossbill, but difficult to tell from Scottish and Parrot. ♂ bright red. ♀ olive, paler on rump and undersides, no white in wing. VOICE loud distinctive 'chip' repeated; song short trills and 'chip's. HAB conifer forest, especially spruce. NEST in canopy of tree; small cup of twigs, lined grass, hair, etc., ♀. EGGS 3–4, very pale blue, spotted darker, 22mm. BROODS 1. INC 13–16, ♀. YOUNG col, 16–25, ♂♀. IMM 12. AGE 1, ?. FOOD conifer seeds, especially spruce.

Bill p. 16–17; Breeding season p. 252–3; Nest site p. 264; Food for young p. 276; Irruptions p. 290–1; Coniferous habitat p. 310.

○☐ **SCOTTISH CROSSBILL** *Loxia scotica* 16·5cm. ?g. Resident in Scottish highlands where replaces Common (order 3). Thought by some to be British race of Parrot Crossbill; similar to Common, but has rather heavier beak; no white in wing. VOICE as Common. HAB conifer woods, especially pine. NEST in canopy of pine; small cup of twigs, lined grass, hair, etc., ♀. EGGS 3–4, pale whitish-blue, spotted darker, 22mm. BROODS 1. INC 13–15, ♀. YOUNG col, 17–20, ♂♀. IMM 12. AGE ?1, ?. FOOD conifer seeds, especially pine.

Bill p. 16–17; Breeding season p. 252–3; Nest site p. 264; Coniferous habitat p. 310.

☐ **PARROT CROSSBILL** *Loxia pytyopsittacus* 17cm. 35–45g. Vagrant. Like Common and Scottish, but bill larger and stouter; no white in wing. VOICE 'chup' deeper than Common; also twanging notes. HAB conifer woods, especially pine. NEST in canopy of pine; cup of twigs, lined grass, hair, etc., ♀. EGGS 2–4, very pale blue, spotted darker, 23mm. BROODS 1. INC 14–16, ♀. YOUNG col, c. 25, ♂♀. IMM 12. AGE ?1, ?. FOOD mainly conifer seeds, especially pine.

Bill p. 16–17; Breeding season p. 252–3; Nest site p. 264; Coniferous habitat p. 310.

☐ **PINE GROSBEAK** *Pinicola enucleator* 20cm. 40–60g. Rare vagrant. Markedly larger than crossbills, mandibles uncrossed, tail longer; two white wing-bars; ♂ pinker than crossbills. VOICE high-pitched whistles and 'tew's, often tri-syllabic; song a mixture of whistling and twanging notes. HAB coniferous forests. NEST in tree, often fairly low; cup of twigs, lined grass, roots, ♀. EGGS 4, pale blue, spotted and blotched dark, 26mm. BROODS 1. INC 13–14, ♀. YOUNG col, 14, ♂♀. IMM 3. AGE ?1, 8. FOOD mainly seeds.

Population movements p. 291.

●■ **BULLFINCH** *Pyrrhula pyrrhula* 15cm. 21–27g. Common resident (order 6). Black crown, very stubby bill, black tail and wings with conspicuous white rump and wing-bar; juvenile lacks black cap. VOICE a soft whistle 'deeu'; song (rare) a short, musical, scratchy, creaking warble. HAB woodland with thick undergrowth, hedges, gardens. NEST in dense bush or brambles; cup of twigs, lined roots, etc., ♀. EGGS 4–6, pale blue, spotted and streaked darker, 20mm. BROODS 2. INC 12–14, ♀. YOUNG col, 12–16, ♂♀. IMM 2–4. AGE 1, 17. FOOD mainly seeds, buds of trees, especially fruit-trees, in spring.

Weight of plumage p. 221; Breeding season p. 252.

○☐ **HAWFINCH** *Coccothraustes coccothraustes* 18cm. 48–62g. Widespread resident (order 4–5). Large, very stocky, thick neck, massive bill, short tail with white tip, white patches in wings. VOICE 'tick' and 'tseep'; song a rather squeaky, high-pitched, quiet warble. HAB woodland, parks, large orchards. NEST on small horizontal branch of tree; cup of small twigs, lined roots, etc., ♀. EGGS 3–6, off-white, streaked and blotched darker, 24mm. BROODS 1. INC 12–13, ♀. YOUNG col, 11–14, ♂♀. IMM 3. AGE 1, 10. FOOD seeds, inc. kernels of large seeds such as cherry, damson.

Bill p. 16–17.

BUNTINGS family *Emberizidae* 281 species in the world.
A very large family of primarily seed-eating birds. Somewhat similar to small-billed finches, most have longer tails. Like the finches, many bring insects to their nestlings. Most live in rather open country with bushes. Many are largely resident, but others are long-distance migrants.

Feeding flocks p. 230.

☐ **LAPLAND BUNTING** *Calcarius lapponicus* 15cm. 18–30g. Regular passage migrant; winter visitor in small nos (order 3); very rare breeder (order 0–2). Breeding ♂ black face, chestnut nape; in winter both sexes resemble ♀ Reed but rufous nape, yellower bill. VOICE 'tick-titick' and 'teu'; song short, musical, usually in flight. HAB SUM tundra and open arctic areas; WIN saltings, fields, etc., usually coastal. NEST on ground, often in shelter of tussock; cup of moss and roots, lined grass, hair, etc., ?. EGGS 5–6, pale greyish-green, streaked and spotted dark, 21mm. BROODS 1. INC 12–14, ♀. YOUNG col, 8–10, ♂♀. IMM 3. AGE 1, ?. FOOD small seeds, insects.

Moult p. 221–2.

○☐ **SNOW BUNTING** *Plectrophenax nivalis* 16·5cm. 26–40g. Rare breeder (order 1–2), passage migrant and winter visitor in small numbers (order 4). Breeding ♂ black and white; distinctive black-and-white flight pattern in all plumages. VOICE 'trrrip' and and 'teu'; song repetitive, high, rapid, musical notes. HAB bare rocky screes, mountains in south to sea-level in north of range; in winter often along seashore. NEST in rock crevice; moss and grass, lined finer, ♀. EGGS 4–6, off-white or greenish, spotted darker, 21mm. BROODS 1–2. INC 12–13, ♀. YOUNG col, 10–12, ♂♀. IMM 1–2. AGE 1, 8. FOOD small seeds, insects.

Moult p. 221–2.

●■ **YELLOWHAMMER (YELLOW BUNTING)** *Emberiza citrinella* 16·5cm. 24–30g. Common resident (order 7). Male bright yellow on head and underparts; all plumages have chestnut rump and much white on outer tail. VOICE 'twit' and 'tink'; song 'a-little-bit-of-bread-and-no-cheeeeeese', last note emphasised and drawn-out. HAB open ground with shrubs, wood edge, hedgerows, etc. NEST in or under bush or in bank; cup of grass, lined fine grass, hair, ♂♀. EGGS 3–5, variable, often off-white, spotted and scribbled darker, 22mm. BROODS 2 (3). INC 12–14, ♀. YOUNG col, 12–13, ♂♀. IMM 3. AGE 1, 12. FOOD small seeds, insects.

Song p. 23.

○☐ **CIRL BUNTING** *Emberiza cirlus* 16·5cm. 20–28g. Local resident (order 3). From Yellowhammer by lack of chestnut rump (olive); ♂ distinctive face pattern, black throat. VOICE 'tsip' repeated; song a monotonous trill of single note, somewhat like Lesser Whitethroat (p. 172). HAB open country with bushes and small trees, hedges; in winter in more exposed areas like downland. NEST usually in bush a little above ground; cup of moss, grass, etc., lined finer, ♂♀. EGGS 3–4, off-white to greenish, blotched darker. 21mm. BROODS 2 (3). INC 11–13, ♀. YOUNG col, 11–13, ♂♀. IMM 3. AGE 1, ?. FOOD small seeds, insects.

☐ **ROCK BUNTING** *Emberiza cia* 16cm. 20–30g. Rare vagrant. Chestnut rump, white in outer tail; ♂ has unmistakeable face pattern; ♀ dark brown, streaky. VOICE quiet 'see'; song short fast warble reminiscent of Reed's. HAB open rocky hillsides with bushes and small trees. NEST usually on ground, in cavity in rocks; cup of moss, grass, lined hair, etc., ?. EGGS 4–6, off-white, streaked darker, 21mm. BROODS 1–2. INC 12–13, ♀. YOUNG col, 11–13, ♂♀. IMM 3. AGE 1, ?. FOOD small seeds, insects.

CINEREOUS BUNTING *Emberiza cineracea* 16·5cm. 20–24g. In Europe only on Greek island Mytilene. A dull greyish to brownish bunting with white outer tail; ♂ has olive to yellowish head; ♀ and juvenile often show trace of yellow on throat; broad buffish edges to secondaries; pale eye-ring. VOICE 'tsip'; song short, rather buzzing notes, repeated phrases starting slow and speeding up. HAB dry rocky slopes in mountains. NEST ?. EGGS c. 3, whitish or pale greyish-blue, streaked darker, 21mm. BROODS ?. INC ?, ?. YOUNG col, ?, ?. IMM 3. AGE 1, ?. FOOD small seeds, insects.

BUNTINGS
Breeding males of most buntings are distinctively coloured. *Look for head pattern, especially.*

Females, juveniles, and winter males can be very difficult, or impossible. *Look for amount and position of white in tail and wing-bars, colour of bill and of edges of flight feathers, presence or absence of streaking underneath, colour of rump.*

201

☐ **ORTOLAN BUNTING** *Emberiza hortulanus* 16·5cm. 17–28g. Regular autumn vagrant, small numbers (order 2). Breeding ♂ greenish head; pale eye-ring, pinkish bill, white 'ovals' in tail; ♀ yellowish throat. VOICE 'tsi-ip'; song slow, 6–8 rich, clear 'tsee' or 'teu' notes, often in song-flight. HAB open scrub. NEST on ground; cup of grass, lined hair, ♀. EGGS 4–6, variable ground, blotched and streaked dark, 20mm. BROODS 2. INC 11–14, ♀. YOUNG col, 10–15, ♂♀. IMM 3. AGE ?1, ?. FOOD small seeds, insects.

Energy for moult
p. 227; Migration
p. 243.

☐ **CRETZSCHMAR'S BUNTING** *Emberiza caesia* 16cm. ?g. Rare vagrant. Male like Ortolan but head greyer, throat rufous; ♀ has rufous not yellow throat. VOICE 'tsip'; song 3–4 'peu' notes, emphasis on last. HAB barren desert edge and rocky hillsides with scattered shrubs. NEST on ground, often at base of vegetation; cup of plant stems, lined hair, etc., ?. EGGS 4–6, off-white or greyish-blue, spotted and streaked darker, 19mm. BROODS 2. INC ?, ?. YOUNG col, ?, ?. IMM 3. AGE ?1, ?. FOOD small seeds, insects.

☐ **RUSTIC BUNTING** *Emberiza rustica* 14·5cm. 17–22g. Rare vagrant. Breeding ♂ has white stripe behind eye, in winter black head becomes brown; ♀ like duller winter ♂, marked eye-stripe. VOICE 'tsip' repeated; song a short warble. HAB scrubby woodland, often near water. NEST near ground in shrub, or on ground; cup of moss, grass, lined hair, etc., ?. EGGS 4–5, whitish-blue or -green, spotted darker, 20mm. BROODS 1. INC 12–13, ♀. YOUNG col, 14, ♂♀. IMM 3. AGE ?1, ?. FOOD small seeds, insects.

☐ **LITTLE BUNTING** *Emberiza pusilla* 13·5cm. 12–16g. Rare vagrant. Small, like ♀ Reed but has chestnut cheeks and crown, pale eye-ring, pinkish legs. VOICE short Robin-like 'tick'; song variable, rich jingle, with repeated section. HAB marshy tundra with small trees. NEST on ground under shrub; cup of moss, grass, lined hair, etc., ?. EGGS 4–5, variable ground colour with darker spotting and streaks, 19mm. BROODS 1 (2). INC 11–12, ♀. YOUNG col, 6–8+, ♂♀. IMM 3. AGE ?1, ?. FOOD small seeds, insects.

☐ **YELLOW-BREASTED BUNTING** *Emberiza aureola* 14cm. 18–28g. Rare vagrant. Female usually yellowish underparts, buffish-yellow eye-stripe, and stripe on centre of crown; often shows slight double wing-bar. VOICE 'tick'; song melodious loud warble. HAB open, shrubby country, often near water. NEST usually in low bush; cup of grass, lined hair, etc., ♂♀. EGGS 4–5, pale greenish-grey, spotted and streaked darker, 21mm. BROODS 1. INC 13, ♀. YOUNG col, 13–15, ♂♀. IMM 3. AGE ?1, ?. FOOD small seeds, insects.

●■ **REED BUNTING** *Emberiza schoeniclus* 15cm. 15–22g. Common resident (order 6). White outer tail, chestnut wing-coverts; breeding ♂ has distinctive black hood with white moustache. VOICE 'tsee' and wistful 'teu'; song series of 'tsee' notes ending 'tissick'. HAB marshes. water-meadows. reed-beds. NEST on or just above ground; cup of grass, reeds, lined hair, etc., ♀. EGGS 4–5, olive to buff, spotted and streaked darker, 20mm. BROODS 2. INC 13–14, ♂♀. YOUNG col, 10–13, ♂♀. IMM 3. AGE 1, 11. FOOD small seeds, insects.

Subspeciation p. 56;
Plumage abrasion
p. 221.

☐ **BLACK-HEADED BUNTING** *Emberiza melanocephala* 16·5 cm. 22–34g. Rare vagrant. No white in tail; ♀ pale with unstreaked underparts, yellow under tail. VOICE 'chup', 'tsee'; song short series of buzzes followed by a brief warble. HAB open ground with trees and bushes. NEST in dense herbage or low in thick bush; cup of grass, lined hair, ?. EGGS 4–5, pale greyish-blue, spotted darker, 22mm. BROODS 1. INC 14, ♀. YOUNG col, ?, ?♀. IMM 3. AGE ?1, ?. FOOD small seeds, insects.

●■ **CORN BUNTING** *Miliaria calandra* 18cm. 38–55g. Common resident (order 5). Solidly built; no white in wings nor tail; flies with legs trailing. VOICE harsh 'chip', 'tsee'; song like shaken bunch of keys. HAB open grassland, usually with bushes. NEST (♂ often polygamous); on ground, often at base of plant; grass, lined roots, hairs, etc., ♀. EGGS 3–5, variable ground, often whitish-purple, spotted and streaked darker, 24mm. BROODS 2 (3). INC 12–13, ♀. YOUNG col, 11–14, ♀(♂). IMM 0. AGE 1, 10. FOOD small seeds, insects.

Baby bird p. 209;
Post-fledging moult
p. 219; Song flight
p. 259.

Part 3

THE LIFE OF A BIRD

THE HATCHLING

A young bird becomes conscious of its surroundings well before it hatches from the egg. Several days prior to hatching, it will notice the chilling and warming as the incubating parent leaves and returns. More chicks hatch in the morning than in the afternoon, and this suggests that, even in the egg, they already have some kind of diurnal rhythm; this may be as a result of the parents' incubating intermittently during the day, but in a long unbroken spell during the night. Doubtless it will also feel its parent turning the eggs at frequent intervals; this is probably done to prevent the egg membranes sticking to the shell, and to aid the uptake of oxygen, though a few species do not turn their eggs.

At first, the developing chick breathes oxygen which passes into the egg through the surprisingly porous eggshell and the albumen (the white); expired carbon dioxide passes in the opposite direction. In the early stages, respiration is by diffusion, but soon a system of blood vessels develop outside the embryo; then the blood takes up the oxygen and carries it into the embryo. Water is also lost through the shell of the egg as the chick develops and, as this happens, the egg membrane contracts and pulls away

from the shell at the blunt end of the egg, leaving an air space just inside the shell. Some time before it hatches the young bird punctures the membrane with its bill. It can then get its nostrils into the air space and breathe air directly through the shell, using its lungs for the first time (although it still relies partly on the external blood vessels). Only after this stage can the young bird begin to call.

Still later, but in some species still several days before the young bird hatches, it may make a tiny hole in the egg which enables it to breathe much more rapidly during its final period in the egg; at this stage the external blood vessels begin to atrophy. By now the young bird has become aware of, and can obviously hear, what is going on outside the shell: if it is cheeping quietly in the egg, it will stop the moment a parent gives an alarm call. For some species this ability to hear and call is crucial. The young Guillemot will hatch onto a very crowded ledge, covered with parents and other youngsters. If it is to be guarded by its parents and fed by them, it must be able to know who they are – and vice-versa. The young bird learns to recognise its parents' calls before it hatches and, likewise, they also learn to recognise their

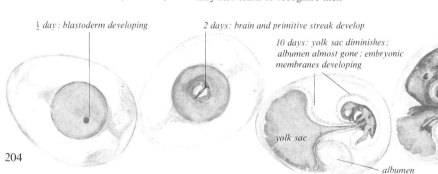

½ day: blastoderm developing

2 days: brain and primitive streak develop

10 days: yolk sac diminishes; albumen almost gone; embryonic membranes developing

yolk sac

albumen

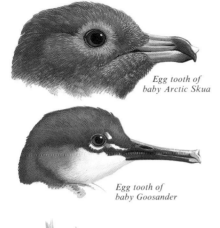

Egg tooth of baby Arctic Skua

Egg tooth of baby Goosander

A hatching clutch of Quail's eggs

14 days: embryo about to change position; yolk sac withdrawing into abdomen

youngster by its call. In gamebirds, where all the young leave the nest together as soon as they are dry, it is important that they are ready to go at the same moment. Young Quails in some way co-ordinate their hatching by listening to each others' calls; hatching is much more closely synchronised if the young birds are within earshot of one another during this time than if they are, artificially, kept out of each other's hearing.

Eventually, the time comes for the young bird to break out of its egg. It does this by chipping a ring of holes around the blunt end of the egg. To do this it uses a particularly powerful neck muscle, the hatching muscle, developed at this time especially for this one purpose, to force the head hard against the end of the egg; it also presses against the shell with a small sharpish spike, the egg tooth. This is a small white protuberance near the tip of the upper mandible (some species also have one on the lower mandible), clearly visible on a newly-hatched chick; in most species it drops off a few days after hatching. Occasionally one finds a chick that has died in the egg at hatching time to be missing the egg tooth, ample evidence of the importance of this small structure for this one essential job.

Once the end of the egg is well cracked, the chick forces its head against the loosened end and, at the same time, presses with its legs against the other end; the top comes off. The actual period of breaking loose is quite short in most small birds, but may take several hours in some of the larger species whose egg's thick shell seems difficult to break; the effort required appears to be considerable, the baby bird having to rest frequently. Eventually however, the young chick breaks free to start its life as a nestling.

22 days: hatching with the aid of an egg-tooth

205

THE BABY BIRD

TYPES OF YOUNG

Newly-hatched chicks vary in appearance considerably. They are usually divided into two sorts – nidifugous and nidicolous – though this is an over-simplification.

Nidifugous (literally 'nest-fleeing') young are the better developed. They are similar in appearance to the chicks of the domestic hen – young which are covered with downy feathers, have their eyes open and are able to run (and swim, if they are water-birds) within 24 hours of hatching. They usually leave the nest within this time and do not return to it. Most nidifugous young are guarded by their parents, but feed for themselves. Species with nidifugous young include divers, grebes, rails, wildfowl, gamebirds – which are the wild relatives of the domestic hen – and waders.

At the other extreme are the nidicolous (literally 'nest-dwelling') young. Such chicks are totally dependent on their parents; at hatching they are usually blind, often naked, and quite helpless. Nidicolous young include shearwaters, herons, birds of prey, woodpeckers, swifts and passerines.

There are a number of species which do not fit neatly into this classification. For example, young nightjars are well-feathered and able to shuffle away from the nest at an early stage, but are not very mobile. Young gulls and terns also hatch well-feathered and with their eyes open, are more mobile than young nightjars and are able to run around from an early stage, but they tend to hide in dense cover near the nest and only run out to be fed when the parents return with food; they cannot collect food for themselves.

The brains and legs of nidifugous chicks are relatively larger at hatching than are those of nidicolous young. Nidifugous young have to be able to run around and think for themselves as well as keep themselves warm, at least for much of this time; it is therefore essential that these parts of their anatomy are well-developed at hatching. Nidicolous young, in contrast, have less need of well-developed limbs and brains; at hatching they have, for their size, very large digestive systems; they are really little more than food conversion units with large mouths and the ability to swallow and metabolise large amounts of food.

Young birds have two main enemies – starvation and predators. Each year enormous numbers of young die from these two causes. The young must be able to get food rapidly and grow quickly to a size where they can

In the nest-hole of a Great Spotted Woodpecker, the young jostle for the best positions when their mother arrives with food.

fly, after which they stand a much better chance of being able to survive. Nidicolous young can do nothing about getting their own food – they are wholly dependent on their parents for this. However, they can and do compete with each other for what the parents bring in. Their legs grow faster than their wings because their first and foremost need is to be able to reach up as high as possible, to stretch over their brothers and sisters in their efforts to get the food. Young Great Spotted Woodpeckers jostle with each other to occupy the position nearest to the nest-hole entrance so that they are in the best position to grab the next meal when the parent arrives with it. In many species, there is little brotherly love; the strongest – which is usually the oldest – chick will grab what food it needs and only when it is satiated will the next be able to get fed. In many species, especially birds of prey, the larger young will fiercely attack the smaller ones and often kill them.

Hungry chicks can induce their parents to feed them faster by begging loudly each time the parents come to the nest. This stimulates the parents to increase their efforts. However, loud begging also carries the risk that a predator may hear the calls. The young's need for food must be balanced against the risks of being killed; it sometimes pays not to be too noisy.

Most nidifugous young are not directly dependent on their parents for food; they find it themselves. The Oystercatcher is a partial exception; the young often follow their parents,

Nidifugous young Oystercatchers, cryptically coloured to resemble their natural habitat, wait while their parent fetches food from the the sea shore.

but wait for the parents to catch food for them. In some cases the parent Oystercatchers may go some distance to the shore to gather limpets and bring them back to the waiting chicks. Likewise, young Water Rails and other crakes are fed by their parents for the first few days. Nidifugous young are dependent on their parents for leading them to food, for keeping them warm in bad weather and at night, and for guarding them against predators.

In some water-birds such as grebes and swans, the young also ride on their parents' backs; young grebes may even stay there during their parents' dives under water. Thus the young not only keep warm, but in addition they are safer from predators than if they were swimming on their own; many young water-birds, including those as large as young cygnets, are taken by pike.

The different types of young have different advantages. It is valuable to be nidifugous if the parent can take the young to the food source. The chicks do not have to wait for the parent to fly back and forth to the food supply; this can take up a lot of time and so the amount of food that can be brought to the young is restricted. In species such as grebes and some of the auks the chicks accompany the parents on their fishing trips. In many species such as the game-birds, each chick feeds for itself; so there are many more pairs of eyes to search for food. Obviously, it is not practicable to be nidifugous unless the food supply is on the ground (or water), since young birds cannot fly.

Nidicolous species gain by not having to expend energy on running about, nor much on keeping themselves warm; they can therefore concentrate more of the food that is brought to them into growth than can a nidifugous chick (need for energy, p. 224). They therefore grow more quickly than nidifugous young. In fact it would be difficult for very small birds to be nidifugous since they might be too small to be able to keep themselves warm.

Other factors will have influenced whether or not a type of bird has nidifugous or nidicolous young. Many freshwater habitats are surrounded by open country where there is little opportunity to nest in trees. So in order to be close to their aquatic habitat many freshwater birds have had to nest on the ground. These sites are very vulnerable to predators and this may be one reason why almost all freshwater birds have nidifugous young. In some cases it may be so difficult to find places which are safe from predators that the parents find

it necessary to nest a long way from the water's edge. The occasional Mallard, for example, nests so far from water that the chicks are faced with a long and hazardous journey after hatching. Presumably the ducks put their nests in such places because they cannot find suitable safe cover any nearer to water. Some ducks nest in holes in trees; baby ducks are so light that they can happily survive a long drop after hatching in a high nest.

GROWTH

Growth rates of young birds – especially nidicolous ones – are extremely rapid. A young Robin weighs about 2 grams at hatching, but within eleven days is more or less fully grown, weighing about 20 grams. Many small birds grow to be as large as their parents in about this length of time, though larger ones take longer, for example: young of Red-throated Diver can fly in about 45 days, Mute Swan in 120 days, Flamingo in 75 days, and Golden Eagle in 70 days. Even at these ages, these young will not be quite fully-grown.

There is a great range of variation in the ways in which young birds develop. For example, if food becomes scarce during the nestling period of small birds like warblers, the young will soon be in great trouble. If the food supply remains

Swifts

Young Great Crested Grebes often ride on their parent's back, and may even stay there when it dives. Before they can even fly, young Reed Warblers leave the nest and clamber around on the adjacent stems.

poor for any length of time, the young will quickly die. However, the Swift chick is fed on small flying insects which are only abundant in fine weather; so the young bird often encounters times when its parents cannot bring it plenty of food. It grows much more slowly than most small birds, but can cope much better with periods of food shortage; it is able to drop its body temperature and 'hibernate' through periods of cold weather; growth virtually ceases during such periods. When the weather becomes warmer and the parents can again bring in food, the young Swift raises its body temperature and growth recommences. In evidence of this essential adaptation to a highly variable food supply, young Swifts grow at different rates in different years, depending on the weather. In warm fine summers, they will normally fledge at about five weeks of age, but in very cold summers (if they survive at all) they may take eight weeks to reach the flying stage.

Young of hole-nesters (such as the tits) spend longer in the nest than those born in open, cup-shaped nests (such as the Blackbird). Nestlings in holes are much safer than those in open nests. Probably the danger from predators is the reason why young in open nests fledge as early as possible, perhaps even before they are really fully ready to do so. In contrast, chicks in holes are safer and so can afford to stay in the nest and develop completely before leaving. Each situation carries both advantages and risks. Birds nesting in the open can usually find a nest site and the females can escape when danger threatens; but their nests are highly vulnerable. Birds nesting in holes are much more likely to raise their brood, but holes can be in short supply and not all birds may be able to find one. Furthermore, if a predator finds the nest while the female is incubating or brooding, she and her offspring are trapped.

Since nidifugous young leave the nest on hatching, their parents do not run the risk of drawing the attention of predators to them by continually bringing food to the same place; and if a predator does threaten, they can scatter and have a better chance of escape than if they were confined to a nest. Indeed, the need to avoid predators, which can find nests more easily than they can find individuals, has led the chicks of a number of ground-nesting nidicolous species, such as Woodlark and Corn Bunting to leave the nest well before they are able to fly, and to separate in the undergrowth so as to reduce the chances of being discovered. They must, of course, be careful not to go too far since it is essential that they can know when the parent has returned with food and be ready to attract its attention.

When a predator does find a nest containing well-grown young, these may leap out and scatter into the cover to avoid being taken. Even if they are too young to fly and have little chance of surviving, it is obviously better to have a small chance than no chance at all. Ornithologists must be aware that it is dangerous to disturb large young in a nest. This tendency to 'explode' is strongly-developed and, however carefully one puts them back in the nest, the young birds will usually just leap out again.

DEVELOPMENT

Most young nidicolous birds stay in the nest until they are ready to fly. Normally they reach roughly the same weight as their parents sèveral days before they fly. Characteristically, their weight levels off several days before they leave the nest and the final days are devoted to completion of feather growth so that they will be well-able to fly. Even so, when the young bird leaves the nest its wing feathers are usually still a little shorter than those of the adult birds and everybody has seen young birds hopping about that are not yet able to fly strongly, having left the nest a little too soon. People find it a great temptation to 'rescue' these young birds and try to look after them. In most cases their parents are usually nearby, and they stand a far better chance of surviving if they are left alone.

In a few species the pattern of growth is quite different. In young Manx Shearwaters, Storm Petrels and Eleonora's Falcons, the young put on enormous amounts of fat so that they become much heavier than their parents; in exceptional cases, young Manx Shearwaters may weigh 800 grams or more, roughly twice the weight of their parents. These young birds are not fed much by their parents in the later stages of the nestling period and depend on these large fat stores to survive and complete their development. This pattern of growth probably evolved because food is more freely available in the early stages of the nestling period than later on; so the young have developed the ability to lay down these great stores of fat rather than risk potential food shortage later on. In the Manx Shearwater at least, this is not the whole explanation: the young birds leave the nest still weighing considerably more than their parents, and probably use these fat stores to enable them to migrate immediately (p. 242). There is one major disadvantage: the fat stores make the young birds attractive to people who take the large chicks for food. For many years the people of St Kilda took fat young Fulmars; young Gannets (known as gugas) are still taken from one Scottish colony (Sula Sgeir) and young Red-footed Falcons are still collected on some Mediterranean islands.

Other species also defy attempts to divide them simply into nidifugous or nidicolous. The young Flamingo stays in the nest for about the first ten days of its life, then leaves and joins small groups of other chicks (crèches) which wander about together in the saline lagoons surrounding their colonies. Gradually, these groups congregate into one enormous crèche in which the individual chick somehow manages to find – and get fed by – its own parents (who learned to recognise the chick's voice in the days prior to its leaving the nest). How they find it in the babel of a crèche of several thousand young remains a mystery.

The auks show a wide range of variation in the stage at which the young birds leave the nest. The Puffin chick grows up in a burrow, which it leaves at about the age of six weeks

A crèche of young Flamingos

Adult Eleanora's Falcons feeding their young in the nest

days of life and then go out to sea; at this stage they are only about a quarter grown. The young bird goes to sea with one of its parents, apparently usually the male, who presumably feeds it while it is growing.

Their departure is an exciting thing to watch, especially at a large colony where many young are going at the same time. They leave in the evening, as the light is fading, probably because the chicks can still see where they are going, but it is too dark for marauding gulls to see them easily enough to catch them. A great deal of excited calling goes on between the chick and its parent and eventually the chick leaps off the cliff, beating its tiny wings and – half falling, half fluttering – goes down the cliff in stages or in one great leap into the sea, depending on the terrain at the colony.

Presumably the young birds are taken to rich feeding grounds, and the parent can feed the chick more frequently because it does not have to fly back and forth to the nesting ledge. This is not the full range of variation in this family: in the Pacific the young of the Ancient and Japanese Murrelets leave the nest even earlier, within a day or two of hatching, and swim out to sea with their parent – a tiny body attached to two powerful legs!

Few young birds can fly before they are nearing full size; hence the premium on rapid growth. Young Guillemots and Razorbills are an exception: though they only fly but once at this stage, the flight is an important one. The 'flight feathers' of the tiny wings are not the real flight feathers, but the primary and secondary coverts (p. 28) which grow precociously. The only other group in which the young can fly at an early stage is the gamebirds; they grow a special set of primaries and secondaries which are much smaller than those they will have when they are fully grown. These enable them to fly when still quite small. The young bird starts to moult these even before it is half-grown and replaces them with a set of full-sized quills.

when still only weighing about 70% of adult weight. It leaves the nest, on its own, in the middle of the night and flies some way out to sea to complete its growth by catching food for itself. (Its parents come into the burrow the next day with food apparently expecting to find it still there.) The Black Guillemot behaves similarly, the two chicks leaving the nest at about five weeks old when they weigh about as much as the adults, and are able to look after themselves. In contrast to these two, Guillemot and Razorbill chicks stay at the nesting ledge for only about the first 14–18

INDEPENDENCE AND SURVIVAL

The amount of care that young birds get from their parents after they leave the nest varies very greatly. Some, such as the Puffin, leave the nest without their parents' knowledge; young Swifts also leave while their parents are away collecting food for them. In neither of these species can there be any parental care after the young have left the nest; they probably never meet again. The same holds true for the Manx Shearwater and the Storm Petrel, though here the parents stop feeding some time before the chicks are ready to leave the nest. The Manx Shearwater chick receives no food at all during the last fortnight or so and almost certainly, by the time it decides to leave its nest, its parents are already some way along their journey to their winter quarters out at sea off South America.

For some species, leaving the nest is a rather gradual affair. For the first week or so after fledging, young Bee-eaters, Goldcrests, Firecrests, and several species of swallow return each night to roost in the nest, thereby benefitting from the safety of the site and the warmth of the brood of siblings.

Most young birds however, need a considerable amount of care after they have left the nest. Whether it be a nidifugous chick soon after hatching or a nidicolous one at the end of the nestling period, its first venture into the wide world is a very dangerous moment for a young bird. It encounters a world of which it has no previous experience and is at great risk from predators which it has to learn to recognise as threats; the chicks of most species do this by responding to the alarm calls of the parents. They must also learn to find food in sufficient quantities to be able to survive. The young of insectivorous species face the added complication that among the food which flies past

Storm Petrel chick in its nest burrow

are insects which are distasteful and others that sting. They have to learn not only to catch the edible ones, but also to avoid the noxious ones.

They may require more food now than they have ever done before. Although they are no longer growing much, they have exchanged the rather inactive life in the warm nest for an active one in a much colder world, where they will need energy both for flight and for keeping warm (pp. 224–7). It is obviously best if they can be raised at that time of year when food is abundant (p. 244).

Small wonder that most young birds need help at this time. However, the length of time for which a young bird can expect to get help from its parents varies greatly. In many small birds, such as the tits, it may last only a week or so, though some individuals will care for their young for longer. It is in the chick's interests to maintain parental care for as long as possible; but there may be a conflict here since the parent may need to get on with another nest (p. 250). Under these circumstances, the young birds may often be seen begging from parents who are no longer anxious to care for them. In some, the female may get on with the building of the next nest and laying of the eggs while, at the same time, the young may be able to continue to get help

212

from the male. But as soon as the young of the next nest hatch, they will be left firmly on their own.

In some passerines, such as the Blackbird, the newly-fledged young quickly become attached to one or other of their parents to such an extent that, after a few days, the other parent will have nothing to do with them. It is not known why this 'brood-splitting' occurs; the young do not divide themselves equally between the two parents nor do they invariably attach themselves to the parent who is the same sex as themselves. Young Sand Martins learn to recognise their parents by call before they leave the nest. If they did not, they would have little chance of finding them afterwards in the milling throng of a nesting colony.

The young of many larger birds need to be looked after by their parents for much more than a week after they have left the nest. In many birds of prey the young leave the nest but do little hunting for themselves for quite some time, merely flying from perch to perch. Almost certainly, it takes time to perfect the complex flying skills that are necessary for such forms of hunting. Sparrowhawk chicks, for example, stay in the vicinity of the nest for up to a month and the parents continue to bring food to the nest where they come from time to time to collect it. Probably during this time they are catching *some* food for themselves, but are not so good at hunting as to be able to maintain themselves;

Adult Tawny Owl feeding fully-grown young several months after it has left the nest

gradually as they become more proficient, they become less dependent on this source of food and drift away. The nocturnal hunting of the Tawny Owl appears to be another skill that is difficult to acquire; although the young birds leave the nest in May or early June, they are fed by their parents until about September.

Adult male Blackbird feeding fully-fledged young after it has left the nest

As spring approaches, the parent Mute Swan becomes more aggressive

Some of the geese and swans stay with their parents for much longer than this. Many of those that are raised in the arctic migrate south in the company of their parents; this enables them to learn the migratory routes and their wintering grounds. Indeed, they stay together as a family unit through the winter. The parents of such family units defend the area around the group from others of their own species, so that the young birds are able to feed more easily; young feeding on their own are persistently harrassed and find it harder to feed.

Some young birds gradually drift away from their parents apparently of their own volition, but in other species the parents may actually have to chase them away. In the Mute Swan for example, the young often stay with the parents in the territory until the parents start to get ready to breed again. In such situations, the parent birds, especially the male, get more and more aggressive to their young until they eventually succeed in driving them off.

SURVIVAL OF YOUNG BIRDS

Young birds emerge into a dangerous environment where innumerable hazards await them. Although predators also take a heavy toll, starvation is probably the greatest danger. The main problem is that young birds, particularly those of small species, are not able to store appreciable reserves of fat (p. 224). The youngsters must be able to get enough food each day not just to survive, but to lay down reserves which will get them through the following night. If they do not, quite simply, they starve to death. Just one day of very poor weather, when feeding is difficult, or of feeling off-colour, can be enough to kill a small bird. Larger birds are a little better off in that they may be able to carry enough food reserves to last a few days, even perhaps a week or more. Some nidifugous young can survive for a few days on the unused portion of the yolk, which they absorb just before hatching. In this way, newly-hatched Mallard ducklings may survive for up to 48 hours without feeding, and Mute Swans may be able to survive up to ten days, although this is exceptional. However, most newly-fledged nidicolous birds must first gather the extra food, surplus to its immediate needs, before it can create such a reserve.

It is perhaps not surprising that, faced with such difficulties, so many young birds perish. In a few well-studied species it has been shown that high numbers die in their first year of life. For example, a pair of Song

and gradually drives its young away from the territory

Thrushes may lay two clutches (each of four eggs) per year. Roughly two chicks per three pairs (or 0.67 chicks per pair) survive to reach breeding age (p. 216). This means that only about 8% of the eggs laid become breeding adults. Even this is probably an overestimate since many birds which lose their nests to predators lay replacement clutches. The average number of eggs laid by each pair of Song Thrushes each year is probably many more than eight; hence the percentage that survive is much lower than that given here. The chances of survival increase if the eggs survive to produce fledged chicks; in one detailed study of Blackbirds, each pair actually raised an average of 4.1 young; about one in six (17%) of these fledglings survived to enter the breeding population the following year.

The loss of five out of every six chicks (or seven out of every eight eggs) may seem extremely high. But the Song Thrush is fairly typical of small passerines in Europe: in most of them only some 10% or fewer of the eggs survive to reach breeding age. Large birds do better, but there are few where more than 15% of the eggs or 20% of the chicks survive to breeding age. (Since many large birds take several years to reach breeding age these figures do not reflect the annual mortality; for example if only 10% of chicks survive to reach breeding age and breeding age is four, the annual survival rate is 56% $[(0.56)^4 = 0.098]$, see p. 284.

Most of the young birds that die probably do so fairly soon after they have left the nest. The weakest are rapidly weeded out; often these are the smallest ones in the brood, or those less successful in finding food or more likely to have it taken away by competing individuals. The fitter ones survive and, as they become more experienced, their chances of survival increase. By about November, the young or most small passerines (see p. 59) have more or less the same chance of surviving as do the adults. The situation is slightly different for long-lived birds which do not breed until they reach the age of two or more. The survival rate of these young and immatures may go on rising steadily for several years before they acquire survival rates as good as those of adults. For example, survival in the immature Mute Swan is about 67% from fledging (September) to the following summer (i.e. only about 9 months), about 67% for the whole of the next year and then about 75% per annum for the next two years, followed by 80% per annum or more when they reach adulthood.

AGE OF FIRST BREEDING

The young bird must survive the winter in order to breed (p. 226). However, by no means all birds breed when they are one year old; many take several years to reach breeding age. For example, most passerines and small waders breed when they are one year old; but many larger waders, a few large passerines and many terns do not breed until they are two years old; small gulls may not breed until three; larger ones may breed first at four, as may Razorbill and Guillemot, Mute Swan and Oystercatcher. The largest gulls such as the Great Black-backed may take five years before they breed, and so does the Puffin; Manx Shear-waters probably breed first at five or six while the Fulmar may not start until it is eight or nine years old.

The period of immaturity of each species is given under its entry in the Directory (pp. 61–203). However, these statements should be used with caution. In order to obtain such information it is necessary to put rings on young birds and then observe them when they start to breed. Since many young birds die before reaching breeding age, and many others disperse over wide areas, this means that a large number of chicks must be ringed if one is to have a chance of finding some of them breeding in a later year. In addition, one has to be prepared to go back and look each year – for many years in some of the species which take a long time to reach breeding age. Such detailed, long-term studies have not been undertaken on many species and the information presented in the Directory has sometimes had to be inferred from the situation in related species.

Another reason for caution is that there tends to be a lot of individual variation; not all individuals of the same species start to breed at the same age. Even with those species which usually start to breed at the age of one, there are some individuals who do not start to breed until the following year. In a study of Mute Swans, 3% bred for the first time at two, 43% at three, 35% at four, 15%

Young male Black Grouse do not participate in the dangerous business of lekking until they are at least three years old.

216

at five and 3% at six, while in another study one still had not bred at the age of eight. Humans, after all, start to breed at a very wide range of ages – if they breed at all.

Some of the variation can be accounted for by sex. In many species males tend to breed a little later than females. For example, in Holland, although most female Starlings breed when they are one year old, about 75% of the males do not breed until they are two; one of the reasons is that there seems to be an imbalance in the sex ratio, resulting in a shortage of females. Hence perhaps one could argue that these birds would have bred if there had been enough females for them to have been able to find mates. The opposite is the case in Sparrowhawks (where the female is much larger than the male); more males than females start to breed at one year old.

Males commonly breed later than females in species where there are communal displays (leks, see p. 256). This is because, since the dominant males in such leks get almost all the matings, there is little point in a young bird trying to breed; the dangers of displaying outweigh the chances of successful mating. In the Black Grouse and the Capercaillie the young males usually defer breeding until the age of three years. (In the Capercaillie, one year old males are not in full adult plumage nor have they reached full size.)

Why should the birds not breed at the age of one? The probable answer to this is that breeding is not only dangerous (p. 246), but also that it takes a young bird time to learn the feeding skills necessary to collect sufficient food to feed itself, never mind the extra food that it needs for producing eggs (p. 244) and raising young (p. 274). It is not only that the young themselves need feeding: the frenzied activity involved in the finding and transporting of the food consumes three or four times the energy that the parent would need if it were just fending for itself. Only skilled, efficient birds can cope with this, and it may therefore be better to defer breeding until these skills have been perfected.

We know that it takes a year or more to acquire these skills. For example, Sandwich Terns at eight months old catch a fish every six minutes, as opposed to every four minutes when they are older. Oystercatchers in their first winter find it less easy than older ones to collect food, and tend to lose weight during the winter, while adults feeding in the same place at the same time can maintain their weight. These figures suggest that young birds find it difficult to collect enough food for themselves, let alone that required to feed a brood.

Young Sandwich Terns are less efficient at catching fish than adult birds.

MOULT

Feathers wear out and have to be replaced (p. 32). The ability to change body covering is valuable since it gives birds the opportunity to change colour.

Since birds have to acquire extra energy to grow new feathers (p. 227), and since they fly less efficiently while growing them, they moult when food is easy to obtain.

PLUMAGES OF YOUNG BIRDS

At hatching, many nidicolous species (p. 206), such as cormorants, woodpeckers and sparrows, are completely featherless; others, such as the tits and flycatchers, have small amounts of feathering, often confined to their upper surfaces, these being the areas from which the young bird is most likely to lose heat. Yet other nidicolous species, such as shearwaters, birds of prey and owls, are covered with a thick coat of down. By far the best covering of feathers is found on nidifugous young, since these have to wander around on their own soon after hatching. Some of these, such as waders, terns and nightjars are extremely well-camouflaged. Nidifugous young are covered with downy plumage, not the contour feathers (p. 28) that they will have later. Many such as the divers, grebes and ducks are beautifully waterproof; they dive, come up, shake themselves and all the water runs off.

Some young which are born naked, such as the woodpeckers, remain so until their first set of true feathers begins to grow. Others, such as the swifts, grow an intermediate downy plumage. Most young which hatch covered in down such as shearwaters, and nidifugous birds like divers and gulls, grow a second downy plumage prior to growing their first set of contour feathers. The reason for this is probably that the down which covers the newly-hatched chick is

Hatchling Green Woodpecker is featherless.

Hatchling Merlin has thick coat of down.

Hatchling Roseate Tern is well camouflaged.

Hatchling Little Grebe is waterproof.

The young Swift grows an intermediate downy plumage.

insufficient to cover a much larger chick; however, by the time this first set of down is no longer sufficient, the young bird is still too small to be able to wear the feathers of a fully-grown bird. Hence a second set of down must be produced to cover the half-grown youngster.

POST-FLEDGING MOULT

The juvenile plumage may resemble the adult one as, for example, in the Wren, or it may be very different, like the scaly-brown of the juvenile Stonechat. A distinctive juvenile plumage is an advantage to the young bird since, if it wanders into the territory of an adult bird, it does not elicit the aggression that a bird in adult plumage might. For example, territorial adult Robins are prone to attack any Robin with a red breast, but tend to leave the brown juveniles unmolested. Similarly, the black collar of the juvenile Kittiwake is recognised by the adults, and they rarely attack a juvenile.

The feathers which most young song-birds have when they leave the nest seem to be of fairly poor quality. Perhaps it is better for a growing chick to invest as much of its food as possible into growth of the body, rather than into the quality of the feathers. Whatever the reason, many young birds soon replace their juvenile feathers. They moult into what is called first-winter plumage. In most small birds this is similar to the normal winter plumage of the adults, but in larger species such as the Herring Gull or Gannet which do not breed until they are several years old there may be a succession of plumages, each of which is progressively more like that of the adult.

One reason for moulting soon after leaving the nest is that, when the bird is moulting its insulation is less good, so it is important to acquire the complete winter plumage well before the weather becomes too cold and the heat loss too serious.

The young bird does not necessarily moult *all* its feathers at this time, many retain their wing and tail feathers, together with the associated coverts (p. 28). These large feathers may represent, by weight, some 20 to 25% of the total feather weight and so it may be uneconomical to replace them. Usually, these large flight feathers are not moulted until after the breeding season the following year; they are retained for a little over a year. However, some small birds *do* moult their flight feathers during the post-fledging moult; these include the woodpeckers, Shore-lark, Skylark and Woodlark, the Long-tailed Tit, the Starling, the sparrows and the Corn Bunting, Young Swallows, House and Sand Martins also moult their flight feathers, but they do so in winter quarters after migration.

Larger birds such as the Lesser

Conflict between adult Kittiwakes does not involve the recognisably young birds.

Black-backed Gull and the Mute Swan also start a moult shortly after they become full grown, but in these species the loss of feathers is gradual and prolonged. Even so, the young gull only changes a proportion of its body feathers after fledging. It has a pause in mid-winter and then starts again in spring. The main wing and tail feathers are not shed until the following late summer when the bird undergoes its first complete moult. In the swan, the moult seems to be more gradual still, with a steady replacement of the brown cygnet feathers by white ones throughout the winter and spring until by late summer of the following year only a few of the brown body feathers remain.

SPRING MOULT

Many of our most familiar birds such as the Dunnock, the thrushes and the tits do not change their plumage between winter and summer, while other species have a pre-breeding moult after which they are more brightly coloured.

It is difficult to generalise about the common factors of those that do and those that do not have a spring moult. The Ptarmigan and Willow Grouse moult out of their white winter plumage into a dappled and

The Ptarmigan changes its plumage from season to season to camouflage it in the prevailing conditions.

well-camouflaged one for the summer. Plainly in these species one major function of both plumages is camouflage. However, divers and grebes moult into bright plumages for the summer; these are obviously important in their displays, but why should they be dull in winter? It seems hardly likely that the winter plumage of the divers has much to do with camouflage; the drakes of many species of duck remain, often on the same waters as the grebes and divers, in bright plumage throughout the winter. The difference can probably be related to the fact that many ducks pair up in their winter quarters whereas, the divers and grebes do not; hence the former need their attractive breeding plumage in winter and the latter do not. But this begs the question as to why one group pairs up in winter quarters while the others do so on or near the breeding grounds.

Within the waders there is great variation in how different the birds become in their summer plumage. Among the sandpipers, Knot, Sanderling, Curlew Sandpiper and Dunlin become much brighter, while the stints change less markedly; the male Ruff (but not the female) in summer plumage is also a particularly striking bird. Among the plovers, Grey and Golden are much brighter in summer than in winter plumage, whereas the smaller plovers, Ringed, Little Ringed and Kentish, show much less change between the seasons. Even the closely-related redshanks differ, the Spotted Redshank changing much more than the Redshank.

In many of the song-birds, only the males acquire bright plumage in the summer, though both sexes have a spring moult. These include the Pied Flycatcher, Yellow Wagtail and several of the warblers of the genus *Sylvia.*

These species do not moult their flight feathers in the spring; they change the body plumage only. Perhaps uniquely among European passerines, the Willow Warbler moults its flight feathers twice a year, once in Europe in late summer before its migration southwards, and once in Africa just prior to its migration northwards. It is not known why it should do this, but it is the smallest long-distance migrant and perhaps its flight feathers become badly worn on the long flights.

INCOMPLETE MOULT AND ABRASION

A few species acquire their summer plumage by means of a restricted moult. For example, the Black-headed and Mediterranean Gulls acquire their brown or black heads by moulting the feathers of the neck and head; it seems that they do not moult the rest of their plumage. The same is also true of terns which derive their black caps for the summer from a restricted moult.

The Brambling has an even subtler way of acquiring its bright breeding plumage without having to undergo an energy-demanding moult. At the end of the summer, the male moults from his bright spring plumage into a much duller one for the winter. In fact the winter plumage looks duller only because each feather has

The brighter appearance of the Brambling in spring is the result of the wearing away of buff feather-tips.

which replaces it weighs about 1.6 grams.

Moult of the flight feathers is a tricky thing for birds. The shedding of old feathers, and the growing of new ones, is staggered so that not too many gaps exist at any given moment; even so, flight is less efficient, and more energy is needed for it.

The timing of the post-nuptial moult varies markedly both between and within species. Only in exceptional circumstances, such as in the short period available for breeding in the Arctic, do many birds get into heavy moult while raising young. The Arctic-breeding Glaucous Gull does so, and even some small passerines, such as Snow and Lapland Buntings, moult while raising young. Further south, most passerines (see p. 59) only begin to moult at about the time when their young leave the nest, though birds with late nests or second broods may have started to moult before their young have flown.

Another species whose moult is clearly linked to the age of the young is the Great Crested Grebe. In the late summer it is often possible to see a pair in full breeding plumage when most of the other adults have already moulted. Almost invariably, it turns out that they are parents of a late brood and still have chicks with them.

a dull brown fringe to it. Since it is only the tips of the feathers that show at any time, the bird looks dull-coloured. As spring approaches, these tips begin to wear off revealing the bright spring plumage underneath. Such a system for getting a bright spring plumage, cheaply in energetic terms, is not confined to the Brambling. It also occurs in a number of other finches and buntings; the black head of the male Reed Bunting is acquired in this way.

AFTER BREEDING

The parent bird's main aim when it has finished breeding is to ensure, as best it can, that it can survive through the winter to the next breeding season. Its feathers, especially the large flight feathers, have become abraded after being in use for a year, and need replacing. It is also possible that some species shed some of their warm winter plumage so that they are not too hot in the summer. The body plumage of a Bullfinch weighs only about 1.0 grams by late summer whereas the new winter plumage

FLIGHTLESSNESS

For those species near the limit of flying efficiency when in possession of their full complement of feathers (in other words those with a high wing loading, p. 43), the loss of some of the main flight feathers must make flying very difficult indeed. The Guillemot is one such bird. It has solved the problem of how to cope with an incomplete set of wing feathers; it drops them all at once and becomes flightless. It does this when out at sea with its chick. This has a number of advantages: by growing all its feathers at the same time it has a wing which is incomplete for a far shorter time than if it moulted the feathers one by one (p. 32). Since it has to stay with its still flightless chick during this

A moulting Guillemot drops all its primaries simultaneously (top); *when the new primaries are half-grown, all the secondaries are dropped* (centre); *the fully-feathered wing* (bottom) *is finally achieved.*

period, it is probably only a very slight disadvantage to be flightless.

A number of other birds also go though a flightless period during the moult. Although many of these might manage with an incomplete wing better than the Guillemot, many of them are also tied to flightless young when they moult. These include ducks, geese and many of the rail family including Moorhen and Crane. The Crane is unusual in that it does not necessarily moult its flight feathers every year; it retains them for two or even more years, but when it does moult it sheds them all at once.

No European passerine becomes completely flightless during moult; being small they would probably be at too great a risk from predation. But the Dipper sheds many of its flight feathers simultaneously and can fly only weakly. Similarly, moulting Snow and Lapland Buntings, in their race against time in the Arctic, shed many feathers together and fly poorly. The Marsh Warbler is only at the southern end of its migration for a short while, and also moults many feathers at the same time; it can only just fly when in full moult.

DIFFERENCES BETWEEN THE SEXES

In some species the two sexes moult at different times. For example, in breeding pairs of Mute Swans, which are flightless during moult, the female drops her flight feathers soon after the young have hatched, but the male retains his for about a further month. Only when his mate's feathers are well-grown does he shed his. Swans rely heavily upon their wings in defence, but they cannot use them while the feathers are growing, because of the risk of breaking them. If this happened, they might be flightless for the whole year. Presumably this is the reason why the pair arranges things so that one of them is always full-winged. Certainly such a suggestion fits with the aggressiveness of the birds: the full-winged one is always the one that seems the more ready to attack. By the time their cygnets are large enough to fly, both parents are full-winged. (It is significant that *non*-breeding male and female Mute Swans moult at the same time.)

In some of the birds of prey the two sexes also have different moult patterns. Female Sparrowhawks and Goshawks sit on the eggs throughout the incubation period and brood the chicks for the first part of the nestling period. During this period the female is fed by her mate and is doing little flying, so she moults her flight feathers. In contrast, the male who at this stage is very active hunting for food, waits until after the young have fledged before he moults. In the Kestrel the male starts to moult about a fortnight after his mate.

OUT-OF-SEASON COLOURS

The adult moult differs from that of the juvenile in that the adults are often changing from a bright summer plumage into a duller winter one. Males of passerines are less conspicuous to predators in the off-season plumage, so it is worth changing into it, even though this involves them in another moult in late winter in order to get back into summer plumage. Adult male ducks show an interesting variation of this theme. They stay in the bright colours of the adult breeding plumage almost the whole year round. However, just before they have their main moult in late summer (during which they are flightless), they change their body feathers to a dull colour, rather similar to that of their mates; this is called an eclipse plumage. As they become able to fly once more, they moult their body feathers again and return to being brightly coloured. The fact that it is worthwhile undertaking two body moults instead of one in the space of a little over a month indicates perhaps the danger that they would be in if they were brightly coloured while they were flightless.

WHERE AND WHEN TO MOULT

Many migrants moult before migrating, but some of those species which breed in the Arctic do not. There, the birds face a very harsh climate and the area is habitable for only a very short period of time. They tend to rush in, lay their eggs, raise their young and leave as quickly as possible so that they are not caught as the winter closes in again. Nevertheless, some species do moult at these high latitudes. Many of the geese (which do not feed their young, but merely accompany them) moult while their goslings are growing up. Most waders, however, move off south before moulting. In many of these, such as the Knot, which may winter as far south as South Africa, different populations moult in different places. Many Knot start their body moult on the breeding grounds, but soon afterwards set off southwards. Some pause in Britain, and moult, before flying on to complete

their migration. Others fly direct to Mauretania before moulting.

Some waders, including Grey Plover, Wood Sandpiper and some Dunlin, moult some of their flight feathers in one area, then suspend moulting, move on and complete their moult elsewhere, perhaps in their winter quarters. Likewise the Turtle Dove starts by moulting some of its flight feathers on the breeding grounds, then suspends moult until it reaches winter quarters.

Some species put off the whole moult until they reach their winter quarters. These include Garden Warbler and Swift (although the closely-related Blackcap and Alpine Swift stay longer in Europe and moult here). One possible advantage of moulting in winter quarters is that the birds can set off southwards sooner than if they have to wait while they complete a moult first. This may be important in species which hold winter territories (p 256), such as the Greenish Warbler. A bird which spent time moulting in Europe might arrive on its winter quarters to find the most suitable areas already occupied.

While the majority of birds undertake their full moult soon after breeding or soon after reaching winter quarters, a few leave it until even later. Those Great Reed and Sedge Warblers which go farthest south delay moult until close to the time for departure, and migrate on fresh feathers. The Red-throated Diver moults its flight feathers in the autumn like most other birds. But the other three divers wait until just before the next breeding season before doing so.

A flock of Knot seen in Britain in the Autumn contains individuals of widely-varying plumage, depending on the age of the individuals and the stage of their moult.

ENERGY AND FEEDING

THE NEED FOR ENERGY

All animals need energy in order to survive. Although it is sometimes possible to get small amounts of energy by warming from the sun, as many reptiles do, this is a slow and unreliable method. Virtually all of the energy used by birds is obtained from their food.

Energy is needed for many purposes. Among the most important, it is needed for:–
(1) maintaining the body temperature (in warm-blooded animals such as birds);
(2) general body maintenance (keeping the body tissues supplied with nutrients, and replacing worn tissues; such maintenance is going on all the time, but may be more intensive at certain times, such as during the moult when new feathers are being formed);
(3) the processing of food (digestion);
(4) locomotion (flight in particular is energy-demanding);
(5) growth (obviously this is necessary in young birds; but adult birds at certain times also grow tissues such as the sex organs and eggs).

FACTORS AFFECTING THE AMOUNT OF ENERGY REQUIRED

The amount of energy used depends on many factors. One of these is the size of the bird. If one compares two objects of similar shape, but different size, the larger one has a smaller surface area in relation to its volume. This has important implications, especially for small birds, since the surface area to volume ratio affects the rate at which heat is lost from an object. The smaller the body, the relatively larger the surface area, and so the faster the heat loss. This is one of the main factors limiting how small birds can be; if they were too small

the rate of heat loss would be too great, and the birds could not get sufficient food to keep themselves warm – they would run out of fuel trying to keep their boiler stoked. The very smallest hummingbirds weigh only about 2 grams. Although they live in hot climates, they still have difficulty preventing excessive heat loss during the night; often they become torpid so as to conserve energy. No European bird is quite as small as that, but the Firecrest and Goldcrest weigh only about 6 grams, the Fan-tailed Warbler about 7 grams, the Long-tailed Tit about 8 grams and both the Coal Tit and the Wren weigh less than 10 grams; all these can have considerable difficulty keeping themselves warm during the night.

The other main factor which affects the rate of heat loss is the ambient temperature; a bird loses heat more rapidly when the air temperature is low than when it is high. Low temperatures in winter have a particularly serious effect on small birds. For example, the small birds mentioned above maintain a body temperature of a little over 40°C. To do this on a cold night, say when the air temperature drops to −20°C, requires a

The largest and one of the smallest birds in Europe: Mute Swan and Fan-tailed Warbler.

considerable amount of energy. Not surprisingly, many small birds perish in periods of extreme cold; they burn up all their food reserves during the night trying to maintain their body temperature. Even so, the fact that they can survive at all is a great tribute to the insulating properties of feathers.

Some birds have found ways of reducing the rate at which heat is lost. The Wren reduces its heat loss by roosting in holes; the air in these warms up around it and provides some insulation. Holes also provide some protection from the chilling effect of cold winds. In the Arctic, Ptarmigan, Siberian Tits and Arctic Redpolls protect themselves against wind chill by roosting in holes in the snow. Ptarmigan dig these for themselves, but the smaller species use mouse tunnels. Although they do not live so far north, the Capercaillie and Black Grouse also burrow into the snow. Siberian Tits sometimes go slightly torpid at night, lowering their body temperature so as to reduce the rate of heat loss. Although this produces some saving, the semi-torpid birds may be less able to react quickly to danger and must use considerable amounts of energy at dawn to regain their normal temperature.

In very cold weather, Wrens often roost together in small groups so as to keep each other warm. Long-tailed Tits also huddle together for warmth; indeed this may be the main reason that they live in flocks in winter.

The activity of a bird greatly affects its energy requirements; the more active the bird, the more energy it uses up. For example, if a domestic hen which has been lying down stands up, its energy consumption increases by 40–50%; walking and running cost yet more in terms of energy to fuel the activity; the ultimate is flight which, compared with resting, involves a bird in roughly a ten-fold increase in energy consumption over the resting state.

A group of Wrens emerge from their roost together in a hole

A Siberian Tit comes out of its roost in a hole in the snow

A Ptarmigan digs a hole in the snow, in which to roost; it is seen below coming out in the morning.

SEASONAL VARIATIONS IN ENERGY REQUIREMENTS

The measurement of the energy required for the different activities is difficult, and much still remains to be learned. However, some indication of the amounts of energy required for various activities are given opposite. It is probably no accident that most of the energy-demanding activities in a bird's life are spread out around the year instead of overlapping; for example most birds do not moult while they are getting into breeding condition, nor while they are incubating, raising young or laying down the fat for migration, nor do they moult while on migration.

One of the first activities for many species as the breeding season approaches is for the males to acquire a territory (p. 254). The energy required to do this will vary with the species, the type of territory held, and other factors. In particular, it probably requires more energy to acquire a territory in the first place than to hold on to it. The Spotted Sandpiper, when defending its territory, increases its energy requirements by as much as 12%. As with many other activities, the picture is complicated by the fact that the bird not only uses more energy, but also has less time to feed; territorial defence takes up a lot of time. Although a woodland bird may be able to snatch food at intervals while singing, a seabird on guard in its territory is away from its feeding grounds and has no opportunity to feed.

When birds start to get into breeding condition their sex organs have to develop from their regressed out-of-season state (p. 34). The male's testes grow over a period of several weeks and do not seem to require more than about a 2% increase in the daily energy requirements. The ovaries and associated organs of the female are larger (in exceptional cases, they may weigh up to 15% of the bird's weight) and take from one to four weeks to grow to full size. Over the whole of this period, the increase in energy requirements averages out at about the same as in the male, only about 2%. However, growth is not always evenly spread throughout this period; at certain stages the female Sand Martin needs about 10% more energy than normal.

The female requires even more energy when she starts to form eggs. The weight of eggs produced by the females of many species (and the energy required to form them) is considerable (p. 268). The increase in energy required has been estimated for several different species: Herring Gull 80%, Rock Dove (which lays relatively small eggs) 25%, and Starling 55%. The eggs of nidifugous species (p. 206) contain relatively more nutrients than those of nidicolous species and so presumably more energy is required to form them.

There is some dispute as to how much energy is required by a bird to incubate the eggs. A considerable amount of heat has to be applied to the eggs, and it would seem that this ought to lead to a marked increase in the energy requirements of the incubating bird. In birds such as waders, which incubate their eggs on bare ground, such a heat loss is probably considerable, and this may be why most species of waders line

The male Spotted Sandpiper defends the breeding territory while the female lays an egg (which he may later incubate on his own).

The variation in a bird's weight gives an idea of how much energy it needs at various times in the year. The graph shows that a Great Tit (green) puts on fat to provide the extra energy needed in cold weather, and that the female in particular feeds more when she is preparing to lay eggs. A Sedge Warbler (brown) doubles its weight in order to undertake migration.

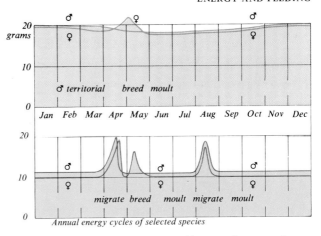

Annual energy cycles of selected species

their nest (p. 265). However, some birds such as Ringed Plovers which lay their eggs on bare shingle (where to line the nest would make it more conspicuous to predators) are known to have high energy consumption when incubating. This is almost certainly because of the lack of insulation.

In contrast, in some species at least, it seems as if any possible heat loss is mitigated by the fact that the bird is inactive, tucked up in a well-insulated nest. Some studies, especially of hole-nesting birds, have indicated that there are no increases in energy consumption during incubation. And yet an incubating Wren is thought to require from 17–50% extra energy (the amount depending on the temperature); and in both the Starling and the Blue Tit it is known that the energy required for incubation increases with the number of eggs in the clutch. Even if the act of incubation itself does not require an increase in energy consumption by the bird, it may still find it difficult to get enough food to provide its basic energy requirement, since it has much less time to feed. Further, when it is off the nest collecting food, it probably has to be very active to get its food in the short periods of time between bouts of incubation.

There is no doubt that great amounts of extra energy are required by the parent birds once the young

hatch. At this stage, they not only have to feed themselves, but also a hungry brood. The increase in energy required by the adults at this stage varies greatly in relation to the number of young which it has and the rate at which they are growing. In a range of species including Herring Gull, Long-eared Owl, Turtle Dove, House Martin and Starling the parents use up energy at 3½ to 4 times their normal rate. Put in human terms this is roughly the equivalent of a man doing a heavy labouring job for all the daylight hours. This calculation relates only to the amount of energy that the parents need to cover their own greatly increased activity (p. 274); it does not include the extra food gathered for the young.

Replacing the feathers also requires extra energy. Moulting Chaffinches and Ortolan Buntings need about 25% extra energy. Some of this may be required because, at this time, the birds are less well-feathered and so lose more heat than when fully insulated; but most of the increase in energy consumption appears to be directly associated with growing the new set of feathers. These 25% increases are for adults which are replacing their complete set of feathers; young birds, which moult fewer feathers (p. 218), seem to require less energy.

ACQUIRING THE ENERGY

DAILY FEEDING RATES

One can get some idea of the pressure that a bird is under to find enough food by observing how much of the day it spends trying to do so. In Europe the days are both shorter and colder in mid-winter than they are in summer; in mid-winter the bird has to find more food to maintain itself, and has less time to do it in, than in summer. Although, at some times of the day, birds may sit about and preen, or do nothing in particular, at other times they feed busily.

The Coal Tit spends about 80% of the day feeding in the autumn; but as the nights lengthen and the temperature drops, they spend more and more time until, in mid-winter, they are feeding for virtually the whole of their day. The proportion of time then steadily decreases through late winter and early spring, until the nesting season approaches. Then, from late April to the end of June, the Coal Tits again spend 90% or more of their day searching for food, either for themselves or for their young. Incubating birds spend all of what time they have off the nest feeding. After breeding, the amount of time spent feeding drops away during late summer until, in September, it starts to increase once more.

Because they lose heat relatively more rapidly, small birds need relatively more food than larger ones. As a result, the smallest species spend the highest proportion of the day foraging. The Coal Tit (which weighs about 9 g) spends a higher proportion of the day feeding than does the Blue Tit (c. 11 g) or the Great Tit (c. 19 g).

The activity of the two sexes may be different; so they may require different amounts of food. This has been measured best when the females are preparing to lay. At this time, a female Mallard may feed almost three times as fast as her mate, a female Spotted Sandpiper about 60% faster than the male. In some of the smaller species, there is not this difference, because the males also increase their feeding rate, bringing much of the extra food they gather to the female.

DAILY WEIGHT CYCLES

Birds cannot feed throughout the 24-hour period; most, except for the owls, feed by day and sleep at night. During their period of sleep, they lose weight because they are not feeding and are using up energy. So, at dawn, they weigh less than when they went to roost. They have to make good this overnight loss by feeding up in the day to reach the same evening weight again. Normally birds feed very busily in the early morning, but then may slacken off a bit during the afternoon, and then have another busy period just before they go to roost. In human terms, the daily changes in weight are quite considerable, but this is largely because we are dealing with small animals whose surface to volume ratio is very high (p. 224). For example, a House Sparrow going to roost may weigh about 26 grams, of which some 2 grams is fat which it can use overnight to maintain itself. Normally it will lose about a gram (4% of its evening weight) by dawn. But in cold weather some birds have used most

A duck Mallard can feed uninterruptedly if the drake stays on the look-out for predators.

of their fat stores by the time morning comes, and will not survive for long unless they can start to feed almost immediately.

Although small birds do not have many reserves over and above those needed to get them through the next night, the amount of those reserves needed varies from season to season. In mid-winter, when nights are cold and long, they use up more energy and lose more weight during the night than is the case in summer. Hence, during the winter they must lay down more fat by nightfall than is necessary in summer.

There is therefore an annual cycle in the amount of food reserves they store up during the day. They do not take just what they need; they take a little more, just to be on the safe side. Apart from anything else, the night might suddenly turn much colder; some spare energy might prove essential.

A number of species reduce the effective length of the night by filling their crops with food just before they go to roost. Finches do this, and consume this extra snack during the night. It is often easy to see the packed crops of Woodpigeons as they head from the farmlands into nearby woodland for the night, taking food to roost.

One is always tempted to ask why birds do not lay down even more reserves than they do – enough, say, to see them through a further 24 hours. Surely it would be safer to be able to survive a day or two without having to be dependent on finding enough food? There are two possible answers to this. First, in poor conditions it might indeed be better to have larger food reserves; but perhaps these are just those occasions when they cannot get them. Second, it is possible that the advantages are outweighed by disadvantages. For example, the House Sparrow would need to lay down about 4 grams of fat if it were to have enough reserves to survive for a further 24 hours in cold weather. But if it did this it would increase its own weight by about 15%. This extra weight would mean that it

would be less manoeuvrable and therefore perhaps more vulnerable to predators. And it would need more energy to fly, because it was carrying the extra fat.

This problem is most acute for the small birds – those whose energy consumption is so high that a day's fat stores represent a high proportion of their body weight. As the size of the bird increases, it becomes more practicable to store food that will last for a longer period. Birds the size of ducks can almost certainly survive for several days without feeding (if they start with good stores of fat), and birds the size of geese can survive a week or more.

SURVIVAL IN THE COLD

Problems of overnight survival are obviously most acute at high latitudes, where the combination of short days and low temperatures makes survival very challenging. Birds have only a short time to find the food they need, and a long time to wait before they can feed again; and the cold conditions mean that they need to take in a lot of food. Birds have evolved a number of ways of trying to cope with these conditions. In the very coldest areas all birds migrate away for the winter (p. 232); it is only their powers of flight that make it possible for them to use these areas in summer. Nonetheless, some birds manage to remain at high latitudes all the year round.

Siberian Tits and Ptarmigan remain at these high latitudes throughout the winter. The Coal, Crested and Willow Tits spend much of the autumn poking seeds behind the bark of trees, and depend heavily on this stored food during the winter. Unstored seeds are often unavailable because they are covered by a thick layer of snow. The tits get some protection from the cold by roosting in holes in trees; even so, they drop their temperature by several degrees while asleep, thereby economising on the amount of energy needed to keep warm.

229

FORAGING BEHAVIOUR

LEARNING TO FEED

Learning to feed for itself is perhaps the most difficult single thing that a young bird has to do, and it is no wonder that so many of them fail the test (p. 214). Young Swifts and Puffins leave the nest when their parents are away, and fly off by themselves; they have never seen their prey in its natural habitat, and they get no help from their parents. Most birds get some sort of assistance from their parents after they leave the nest (p. 274). We know very little about how they actually learn to catch their prey.

Even parental tuition cannot cover all situations. Resident European birds may switch from insects in summer to seeds in winter, while the warbler which leaves a European woodland for an African forest, or the wader which moves from its tundra birthplace to a seaside sand-bank, faces a whole range of changes. The habitats, the prey and the predators all change; all must be learned if the young bird is to survive.

The individual seems to develop its hunting skill in response to reward and failure – continuing to hunt in places where it has been successful and tending to give up places where it fails to find food.

The evidence suggests that birds often make very subtle distinctions between the foods that are available, choosing the ones that are of better quality or more easily gathered. For example, Red Grouse take those heather shoots which are richest in nitrogen and phosphorus.

A hunting-party of four different species of tit

FLOCKS AND FLOCKING

Many species feed in flocks at rich supplies of food – such as gulls on rubbish tips, seabirds on shoals of fish, and vultures, kites and crows at carrion. Birds that feed in this way can learn from others on the food. Many other species hunt in loose flocks – such as mixed parties of woodland birds, flocks of pigeons in fields, and gatherings of Rooks and Jackdaws or of buntings and finches.

At least in many of these cases, the young bird may be able to learn the whereabouts of food by watching others in the flock.

For many birds there is another

Lapwings, Golden Plovers and Black-headed Gulls feeding together; the two plovers are sometimes robbed of their food by the Gulls.

advantage in living in flocks. The larger the numbers of birds the more likely it is that one of them will spot an approaching predator before it gets dangerously close. Goshawks get closer to Woodpigeons in small flocks, before the alarm is given, than is the case with large flocks; hence they are more likely to be able to make a kill from a small flock than a large one. Birds spend an appreciable amount of time scanning round for predators, but individuals spend less time on the look-out in large flocks than in small ones and so have more time for feeding.

There is however, a disadvantage of being in a flock. When an individual in a flock finds an item of food, a nearby bird may come and snatch it before the finder can eat it. This is not usually important where small food items are being taken since the bird that finds them can swallow them quickly. But a large worm, or a large seed which takes some time to deal with, may easily be snatched by another bird.

Food stealing of this type is quite common in birds in winter. Robbing often occurs between individuals of the same species. In small flocks there is usually a clear peck-order among the birds in a flock. Individuals know each other. When birds have previously squabbled they remember who won, and a hierarchy develops. The advantages to the winner are obvious, but to the losers the system may have certain benefits: it is better to give up swiftly and avoid injury than to risk a prolonged and possibly damaging battle. In such dominance hierarchies, older birds tend to dominate younger ones and the males usually dominate the females. These hierarchies are probably established partly on the basis of the experience of the birds concerned, but also partly on their size; for example, large female Rooks dominate the smaller ones.

In mixed species flocks larger or more aggressive species often take food from the slower or less aggressive species. For example, Black-headed Gulls, Lapwings and Golden Plovers often feed in mixed flocks on grassland in winter. The gull is good at robbing the Lapwing of prey (though less good at robbing the Golden Plover). Similarly, Great Tits snatch beech seeds from Blue Tits before the latter can open them and eat the contents. Both Great and Blue Tits rob Coal Tits. As a result, Coal Tits try to avoid direct confrontation; often, at a bird-table, Coal Tits sneak in underneath and wait for the other tits to drop a small piece of food which they then rapidly grab and fly off with.

Black-headed Gulls feeding on a rubbish-tip; there are distinct advantages in feeding in a flock.

MIGRATION

Flight enables birds to travel great distances, over both land and water, in a short time. Flight enables birds to exploit many places where food is plentiful at certain times of the year, but absent or unavailable at others.

Migration may be defined as 'a regular, large-scale shift of the population between a restricted breeding area and a restricted wintering area'. This is not a completely watertight definition, since, as we shall see, not all migration is between breeding and wintering areas. Nonetheless it covers the great majority of cases.

EVOLUTION OF MIGRATION

Migratory habits have arisen as a result of a set of complex 'pros' and 'cons'. In Europe, we tend to think of the Swallow as leaving its home and going to a warmer area, with more insects, until home is habitable once more. In fact this is the wrong way about; it is nearer the truth to say that Africa is the Swallow's home and that it comes to Europe for our summer so as to cash in on the rich supply of insects for its young. Certainly this is the way its journeys came about.

If we look back some 15,000 years, a mere twinkling in evolutionary time, the whole of central and northern Europe was covered by a thick layer of ice; the last glaciation (Ice Age) was at its peak. Even much of southern Europe was a treeless, arctic tundra. After that date, the ice started to melt; the ice-cap retreated. Over many thousands of years each type of vegetation spread slowly northwards, occupying that climatic area to which it was best suited. Effectively, the same thing happened to the birds; they followed their habitats, the oakwood birds moving northwards as the oaks spread north and so on.

Such a northwards spread was fairly straightforward for the resident species, but for others, there was a different reason for heading north. Our Swallow, for example, had been living perfectly successfully in the southern areas and could doubtless have gone on doing so. Since they

Europe 15,000 years ago

232

could not survive the winter in the north, why should they bother to go there? One reason was that they were living in these southern areas in close association with many other birds, and competition for food was intense. As the ice retreated to the north, new areas became available to them, areas that were, to start with, empty of birds. A Swallow that migrated northwards to these areas found plenty of food, little competition, and longer days in which to hunt. The

Europe today

bird which migrated was able to raise more young than the one which stayed behind. Natural selection favoured the migrant.

As the ice retreated further still, the winter and the summer places for the migrant moved progressively further apart. However, as long as the migrant continued to raise more young than the bird that did not migrate, it was still at an advantage.

As the two areas moved further apart, the birds faced another problem. Was it worth the effort of returning to the southern area for the winter? Presumably (though there is little actual evidence) migration is difficult and dangerous; the bird must lay down large reserves of fat for migration, and birds blown off course may perish. Birds should only migrate when the chances of dying on migration are lower than the chances of dying as a result of food shortage on the breeding grounds in winter.

In the event, many species which moved into the areas vacated by the ice stayed there, while others continued to return to their ancestral areas in winter, and yet others split the difference by migrating some distance from the breeding grounds, but not the whole way back.

Hence we may regard the habit of moving northwards as resulting from natural selection favouring those members of a species which raised the largest number of young, and the habit of migrating southwards as an adaptation which gives the bird the best chance of surviving so that it may breed the following year. We can see in some species evidence of the ways in which both these habits may have come about.

EVIDENCE FOR THE EVOLUTION OF MIGRATORY ROUTES

The first of these two habits, that of northward migration in spring, developed a long time ago, so we cannot observe it in the making. However, there are a few migration routes which are best explained by a gradual extension of a route that might have

233

been, originally, quite simple. For example, the Wheatear breeds from Scandinavia eastwards across the whole of northern Asia; a small number even cross the Bering Straits each summer to breed in Alaska. Yet, as far as is known, all these birds migrate to Africa for the winter. It seems odd that the birds breeding in Alaska should go all the way back to Africa (a distance of some 16,000 km). One might think that they could find suitable areas in temperate North America – only half as far away as Africa. This seemingly odd migration route makes sense if looked at as a gradual extension of a route which took place over a long period of time. Birds heading up to breed kept finding new areas – on the fringe of traditional breeding grounds – where they could breed successfully with little competition. So, slowly, they and then their descendants spread eastwards. At no time have they succeeded in breaking with their old route to Africa for the winter. Presumably any that have tried have not been successful. Perhaps one day

some birds will make a mistake and fly down into temperate North America for the winter, find a suitable wintering ground and survive there; then a new and shorter route may evolve.

As well as spreading eastwards to Alaska, Wheatears have also spread westwards from Europe to Greenland and eastern Canada. Again, the birds breeding in these areas would have a shorter journey if they went south into North America, but they stick to the tried and tested routes back into Africa for the winter. This route is not only very long, but involves some of the birds in sea crossings of more than 3,000 km.

In some species some individuals have at some stage broken with tradition. Like the Wheatear, Yellow Wagtails also breed right across the Old World and into Alaska; almost certainly they too spread eastwards from a European origin. However, not all Yellow Wagtails return to Africa for the winter; many of those that breed in eastern Asia find suitable wintering sites in south-east

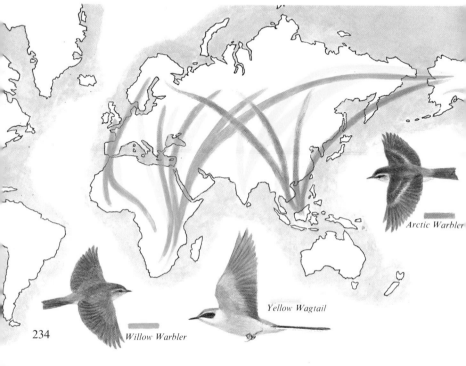

Arctic Warbler

Yellow Wagtail

Willow Warbler

Asia and India, so greatly reducing the journey; none however, is yet known to winter in the New World. Similarly, the Red-backed Shrike and Red-throated Pipit breed over a wide area of Eurasia; in both these the western populations spend the winter in Africa, the eastern ones in southern Asia. The European Swallow occurs throughout most of Eurasia and, at some stage, spread into North America where it is known as the Barn Swallow. Barn Swallows migrate into South and Central America for the winter, a far simpler and shorter route than continuing to return to Africa. Perhaps, one day, the Yellow Wagtails and Wheatears will do the same.

Some species seem to have survived the Ice Age in the south-east Asia and spread westwards; like the Wheatear, they cling to their ancestral wintering grounds, heading back to south-east Asia instead of making the shorter journey to Africa. Amongst these are the Red-breasted Flycatcher which winters in India and the Arctic Warbler which winters in the ex-

treme south-east of Asia. The latter is particularly interesting since it is a close relative of the Willow Warbler which winters in Africa. Both species breed in northern Scandinavia, yet winter in very different places. The Arctic Warblers which fly over the Himalayas en route to their winter quarters, meet Willow Warblers from eastern Siberia on their way to Africa!

PARTIAL MIGRANTS

Another group of birds which give us some insight into the evolution of migration are the so-called partial migrants. These are species in which different populations, and indeed different individuals in the same population, show marked differences in migratory behaviour. In Finland the Robin is almost wholly migratory, whereas in England only a few migrate, and in Spain they are all resident. The tendency to migrate is related to the harshness of the winter: the more difficult it is to survive the winter on the breeding ground, the

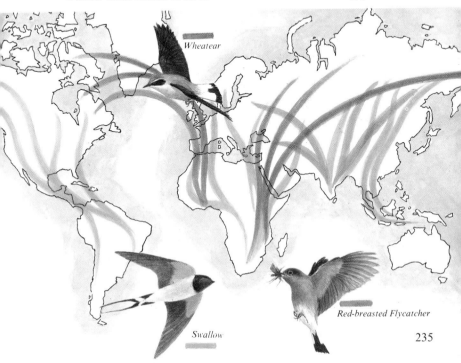

Wheatear

Red-breasted Flycatcher

Swallow

235

more advantage there is in being a migrant.

In another partial migrant, the Chaffinch, the individuals of the same population differ in their tendency to migrate. In Scandinavia the migratory tendency seems to be related to the severity of past winters. After a series of hard winters, most of the Chaffinches migrate in winter whereas after a series of mild winters a much higher proportion spend the winter on the breeding ground. What happens is that, in these northern areas, the balance between the advantages of staying put and of migrating is fairly even. During a severe winter the migrants survive better than the residents, whereas in mild winters the advantage lies with the residents. The individual birds are not making a choice; rather, when there is a severe winter, those with the migratory tendency survive better and so leave more offspring (which inherit the same tendency to be migrants), whereas in a mild winter the residents survive better and leave more offspring.

In the Blackbird, another partial migrant, females are more likely to migrate than males, and juveniles more likely to migrate than older birds. This is the opposite of the peck-order noted in birds feeding in winter (p. 231). Since males are more likely to survive on the breeding grounds than females, and adults than juveniles, the old and the males stand to gain less by migrating than the young

Many Robins, which have bred in mainland Europe, arrive on Britain's east coast in the Autumn.

and the females. Hence the pattern noted is in keeping with the relative chances of surviving on the breeding grounds. In Germany it has been shown that the tendency to migrate or stay is inherited. Because the advantage of staying versus migrating varies markedly between years, the population of Blackbirds can swing from being mainly migratory to being mainly resident over a few years, depending on the harshness of the winters.

These studies show that the migratory habits of some species may vary over even a short span of years. If conditions change permanently, the habits may also change permanently. One species where this appears to have happened is the Hooded Crow. In the early part of this century, many of them used to migrate southwards in western Europe, coming down as far as the southern end of the North Sea. Nowadays, such sightings are extremely rare. It seems that the migratory habit has become less, possibly because feeding conditions (such as the spread of rubbish-tips) have improved.

MIGRATORY SPECIES AND ROUTES

It is difficult to generalise about those European birds which are migrants. Most insect-eating groups, such as the warblers and swallows, leave Europe for the winter (though Dartford and Fan-tailed Warblers and Crag Martins are largely sedentary). Other groups which are mainly sedentary contain migrants. For example, the Quail, Turtle Dove, Scops Owl and Wryneck go to Africa for the winter, while the other gamebirds, doves, owls and woodpeckers are mostly non-migratory. Most pipits and wagtails stay in Europe; but Red-throated and Tree Pipits and Yellow Wagtails are long-distance migrants. Most of the rails, which one thinks of as skulking and weak fliers, are in fact long-distance migrants. Although some Baillon's, Little and Spotted Crakes winter in the Mediterranean areas of Europe, most go to Africa

Migratory behaviour may differ between species in the same family; in much of Western Europe, Water Rail and Great Spotted Woodpecker are highly sedentary, while the respective close relations, Spotted Crake and Wryneck, are long-distance migrants.

for the winter; as do all the Corncrakes.

Three other members of the rail family, Water Rail, Coot and Moorhen provide another reason why it is difficult to generalise about the migrants. These three species are largely resident over much of southern and western Europe, but are strongly migrant in the northern, colder areas.

ECOLOGY OF MIGRANTS

Most of the major migrants fall into one of two categories. One contains species in which almost all individuals leave Europe for the winter. Although a few of these species go to India and south-east Asia (e.g. Red-breasted Flycatcher, Arctic Warbler, Greenish Warbler), most go to Africa. Some 600 species of land-birds breed in Europe and Asia, and about 40% of them leave the area completely for the winter (though a few stragglers may stay behind in some cases).

The second category consists of a large number of species which migrate into Europe for the winter, or migrate within Europe. Many migrate particularly to western Europe (North Sea, British Isles, Western France); these areas are much milder than central and northern Europe in winter, thanks to the Gulf Stream, so it is easier both to survive (less food is needed at higher temperatures – p. 224) and to find food (the land is

less likely to be frozen or covered with snow). It is for this reason that one finds that the northern populations of Coot and Moorhen migrate, but the southern ones do not. Similarly, Grey Heron, Mute Swan and Kingfisher are largely resident over much of their range, but tend to leave the northern areas which freeze over during the winter.

Although there is overlap, there are some ecological differences between these two groups of birds. Those that go to Africa include almost all the true insectivores (swallows, swifts, flycatchers, wheatears) and most of those that rely largely on insects (warblers). Most of those that come into Europe for the winter are ducks, geese and waders from the far north or a long way east in Russia. These birds feed mainly on grass or other vegetable material or invertebrates along the shore or in fields; the last group includes Lapwings, Starlings and even Blackbirds from further east in Europe. These benefit greatly from the lack of snow cover; ground, shore and water are only infrequently frozen over in the west of Europe compared with the east. Equally, many of the birds that live near to or on fresh water migrate for the winter to salt water or coastal habitats which are much less likely to freeze over. Such species include the divers, grebes and many of the arctic waders.

MIGRATORY ROUTES

There are almost as many migratory routes as there are migratory species. In most cases, especially where the birds are night migrants, there are no specific routes on which the birds are concentrated. Most warblers, for example, migrate on a broad front, spread out over wide areas of Europe. The same is probably true for many of the diurnal migrants; they do not concentrate in flight lines. Seabirds and sea-ducks often try to keep out over the water, but may become concentrated as they pass over headlands. Many of the soaring birds concentrate at the short sea crossings (p. 41); but after that they spread out on much wider fronts.

There are differences in the directions flown by different species. For example Garden Warblers and Nightingales tend to go south-west from much of western Europe, entering Africa via Iberia, whereas the Lesser Whitethroat and the Marsh Warbler tend to go south-eastwards, flying across the eastern end of the Mediterranean, or even round it, and thence southwards into East Africa. Both these routes possibly give the birds better opportunities of stopping to refuel, and involve shorter distances across sea or inhospitable land than if they took the most direct route.

In most cases, all the individuals of a species go in a specific direction, such as south to Africa; but in some species different populations may take different routes. The White Storks from western Europe fly south-west and cross the Mediterranean at the Straits of Gibraltar, whereas those from eastern Europe fly south-eastwards and leave Europe across the Bosphorus. Similarly, the Blackcaps which breed in western Europe tend to migrate south-westwards while those that breed in eastern Europe go south-eastwards.

Some species have no true migratory routes, but nevertheless manage to move to much milder areas for the winter. These are those species that live high in the mountains in summer.

such as the Alpine Chough, Alpine Accentor and Snow Finch. The individuals make only short migrations, moving down mountains from their summer quarters at high altitudes to lower altitudes for the winter; they do not go in any particular direction.

Some seabirds, such as the Puffin, Fulmar and Kittiwake, disperse over wide areas of sea during the non-breeding season. Many European Puffins fish on the Grand Banks off Nova Scotia. Shag, Cormorant, Guillemot and Razorbill seem to stay in inshore waters, merely moving southwards down the European coast. Other species go further south, some Storm Petrels as far as the southern tip of South Africa. The Arctic Terns which breed in north-east Canada cross over the Atlantic by way of

The Spotted Flycatcher which breeds in an English garden and leaves in the Autumn for Southern Africa encounters two summers' food supplies each year.

Lesser Whitethroat
green

Garden Warbler
salmon pink

Blackcap
purple

Some migratory routes in autumn

White Stork
blue

Greenland, and head southwards down the European and west African coasts.

Some species use different routes in spring and autumn. The Sand Martin tends to fly south-westwards in western Europe in the autumn and take a route similar to that of the Garden Warbler, going round the western edge of the Sahara. However, in spring many of them fly more directly northwards on a route which takes them across the centre of the Sahara. In autumn the White-fronted Goose, after breeding in northern Russia, flies to western Europe by a fairly direct route through Sweden and Germany. In spring, however, they take a more easterly route as far as about the longitude of Moscow, and then turn north and head up to their breeding grounds. In this way they encounter warmer climates along much more of their route than they would if they went through the southern Baltic.

One of the most extraordinary routes used by any European bird is that taken by the Eleonora's Falcon. This species breeds mainly on islands in the Mediterranean (p. 246) and most birds seem to spend the northern winter in Madagascar. Apparently, in autumn, most birds fly eastwards along the Mediterranean, then down the Red Sea and the East African coast.

ODD MIGRATIONS

Some birds make odd seasonal movements which are hard to define as migration. For example, many tits and finches come into gardens from the woods in winter, moving only a few miles to do so. Are these migrants? In many cases they make the move each day returning to the wood to roost; these are more commuters than migrants.

Others change habitat in a more marked way. The Capercaillie lives in areas which are covered with thick snow for part of the winter. In summer it feeds on seeds and leaves on the forest floor. In winter these foods become buried under snow and the birds turn to eating pine-needles

239

from the tops of trees which are well above the snow. This switch may involve the birds in considerable local movements. In certain areas of Europe they migrate *northwards* in autumn from deciduous woods to the conifer forests.

Non-breeding White-fronted Geese migrate up to the breeding grounds with the breeding birds, then fly still further north to tap rich grazing which is available for too short a time for breeding to be possible there. By doing this they can make use of a food supply with little competition from the majority of other geese.

The ducks and geese become flightless during the moult (p. 221) and are therefore at particular risk then from predators. Most Shelduck in northwest Europe have a moult migration in late summer, flying to the Friesian islands off northern Germany to moult. These low-lying, sandy islands provide good offshore feeding in relative safety. After moulting, the birds slowly make their way back to their breeding grounds.

Although many birds which breed in north temperate areas migrate to the southern hemisphere for the winter, the reverse is not the case: no species which breeds in South Africa migrates north to spend the southern winter in Europe. One reason for this may be that there is virtually no land habitable for birds south of the Cape of Good Hope which at 35°S is the latitudinal equivalent in the southern hemisphere of the Mediterranean Sea in the north. Cold weather conditions and shortage of food do not therefore occur in the way that they regularly do in the north; so for land-birds there is not the same compulsion to migrate. However, this is not the case for seabirds – there are larger areas of sea in the south than in the north. Even so, few seabirds come into the high latitudes of the northern hemisphere for the southern winter. The Great and Sooty Shearwaters, which breed in the South Atlantic, are the only major exception, being quite common in the North Atlantic waters in late summer, straying as far north as Iceland.

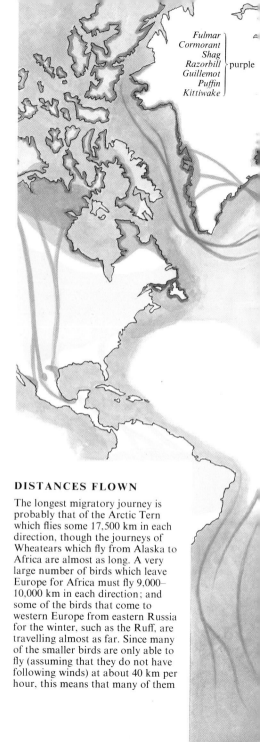

Fulmar
Cormorant
Shag
Razorbill ⎱ purple
Guillemot
Puffin
Kittiwake

DISTANCES FLOWN

The longest migratory journey is probably that of the Arctic Tern which flies some 17,500 km in each direction, though the journeys of Wheatears which fly from Alaska to Africa are almost as long. A very large number of birds which leave Europe for Africa must fly 9,000–10,000 km in each direction; and some of the birds that come to western Europe from eastern Russia for the winter, such as the Ruff, are travelling almost as far. Since many of the smaller birds are only able to fly (assuming that they do not have following winds) at about 40 km per hour, this means that many of them

White-fronted Goose
orange-brown

Sand Martin
yellow

Eleonora's Falcon
bright green

Arctic Tern
blue

are undertaking journeys involving them in about 200–250 hours of flying. In many cases they cannot stop whenever they want, since they may be over sea or other inhospitable country; they must be prepared to make some very long flights.

DISTANCES FLOWN IN A SINGLE FLIGHT

Most of the birds which cross the Mediterranean in autumn arrive in North Africa to find it almost at its driest. Almost certainly, for most of them, there is little chance of finding food, especially when one considers how very many birds are making the journey (p. 242). Although some species may stop and try to feed, for many there is no option but to fly on across the Sahara and into the Sahel zone before they reach a reasonable food supply. The distance across the Mediterranean can be as much as 1,000 km and it may be a further 1,500 km across North Africa. Many birds must cross this area of sea and desert in a single flight.

This may seem an enormous distance for a small bird to fly, but we know that some small birds can do it. One example concerns the Wheatears which breed in Greenland. Although in both spring and autumn some of these birds may touch down in Britain or other parts of western Europe on their journey, in autumn some fly south-eastwards from Greenland and make no landfall until they reach the north Spanish coast, a distance of some 3,000 km.

Since many of the smaller birds, such as the warblers, fly at only about 40 km per hour, such long distances pose great problems for them; they must expect to have to fly non-stop for perhaps 72 hours. At these speeds, even a light headwind may prove disastrous. For example, a 15 kph headwind would slow a warbler down to 25 kph and make a 2,500 km journey take 100 hours instead of 62; this might well mean death.

On the other hand, if the birds can judge it right, a tail-wind would make

241

life a great deal easier for them. We know very little about whether European birds are able to make use of favourable winds for these long flights, but one American species, the Blackpoll Warbler, which flies non-stop from the New England coast to northern South America, a flight of some 4,000 km or more, changes altitude several times on route apparently to take advantage of favourable winds; even with this help, it still takes over 100 hours to make the journey.

An example of the effects of wind can be seen in the Wheatear. Birds leaving Greenland in the autumn weigh about 40 grams. Those that make landfall in northern Britain weigh about 25–27 grams if they had a strong following wind, but only 21–23 grams if they had a light wind or a head-wind.

FAT RESERVES FOR MIGRATION

To be able to make these long flights, the migrant birds have to lay down fat reserves. Fat is a particularly good source of energy for a flying animal because it produces more energy per gram than do stores of protein or carbohydrate. In addition, as it is used up, one of its by-products is water; for a migrant which is on the wing for two or three days at high altitude, and without the opportunity to drink, this may be crucial.

The Sedge Warbler which weighs about 10–12 grams at normal times may take on this amount of fat, thereby doubling its weight, and enabling it to fly for as long as 115 hours. The Lesser Whitethroat normally weighs about 10 grams, but may weigh as much as 18 grams just prior to departure. The Sanderling and Knot, which normally weigh about 55 and 120 grams respectively, may double their weight just prior to their long flights to their arctic breeding grounds.

Even seabirds may lay down large fat reserves for migration. The young Manx Shearwater may fly from the nesting colony weighing considerably

more than its parents (p. 210). It relies on this store of fat to see it through the major part of its journey to South America.

In order to lay down these reserves, the birds must find a good feeding place; in ideal circumstances, they may be able to put on weight rapidly. Some Pied Flycatchers from northern Europe fatten up in Spain and Portugal for the long crossing of the Mediterranean and Sahara. They put on 0.25–0.3 grams of fat per day, taking some 4–5 weeks to acquire the necessary reserves. Sedge Warblers which fatten up in southern England may put on 0.5 grams per day.

The ability to find good areas for fattening up may influence the types of journeys which birds make. For example, the Sedge Warblers which fatten in southern England put on large amounts of fat which enable them to fly 4,000 km or more; even so, they probably need to set off with a following wind. During this flight they overfly southern Europe without stopping. Yet the closely-related Reed Warblers fly from England to Iberia where they fatten up before making the shorter journey across the Mediterranean and North Africa. The Great Reed Warbler puts on fat on its breeding grounds and migrates rapidly, taking only some 10–14 days to reach its wintering grounds. The Marsh Warbler, in contrast, sets off from Europe in August, but stops for some time in various areas, and eventually arrives on its wintering grounds (as far south as South Africa) in December or even January. It has just enough time to moult before setting off northwards again.

THE NUMBERS OF MIGRANTS

The scale of migration is sometimes difficult to comprehend. The number of birds which leave Europe and western Asia for Africa each year is very large indeed (and the figures given below do not include those birds that migrate into or within Europe). In many European countries bird censuses have been undertaken and these, coupled with measurements of the extent of the relevant habitats, can be used to obtain the approximate numbers of breeding pairs and their offspring. Rough estimates (in millions) for a number of common species in Europe are as follows: Willow Warbler 900, Sand Martin 375, Tree Pipit 260, Spotted Flycatcher 250, Swallow 220, Blackcap 200, Garden Warbler 200, Lesser Whitethroat 150, Wheatear 120, Redstart 120, Whitethroat 120, Ortolan Bunting 120, House Martin 90, Yellow Wagtail 70, Whinchat 45, Pied Flycatcher 30.

These 16 species alone account for 3,300 million migrants going into Africa. On top of these there are about another 50 species of songbirds which go to Africa in varying numbers. There are also the larger birds; perhaps 40 million birds of prey go to Africa for the winter. This figure is made up largely of falcons, but up to 1 million of the eastern race of the Buzzard also migrate to Africa, as do some 700,000 White Storks. Other smaller non-passerines may add up to perhaps another 200 million. Included in this last group is a very large number of Swifts, but no estimate of numbers has been made for this species.

In total, perhaps some 5,000 million birds migrate to Africa (excluding water-birds, waders and seabirds for which no estimates are available). On average this means that one bird from every five acres (2 ha) of Europe goes to Africa for the winter.

We can use these figures to get some idea of the scale of migration into Africa. The birds migrate across a front of some 2,500 miles from the western tip of Portugal to the eastern side of Turkey. 5,000 million birds equals, on average, 2 million birds per mile of coastline each autumn. The main migration period lasts about six weeks, therefore some 50,000 birds cross *each mile* of coast *each night*. These figures are, of course, averages and at certain places at certain times the numbers will be very considerably higher. The numbers returning in the spring will be much lower after winter mortality, possibly about a half.

Birds of prey in a flock gaining height over the Rock of Gibraltar prior to migrating across the mouth of the Mediterranean.

243

THE HAZARDS OF BREEDING

Breeding may arguably be thought of as the only part of a bird's life that really matters, for without breeding no offspring is left to produce future generations; the line dies out. All aspects of life – feeding, roosting, migration, moult, etc. – are but attributes by which the bird may survive long enough to breed again. If this is really the case, then why, one might ask, do birds not breed all the time? The answer is quite simple: breeding is both difficult and dangerous. If, as is usually the case in temperate regions, it is difficult to breed at many times of year, it is better for the bird to put its efforts into surviving to the next period of the year when it has a reasonable chance of breeding successfully. The biologist tends to refer to these conflicting forces as the costs and benefits of breeding (p. 247). There are many costs, the main one being that the bird may endanger its own life either through food shortage or by putting itself at risk from predators.

At some stage in the young bird's life, older individuals of the species prepare to breed again. The young bird will have to decide whether or not to join them. What influences this decision?

The female Grey Partridge lays the largest clutch of any European bird.

THE FOOD REQUIRED FOR BREEDING

Part of the answer lies in the fact that breeding requires the bird to collect a great deal more food than it needs if it is only fending for itself. Young birds are often less skilled at finding food than older ones and may therefore find this difficult. Not only do they have to find more food, but their nesting duties often mean that they have less time to look for it, though most European birds have their young in the nest when the days are nearly at their longest and there is more time for feeding.

The time for feeding is curtailed in a number of ways. The males spend a lot of time singing to attract mates or defend their territories. The females, and in many species also the males, must spend much time incubating the eggs and brooding the young. All these duties take time which the parent birds cannot therefore spend in their search for food.

The amount of energy required for breeding is considerable. The weight of a clutch of eggs is often very large in comparison with the weight of the female. A range of weights of eggs, clutches and female birds is shown in the table on the right. In some species, the females produce about their own body-weight of eggs or even more. Since it takes about 4–5 days to form an egg (more in larger birds), and eggs are usually laid daily, this means that the material required for egg formation must usually be obtained in about 10 to 20 days. The Grey Partridge, whose clutch is the largest of any British species (the Red-legged Partridge probably lays even more eggs, though not in a single clutch, p. 283), takes a little longer still.

244

EGG AND BODY WEIGHTS OF SELECTED SPECIES

Weights in grams

Species	Weight of one egg	Average clutch size	Weight of clutch	Weight of female	Clutch as % of female's weight
Blue Tit	1·3	11	14·3	11	130·0
Dunlin	10	4	40	50	80·0
Tufted Duck	53	10	530	700	75·7
Robin	2·4	5	12	18	67·0
Moorhen	25	7	175	300	58·3
Mallard	51	11	561	1,000	56·1
Kingfisher	4·2	6	25·2	45	56·0
Meadow Pipit	2·1	5	10·5	19·5	54·0
Grey Partridge	14·5	14	203	400	50·7
Whitethroat	1·8	4	7·6	16	47·5
Chaffinch	2·5	4	10	22	45·5
Starling	7·2	5	36	80	45·0
Kestrel	20	5	100	250	40·0
Little Grebe	14	5	70	187	37·0
Blackbird	7·2	4	28·8	90	32·0
Herring Gull	90	3	270	850	31·8
Oystercatcher	47	3	141	525	26·9
Tawny Owl	40	3	120	500	24·0
Swift	3·6	3	10·8	45	24·0
Mute Swan	345	6	2,070	9,600	21·6
Nightjar	8·2	2	16·4	85	19·3
Grey Heron	60	4	240	1,500	16·0
Fulmar	101	1	101	800	12·6
Guillemot	108	1	108	1,000	10·8
Woodpigeon	18·5	2	37	490	7·6
Griffon Vulture	252	1	252	9,500	2·6

There are problems associated with getting so much extra food. It may well not be easily available. One possible way of getting it would be to store it up in its tissues gradually over a long period. In practice, most small British birds do not do this; one reason why they do not do so may be that it imposes weight problems for the bird (p. 43). For example, a female Blue Tit may weigh about 15 grams while it is laying eggs, as opposed to about 10 grams at most times of the year; this weight includes the weight of one egg, plus a small amount for the eggs to be laid on subsequent days, but not the reserves for all the other eggs: this would increase the bird's weight still further (p. 34).

Obtaining the food necessary for egg-formation is only one of the problems facing the laying female. Not only does she have to collect this extra food, but the time which she has available for hunting for it is restricted. She must take time off to build the nest; this may occupy many hours a day for several days. On top

of this many females have to hunt for calcium-rich objects so as to obtain the calcium required for the egg-shells. Many collect snail shells for this purpose; Dunlin on their arctic breeding grounds are known to eat lemming bones. On top of all this, the female herself needs more energy in order to be able to fly since she is much heavier than at other times. The female Common Tern weighs up to about 180 grams when she starts egg-laying, as opposed to about 125 grams when she has finished. The difference in weight indicates that the problems faced by a laying female may be severe. For example, a female Purple Sandpiper walks awkwardly while carrying well-developed eggs; she is probably more easily caught by a predator at this stage. There may also be a danger that a female with a fully-formed egg within her may break it if she is very active; this might be a particular hazard for birds like terns, which plunge-dive into water for their food.

The female Common Tern, and the female of some other species, has solved this problem, at least to some extent, by having her mate provide her with food. Often referred to as 'courtship feeding', the feeding of the female by her mate occurs in most species long after pair-formation, mainly just prior to and during egg-laying, though often also during incubation in species where the female alone incubates. The female Common Tern gives up hunting completely during the egg-laying period, and is wholly dependent on the male for

A female Purple Sandpiper cut-away to show the space occupied by its egg

A drake Shelduck guards a feeding duck; a male Common Tern presents a fish to its mate in courtship.

food. In many small passerines, the females themselves continue feeding and the males bring them *extra* food. In the Pied Flycatcher the male brings about 40% of the female's diet, which is approximately equal to the increase in her needs, so that she has only to continue to collect food at the normal rate.

In a number of species the males may help the female less directly. In many ducks and geese, the male guards the female very assiduously, making sure she is not disturbed and so allowing her to feed uninterruptedly. In the Shelduck for example, a female so guarded feeds about 80 to 90% of the time, relying on her mate to chase other Shelducks away and keep an eye open for predators. In the Manx Shearwater, and probably some other seabirds, the male's help is even more indirect. After mating, the male stays at home, making nightly visits to the pair's chosen burrow – apparently to ensure that it is not taken over by another pair. The female goes off on her own to rich feeding grounds where she spends about two weeks feeding up. She then returns to the nest, lays her large single egg, about 16% of her body weight, and once more goes off to sea to feed up, leaving the male to undertake the first incubation stint. Similarly, the female Fulmar goes away for about three weeks while forming the egg; the male also goes, but only for a week or so, and he is back at the nest ready to undertake the first incubation stint when she returns.

THE DANGERS OF BREEDING

The act of breeding is dangerous in a number of ways; it ties a bird to a particular site (the nest and eggs or young) with a regularity of behaviour that may make it easier for a predator to catch. A singing or displaying male gives away his position to predators at the same time as advertizing himself to potential mates; similarly, the bird that is incubating the eggs or brooding the young may be at high risk from predators in a way that it is not at other times of year. There are not very many quantitative measures of the mortality at different times of year, but Sparrowhawks may take about 15% of the local adult Great Tits during the tits' breeding season; the loss from this cause alone is greater than the death rates at other times of year, without even taking

The song from the male is an essential part of the breeding process for a Great Tit; but it can attract the attention of predators!

into account any other forms of mortality during the breeding season. Many of the longer-lived seabirds seem to suffer as high or higher mortality during the breeding season as when they are out on the high seas for the rest of the year.

Breeding birds are not just at higher risk from predators. As we shall see, successful breeding requires that the parent birds find a lot of extra food. The food which they bring to their young may be food which they would otherwise have eaten themselves. As a result, they sometimes run themselves so low in food reserves that they may die. They may also have to delay migration or moult, or forego opportunities to build up enough fat reserves for periods of food shortage; any of these may bring about their deaths.

THE COSTS AND BENEFITS OF BREEDING

If a bird is to maximise the number of young which it produces in its life, it must try to breed as many times as possible. On each occasion it should weigh the benefits against the costs. It is no good trying to breed if there is little or no chance of raising young

or of the young surviving after they have left the nest. Birds should only breed when the probability is that the number of offspring which themselves survive to breed will exceed the number of parent birds that die as a result of the risks of breeding. Of course, no bird consciously weighs all these probabilities, but many aspects of breeding have evolved in such a way that, on balance, the benefits of breeding (in terms of the number of young which should survive to breed) outweigh the costs (the reduction in the survival chances of the adults).

It is important also to realise that the amount of risk that birds should take will be assessed – by natural selection – in relation to the gain. If the act of breeding involves the bird in only a small risk, then it may pay it to try to breed even though the chance of success is small, whereas it will not be worth trying to breed if the chances of success are small *and* the risks are great. The probability that the parent will survive to breed again is another variable. A small bird such as a Blue Tit has less than a 50:50 chance of surviving to the next breeding season. Therefore it should not desert its nest too easily: there is rather little chance of it breeding again and so, if it is threatened, it may have to accept the risk. In contrast, a large bird of prey or a large seabird has a very high chance of surviving to breed for many more years; it should not risk much to save a single brood.

The timing of breeding, the number of eggs laid and the number of broods in a season are all things that have been influenced by natural selection in this manner, and we shall see how these have influenced the breeding biology of the birds (pp. 248, 250, 270). Although there are as yet few studies, it has been shown for a number of species that the laying dates and the clutch sizes of female birds are characteristics which are inherited from their parents and thus open to evolution in the ways that we have been talking about.

BREEDING SEASON

THE TIMING OF BREEDING: FOOD SUPPLIES

Birds can only breed when food is plentiful. The breeding seasons of all birds seem to be closely tied to the availability of their main food supplies: they breed at that time of year when that food is most plentiful. Even more precisely, birds probably try to time their breeding so they actually have their young in the nest, or possibly just fledged, when food suitable for them is at its most plentiful. This is obviously a good strategy, since it enables the parents to find food for their young most easily, or the inexperienced young themselves to learn to forage when there is plenty of food about.

However, for many birds there are complications about breeding at such a time: the breeding parents, especially the female, *also* require a plentiful supply of food *for themselves* in order to be able to breed at all. If, however, their young are to be in the nest when food is most plentiful, the parents must start to breed considerably earlier, when food is *not* so plentiful. In the case of most small birds, such as the Chaffinch, it takes about four days to form an egg, a further four days to lay a clutch of five eggs at daily intervals, and 12–13 days of incubation to hatch them. So a period of about three weeks must elapse between the time at which the female Chaffinch starts to form her eggs and the moment when the chicks hatch. In

SOME AVERAGE INCUBATION PERIODS

Eggs may take longer to hatch if they are not properly incubated for some of the time.

Species	Incubation period in days
Lammergeier	55
Griffon Vulture	52
Fulmar	52
Mute Swan	35
White Stork	33
Red-throated Diver	28
Greater Flamingo	28
Gannet	28
Kestrel	28
Mallard	27
Herring Gull	25
Oystercatcher	24
Moorhen	21
Raven	21
Swift	19
Kingfisher	19
Woodpigeon	17
Great Spotted Woodpecker	15
Robin	13
House Sparrow	13
Blackbird	13
Reed Warbler	12
Skylark	11

fact, this is an underestimate of the time required, since the ovaries and associated organs must grow from their winter resting state (p. 34) to full size before egg-formation can begin. The time which this takes is not known, but is unlikely to be less than a week or two; in practice they seem to grow, slowly, over a much longer period.

This minimum period of 4–5 weeks is probably typical of many of the smaller European birds, though some

A flock of Pink-footed Geese graze on stubble in Scotland in winter.

such as the tits take up to ten days or so to lay their larger clutches. In many of the larger birds the interval between starting to get into breeding condition and having young in the nest will be considerably longer than this, since most of them have much longer incubation periods than the Chaffinch; the longest for any European breeding bird is probably that of the Lammergeier which takes about 8 weeks to hatch its eggs.

So the female must get into breeding condition and lay her eggs at a time of year when food is *not* at its most plentiful. For some species, such as the Great Tit, there is evidence that the bird may not find it easy to do this. In this and other species the individuals which breed earliest raise the largest numbers of young; those that breed later raise fewer. It is difficult to escape the conclusion that all the birds which breed later would have raised more young had they bred earlier. If this is true, why did they not do so? The answer seems to be that they were not able to get into breeding condition any earlier. Are the very earliest breeders laying at the best time, or would they breed even earlier if they could? Again we do not know, but in a few experiments where wild birds have been provided with plentiful food just before the breeding season, the birds nested earlier than others who were not provided with extra food. This strongly suggests that the date of laying is – at least sometimes – influenced by the food supply for the parents.

Migrant species may be able to 'cheat' by feeding up in an area on the way to their breeding grounds, and arriving with the reserves necessary for breeding. Some of the geese which breed in the high Arctic are known to do this. The Snow, Brent, Barnacle and Pink-footed Geese feed up on the way to their breeding grounds, the last three partly in Scotland as well as in other parts of Europe. They arrive on their breeding grounds weighing up to 20% above their normal weight. Their breeding grounds are usually almost completely snow-covered at this time. As soon as the thaw begins, the birds build a nest and lay their eggs. Their body reserves are sufficient for them to complete their clutch and incubate their eggs without the need to feed much. If all goes well, the spring growth of grass starts at about the time the goslings hatch.

It is unlikely, however, that most of our migrant birds put on reserves in this way. As we have seen, they increase weight very considerably prior to breeding; yet, unlike the geese, this is insufficient for the full clutch. In addition, the birds have to lay down large quantities of fat for migration (p. 242); the amount required in some smaller species is so great that they probably could not also store enough reserves to last them through the early part of the breeding season as well. (Their small size means that they require relatively more reserves than birds as large as geese.)

Even in the same area, breeding may start at different times in different years. We talk of early and late springs; early springs are ones that are unusually warm and in which food becomes plentiful sooner than in late springs. The breeding seasons of many birds reflect the earliness or lateness of the spring: in some species the birds may breed as much

Pink-footed Geese on their nests in Iceland in the summer breeding season

as a month later in a cold spring than in a warm one.

The spring temperature may affect the timing of laying in other ways too. In the Arctic, waders must wait until the snow has thawed off large areas of tundra before they can nest successfully. Although they can lay eggs on the first tiny patches of cleared ground, their nests are then so easily found by predators that it is not worth trying. Similarly, many Eiders and other birds nesting on small offshore islands are safe from predation by Arctic Foxes only after the ice has thawed and removed their access. So these birds should wait for the ice to break up before they start to nest.

LENGTH OF BREEDING SEASON

The length of the breeding season is highly variable. The number of broods normally raised by each species is given in the Directory (pp. 61–203). Many species are single brooded and, in these, most individuals breed at roughly the same time of year, though there may well be a span of a month or more between the earliest and the latest breeders. The spread of time may be larger still when a bird loses its clutch and replaces it with another one. However, birds become progressively less and less likely to replace their clutch the later in the season that it is lost. Indeed, some such as the shearwaters and petrels scarcely ever lay a replacement clutch, even if they lose the eggs immediately after laying.

Almost all the non-passerines are single brooded. In the main they are larger than the passerines and take longer over their breeding; so there is less opportunity for them to have a second brood. Time is too short. For example, for both the Osprey and the Crane there are over three months from the start of laying to the moment at which the chicks start to fly, and even then the parents continue to care for the flying young for some time; there is simply no time for a second brood.

Among those non-passerines that regularly have second and even third broods are the Little Grebe, several crakes and rails including both Moorhen and Coot, and the Kingfisher. Most doves and pigeons have two or more broods in a season; indeed, feral pigeons may make five or more breeding attempts in a year, perhaps because they have access to a rich food supply around most of the year, from man's waste in urban areas, or because they are fed carefully by their owners. Some Nightjars also have a second brood.

Many more passerines than non-passerines have second broods. Among those which do not are the largest – the crows. But some such as House Sparrows and Blackbirds may exceptionally even manage to raise four or five broods in a single season.

FACTORS AFFECTING THE NUMBER OF BROODS

One of the main factors affecting the number of broods raised is the latitude at which breeding takes place. There is much more scope for prolonged breeding at southern than at northern latitudes; in the latter it is often a race against time to raise a single brood, let alone attempt a second one. The same species may have different numbers of broods at different latitudes; the Ringed Plover, as one of the non-passerines which frequently raises two and sometimes even three broods, only does this in southern Europe; in the arctic it has only a single brood.

The food supply must be particularly favourable for prolonged breeding. For example, the Blackbird is dependent on soft ground if it is to be able to get at its main food supply – worms. Frost in spring, or drought in summer, means hard ground and difficult feeding. As a result, Blackbirds tend to start breeding early in mild springs rather than cold ones and go on breeding later into the summer in damp summers as opposed to hot, dry ones; the number of broods which it attempts is closely related to the weather since this affects the food supply.

Two species of owls, Barn and Short-eared, may have second broods if small mammals, such as voles, are unusually plentiful. The Tawny Owl also varies the number of broods it has in relation to the abundance of small mammals. But this owl normally only has a single brood; in years when the small mammals are very scarce, it may not breed at all.

THE BREEDING SEASONS OF INDIVIDUAL SPECIES

The breeding seasons of most European species are well-documented and, in general, correlate well with what was suggested above, namely that birds tend to have their young in the nest at that time of year when food is most plentiful.

The timing of the breeding season obviously varies with latitude since spring comes much earlier to southern Europe than it does to the northern areas. For example the Yellow Wagtail may start laying in early March in southern Spain when in the northern part of its range, in Fenno-Scandia, the ground is still thickly covered with snow; breeding at this latitude does not start until early June. Interestingly, the wagtails which breed in these different areas spend the winter together in Africa. Because they belong to different subspecies which can be distinguished in the field (p. 60), we can see that those birds which breed in southern Spain set off from Africa on their spring migration several weeks before those which breed in Scandinavia, for whom arriving on the breeding grounds at such an early date would be disastrous.

It is more important that the food be easily available than necessarily at its most abundant; it is the speed with which the parents can collect it which matters more than how many prey are present. For example, the Grey Heron starts to breed quite early in the year, often in March or

Different subspecies of the Yellow Wagtail start breeding at different times in the year, depending on the latitude of their breeding-grounds.

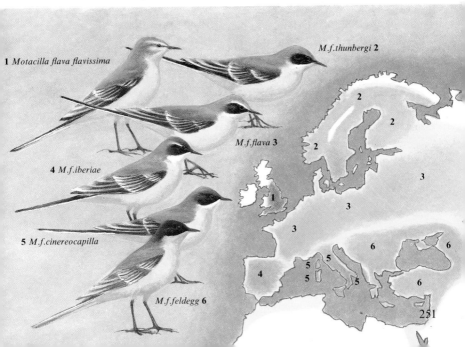

1 *Motacilla flava flavissima*

M.f.thunbergi 2

M.f.flava 3

4 *M.f.iberiae*

5 *M.f.cinereocapilla*

M.f.feldegg 6

251

even February. As a result, they may have their young in the nest by late April. The advantage of such early breeding is probably not that prey is more abundant then than later on, but that the aquatic vegetation has not yet grown up and their prey is much more easily visible. Similarly, the Tawny Owl is an early nester. It feeds mainly on voles and mice; although these are more abundant later in the year, by then the ground vegetation is much thicker and the prey much more difficult to catch.

The breeding seasons of many woodland species fit well with the suggestion that they are broadly timed to coincide with the period when food is most abundant for the growing young. For example in woodland the Blackbird, which feeds the young of its first brood primarily on worms from the soft soil, lays first; the tits and Robin, which feed their young primarily on caterpillars, lay next; the birds that feed their young on flying insects, the fly-catchers (and outside woodland the swallows and martins), lay later. This is the order in which the specific foods are most abundant; worms are most easily collected before the soil starts to dry out and the larval stages of insects appear before the flying stages. The Redstart is of interest since the female collects caterpillars while the male takes mainly flying insects; Redstarts lay a little later than Robins, but before the fly-catchers.

The small birds of prey exhibit an interesting array of breeding seasons. The Kestrel, which feeds on small mammals, lays first; like the Tawny Owl, it has its young in the nest before the grass has grown long and the voles and mice have become difficult to find. The Sparrowhawk lays later; it has its young in the nest when the young of small woodland birds, the tits and warblers, are on the wing. The Hobby and the Red-footed Falcon feed primarily on young swallows and martins and also take many large insects such as dragonflies; they are the last to nest since their main food is available

later. One of the most fascinating of the small birds of prey is the Eleonora's Falcon. This Mediterranean species does not lay its eggs until just after mid-summer; these hatch just as the first of the huge numbers of small migrant birds start to pass through the Mediterranean on their way *back* to their African winter quarters. Having young in the nest in the autumn migration rather than the spring has a number of advantages; spring migration is faster and spans a shorter period than autumn – birds are in a hurry to get to their breeding grounds – and fewer birds pass through because many have perished in their winter quarters. In contrast, the autumn migration includes large numbers of naïve juveniles on their first migration.

The finches show the greatest range of breeding seasons. The Chaffinch and the Brambling feed their young primarily on insects and their breeding seasons are similar to those of the other woodland insect eaters such as the tits. Others, however, feed their young mainly on seeds. Some of these, like the Linnet, Bullfinch and Greenfinch, have extended breeding seasons, changing their diet from one type of seed to another as the season progresses. The Goldfinch, which feeds its young mainly on the seeds of thistles is the last to breed; indeed it is probably the latest of all European species to breed.

One other group of finches, the crossbills, have very distinctive breeding seasons. Although each different species tends to prefer the seeds from one particular type of conifer, they may take those of other conifers if these are particularly abundant. The easiest time for the crossbills to get the seeds is when they are ripening and the cones just beginning to open. This happens at different times of year for the different species of conifer; spruce tend to open from late autumn through to spring, and pines during spring and early summer. As a result the Common Crossbill, whose preferred diet in Britain is pine seeds (but which will also take those of spruce), has a very

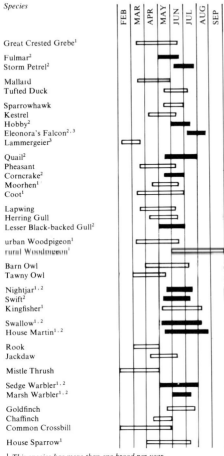

MAIN EGG-LAYING PERIODS OF SELECTED SPECIES
FOR MID-LATITUDE EUROPE

Species

	FEB	MAR	APR	MAY	JUN	JUL	AUG	SEP

Great Crested Grebe[1]

Fulmar[2]
Storm Petrel[2]

Mallard
Tufted Duck

Sparrowhawk
Kestrel
Hobby[2]
Eleonora's Falcon[2, 3]
Lammergeier[3]

Quail[2]
Pheasant
Corncrake[2]
Moorhen[1]
Coot[1]

Lapwing
Herring Gull
Lesser Black-backed Gull[2]

urban Woodpigeon[1]
rural Woodpigeon[1]

Barn Owl
Tawny Owl

Nightjar[1, 2]
Swift[2]
Kingfisher[1]

Swallow[1, 2]
House Martin[1, 2]

Rook
Jackdaw

Mistle Thrush

Sedge Warbler[1, 2]
Marsh Warbler[1, 2]

Goldfinch
Chaffinch
Common Crossbill

House Sparrow[1]

[1] *This species has more than one brood per year.*
[2] *This species is a migrant.*
[3] *Mediterranean (not mid-latitude Europe).*

variable breeding season. It most frequently inhabits areas of pine, and there it may start breeding very early in the year. It has been recorded incubating when the air temperature was down to −20°C! Occasionally, when both spruce and pine produce heavy seed crops consecutively in the same area, Common Crossbills may start nesting in the early autumn, and

have a series of broods right through to the following summer, perhaps breeding for ten consecutive months. Likewise, the Two-barred Crossbill, whose preferred diet is larch (which produces its seeds in late summer), also has a very varied breeding season, and has often been recorded breeding in autumn.

MOVEMENT BETWEEN BROODS

Most species that raise more than one brood raise the subsequent broods in the same territory as the first; indeed, some species use the same nest. However, some finches undertake local movements in between broods. For example, the proportion of Linnets nesting in gorse areas declines as the season progresses, and the proportion nesting in deciduous shrubs goes up. Similarly, in north Europe Goldfinches first nest in conifers in woodland, but later move into gardens and orchards. These movements are probably associated with changes in the areas where seeds are most abundant.

In one or two species, individual birds may raise young in two very different areas, involving much longer movements between breeding attempts. The Quail breeds in north Africa in April and, having raised its young, disappears from there in May when its habitat is starting to dry up. At about this time Quail arrive in Britain and other parts of north-central Europe, and breed there. It seems not at all unlikely that these may include the individuals which have bred in north Africa earlier. Similarly, when Redpolls disappear after breeding in central Europe, Redpolls arrive at about the same time in northern Scandinavia and start to breed. The theory that these are the very same birds is supported by the fact that some of them arrive accompanied by young, presumably the offspring from their previous nesting.

TERRITORIES, SONG AND MATING

A Golden Eagle soars over its large territory.

TERRITORIES

Once a male bird is ready to breed, it must find a place to do so – a territory. The purpose of territories varies so much between species that it is difficult to define them simply. They are, however, all fairly vigor-

Brünnich's Guillemots on nesting cliff

ously defended and some people have therefore just defined a territory as any defended area. Most territories are associated with breeding. But a few birds establish territories, briefly, on migration, and others do so in winter quarters (p. 256); and some birds may defend other areas for other purposes.

Territories vary from tiny spaces just around the bird (in the case of a Guillemot) to areas of many square miles (for a pair of Golden or Short-toed Eagles). Even birds living in the same habitat and with roughly similar feeding habits may differ in the type of areas that they defend. A Chaffinch may defend one or two acres of woodland containing any number of possible nesting sites whereas a Pied Flycatcher selects a suitable nesting hole and defends that vigorously, but does not defend a large area around it.

In most species, if the individual fails to establish a territory, it will not be able to breed. If a bird fails to obtain a territory, why doesn't it breed without one?

THE FUNCTION OF A TERRITORY

Three main explanations of the importance of having a territory have been put forward. It is a place where the pair can mate and live without interference; it is an area where the pair can get food for their brood without competition from others of their kind; territories lower the nesting density and this reduces the dangers from predators.

The suggestion that a territory is necessary for pair-formation is probably true for some species, but cannot be for others. For example, in a number of ducks and geese, the pair may be formed in the winter quarters and the pair fly to their breeding ground together, already paired; a pair of Goldeneye returns to where the female was raised and not, as one might expect (since in most species the male selects the territory), to where the male was raised. Other species, such as Wood-chat Shrikes, also tend to arrive on the breeding grounds already paired. In these cases, it may be important for the male to maintain a territory in order to prevent rival males from coming and mating with his female.

The suggestion that the territory is established to secure a food supply for the family also does not seem very likely. In many species the parents do not make use of the whole area of their territory when they are feeding young; indeed, in most, territorial behaviour *breaks down* when the young are being fed; the parents are just too busy to defend the area. A more serious objection to this explanation is that most seabirds, and a few other species also, do not feed in their territories! For example, the Gannet cannot feed on its tiny patch of rock; and the same goes for almost all seabirds, even though many of them defend much larger territories than the Gannet. Some Great Black-backed Gulls do defend large territories and get at least some of their food (such as other seabirds and rabbits) from within it; but territories of this size are exceptional in seabirds. (And in these cases, territories are still important in enabling the pair to find each other and hence enabling them to maintain the pair-bond.)

The suggestion that by restricting the breeding density the birds may reduce the chances of losing their nest to predators may have some merit. When woodland birds nest at particularly high densities, they increase the risk from predation. What seems to happen is that a predator may start to hunt in a particular way or to look in particular places; if there is a nest there and it finds it, it will start to look even harder in such places. If it finds other nests in the same sort of place, it will be rewarded again and will look harder still in such places. However, if it looks in those kinds of places on a number of occasions and fails to find another nest, it will be more likely to give up and try elsewhere. Since it will start hunting again near the first nest it found, it follows that the nearer nests are to each other the greater the risk of them being found. It is therefore in the individual's interests to try to keep others of its species as far away as

A Great Black-headed Gull predates a breeding colony of Arctic Terns.

After the female has visited the lek for mating, the male Capercaillie takes no part in the nesting activity.

possible; it is of no concern to that individual if this means that other individuals cannot obtain territories. That this theory is probably sound is evidenced by studies of tits in woodland and of nesting Mallard and Tufted Duck: the nests were safer from predators the farther they were situated from the adjacent nest.

But this explanation cannot be true for all species: it does not hold good for the Guillemot with its tiny cliffledge territories; nor does it explain the territories of species such as Blackcock and Ruff whose males defend tiny areas at a communal display ground called a lek. The females come to these areas to mate, usually with one of the dominant males defending a central position on the display ground. The females then go away and lay the eggs, incubate them and raise the young without any help from the male; as far as is known, the females do not defend territories and so the nests are not spaced out by territorial behaviour.

INTERSPECIFIC TERRITORIES

It seems at first somewhat surprising that, usually, a species will only defend its territory against other members of its own species. For example Blackbirds maintain territories against Blackbirds, and Song Thrushes against Song Thrushes, but Blackbird and Song Thrush territories overlap completely. Since the type of food that the two species eat also overlaps, one could have thought that, if food for the young was an

important function of territorial behaviour, the Blackbird would have tried to establish a territory that excluded both neighbouring Blackbirds *and* Song Thrushes; but this does not happen.

In most cases pairs of closely-related species seem to ignore each other when they are establishing their territories. This is not always the case; in the two species Blackcaps and Garden Warblers, which to many people have very similar songs, the birds do establish territories which exclude members of both species. The two species defend only small territories and take similar food, so possibly this is to reduce competition between them. Chiffchaff territories overlap with those of the Garden Warbler and Blackcap, but since this species takes much smaller insects than the other two perhaps competition does not occur.

PROPORTION OF THE YEAR SPENT ON TERRITORY

Different species occupy and defend their territories for varying lengths of time. In some species, such as the Marsh Tit and the Golden Eagle, the older birds stay in their territories from year to year, virtually never leaving them. Some migrants, such as the Marsh Warbler, may be away from the breeding territory for most of the year. Great and Blue Tits, are present for most of the year, but are only strongly territorial in late winter and early spring (though there is some resurgence of territorial behaviour for a brief period in autumn). Blackbirds

and Robins hold territories throughout the winter, but they differ in the
way they do it. Female Blackbirds
remain on territories defended by
males, whereas both male and female
Robins defend territories separately,
each keeping to their own; in spring
the females give up their territories,
often mating with the male in an
adjacent territory.

ESTABLISHING A TERRITORY

The young bird which is trying to
stake out a territory for itself for the
first time faces a number of problems.
Old birds can usually successfully
defend their territories against other
birds that try to usurp them; the old
adage 'possession is nine-tenths of the
law' seems to hold strongly. Even in
migrants, the older males seem able to
get back to the breeding grounds before the younger ones, and they
ɐstablish territories that cover much
the same areas in successive seasons.
The young bird seeking a territory for
the first time really only has two
options (since he is unlikely to wrest a
territory in direct combat); either he
has to find one whose previous holder
has died or he must try to squeeze in
by making himself a little territory on
the border of two others and expand
it little by little. He has the best
chance if the territories are large and
the owners are hard-put to defend
them easily. If he persists he may have
a good chance of becoming accepted
by his neighbours. He has established
himself.

MAINTAINING A TERRITORY

Once he has successfully established
his territory, a bird defends it
vigorously against intruders, adver-
tising his presence by song or display.
Though there is wide overlap, displays tend to be used more in open
country or at close quarters, while
song is more important in situations
where visibility is limited, such as
woodland.

The response of a territory owner

*A male Wood Warbler sings to establish his
woodland territory.*

to a strange song can easily be seen
by playing a tape-recording of a song
in a territory. The owning male
quickly appears and sings at the
'intruder'.

It has been suggested that the
reason why birds have several different song-types (p. 22) is in order to
confuse would-be invaders. Is a bird
moving round its territory singing
different songs in different places *one*
bird, or is it several? This type of
behaviour may confuse a would-be
intruder into thinking that there are
many birds holding small territories
in an area and that it will be difficult
to squeeze in there. Some experiments
with Great Tits have shown that, if a
territory holder is temporarily removed, his territory, will rapidly be
taken over by a new bird. However, if
the empty territory is 'filled' with the
songs of the original territory holder,
played from tapes in different parts of
the territory, it takes far longer for a
new territory holder to become established. The presence of the song
confuses the newcomer into thinking
that the area is still full.

It is probably of value to the
established individuals to be able to
recognise their neighbours. If they
are able to do this, then they do not
have to waste a lot of time going to
see who it is singing on the border of
their territories. It may equally be of
value to be recognised by one's
neighbour since this reduces the
chances that he will come charging in
every time one starts to sing, just to
see who it is.

Usually just singing is sufficient to deter would-be intruders who would like to take over the territory. If singing is not enough and an intruder enters the territory and sings himself, the owner will fly towards him, display to him and chase him off. On the whole, intruders do not push their luck beyond this; physical fights are rather rare. One reason for this is that the established territory holder usually wins such encounters: possession seems to put the defender at an advantage over the intruder. It is not in the interests of the intruder to run the risk of physical injury in a battle if the chances of gaining the territory are slight.

DISPLAYS

Although song plays an important part in maintaining a territory and acquiring a mate, it is not the only method which is used. (Indeed, even some of the sounds used are not songs; a few species make noises in other ways. For example, the Snipe's drumming is made by the tail feathers.)

The other main method of advertisement is display. Displays are any movements which have become specialised (and usually exaggerated) so as to be used as signals; they are the visual equivalents of song. In certain ways song and display perform the same functions; both may be used

Snipe drumming

to deter rival males, and both may be used to attract mates.

As with song, where those of related individuals are often markedly different, so the plumages of closely-related species which rely mainly on display tend to be different. This reduces the chance of the bird pairing with a member of a different species. For example, Marsh and Reed Warblers look quite similar, but their songs are very different. Lesser Black-backed and Herring Gulls, on the other hand, have rather similar displays, but very different coloration of the back and eye-rings, both of which show up prominently in their displays.

As mentioned many birds in open country rely partly on displays, rather than songs, to defend the territory. Mute Swans defend an open stretch of water and are clearly visible to potential intruders from a long way off, and these are chased off as soon as the territory owner sees them. Similarly many birds of prey, such as the Peregrine, rely on seeing and

The courtship-displays of Eider, Lesser Black-backed Gull and Herring Gull

being seen as they fly over the top of their extensive territories. Even the Goshawk and Sparrowhawk, which live primarily within woodland, have soaring display flights with which they advertise their presence.

A great many species couple the use of sound and displays in order to attract potential mates; for example, many ducks and seabirds call while at the same time displaying elaborately; the drake Eider throws its head back, inflates its white throat and stretches out its neck while making a loud cooing noise. Many passerine birds that live in open habitats such as Skylark, Corn Bunting, Whitethroat and Tree Pipit have elaborate song flights in which they fly in an exaggerated fashion above their territories while singing.

Goshawk in soaring display

OBTAINING A MATE

As well as acquiring a place to breed, the young bird must find a mate. Songs and displays are used not only for driving off rivals, but also for attracting mates. Birds vary widely as to whether they pair up before finding a territory, or take up a territory and then try to acquire a mate.

Many migrant males tend to arrive back on the breeding grounds and take up a territory before the females get there. Other migrants, such as geese and many of the ducks, pair up on the wintering grounds before migrating together to their breeding areas. Similarly, Blackthroated Divers pair up at sea and arrive on the breeding lochs together.

Indeed, the males of some species seem unable to defend a proper territory in the absence of a mate. Great Tits that take up territories seem to have paired already, and solitary males seldom seem to set up a territory effectively.

There is often a dramatic change in the male's behaviour after he gets a mate. Both Reed and Sedge Warblers sing throughout the day until they find a mate. Thereafter, the male Reed Warbler only sings a little at dawn and dusk, and the male Sedge Warbler virtually stops singing altogether. If a bird loses its mate, it immediately starts singing again. So it is with many other species: one can identify those birds who have failed to obtain, or who have lost, a mate by the fact that they continue singing long after the others of their species have stopped.

Whitethroat male in song flight

Ruffs at the lek

CHOICE OF PARTNER

Little is known about how a bird
selects a mate. Obviously, natural
selection would favour birds which
selected a mate of good 'quality' since
their offspring are likely to be better
fitted for survival than those of birds
with less vigorous mates. There is
some evidence that many birds do not
just choose the first bird of the
opposite sex that comes along. In
particular, birds seem to be able to
choose mates which are experienced
breeders, in preference to young ones.
Since the former are usually more
successful parents than the latter,
natural selection will favour such a
choice wherever it is possible for the
birds to distinguish between the two.

There are many circumstances
where birds have the opportunity of
making such choices. In those species
where the males take up the territory
by themselves, the females may move
around several territories before they
find a mate who is acceptable to
them. This is likely to be the case in
most small passerine migrants, where
the males return to the breeding
grounds first, find themselves a territory and sing to attract the females
who arrive a few days later. In some
of the ducks that pair up in the winter
quarters, the males display there,
singly or in groups, on the water in
front of the females, and the females
make the choice. The female's
ability to discriminate between males
includes their being able to choose the
right *species* of mate (p. 23). In ducks,

where the females of several species
may look rather similar, but the males
quite different, it is the females who
choose the right species of mate; the
males are much less good at knowing
whether their mate is of the right
species or not and are much more
likely to accept the attentions of a
female of the wrong species (isolating
mechanisms p. 57).

In those species in which the males
have a communal lek, the females
also tend to choose the mate. Often,
they stroll through the outer territories ignoring the solicitations of the
males there and mate with one of the
birds holding a central 'court'; these
are usually the older, more dominant
males and so are probably a good
choice by the female as the father of
her offspring. Something similar
occurs in many seabirds too. In
many of the gulls and the Gannet, the
male takes up a territory and displays
at passing females who may well
consider many males before they
descend and land in a territory. As
one might expect, in contrast to birds
in woodland where vocal communica-
tion is important, these seabirds rely
to a considerable extent on visual
displays. Nocturnal seabirds, however,
rely greatly on calls. The calls of the
two sexes of the Manx Shearwater
are readily distinguishable. The calls
of females passing over appear to
stimulate the males, who are defending
burrows on the ground, to call; this
in turn encourages the female to land
and investigate the calling male and
his burrow.

COPULATION

The final stage of the pairing is of course the actual mating, the moment during copulation when sperm is passed from the male to the female to fertilise her eggs. Not surprisingly, the female is most prepared to copulate during the period of egg formation.

In a few species the males display at leks (Black Grouse, Capercaillie, Ruff) or form no lasting pair-bond with the females (Pheasant). Females of these species only approach the males when they are ready for copulation. Copulation takes place after a brief, but often very frenzied, display, and the female goes off afterwards and raises the young on her own.

In most species, however, the pair-bond has been firmly formed, often for some time, before copulation takes place. This may be many weeks after pair formation or, in the case of some of the long-lived species, the birds may remain together throughout the year (some eagles), or meet again on the nest site in successive years (Kittiwake). In all these cases copulation tends not to occur unless the eggs are being formed.

Most male birds do not have an organ equivalent to the mammalian penis (though the ducks and geese have an extendable organ rather like a penis). The transfer of sperm is achieved by the male putting his cloaca into contact with the female's. To do so, he has to mount her and, while balanced on her back, bend the rear end of his body over and round until his cloaca comes into contact with hers. Both birds have to turn their tails to the side and the female has to remain very still for copulation to be successful; even then in some long-legged species such as herons and the Flamingo copulation looks to be very much of a balancing act!

In most species copulation takes place while the female is standing on the ground, but in the waterfowl and auks it may take place on the water. The Swift, perhaps the most aerial of all birds, may even copulate on the wing.

Little is known about how long the

Different methods of copulation:

Bar-tailed Godwits standing on the ground

Swifts on the wing

Teal in the water

sperm remains viable after copulation. In some species, such as the Willow Grouse, eggs may be fertilised by sperm from a copulation that took place as much as two weeks earlier, but this is probably unusual; moreover, the percentage of infertile eggs seems to increase with the time since copulation. Normally the pair copulates many times; the frequency of copulation is often highest a day or two before the first egg is laid, but probably varies a great deal between species and with how many eggs there are in the clutch.

In many species the male guards his mate most closely during this stage of the breeding cycle; this is almost certainly to ensure that no other male takes advantage of his absence and fertilises the eggs. In a number of species, such as the Mallard, males will quickly pursue, and try to mate with, any unguarded female.

NESTS AND NEST DISPERSION

Birds must have a safe place in which to nest and raise their young. The site must be one where the eggs and young can be kept together, kept dry and kept as safe as possible from predators.

The siting of the nest is clearly of great importance. Most birds are vulnerable to predators of one sort or another. The best defence is to have a nest which is well-concealed; for most small birds this is their main hope of success. In many larger birds concealment is difficult and the best strategy is to place the nest in a site which is as inaccessible as possible.

COLONY NESTING

Some seabirds which nest in colonies on islands may simply be packing into a limited area of suitable safe nesting sites. In other species the colonial nesting provides positive defence against predators. As danger threatens – from a Carrion Crow, a Herring Gull or even a fox – the birds gang up to mob the predator and may well succeed in driving it off. Some of the terns are good at driving off predators – many a person has strayed too close to a colony of Arctic Terns and ended up having blood drawn from his scalp! The Black-headed Gull also nests in dense colonies in marshes; Black-necked Grebes often nest within these colonies apparently in order to make use of the gulls' defences.

Some seabirds nest so close together that there is almost no room between them. No gull can land between the nests in a Gannet colony where the individual Gannets are barely, but deliberately, just out of pecking range of each other. The tight packing of Guillemots, exceptionally up to 70 pairs per square metre, provides good protection against marauding gulls; they can land only at the edge of the colony and even there are faced with a serried row of stabbing beaks.

For several species of herons, and the Rook, which nest colonially, the advantage is less clear than in the case of the seabirds. Often the particular colony has been in the same place for many years, so for any young bird looking for a safe place to nest it is probably advantageous to nest alongside other established birds; any other place may have unknown dangers. In addition, young Rooks can follow the established birds as they fly out from the rookery in the morning and so discover the best feeding sites in the area. (This does not work, however, for herons, since they are solitary feeders, each indeed maintaining a feeding territory where their prey is not disturbed by other herons; any young bird following an older heron out to its feeding area would not be welcome.)

Few small European birds are colonial, perhaps because even a group of them would not provide a substantial deterrent to a predator.

Black-necked Grebes sometimes nest in the middle of a dense colony of Black-headed Gulls in a marsh.

Yellow Wagtail on nest; in the distance a Lapwing chases away a Carrion Crow.

The Fieldfare is an exception. Adult Fieldfares sometimes attack predators *en masse*, bombing them with faeces. This plainly works, for predators have been found plastered with faeces and incapable of flying.

Lapwings, too, are effective in chasing off potential predators such as crows. Yellow Wagtails and Meadow Pipits, both small birds, often nest in Lapwings' territories, apparently to benefit from this defence.

NEST SITE

The nest site itself needs to be chosen carefully. For many species which live in open country or on water there is often little opportunity to make the nest in dense cover. A small amount of concealment by nesting alongside a grass tussock may be all that is possible. Many waders try to slip away from the nest unnoticed as a predator approaches, so as not to give away its position. Divers do this by slipping into the water and making a submerged getaway; to do so swiftly and inconspicuously they need to nest very close to the water's edge.

Waders and gamebirds have interestingly different ways of trying to conceal their nests. Waders, which usually nest in rather more exposed places than do gamebirds, keep a close watch for danger and, as soon as it threatens, the incubating bird leaves the nest – long before the predator gets anywhere near. The bird is fairly conspicuous, but the eggs are very well camouflaged and

hard for the predator to find. Most gamebirds lay their eggs in slightly thicker cover. The eggs themselves are quite easy to see, usually palish in colour and not camouflaged. They get their protection from the parent bird, who is well camouflaged, sitting tight on the eggs and hoping to avoid detection. Only when the predator is almost on top of it does the bird flee from the nest.

For birds nesting in thicker cover, concealment is easier and remains the most important method of defence used by most small birds, such as the warblers. Larger birds try to make their nest inaccessible – in the top of a tall tree (for a Carrion Crow) or on a cliff (for a Raven or a Peregrine). This tends to make the birds fairly safe from most mammalian predators (though martens remain a hazard to many birds). But large nests in inaccessible sites, especially in trees, tend to be fairly conspicuous; such sites are probably not much use unless the bird can defend itself against other birds. For this reason, rather few *small* European birds nest in the tops of deciduous trees: even small

Female pheasant sitting on her nest

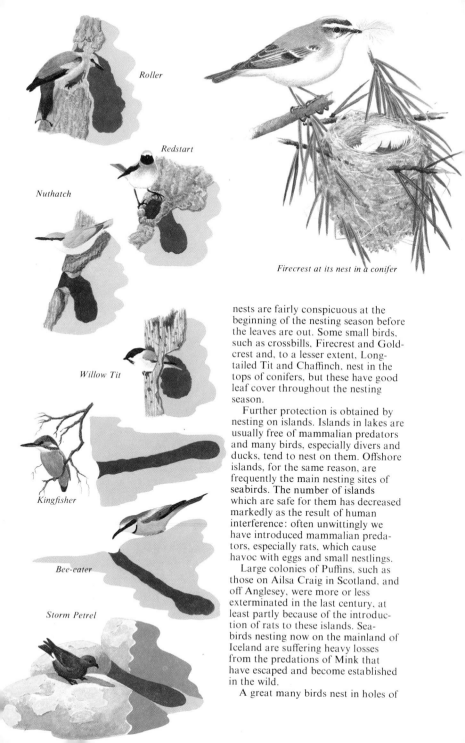

Roller

Redstart

Nuthatch

Willow Tit

Kingfisher

Bee-eater

Storm Petrel

Firecrest at its nest in a conifer

nests are fairly conspicuous at the beginning of the nesting season before the leaves are out. Some small birds, such as crossbills, Firecrest and Gold-crest and, to a lesser extent, Long-tailed Tit and Chaffinch, nest in the tops of conifers, but these have good leaf cover throughout the nesting season.

Further protection is obtained by nesting on islands. Islands in lakes are usually free of mammalian predators and many birds, especially divers and ducks, tend to nest on them. Offshore islands, for the same reason, are frequently the main nesting sites of seabirds. The number of islands which are safe for them has decreased markedly as the result of human interference: often unwittingly we have introduced mammalian preda-tors, especially rats, which cause havoc with eggs and small nestlings.

Large colonies of Puffins, such as those on Ailsa Craig in Scotland, and off Anglesey, were more or less exterminated in the last century, at least partly because of the introduc-tion of rats to these islands. Sea-birds nesting now on the mainland of Iceland are suffering heavy losses from the predations of Mink that have escaped and become established in the wild.

A great many birds nest in holes of

one sort or another. Many, such as Kestrel, Stock Dove, some owls, Roller, Hoopoe, Redstart, Jackdaw and Starling, usually nest in holes in trees. The Nuthatch does too, and it carefully plasters mud around the entrance until it is so small that the Nuthatch itself can only just squeeze through. When the mud hardens it discourages larger birds such as Starlings from trying to take over the site. None of these birds makes the hole itself: it relies on finding a natural hole or one made by another bird or by a mammal. But both Willow and Crested Tits excavate nest-holes of their own in a trunk of rotten wood; and all woodpeckers excavate their own holes.

Kingfishers and Sand Martins use holes in vertical banks. Bee-eaters may nest in banks, but will also dig burrows in flat ground. Manx Shearwaters, Puffins and Storm Petrels may nest down burrows in the ground, although they can dig these themselves, they tend to find it easier to take over rabbit burrows. Wheat-ears nest in holes in walls or rock scree, but also readily take to rabbit burrows in some areas.

Hole-nesting carries certain advantages; most mammals cannot reach the nests (though foxes can sometimes dig out underground nests). Those in holes up trees are safer still; larger birds cannot normally reach the contents of the nest. As a result many birds that nest in holes tend to be more successful at raising young than birds that nest in the open. So why

do not all birds nest in holes? The answer is that, whereas birds which nest in the open may have an almost infinite choice of nest-sites, holes tend to be in short supply. They are competed for, sometimes fiercely, and some birds may fail to nest because they cannot find a suitable nest-site.

TYPE OF NEST

For birds which nest in exposed sites, the use of nesting material is risky. Divers, most waders and many game-birds merely make a modest scrape in which to place their eggs, and use almost no nesting material at all. Nevertheless, for species such as the Ringed Plover which at best only line the nest with tiny pebbles, there is a problem of heat loss through the eggs into the ground (p. 226). Many waders put at least a little lining into the nest cup to provide insulation against such heat loss. Usually this is grass or leaves, but for some such as the Knot, which nests in very ex-posed areas, it is usually lichens. The larger species may have more prob-lems concealing their nests if they are in exposed places, simply because their eggs are larger; the Lapwing and the Oystercatcher may put a few objects around the nest, possibly to help break up the outline of the eggs.

Most ducks and geese also make only rather simple nests, but these are well-insulated, with a lining of down plucked from their own breasts. Some of these birds will pull in other material such as grass and other

An Oystercatcher may site its nest up against a rock or log to make it less conspicuous, and place pebbles around it to break up the outline of its eggs.

Magpie arriving at its nest

Two young Wood Pigeon 'squabs' on their flimsy nest

vegetation that is within reach of the incubating bird. Swans pull in great quantities of reed and make a substantial mound on which to lay their eggs; the height of this mound gives them some protection from changes in level of the water. Grebes and the marsh terns also use vegetation for their nests which float anchored to reeds or other aquatic vegetation and can move up and down a little with changes in the water level. Ducks and grebes cover their eggs (with down and weed respectively) when leaving the nest so as to make them harder to find.

Many birds build more intricate nests. Even the simple twig nest of the Woodpigeon has to be built carefully. The birds must find a place on a branch where twigs can be placed so that they will form a firm platform. Many places may be tried

and the first twigs are often hard to anchor, but gradually a platform is constructed which is strong enough to hold not just the eggs, but the incubating adult and, later, two large chicks. The pigeons are not highly expert builders; but crows and jays interweave the sticks more carefully and make a deep cup which they line with woven rootlets. The Magpie takes this development one stage further and builds a nest with a strong dome. In this species, the dome probably gives the Magpie protection against raids from other members of the crow family, though the disadvantage is that it makes the nest larger and therefore more conspicuous.

Open, cup-shaped nests are made by many species of passerine birds such as the thrushes, finches and warblers. Most make the outer structure of small twigs and line it with finer material such as hair or feathers. Feathers are a particularly valuable form of insulation and are used by many birds for lining their nests. Unlike the ducks and geese

Before departing a Little Grebe covers its eggs with weed.

which pull out their own feathers to line the nest, the passerines depend on finding moulted feathers of other species, or whole dead birds from which they can pluck feathers. The Goldfinch and the Redpoll build very neat, compact nests made mostly out of wool, lichens and moss, and lined with feathers.

The ground-nesting passerines such as the larks and pipits also build cup-shaped nests, usually well concealed and tucked into the side of a tussock of grass. In those such as the Tawny Pipit, which breeds in areas which become quite hot in the middle of the day, the way in to the nest tends to be oriented towards the north or east, presumably in order to prevent overheating of the occupants.

Among the most complex nests built by European birds are those of the Wren, Long-tailed Tit and Penduline Tit. All build domed nests, the first of leaves, the other two of spider's-web and lichen, or the furry seeds of reed-mace. The nests are beautifully warm, lined as they are with many feathers; as many as 2,000 have been counted in a single Long-tailed Tit's nest.

The nests of Goldcrest and Firecrest look as if they are just open cup-shaped nests, but they have a ring of feathers protruding over the top of the cup; these act as a thin cover, reducing the amount of heat lost from the nest. This 'door' over the nest is particularly well built in some northern areas.

Some birds use mud for building. Several species of thrushes use mud in the construction of their nest, though only the Song Thrush lines the nest entirely with mud. The House Martin

A Penduline Tit builds its nest.

and the Red-rumped Swallow build intricate nests of mud lined with feathers; the birds may fly some distance to collect the mud. The Flamingo's characteristic nest is also built of mud; the bird does not carry the mud, but leans over the edge of the nest and pulls it in from the surrounding ground.

SPEED OF NEST-BUILDING

Some resident birds may build their nests slowly, taking up to two or three weeks to complete it. Some of the large birds of prey may add sticks to a nest used in previous years, until a very large structure develops.

Some migrants, such as the Brambling and Marsh Warbler, may pair up within hours of arrival on the breeding grounds, and start to build almost immediately, completing a nest within only a few days. The same can be true of resident species which have lost their first nest: a replacement may be built much more rapidly.

The entrance to a Tawny Pipit's nest is usually oriented towards north or east.

EGGS

Once birds have selected a nest site and built the nest, they are ready to produce the eggs.

EGG SIZE

Two generalisations can be made about the size of eggs in relation to the size of the female's body. First, egg size varies very markedly between families, but less so within families. Second, within families smaller birds tend to lay proportionately larger eggs than larger birds do.

For example, the European species of shearwaters and storm-petrels, which both belong to the same Order of birds, lay very large eggs weighing between 16 and 25% of the female's weight, whereas in the gamebirds the eggs weigh between 3.5 and 9% of the female's weight. However, in both groups the smaller birds lay the relatively larger eggs. The storm-petrels lay eggs which are about 25% of their body weight while the shear-waters' eggs are only about 15 to 16% of the female's weight. Similarly, the eggs of the Quail are about 9% of the bird's weight while those of the Capercaillie are about 3%. The eggs of the small ducks are about 7 to 8% of the female's weight compared with those of swans which are about 4%.

The relative size of the eggs has sometimes been related to the type of young which hatch from them. Some species, such as the waders which have nidifugous young, lay large eggs (the eggs of the Ringed Plover are about 18% of the female's weight, those of the Lapwing about 12%); this may be related to the need for well-developed chicks at hatching. However, the eggs of ducks, game-birds and rails are not particularly large, even though they also have nidifugous young. Large size may be related to the need of the adult to be able to leave the young untended for considerable periods of time; larger birds lose heat more slowly than smaller ones (p. 224). Shearwaters and storm petrels lay very large eggs, and the parents leave the young alone from the early stages while they make long sea journeys to collect food.

A Fulmar (above) *and a Storm Petrel with their eggs*

The somewhat conical shape of waders' eggs means that a normal clutch of four form a neat group if they are positioned so that their pointed ends face inwards. The incubating female could not cover effectively as many eggs of such a large size if they were any other shape. If the Guillemot's single very pointed egg is accidentally knocked it turns round in a small circle as opposed to rolling any distance; this reduces the chance that they will roll off the cliff ledge. Many eggs of hole-nesting species such as the owls and kingfishers are rounder, but it is not known why this should be.

The four eggs in typical arrangement in a Lapwing's nest

268

EGG COLOUR

The eggs of different species are very variedly coloured and patterned. The usefulness of some egg colours seems clear, but the value of others is puzzling. The camouflaged eggs of ground-nesting species such as the waders and nightjars are obviously adaptive, since they are difficult for the predators to find. On the other hand, some species lay eggs that are not well-camouflaged at all – such as the white eggs of Woodpigeon and Turtle Dove, and the pale eggs of pheasants. These eggs are normally covered by the incubating birds (both members of the pair taking turns in the Woodpigeon, the female only in the Pheasant), and so there is probably no need for them to be well-camouflaged (p. 263).

In fact, most species that nest in holes lay white eggs (storm-petrels, Puffin, owls, Kingfisher, Bee-eater, Roller, woodpeckers, swifts, House Martin, Black Redstart, Dipper) or pale blue ones (Starling, Wheatear, Redstart, Pied Flycatcher); most probably this is to help the parents to see them in the dark, and avoid breaking them.

Apart from the well-camouflaged eggs of birds which nest on the ground, it has generally proved difficult to correlate the colours of eggs with any particular aspect of the nesting behaviour of a species. The nest itself is necessarily a bulky object, much larger than the eggs, and, in the vast majority of cases, it is the nest that is found by the predator, and not the eggs. Building a nest that is well-camouflaged or inconspicuous is important; inconspicuous eggs are not necessarily advantageous.

In a few other cases however, the colour of the eggs is known to be important. The parent Guillemot learns to recognise its own egg by the combination of colour and patterning; so it is less liable, in the turmoil of a densely-packed ledge, to end up incubating the wrong egg by mistake. The Cuckoo is also another species where the colour of the eggs is important (p. 278).'

INTERVAL BETWEEN EGGS

The laying female needs to find a lot of food to form the eggs (p. 226). In many small species, the female lays her eggs at daily intervals; in those that lay a large clutch (p. 270), the female may have to find the food required to form one egg every day (since she cannot store the nutrients required for all the eggs, see p. 34). In some larger birds the interval between the eggs is longer. Canada Geese lay at about 36-hour intervals and swans have a two-day interval between eggs. The Swift, which is dependent on flying insects for its food, also lays its eggs at two-day intervals; but if the weather is bad, and therefore food is scarce, it may lay at three-day intervals instead. The Manx Shearwater and the Fulmar go away to sea for up to two weeks just prior to egg-laying, apparently to rich feeding grounds. In the former species it is known that they go down to the rich fishing areas in the Bay of Biscay, a return journey of some 1,000 km.

Nightjar's nest

Stock Dove's nest

Woodpigeon's nest

CLUTCH-SIZE

A Puffin has a single chick, a Blackbird three or four and tits many more, often eight or ten. Why should there be such big differences between species? What factors effect how many eggs a bird has in its clutch?

Once again the answer is an evolutionary one. Within a species, natural selection will favour those individuals which raise the largest number of young (and thus pass on more of its genes). If its offspring are also successful at raising young, the characteristics of these individuals will come to predominate in the population – this is what evolution is all about.

However, it may not always be easy for the parent birds to lay that number of eggs which results in them raising the largest number of young. If they lay too small a clutch, then others, which lay a larger clutch, will raise more young. If they lay too many eggs, they may end up with more young than they can feed properly; either all the young will die in the nest or they will leave the nest undernourished and with poor chances of surviving to breed. Birds that started off with fewer eggs may actually raise more young; there is a clutch-size for each species which is best.

Swifts feed on flying insects which are more abundant in fine than in cold weather; it is harder to get food in cold, wet summers than in warm ones. In Britain, Swifts usually lay either two or three eggs; occasionally in Continental Europe they may lay a fourth. In one study in Britain, birds which were given a fourth chick were unable to raise four young; even in a very fine summer when food was plentiful, birds starting with four young raised on average only 2.75 of them, whereas those which started with three raised them all. It is clear why broods of four are not produced in Britain: they result in fewer surviving young than broods of three. On the Continent, in finer

A Swift arrives at the nest with food for the young.

weather with perhaps a richer insect fauna, they may be more successful. Furthermore, in Britain, in cool summers, more chicks die in broods of three than in broods of two; in one study, broods of three raised an average of 1.6 chicks in poor summers while pairs starting off with only two chicks raised an average of 1.8.

So, in fine summers birds starting with three chicks are more successful than those starting with only two (2.75 young compared with 2.0). Hence in some years it is better for Swifts to lay two eggs, in others better to have three. Which is best depends on the weather during the nestling period – something the parent birds cannot forecast at the time of laying.

The Swift's situation is fairly clear-cut because many of the young which die do so in the nest. In many other species most of the young leave the nest successfully and so, to the casual observer, it may seem as if they were successful. But the situation is more complex than it seems. Comparing two nests of the same species with different numbers of young, the individual chicks in the larger brood receive less food than those in the smaller one. As a result, chicks in large broods tend to leave the nest less well-nourished and lighter in weight than those in smaller broods. In several species it has been shown that the weight of the chick at fledging markedly affects its chances of survival. Hence the lighter chicks in large broods have less chance of surviving than do the heavier ones in smaller broods.

In many species the number of eggs laid by different individuals may be quite variable. The reason for this is often that there are different local conditions which may affect the number of young which can be raised. Many species, such as the Robin, tend to lay larger clutches further north in Europe than they do in the south. This is because there is a longer period of daylight in the north and a richer supply of food available in mid-summer; hence northern Robins can raise larger broods than southern ones. Birds laying in poor habitats may have smaller clutches than others laying nearby in better habitats. Tits in gardens have lower clutches than those in nearby woodland where there are many more caterpillars for the parents to feed to their young. Magpies lay smaller clutches in territories where other pairs have had low breeding success in earlier years than do those laying in territories where previous birds have had good breeding success; they seem to be adjusting their clutch to local environmental factors which they can detect, but which we cannot.

The same bird may also lay a clutch of a different size at different times in its life or in the year. Many birds breeding for the first time have slightly smaller clutches than those which are older and have bred before. These birds are inexperienced at raising young and so are less likely to be successful than the older birds.

Blackbirds lay small clutches at the beginning of the season, larger ones in the middle and smaller ones again at the end. Only in the middle of the season is there an abundance of both caterpillars and worms for them to bring to their young.

In most cases the birds are presumably laying that number of eggs which, on average, has been most successful in the past and so has evolved through natural selection.

There is the added complication that the birds have to lay their clutch some time before the food that they will bring to the chicks is available (p. 248); so they cannot gauge the food abundance accurately. In only a few cases do birds lay a clutch which is immediately related to the amount of food that will be available for the young. In several species of owls, which take small mammals like voles and lemmings, the clutch-size varies markedly in relation to prey abundance. The Long-tailed Skua may not breed at all in years when lemming numbers are very low.

Tawny Owls may lay two or three eggs in years when prey is of average abundance, but four in a year when voles are particularly plentiful. In years of very poor vole numbers, they may not breed at all – like the skua, their clutch-size is zero. The Ural Owl responds to a shortage of voles by starting to breed later on in the season, laying a smaller clutch, and stepping up the proportion of birds in its diet.

The abundance of its Lemming prey influences the breeding of the Long-tailed Skua.

INCUBATION

After the eggs have been laid, the parents must keep them warm so that they can develop. Incubation takes quite a long time; the shortest incubation period of any bird is 11–12 days; most species take longer than that (see table on p. 248). The longest incubation period of any European bird is probably that of the Lammergeier which takes about 55–60 days, but Cory's Shearwater, Fulmar and Griffon Vulture all take about 52 days to hatch their eggs.

In order to hatch the egg, parents must apply heat to it. They cannot do this properly through their thick (and insulating) feathers, so they have to develop a special brood-patch; this is an area of the belly from which the feathers are shed and which develops large blood vessels just underneath the skin. By applying the brood patch to the eggs, the bird can maintain the egg at close to its own body temperature.

In some species both sexes develop brood patches; in others only the female does so. In a very few, such as the phalaropes, only the male develops a brood patch. In some seabirds, only small areas of skin are bared; for example gulls have three small, separate brood patches, one for each egg, rather than a single large one. Presumably this helps the bird to minimise its own heat loss when it is off the nest, especially when it is on the water.

In most species, the egg is very vulnerable to chilling; if it is left unattended too long in cold weather the embryo will die. There are however, a few species in which the eggs will withstand quite an amount of chilling and yet still hatch. Such birds include the shearwaters, storm-petrels and swifts. In all these groups, the parents find it difficult to feed themselves in hard weather and so may be forced to be away from the nest for prolonged periods; for the seabirds unusually rough weather at

sea means that it takes the bird a long time to find food, while for the Swift cold weather means that there are few insects flying. Bad feeding conditions happen sufficiently frequently that such an adaptation is more or less a necessity.

SHARE OF SEXES IN INCUBATION

The parent must not only keep the eggs warm, but must keep the whereabouts of the nest secret. Nonetheless, the parents usually need to feed, so they must make visits to and from the nest. Going to feed is obviously less of a problem for species in which both parents incubate: one can take over directly from the other. When only one of the parents incubates (usually it is the female), the eggs may chill when left untended; so the bird must keep its foraging trips short, especially in cold weather. It is not always clear why the male does not incubate; differences occur between closely-related species. For example both sexes incubate in the Sand Martin, House Martin and Red-rumped Swallow, but only the female incubates in the Swallow and the Crag Martin.

Even when both parents incubate, the female often takes more of the time; in particular, she often incubates throughout the night as well as taking a share during the day. The parents may switch over every half-hour or so in small species or only once or twice a day in larger ones. In shearwaters and storm-petrels, which only come to the nesting colony at night, the birds only switch over every two or three nights and exceptionally one bird may have to incubate without a break for eight or nine days. In some of the Arctic geese and the pheasants, the female may not move off the eggs at all for many days; the female Golden Pheasant sometimes does not move from the clutch for the whole of the incubation period. In most species, however, the females leave for a little while each day to defaecate; the very large pheasant faeces that one finds in woodland in spring are evidence of an incubating female nearby.

HATCHING SYNCHRONY

The moment at which the parents start to incubate their clutch has important implications for the brood. In many species the parents do not start to incubate the eggs until the clutch is complete. Where this happens all the young hatch at more or less the same time (synchronously). In some species, especially ones where the young are nidifugous, it is very important that the young are ready to leave together or they become difficult to look after.

In contrast, some parents start incubation before the clutch is complete, so that the eggs do not all hatch together (asynchronously). For example, many owls, such as the Barn Owl, start to incubate the first egg as soon as it is laid. Since the eggs are laid at roughly two-day

intervals and each takes the same number of days to develop, the chicks hatch roughly two days apart. The earlier-hatched chicks are at a great advantage over their later brethren. The larger the chick, the greater the chance that it has of getting the food it needs; if food is in short supply, the first chick to hatch may flourish while the later ones starve to death

At first sight, this may seem to be an inefficient way of breeding, since it leads to the death of many young. Almost certainly, however, the opposite is the case: it is, for the parents, a way of ensuring that they raise as many young as possible. If food is scarce, the parents raise more young if the small ones die quickly and so do not compete with the largest. If they were all of equal size, then all would be equally emaciated, and none might survive. This habit is often referred to as the brood-reduction strategy. It is most commonly found in birds where the food supply is unpredictable; we have already seen that birds cannot easily adjust the number of eggs they lay to match the food supply. Such species include: herons, cormorants, pelicans, birds of prey, owls and swifts, kingfishers and bee-eaters.

An adult Barn Owl feeds its family of young, which hatched at roughly two-day intervals.

EGG-SHELL REMOVAL

Once the chick emerges from the egg the parents' behaviour changes to deal with young which must be fed. In many species the parents have a special duty to the hatching chick: they must remove the egg-shells. This is particularly important in species which nest out in the open. In these the startling white of the inside of the shell contrasts markedly with the camouflaged outside. It is dangerous for the parent to leave the eggshells near the nest, these may well draw the attention of predators to the nest-site; so the parents pick up the shells and fly with them some distance from the nest before dropping them.

PARENTAL CARE

Once the young bird has hatched, the parent must bring it food or lead it to where it can feed itself. Nidicolous young may still need a lot of brooding – they will not be able to maintain their own body temperature until they are much larger, especially in cold weather. This can pose a problem for the parents of small passerines where both parents normally collect food for the young. They need to go and hunt for food for the chicks, but the chicks may chill if they are away too long. In warm weather the chicks need little brooding and so both parents can collect food, but in cold weather one of the parents may have to brood the young and this effectively cuts the feeding rate by half. Even though they are kept warm, the young may die of starvation.

We know rather little about the detailed behaviour of birds with nidifugous young because they are rather difficult to observe. In most species they are led away from the nest within a few hours, a day at the most, of hatching, and in most it is important for them to hatch synchronously. However, in a few species this does not seem to be so important. In the Mute Swan the young which hatch first may be taken off and cared for by the cob (male) while the pen (female) continues to incubate those eggs that have not yet hatched; hatching of the whole clutch may be spread out over 24 hours or more. Another exception is the Crane which lays its two eggs at 48-hour intervals

and starts to incubate as soon as the first egg is laid. The first chick often leaves the nest before the second hatches. However, since, again unusually for nidifugous birds, there are only two young, each can be cared for by one of the parents, and asynchronous hatching does not therefore lead to problems. The crakes and rails, distant relatives of the Crane, are also nidifugous and hatch their young asynchronously. These include Coot, Spotted, Baillon's and Little Crakes and Moorhen, though the latter is highly variable, often hatching first broods synchronously and later ones asynchronously. In both Coot and Baillon's Crake (and probably the others), like the Mute Swan, the female continues to stay on the nest while the male brings food and cares for any young that leave the nest.

In most nidifugous species the young never go back to the nest again; but in some of the aquatic species, such as the Coot and Moorhen, the chicks spend the night on platforms of vegetation, made for them by their parents, and where they are brooded.

The duties of parents of nidifugous young are mainly to keep them dry and warm, especially when they are very small, and safe from predators. Relatively few bring food to their young (though Oystercatchers do, p. 207). Most take them to good feeding places where they feed for themselves.

On the left of the picture, an adult female Coot incubates its second clutch of eggs, while on the right the male attends to the first brood of young on a temporary platform of reeds.

In the Eider, broods may gather together into crèches, guarded by several females (often referred to as aunties). This may be because several adults may be more effective in guarding a pack of young against predators than each individual mother is in guarding just her own brood. The habit may also have arisen because the females' own fat reserves become so depleted during incubation that they need to take time off to feed.

This is not the case with the parents of nidicolous young whose babies are wholly dependent on them for everything including food. Such parents may be faced with a very heavy workload. If all is well, food may be plentiful and close at hand; but it still has to be collected and brought to the nest. This may involve a great deal of flying. The extremes of feeding behaviour are perhaps exemplified by the Manx Shearwater and the Blue Tit. In the former species the parents may only come in to feed the young every third night or so at the beginning of the nestling period and are probably flying several hundred miles to good fishing grounds to find food. In the Blue Tit, the pair may bring a food item to the nest every minute of the daylight hours – making more than 1,000 visits in the course of a 16-hour day. The birds are clearly not going very far to find the food, which is just as well because they must be able to find it very quickly. Nevertheless they too spend a great deal of their day in flight.

It is obviously important to bring to the nest as much food as possible in the time available, and at the same time to reduce as far as possible the amount of effort involved in doing so. Some birds that make infrequent visits to the young, such as the Storm

A Buzzard brings a dead rabbit to its nestlings.

Petrel and the Fûlmar bring in the food partly digested in their stomach. By predigesting it to some extent they are able to get rid of some of the water (which forms a high percentage of their marine prey); so they bring back a quantity of food which, for its weight, maximises its nutritional value.

Many other birds use their crops to bring food back to the nest. They can bring large quantities at each visit; hence they need to make fewer flights between food and nest, and so save energy. A bird that brings in a large prey, such as a Buzzard with a rabbit, needs to make few visits to the nest each day; the Gyrfalcon brings in only some 180 to 200 prey (mostly grouse and Ptarmigan) in the 75 days during which the young are dependent

Feeding the young in the nest; a House Martin will bring a mouthful of insects, while a Spotted Flycatcher brings only one at a time.

on their parents for food. It is birds that bring small prey that need to carry as many as possible on each trip.

Finches bringing small seeds, and swallows small insects, would waste an enormous amount of time if they brought in each item individually. A swift, for example, may carry in its huge gape more than 1,500 insects each time it visits the nest. Nevertheless, many insectivorous species, like tits, flycatchers and the Bee-eater, do bring in only a single item on most visits. Apparently this is because many insects have to be beaten and killed so that they do not sting or bite the young birds. Even the jaws of caterpillars must be broken so that they cannot bite the chick after being swallowed. Since it appears to be too difficult for the adult to hold one prey while preparing another, the items have to be brought in one at a time. But these birds do try their hardest to be efficient: they eat the

small prey they find themselves, and take only larger ones to their young.

The Puffin is particularly adept at carrying large numbers of small fish in its bill; as many as 62 have been recorded. The bird catches each fish between the two mandibles, and kills it; it then moves it so that it is held between the tongue and the upper mandible (stacking them from the back forwards); this leaves the bird able to open the bill and catch the next fish.

The size of prey brought in is obviously important. It may be necessary to catch small prey for tiny chicks; they may not be able to swallow larger prey. This is not usually a great problem since many of the parents which bring large food items, such as the birds of prey, can tear them into small portions if necessary.

The quality of the food may also be important. In general it seems that a vegetable diet is not a good one for raising small, rapidly-growing young. Almost all birds which feed on vegetable material when adult feed insects to their young. For example, young Red Grouse and Capercaillie, which later in their lives will eat heather shoots and conifer needles, seek out and eat insects during their main period of growth. Most finches feed their small young on insects; later they may bring increasing amounts of seeds. There are exceptions to this; the Crossbill, which eats the seeds of conifers, feeds its young almost exclusively on the same diet; seeds are more nutritious than leaves and so young can be raised on them.

Two groups of birds, the pigeons and the flamingos, feed their young in an entirely different way from other birds. The parents produce crop-milk for their young. This substance is formed from cells which are sloughed off from the inner surface of the crop and is very rich in fat and protein. These cells are regurgitated to the chicks and form the whole diet of the very small young. In the Flamingo, there is a small quantity of red blood cells amongst the milk. It is not known whether these are an

A Puffin catching fish holds them with its tongue at the back of its mouth, in order to be free to catch more.

important part of the diet or how they get into the milk. In the case of the pigeons, this diet is much more nutritious than the vegetable diet of the parents, presumably this is why the birds have evolved the habit. In the case of the Flamingo, the reason is less clear because the adults often feed on animal plankton; it is however, sieved from very salt water and the high concentration of salt might be difficult for the young to cope with. It is thought that the birds are probably producing crop milk as quickly as they can and this may be why all species of pigeon (there are some 280 species throughout the world in a wide variety of habitats) have either one or two chicks at a time; it might be impossible to provide adequately for more. Both flamingos and pigeons start to bring their normal diet to the young as they get older.

The parents bring food to the nest in response to begging by the chicks; the more begging the chicks do (i.e. the hungrier they are), the greater the likelihood that the parents will work harder to provide more food for them. However, there is a point beyond which they do not seem able or prepared to go. Clearly it is of little value if they endanger themselves too much; if they die, there is little or no hope for the young anyway.

As well as bringing food to the nest, most passerines keep the nest clean by removing the faeces produced in a gelatinous sac by the young. These are carried some way from the nest before being dropped, so that the site of the nest is not revealed to a predator by a pile of conspicuous droppings.

In almost all species parental care continues for some time after the young have left the nest (p. 210). There may be a conflict between the interests of the parent and the young at this time. It is in the interests of the young to stay close to the parents, benefit from the safety of the territory, and perhaps get fed. There comes a time, however, when these benefits no longer greatly increase the probability that the young will survive, and when the continued feeding of the young may impair the adults' freedom to get on with having another brood.

Parent Spotted Flycatchers feed their young for as much as a fortnight after they leave the nest. But gradually they become more reluctant to do so, and the young have to chase after their parents more and more in order to get fed. Eventually, as the young's own hunting skills improve, bothering their unwilling parents ceases to be worthwhile; it is easier to go and catch their own food.

From the evolutionary viewpoint it is obviously more important to the adult that there is another brood than it is to the young; hence the conflict of interests. In due course the chick will be ignored by the parent, or actively chased away. The parents will then be free to see to their own affairs, which may involve the raising of another brood, undertaking a moult, or preparing for migration.

277

ODD BREEDERS

A number of species have particularly unusual breeding habits and some of these are described here.

CUCKOOS

The two European cuckoos are parasitic on other species of birds, laying their eggs in their nests and leaving the other birds to raise the cuckoo's young.

Why should they do this? The answer lies in the bird's need to leave as many offspring as it can. In most species, the birds lay their eggs and then have to incubate them and raise the young. All this takes time; most birds the size of a Cuckoo only raise a single brood of about 3–5 young each year. If a bird could break away from this system in some way, say by getting other birds to raise their young for them, then there would be more time and more opportunities to lay more eggs. This is exactly what the cuckoos have managed to do; many female cuckoos lay about 12–15 eggs during the nesting season.

The cuckoos' nesting habits raise a lot of questions, especially those relating to how such habits could have evolved and why the species which are parasitized (the hosts) allow themselves to be used in this way. The habit of laying in other birds nests is more widespread than one might expect, being particularly common *within* species; Coots,

Moorhens, House Sparrows and Starlings all commonly lay eggs in their neighbours' nests, and then lay a clutch for themselves. This has an obvious advantage: individuals may be able to increase the number of their offspring by doing it. It is not a very big step to laying one's eggs in the nests of *another* species and, providing the host parents can raise the young, the advantage is clear.

Equally, and oppositely, it is advantageous to the host to avoid accepting the parasite's egg, because then it too will be able to raise more of its *own* young. What ensues, over a long period of time, is a sort of evolutionary arms race. The host evolves the ability to recognise the parasite's eggs and eject it, or desert the nest altogether and start again. Natural selection favours those parasites whose eggs best match the host's: egg mimicry evolves and the host finds it progressively harder to discriminate between the eggs of the parasite and its own. It may then pay the host to develop very variable eggs so that the parasite cannot easily mimic them. This may explain why Meadow Pipits are heavily parasitised by Cuckoos, but the Tree Pipit only lightly so. One Meadow Pipit's eggs look much like another's; but the variation of colour and pattern between the eggs of one Tree Pipit and another is considerable. Since each individual female Cuckoo can probably only produce a single

The early history of a young Cuckoo; after the egg hatches, the baby Cuckoo ejects the eggs or young of its host, so that thenceforward it can receive all the food brought by its foster-parents, even after it has left the nest.

pattern of eggshell (see next page), it is statistically likely that this will not be a good match to the pattern on the eggs of any Tree Pipit whose nest the Cuckoo might find. If the Cuckoo laid an egg, the Tree Pipit would almost certainly recognise, and eject, it.

In Europe there are only two species which are fully parasitic, the Cuckoo and the Great Spotted Cuckoo (which parasitise a range of small passerines and some of the crows respectively). The Cuckoo shows a number of adaptations for the parasitic habit. It has unusually good control of the moment of egg-laying: it can often dash in and lay an egg while the host is away for only a few moments. It often removes one of the host's eggs at the same time, perhaps to make it harder for the host to notice a change. This cuckoo is much larger than most of its hosts, so it lays an egg which is very small for its size (only about 2.5% of its body weight, see p. 261). The shell of the egg is unusually thick, apparently because it has to be dropped a few centimetres into the nest, the female Cuckoo being too large to fit into the small nests of her hosts. The eggs match those of the host in colour, often very closely. However, the Cuckoo parasitises several different species of host, each of which lays eggs of different colours. How does the Cuckoo lay eggs which match those of each of these hosts? It is thought that each female lays eggs of one colour only and that she special-ises in laying in one species of host, choosing the species in whose nest she herself was raised. Hence if the egg

Cuckoo's egg in a Meadow Pipit's clutch

Cuckoo's egg in a Reed Warbler's clutch

Cuckoo's egg in a Great Reed Warbler's clutch

Cuckoo's egg in a Dunnock's clutch

Cuckoo's egg in a Pied Wagtail's clutch

An adult Magpie feeds two of its own young, and two young Great Spotted Cuckoos.

from which she hatched was accepted by a host and she lays an egg of similar colour in a nest of the same host, this too is likely to be accepted. Thus female cuckoos belong to a series of lines (called *gens*, plural *gentes*) each of which lays eggs of different colours. The chick usually hatches ahead of the host chicks. Because it will eventually be so much larger than the chicks of the host, it needs all the food that the parents can bring in. It eliminates the competition by getting under the eggs or newly hatched chicks of the host and very slowly stretching up and tipping them out of the nest.

In contrast, the Great Spotted Cuckoo parasitises birds which are its own size or slightly larger – crows, especially the Magpie. Its egg is proportionately much larger than that of the Cuckoo, weighing about 7% of its own weight. Since the hosts who raise its young are much larger than those which raise the Cuckoo chick, they can raise both the young Great Spotted Cuckoo and their own young; the young Great Spotted Cuckoo does not eject the host's eggs. Indeed, the Great Spotted Cuckoo often lays more than one egg in each host nest (like the Cuckoo, it often removes a host egg at the time of laying).

There are many other cuckoos, in other parts of the world, which are parasitic, but there are also many cuckoos which behave normally, raising their own young. There is also a range of birds in other families which have evolved the parasitic habit; indeed, the habit is thought to have evolved separately on no fewer than eight occasions.

CO-OPERATIVE BREEDERS

In Europe, the very large majority of species breed monogamously, the pair defending a territory and raising their young together. In other parts of the world, particularly the warmer areas, a large number of species breed co-operatively. This means that there are more than a single pair in a territory, and more than two birds bring food to the young.

Co-operative breeding is very rare in European birds, but it does occur in a few species. It is not at all uncommon, for example, for young Moorhens and young House Martins from early broods to stay and help their parents to raise later broods in the same season. One can also find more than a single pair of birds at some Bee-eater nests. The extra bird seems to be usually a male and is often an offspring of the breeding pair from the previous year.

There are two other European species whose breeding is sufficiently aberrant to warrant further description.

Dunnock
This common small bird of our back-gardens turns out to have some very unusual habits. There are more males

than females in the population in spring. Probably as a result of this, the birds do not form normal monogamous pairs – at least not all the time. It is possible to find territories with just two males, with two males and a single female, with a normal pair, with two males and two females and – rarely – with a single male and two females. Where there is more than one male in a territory, one male is clearly dominant over the other; but where there are two females, they tend to subdivide the territory and each keeps to her own section.

It is obviously advantageous to the male to establish its territory and acquire a mate. However, there are surplus males also trying to obtain mates and territories. It seems better for these males to accept an inferior position in a territory than not to get into a territory at all; indeed in spite of the dominant male's jealous guarding of his mate, these secondary males do manage to mate with the female on occasions and so may leave offspring. And they stand a chance of inheriting the territory if the dominant male dies before they do.

Why then does the dominant male allow the second male into his territory? The answer is probably that two males can defend a large territory more successfully than a single one can and this may even increase the chance that two females may come into the territory. From the female's point of view the arrangement seems satisfactory since in most cases both males help to raise the young; she may therefore be more successful at raising young in a territory where there are two males than where there is only one. Where there are two females in a territory, they often do not have synchronised broods, so both may get help from both males.

Long-tailed Tits

Long-tailed Tits live in groups throughout the winter; these groups are usually based on a pair and its offspring, but other birds may be included. These flocks defend a territory against other flocks throughout the winter. In very cold weather,

they huddle together and so help to keep each other warm. This probably means that they have a much greater chance of surviving the night than if they were roosting separately.

When spring comes, the young females leave the flock and pair with males in any one of several adjacent flocks (probably so as to avoid inbreeding). The flock splits up into pairs which subdivide the winter territory between themselves (though they do not seem to defend these areas very vigorously). Each of these pairs builds its own nest and, if all goes well, raises their own brood. However, losses of nests are very high. The birds may replace their nest if it is lost early in the season, but later on they do not do this: instead they go to another nest and help the parents to raise their young. Losses are sufficiently high for most broods to have one or more extra birds helping to raise the young by the time that young are in the nest. The presence of the extra bird means that the young receive more food and are more likely to survive. In particular, they get added attention after they have left the nest.

So, once it becomes too late in the season for there to be much chance of the birds raising a replacement brood, the best thing to do is to go and help a relative raise its young. However, it will be remembered that the females have changed flocks: all the males in a flock area tend to be related, but the females are usually not. The females do not usually seem to go with their mate to the nest of one of his relatives. At least sometimes (but how often has not been fully established) they return to the area where they lived in a winter flock and help at a nest there; nests in that area are likely to belong to the female's brothers. This is exactly what theory would predict, since the young in adjacent nests are related to the males, but not to the females, but a female who went back to the winter flock area would encounter *her* relatives.

PAIR BONDS

The bond between the male and female of a pair may last for only a few minutes as in the Black Grouse and the Ruff whose males display in leks (pp. 256, 260–1). The females come to the display ground for mating and go away to lay the eggs and look after the young on their own.

At the other extreme, many species stay mated to the same spouse year after year. Some Mute Swans may stay with the same partner for the whole of their lives. In other long-lived birds, such as geese, birds of prey and many seabirds, individuals may breed together for many years in succession. Kittiwakes, which do this are more successful than those that change partner; natural selection appears to favour those birds that find the same mate again in successive seasons.

In the large majority of birds a male and a female pair up and spend at least one breeding season with each other and raise the young together; they are monogamous. Often, there is a clear need for two birds to take part in the rearing of the young. For example, in many seabirds, such as the Lesser Black-backed Gull, the eggs or the young are in exposed sites and would be very vulnerable to predation if they were left on their own. The parents take it in turns to forage while the other bird stays on guard. In almost all birds of prey, however, the birds do not take it in turns: when the young are small, the female broods and guards the young while the male provides the food. In such species, the need for two birds to rear the young is fairly clear.

However, this is not always the case. In quite a number of birds (such as the tits and most thrushes), although the male helps considerably to feed the young, he does not incubate the eggs nor brood the young.

In species where the female can get enough food for herself sufficiently quickly that she does not allow the eggs to chill, she may even be able to raise the young by herself. This has allowed the male, in some species, to do little or no helping at the nest, or even to take another mate.

Bigamy has been recorded in a number of species, but in only a few is it a regular feature. The male Pied Flycatcher displays and attracts a mate in the normal manner in the spring. When the females have built their nests and started to incubate, some males may move off and display at another nest-site. If a male successfully attracts a second mate, he deserts her as soon as she has laid her clutch and goes back to help his first mate raise her brood. Some male Wood Warblers also behave in this way. The first female does not suffer too badly from this arrangement, since she gets help with raising the brood. However, the second mate does not fare so well since she has to raise her young largely on her own. It is easy to see why natural selection might favour males who are bigamous because they leave more offspring than if they had only one mate, but what benefit is it to the females? Possibly in the case of the second female, her alternatives may be either to breed in this way, with low chances of success, or not to breed at all. It is not usual to find any unmated males; indeed, there may be an excess of females.

This type of bigamy, known as successive polygyny, is taken one stage further in the Wren. The male sets up a normal territory in a piece of woodland, builds a series of nests and sings loudly to attract a mate. When one arrives, he leads her to his nests and tries to get her to accept one. If he is successful, he then goes off and sings to attract another female to his nests.

The advantage for the female Wren may be rather different from that for the flycatcher. The male Wrens who get most mates are those with the largest territories. Possibly a female is still better off in a large territory with plenty of food and cover, as the second or even third mate, than she would be as the only mate of a male with a poor quality territory.

Seabirds and birds of prey normally breed monogamously, but the game-birds show a wide range of breeding behaviour. The Grey Partridge and the Red Grouse maintain territories and mate monogamously, the males even staying with the broods after hatching and helping to guard them. The Black-cock and the Capercaillie have leks and no pair-bond. The male Pheasant defends a large territory and tries to attract a number of females to come and mate with him and nest within his territory (harem polygyny). One of the more extraordinary is the Red-legged Partridge. The female lays a clutch of 12 or more eggs and then goes on to lay a second clutch of about the same size in another area. On completion of the second clutch, she returns to the first and starts to incubate it, leaving the male to look after the second nest.

The waders, too, show a wide range of variation in pair-bonds. Some such as the Lapwing and Curlew are normally monogamous, and Oyster-catchers may stay paired together over many years. In others one sex may undertake most of the parental duties. The female Spotted Redshank normally leaves the area about a week before the eggs hatch and lets the male do almost all the incubation and all the rearing of the young. The position is even more extreme in the phalaropes. In these the female is the brightly coloured one and she lays the eggs and leaves the male to do all the incubation and care of the young.

The female Temminck's Stint also lays a clutch for her mate to incubate, and another which she incubates herself. If there is a second male about she may leave him to incubate the second clutch and lay a *third* for herself. The female Spotted Sandpiper lays up to four clutches to be looked after by a series of males; she may share the duties at the last clutch, but she has nothing to do with the raising of the others. The Andalusian Hemi-pode is thought to breed in the same way, each female laying a succession of clutches for different males.

Both Great Snipe and Woodcock are polygamous and have communal displays. Male Great Snipe gather together at display grounds at night; there they attract females by fanning their white outer tail-feathers, and with twittering calls. Woodcock display by flying over a piece of woodland and calling (this behaviour is known as roding); several males may rode over the same area simul-taneously and an individual may rode over several adjacent areas of wood-land in a single spring. Once a bird has attracted a mate, he will stay with her until she has completed the clutch and then return to roding.

Almost all birds of prey and owls are monogamous. But some male Tawny Owls have two mates who, for the most part, defend separate territories. The Hen Harrier is un-usual in that, while most young males are monogamous, older ones may have as many as five mates.

A Woodcock roding over woodland

ADULT SURVIVAL

One of the most frequently asked questions is perhaps 'How long does such-and-such a bird live?' There is no short answer to this, because the life cycle of birds is very different from that of most other animals, including ourselves. Birds suffer a very high mortality in the juvenile stages (p. 214), but once they have become adult they have a constant mortality for many years with little or no signs of an increase in mortality resulting from old age. This is the same as saying that a fixed proportion of them die each year. For example, about 50% of adult Robins die each year. If we could observe 1000 adult Robins, about 500 would be alive a year later, 250 the year after that and then approximately 125, 62, 31, 16, 8, 4, 2 and 1 in successive years. This constant death rate contrasts with that in ourselves where there are few losses during the ages 10–60, after which the proportion dying increases sharply.

Indeed, there is no good evidence from field studies that old age is an important cause of mortality in birds. This may be the same as saying that life is so dangerous that virtually no birds live long enough to reach old age; we simply do not know. What it does mean is that we cannot easily answer the question 'How long does a Robin live?'. We can say that only

about one in ten of the eggs laid will survive to become a breeding bird (p. 215) and that, once it is a breeding bird, it has a 50% chance of surviving to the next year. It is also possible to convert this figure into one which gives the average length of time for which such a bird will survive. This can be done by using the formula:

average expectation of further life =
$$(2 - m) \div 2m$$

where m is the mortality.
In our Robin example this converts to:
$$(2 - 0.5) \div (2 \times 0.5) = 1.5$$

So the average expectation of further life of an adult Robin is only about $1\frac{1}{2}$ years. Some people are surprised that Robins have such short lives and claim to know individuals that have lived much longer than that. This is quite possible; the figure of $1\frac{1}{2}$ years is an *average* expectation of *further* life; this means that some birds will live much longer, others much less time. In our example above, one bird in every 1,000 lives to be ten years old. (It is also not unlikely that some individuals that are well-known to people will, because they are very tame and rely on human subsidies in winter, live longer than the average anyway.)

Many small birds in Europe have the same sort of lifespan as the Robin; adult Blut Tits have even shorter lifespans with an annual

Adult Robins (left) *have only a fifty percent chance of surviving until the next year; for juvenile birds, the survival is even lower!*

Some Puffins have been known to live for well over twenty years.

mortality of about 70%: their average expectation of further life is just under a year. Most larger birds live longer than these small species. Indeed recent studies show that small birds in tropical areas have much longer life-spans than those of small birds in Europe; it seems that small birds may live much longer in more equitable climates. The table gives the annual survival rates and average expectation of life for a range of European species, and many more are given in the Directory.

At the other extreme to the Robin are some of the larger birds such as the Gannet, Flamingo and Puffin; these birds may live for a considerable time. The highest survival rate as yet established for any European bird is that for the Puffin which, with an annual survival rate of about 95%, has an average expectation of further life of almost 20 years. Again, this is an average figure; many individuals will not live as long as this, and many will live longer. We do not know how long the oldest of these birds live, since studies have not been going on long enough; but it seems likely that some Puffins must live to be forty years of age. There are now quite a

few records of ringed birds which have lived to be well over 20 years. It is likely that these figures will be exceeded in the future. Not only are more birds being ringed, but also the rings used nowadays are made of stronger metals; the early rings, made of aluminium, often became weakened with time and fell off the birds long before they died. Many other large birds are almost certainly very long-lived, but detailed studies of them have yet to be undertaken.

The reader should be aware of the areas of uncertainty when consulting the information on survival rates and longevity in the Directory. The longevity figures for many species will doubtless be exceeded when more detailed studies have been conducted over longer periods. Indeed, for many species such studies have not yet been undertaken and so their longevity can only be inferred from our knowledge of other, related species where studies have been made.

ANNUAL SURVIVAL RATES
OF ADULT BIRDS OF SELECTED SPECIES

Species	% Survival	Average expectation of further life in years
Fulmar	95	19
Flamingo	95	19
Puffin	95	19
Herring Gull	92	12
Manx Shearwater	90	9·5
Gannet	90	9·5
Swift	88	8
Mute Swan	82	5
Buzzard	80	4·5
White Stork	79	4·3
Woodpigeon	65	2·4
Blackbird	65	2·4
Kestrel	60	2
Robin	50	1·5
House Sparrow	50	1·5
Blue Tit	30	1

Part 4

THE ECOLOGY OF BIRDS

BIRD POPULATIONS

SURVIVAL RATES

The number of birds in a population depends on the survival rates of the individuals and the success they have at raising young. We have seen that many young birds die before they reach breeding age (p. 214), and that the annual survival rates of breeding adults varies markedly between species – from as low as about 30% in the Blue Tit to as high as about 95% in the Puffin and other long-lived birds (p. 285). Where known, such information is given for each species in the Directory. Such information is often presented in different ways: an annual *survival rate* of 95% is the same as an annual *death rate* (or *mortality*) of 5% (100 – 95). These figures are also sometimes presented as proportions of a unit (1.0), i.e. in this example as a survival of 0.95 or a mortality of 0.05 (1.0 – 0.95).

Pairs of Tawny Owl recorded in Wytham Wood, Oxfordshire; the graph shows a gently increasing population until, apparently, the maximum carrying capacity of the site is reached

STABILITY OF NUMBERS

In nature, the populations of most species remain remarkably stable. This does not mean that there are no changes in numbers – populations may decline after a very cold winter, for example – but over a longish period of years the numbers remain more or less the same. There are usually one or two pairs of Blackbirds or Robins in our gardens, seldom none or many pairs.

These casual observations are borne out by detailed studies of particular species; such populations tend to fluctuate remarkably little. Similarly, although the numbers of smaller birds, such as tits, fluctuate a little from year to year, sometimes even doubling or halving between years, over the longer term the numbers remain fairly stable. In the tits and some other seed-eating species, the numbers fluctuate in proportion to the seed crops available during the winter. When there is a good crop, survival is good; when the crop is poor, so is survival.

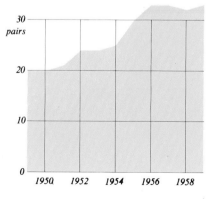

BALANCE OF NUMBERS

The reason why most bird populations are stable is that the number of birds born into the population is matched by a similar number which die. In any given year:

Number born = Number dying

Since the death rates (mortality) vary markedly in eggs and in young of different ages (p. 214), and these figures are often difficult to gather, it is usually simpler to deal just with those youngsters who survive long enough to enter the breeding population and say:

Number entering breeding population = number of adults dying

This equation has certain advantages: one can use it to calculate the number of young which must survive to reach breeding age if the population is to remain stable. For example, the annual adult survival rate of the Herring Gull is about 90% (or 0.9); this means that 0.2 birds per pair die each year $(1.0 - 0.9) \times 2$ (because there are two birds in a pair). If such a population is to remain stable, then each breeding pair must, on average, raise enough young each year for 0.2 per pair to survive to reach breeding age.

These sorts of calculations assume that a population is more or less stable; if its numbers are decreasing, then either too few adults are surviving from one year to the next, or too few young are surviving to reach breeding age, or both. If the population is increasing, then the reverse must be the case.

Because of the large differences in lifespan, the proportion of birds breeding for the first time varies greatly between species. For example, in the Blue Tit where only about 30% of the adults survive from one year to the next, only about 0.6 birds in each breeding pair (0.3×2) are birds that bred the previous year. So, about 1.4 birds per pair $(2.0 - 0.6)$, roughly two-thirds, are young birds breeding for the first time. In contrast, in the Puffin where there is a 95% adult survival rate, 1.9 birds per pair (0.95×2) are birds that have bred

before and only 0.1 birds per pair $(2.0 - 1.9)$, or 5%, are breeding for the first time.

CARRYING CAPACITY

Some of the year-to-year changes in numbers are predictable, such as population fluctuations in tits because of the seed crop. Changes in the breeding numbers of the Grey Heron can also be related to winter conditions. Numbers decrease during cold winters. This happens because ice makes it difficult for the herons to hunt for fish.

However, in the case of the heron, it is interesting to see what happens after the cold winter. Given a series of normal winters, the herons increase in numbers and soon reach their earlier levels. The interesting thing is that they do not go on increasing; they seem to reach a maximum beyond which numbers do not rise. It is as if there is only room for a certain number of herons. This upper limit to the numbers of a species is referred to as the carrying capacity of an area.

In any particular area, there is only a certain amount of fishing space available for herons. When the population goes down, more fishing space becomes available for each bird and so they have a relatively easy time and survive well. Numbers

Occupied nests of Grey Heron in two parts of Britain; hard winters occurred at the starts of 1940, 1941, 1942, 1945, 1947, 1962 and 1963.

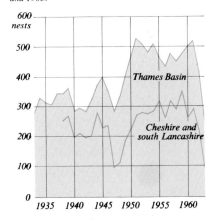

increase because more young birds are surviving to enter the breeding population than are needed to replace the number of adults that are dying. But as the population increases, so the space for each bird becomes more restricted, and survival is harder. Eventually, numbers reach a point where young birds are no longer surviving to enter the breeding population in greater numbers than adults are dying; at this point the population stops increasing. Such a form of mortality is called density dependent, because the proportion of birds dying is dependent on the density of the birds themselves.

POTENTIAL RATE OF INCREASE

This stability of populations is surprising when we consider the remarkable potential birds have for raising young. A Blackbird can have three broods, each of three or four young, in a single season; and a Robin can have two broods, each of five. If all these young, and their parents, were to survive to the next year, there could be six pairs where there had been only one the previous year. If, in their turn, all these birds and their offspring survived and bred for a mere five years, there would be 7,776 pairs where there had been but one!

We all know that this does not occur. But what *does* happen to this enormous production? As we have seen (p. 212), most of these nests fail, or the young die during their first few weeks of life. Many others, together with some of the parents, also perish before the next breeding season.

Although in the long term the number of young birds which survive long enough to breed matches the number of adult birds which die, there are inevitably differences from year to year between these two numbers. As a result, populations often increase or decrease slightly between years.

In theory, increases and decreases in numbers can be the result of changes in the survival rates of either the adults or the juveniles or both. In practice, survival rates of adults tend to be much less variable than those of young birds. For example, in a long-term study of Great Tits, the annual adult survival rate varied from about 40% to 75% – less than a two-fold variation – while the number of juveniles surviving to breed the following year varied from a high of about 20% to a low of about 1%. So changes in breeding numbers in small bird populations are more likely to be caused by variations in the survival of young birds than of adults. The same is true of populations of large, long-lived birds except that, because the number of young birds breeding for the first time in any year is small, marked increases in numbers do not usually occur, and big decreases are likely to be due to high mortality of adult birds.

The potential for extremely rapid increase in numbers is not, of course, normally realised. Numbers are kept in check. However, such calculations are not just figments of the imagination. Under exceptional circumstances, such as when a species is introduced to a new area, birds may increase very rapidly indeed (p. 310). Several species, introduced from Europe to other parts of the world, have shown dramatic increases in numbers. Eight Pheasants were introduced to an island in the State of Washington, U.S.A.; after six breeding seasons there were 1,989. Both Starlings and House Sparrows have shown similar rapid changes in numbers after being introduced to the New World. Either 120 or 160 Starlings were released in New York in 1890 and 1891. By 1950 they had spread across the whole of the United States and were estimated to have increased a million-fold!

Starlings

LONG-TERM CHANGES IN NUMBERS

Although, in the short term, populations may be remarkably stable, long term changes occur in many species. The number of White Storks breeding in western Europe has declined markedly during this century. This is apparently because of the draining of the wet meadows which the storks use for hunting, though changes in their winter quarters (in Africa) may also have had an effect. Another species which seems to have declined as a result of changes in its winter quarters in Africa is the Whitethroat. Its numbers showed a very sharp decline during the middle 1970s; this has been associated with the series of droughts in the Sahel area of Africa where the birds spend the winter.

Changes in habitats can also lead to a change in numbers. The numbers of pairs of Great Tits breeding in a Dutch wood increased over a period of 30 years. The wood was a young plantation when the study started; but it had matured into rich woodland and by the end of the study. Apparently the carrying capacity of the wood increased as the trees grew up.

One of the most remarkable changes in the population of any species in Western Europe during the last century has occurred in the case of the Collared Dove. This species has spread from the east and colonised most of Western Europe during the last 40 or 50 years. It first nested in Britain in 1955, yet by 1972 – just seventeen years later – there may have been 40,000 *pairs*! It is now so common in many areas as to be virtually uncountable. It is not known why this bird has increased so strikingly, but it lives in close association with man and seems to have, quite suddenly, found that this habitat was a very suitable one.

Another remarkable increase has occurred in the population of the Fulmar. This species is known to have started to increase in number in Iceland from about 1750, and birds first colonised the Faeroes about

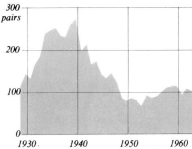

Pairs of White Stork recorded in Oldenburg province, Germany

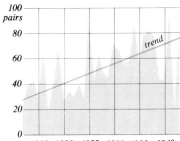

Population index of Whitethroat on farmland in Britain, based on the Common Birds Census of the British Trust for Ornithology; population measurements are relative to 1966, which is taken as 100%

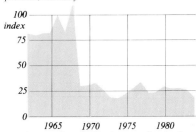

Breeding pairs of Great Tit on 129 hectares of woodland near Arnhem, Holland

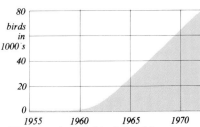

Minimum estimates of the Collared Dove population in Britain and Ireland; after 1964 these doves became almost uncountable, although recently the rate of increase has slowed down.

1820. In Britain, Fulmars bred on St Kilda, off north-west Scotland for many centuries; but they were not recorded breeding elsewhere in the country until 1878 when some were found in Shetland. The colonisation of other parts of Britain followed rapidly, the population increasing at the rate of about 7% per annum. Today, the birds breed on virtually all the coastal cliffs. The last census (1970) estimated that there were just over 300,000 occupied sites and the bird has gone on increasing since that date, though possibly not at quite so rapid a rate. This increase is all the more remarkable when one considers that each pair only lays a single egg per year, and that the young take eight or nine years to reach breeding age (p. 216). The reasons for this increase are not clear, but may be related to the fact that the young birds have been able to feed on offal thrown overboard from fishing boats; this will have helped them through the crucial early months of independence.

CYCLES AND IRRUPTIONS

There are two groups of birds whose populations fluctuate to a greater extent than most others. Both have highly characteristic increases in numbers, followed by crashes when the species becomes much less abundant.

One of these groups contains those species whose populations show cycles of increases and decreases anyway. The most marked cycles in birds are found in some of the gamebirds, especially the Red/Willow Grouse and Ptarmigan. The numbers of these two species show increases and decreases over roughly ten-year periods. The changes in numbers may be linked with nutrient cycles in the soil affecting the plants on which they feed.

The other group of birds whose populations frequently increase and then crash are the so-called irruptive species. These birds increase during a run of years when food is plentiful

and then, when the food supply fails, move to other areas in search of food. One of the best-known of them is the Common Crossbill. These birds live mainly on spruce seeds in continental Europe, though they will also take pine seeds when these are plentiful. The species breeds in large numbers in the northern forests of Norway and from there eastwards into Russia. If there is a plentiful supply of seeds, the crossbills breed well. However, spruce virtually never has a heavy crop of seeds in two successive years: after a good crop there will be a poor one. The crossbills tend to move through the conifer belt settling to breed wherever they find plenty of seeds. Thus in any one area the birds may show enormous increases in numbers (initially due to immigration, then by a build-up from breeding), followed by a sudden decline when they leave the area. Seemingly, the birds can usually find somewhere where the seed crop is reasonable. But their troubles start when, usually after a series of years with good seed crops, no area has a good crop. Large numbers of crossbills are then faced with a great scarcity of food. At this stage they pour southwards across Europe looking for other sources of food, and appear in areas where there are normally no crossbills. Such irruptions take place quite often, over 60 having been recorded since the beginning of the nineteenth century.

The numbers of Ptarmigan shot and sold from year to year in part of northern Iceland reflect the population cycle of this gamebird.

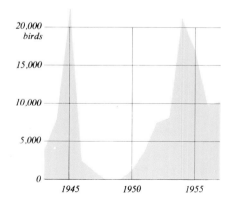

Crossbills are unusual in that individuals may breed each year in a different place. Irrupting birds which find a suitable area in southern Europe may breed and then move back to the north in later years.

The lemming is particularly famous for its population cycles, which normally have a period of about four years. Since it is an important prey of several species of birds, its abundance has considerable effect on their movements. Three of the birds which feed largely on lemmings when they are abundant are the Rough-legged Buzzard, Snowy Owl and Long-tailed Skua. The buzzard and the owl behave rather like the crossbill, moving across the arctic tundra and settling to breed where the lemmings are abundant. In years when the lemming population crashes, both Snowy Owl and Rough-legged Buzzard come south in larger numbers than usual in search of other prey.

Another irruptive species which not infrequently appears in central Europe is the Waxwing. This bird also lives in the northern forests, feeding on berries during the winter, especially those of rowan. When these fail it may move south.

Pallas's Sandgrouse lives on the steppes of Asia, but moves westward into Europe on occasions. It did so during the last century in great numbers, even reaching as far west as Britain on occasions and breeding there in some years. In this century irruptions have become less frequent, and the numbers of birds smaller, apparently because of a general reduction in the species numbers following habitat changes. There was a small irruption to Europe in 1975. Another species which normally lives in the same general area, but irrupts to eastern Europe and breeds there, and occasionally spreads as far as western Europe, is the Rose-coloured Starling.

Irruptive species occur most commonly in the higher latitudes, either in the tundra or the taiga forest. These habitats contain fewer species of trees and other plants than habitats further

Waxwing feeding on rowan

south, and many of the bird species tend to be heavily dependent on one or a very few sources of food. They are likely to find it difficult to switch to another source of food when their mainstay fails – so they move.

Nutcracker, Jay, Great Spotted Woodpecker, Brambling, Pine Grosbeak, Great, Coal and Willow Tits all move out of the northern forests in large numbers in years when their main food fails. However, since most of these species occur over wide areas of Europe, their irruptions are less remarkable than those of the Common Crossbill or the Waxwing which, because they move outside their normal range, are more easily noticed.

As with the mass movements of lemmings, it has sometimes been thought that the irruptions of birds are a way in which a species reduces its numbers when it becomes too abundant, and that the birds that moved were the outcasts which were, effectively, committing suicide. Not so. Such events are mass movements of a species from an area where the food supply has failed more or less completely. It is true that a great number of such irrupting birds will probably die; but they would have died anyway if they had remained on their breeding grounds. They have a better chance of survival by looking for food in new and milder areas than if they had remained in the northern, foodless areas. In fact we now know that at least some of the birds survive their irruptive movements and return to their normal breeding grounds in later years.

IMMIGRATION AND EMIGRATION

A very high proportion of the deaths of young birds occur during the late summer, soon after they become independent. Since birds are small and dead ones rapidly consumed by other animals, this loss is mainly noticed as a drop in numbers. The birds simply disappear.

Many people find it hard to believe that so many young birds die before reaching breeding age. They suggest that when young birds disappear from an area, they have not died, but have emigrated to other areas. Birds do, of course, move between areas: any piece of habitat has both immigrants and emigrants. However, emigration (as opposed to death) is not likely to be the explanation of local drops in numbers. This is because, in most species, local populations tend to fluctuate in synchrony with one another. For example Blackbirds tend to have good breeding success in years when the ground is damp for long periods (so the parents can easily get food for the young). Since such conditions tend to obtain over wide areas at the same time, Blackbirds over wide areas have good or poor breeding success together. The disappearance of the young from one area is likely to be accompanied by similar disappearances in other areas. The birds cannot be emigrating from all areas at the same time.

Of course, ebb and flow on a local level can sometimes have an effect. In an area of mixed woodland and suburban habitat, for example, breeding success of tits will tend to be higher in the depths of the forest than in somebody's garden, where sources of disturbance (like children) or predators (like cats) abound. After a typical breeding season, the woods will be thronged with young and mature tits, and many of them, under pressure from competition for food, may naturally stray into gardens outside. These immigrants will find fewer tits to compete with, and more to eat.

Immigrants also play their part in populations which are newly establishing themselves. In both the Fulmar and the Collared Dove (p. 289) which spread so rapidly through parts of Europe, it was clear that, at least in the initial stages, the pioneering new colonists were being augmented by other immigrant recruits over the ensuing years. The rate of increase was too rapid for the newly arrived birds to have been able to achieve it by reproduction.

Gardens are exploited by birds; but breeding success can be adversely affected by disturbance and poor natural food supplies.

POPULATION REGULATION

We have seen that bird populations are usually stable over quite long periods of time and that, in spite of there being a large production of young, most of these die before reaching breeding age. What factors affect the way in which these numbers balance? The answer is that populations are regulated largely by their own numbers. Such numbers affect the survival of the individuals present. For example, in the population of the Grey Heron cited above, the proportion of young which survive depends on the numbers of birds present. Herons need to be able to feed in solitude so that they can find fish. The more herons present, the greater the disturbance and the more difficult it becomes for an individual to find food. As a result, when numbers are low, each young heron finds it easier to establish a satisfactory feeding area for itself than when heron numbers are high; there is less competition. Hence numbers increase when densities are low. As the population increases, the young birds find it progressively more difficult to obtain a suitable feeding area. Consequently, their survival rate declines until the numbers which survive are only just enough to replace the adults which are dying, and the population becomes stable.

Although food is often the most critical factor affecting the survival of the birds, other factors may affect the chances of birds surviving. For example, at high densities Red Grouse become crowded and each bird can only obtain a small piece of moorland. Competition for territories becomes severe and some birds are unable to establish one at all. Hence, more birds are prevented from breeding in years of high, than in years of low, density.

Population regulation through density dependent factors is a very important concept. Putting it simply, it means that there is only enough room in the environment for a certain number of individuals of any species to survive. If this number is exceeded,

a higher proportion of the birds die than if the numbers are lower. This leads to numbers oscillating about an average figure. When numbers get higher they tend to decrease, when they get lower they tend to increase. We say that the population is regulated.

An important aspect of such a form of regulation is that, because there is only enough room for a certain number of individuals, if one individual dies, another that otherwise would have died will survive because there is room for it. This form of population regulation has a

To feed successfully, Grey Herons need to fish alone.

number of important practical consequences.

A population remains stable because a balance is achieved between *numbers born* and *numbers dying*. For this to happen, one must match the other. Which way round is it? Do the numbers dying match the number born, or do the birds adjust their birth rate to make good the numbers dying? The latter is not the case; birds do not adjust their reproductive rates to compensate for variations in adult mortality. They breed as rapidly as possible so as to maximise their contribution to succeeding generations (p. 250). The number of these young which survive is controlled by density-dependent mortality.

The extra birds for which there is no room in the environment are often referred to as the 'doomed surplus'. Between such youngsters, competition is intense. If a territory falls vacant, it is rapidly filled by a new bird. This is important in that it shows that at least many of the doomed surplus are not intrinsically inferior: given the opportunity, they can survive and breed successfully.

MAINTAINING NUMBERS

The fact that birds produce more young than seem to be needed to maintain their numbers is one of the most important aspects of their biology. Without this overpopulation they could not quickly increase in numbers when conditions are favourable. This is not merely useful when the opportunity occurs, such as when the Collared Dove spread rapidly into new areas (p. 289), but it is essential to all populations. From time to time, all populations encounter poor conditions and their numbers decline. The fact that they are able to produce so many young enables them to make good their numbers as soon as better conditions prevail. Many species go up and down in numbers quite frequently; it they could not rapidly increase in the good years, they would become progressively scarcer.

Farming provides food and habitat for some species of birds such as Woodpigeon. Collared Dove and Wren.

THE BASIS FOR EVOLUTION

Overproduction is the very basis on which evolution operates. Charles Darwin was the first to point out how many young animals failed to reach adulthood and he realised the importance of this. There is great variation between individuals, and they compete for the opportunity to survive to breed. Those individuals which are fittest will be those that survive to leave offspring which will, in their turn, bear many of their parents' characteristics. Thus, over many generations, the characteristics of a species can change to enable it to cope with a changing environment; eventually new subspecies and new species may evolve. Darwin called this process natural selection.

most species if their numbers drop sharply after some difficult period such as a very cold winter. Even birds such as Wrens which are very sensitive to cold winters can make good their numbers after bad periods quite quickly.

What does matter to such species is any change in habitats which affects survival rates or reproductive rates (p. 286). A change in habitat is likely to be permanent and so the balance of numbers may be permanently affected.

Hunting

The same arguments apply as above, but in reverse. Here the aim of the hunter is to take only the doomed surplus. If this can be done, breeding numbers will not be reduced, and hunting at the same level can continue indefinitely. Obviously, such hunting should take place early in the year, soon after breeding, when the population is at its highest. As the season progresses, and more natural mortality has occurred, the crop that can be taken declines. If the hunting is carried out after the main period of natural mortality, not only would there be fewer birds available, but the breeding population might also be reduced, and hence the numbers that could be hunted the following year.

PRACTICAL IMPLICATIONS

A clear understanding of the ways in which populations are regulated is essential if we are trying to control a pest species, protect an endangered species, or hunt a gamebird.

Control of pest species

Pest species have proved very difficult to control because, to do so, we must kill more than the doomed surplus. For example, much money was spent in Britain trying to control the numbers of Woodpigeons. However, studies showed that hunters only killed about one bird per five acres (2 ha.) whereas about four times as many as this died from natural causes. Not surprisingly, hunting failed to reduce the breeding population.

Hunters must not only kill more birds than the doomed surplus, they must do it every year. As soon as they stop, numbers will rapidly return to what they were before. It is particularly difficult to persuade hunters to spend a lot of time searching for a species when it has become scarce; yet it remains important to do so since the numbers tend to increase most rapidly when the density is lowest.

Bird Protection

As we have seen, birds will quickly make good their numbers after some natural disaster. They have been doing so for millions of years. Hence there is no real reason to worry about

Pheasant-shooting in autumn

BIRD COMMUNITIES

Species of birds do not live alone: they live in communities, sharing their habitat with other species. Only a few of these species may inter-act directly with each other; hawks hunt small birds; Puffins compete with Manx Shearwaters, and Starlings with woodpeckers, for nesting holes.

Many members of a community may hardly interact with each other at all. Others may have important influences on each other by taking the same food.

NICHES

Within each community, each species has a separate way of life; it has its own place in the environment, its own separate relation to the other species, to food and to predators. This place in the community is called its niche. Each species has a separate niche because no two species with *exactly* similar requirements could co-exist

(p. 55). Either one will eliminate the other, or they will evolve differences which enable them to co-exist.

Closely-related species are the most likely to compete with one another, because they are most similar in size and habits. In all pairs of species, each is always slightly better than the other at *something*. The closely similar Common and Arctic Terns have slightly different fishing skills, the former being better at fishing on cloudy days, while the latter is better when it is windy. There are several ways in which competition between pairs of closely-related species is avoided or reduced.

Range
Where the niches of two species are very similar, the birds tend to have different ranges. One of the most striking examples of such a situation in Europe is seen in the partridges of

Breeding distributions of the 'Red-legged Partridge group' of species

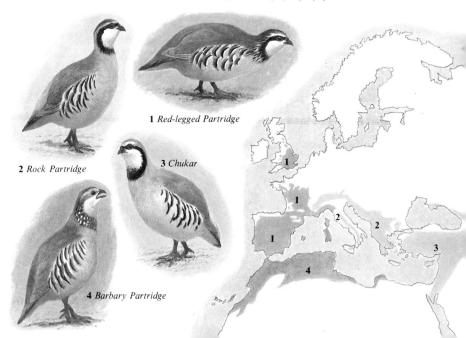

1 *Red-legged Partridge*

2 *Rock Partridge*

3 *Chukar*

4 *Barbary Partridge*

the genus *Alectoris*. Even where the Rock Partridge comes into contact with the Chukar in the east and with the Red-legged Partridge in the west, the contact between them is less than it might seem from the map since the Rock Partridge (in the areas of overlap only) tends to occur at higher altitude than the other two species. Similarly, the closely similar Icterine and Melodious Warblers have ranges which hardly overlap.

Habitat

Many pairs of species live in the same general area, but occupy different habitats. One can often hear White-throat and Lesser Whitethroat singing in the same area, but the former is largely a bird of open scrub, the latter a bird of tall scrubby bushes and low trees. Three other small species of this genus occur commonly in southern Europe: the Sardinian Warbler is a bird of tall bushes and open woodland, the Subalpine a bird of open, lower shrubby growth and the Spectacled occurs in very short vegetation on open dry areas – usually completely devoid of shrubs. Crested and Coal Tits are birds of conifer forest, whereas Blue and Marsh Tits prefer broad-leaved woodland.

Within habitat

Even closely-related species living in the same habitat tend to feed in different places. The Lesser-spotted Woodpecker feeds on the fine twigs and upper branches of the trees, while its larger cousin, the Great Spotted, forages primarily on the main trunk and larger branches. The two closely similar seabirds, Shag and Cormorant fish in the same general areas, but the former hunts in open water while the latter does so on the sea bottom; hence they tend to take different foods.

Segregation by prey size

Many closely-related species which live in the same habitats are some-what different in size and, as a consequence, take food items of different size. The finches provide a

particularly good example of this kind of difference; the birds' bills are specially adapted for husking seeds, and bills of different sizes mean that they tend to take seeds of different sizes. Although each species has a preferred food size which is different from that of each of the others, each can also take seeds that are the pre-ferred food of one of the others. Hence, although they are, to a large extent, avoiding competition, several have a small effect on the preferred foods of other species.

The sizes of the bills of various Finches (Greenfinch, Goldfinch, Linnet, Siskin, Redpoll) are related to the size of their main food items.

We have been considering the situation where one or two species are competing with each other. However, often many species live in the same area and feed on the same sorts of foods (such groups in a community are called guilds), and each may be having some effect on the others. In any piece of woodland, for example, there are often flycatchers, tits, Redstart, Goldcrest, Robin and Dunnock, all of which feed primarily on insects in the summer. How much effect are they having on each other's main prey? We know very little about the effects of such competition (called diffuse competition), but it may explain why the edges of the ranges of many species do not coincide with any obvious geographical or ecological barrier. The birds just fade out in a continuum of apparently suitable country, perhaps because of the combined opposition presented by the other birds in the habitat.

In some species the two sexes feed in different ways. This may be a neat way of broadening the niche of the species, allowing a larger number of individuals to survive. Male Goldfinches have longer, more pointed bills than the females and are more adept at taking the small seeds out of teazels. In both the godwits (Bartailed and Black-tailed) the females have appreciably longer bills than the males, and are better at probing deep into sand or mud.

The most striking differences between the sexes are seen in the Goshawk and Sparrowhawk. The female and male Goshawk weigh, respectively, about 1,250 and 750 grams; the comparable weights for the Sparrowhawk are 250 and 140 grams. Since these birds take a prey of a size related to their own size, both species have a much wider range of prey than they would if the two sexes were of the same size.

More subtle differences exist in other species. Female Three-toed Woodpeckers forage higher up than the males, in smaller trees, and more often in live trees. Similarly, White-backed Woodpeckers feed in different parts of the territory, the females

higher up, searching smaller twigs, while the males hunt lower down, on larger trunks.

ISLAND COMMUNITIES

Communities of birds on islands contain fewer species than those on adjacent large land-masses. About sixteen species which breed close to the north coast of France, or in Holland or Belgium, do not breed regularly in the British Isles. Some of them (like Tawny Pipit and Icterine Warbler) are seen in Britain regularly every year. Some (like Hoopie and Serin) have bred here at one time or another, but have not established themselves (with the possible exception of Golden Oriole).

Likewise, some 32 species of landbird, a third of the total which breed in England, Wales and Scotland, do not breed in Ireland. Some of these have northerly distributions, and some only just get from Europe into south-eastern England; so it is perhaps not really surprising that they do not reach Ireland. Amongst the missing species are birds common in England, such as Tawny Owl, all the woodpeckers, Reed Warbler, Nightingale, Marsh and Willow Tits, and Nuthatch; Redstart and Yellow Wagtail also breed only locally or infrequently. The absence of some of the woodland species is particularly mystifying, since there are many fine areas of woodland in Ireland.

Why have such species not become established in these islands? A number of factors probably contribute to their absence.

Island size

One reason why a species may not occur on tiny islands is that such islands are too small to hold a viable population. Small populations are much more likely than large ones to die out, just by sheer chance; they are always vulnerable to extinction (p. 294). The larger the island, the greater the population of any species that it can hold, and the greater the chance that such a population can be self-sustaining over long periods.

The Black Woodpecker has been breeding for centuries just a hundred miles away across the sea in Holland; but the species has never been seen in Britain.

which is near to a large land mass. In such cases habitat impoverishment also plays a part. Other animal groups and plants also have lower numbers of species on islands. For example, there are no snakes in Ireland, nor are there any short-tailed voles, a factor which doubtless explains the scarcity of the Short-eared Owl since these are its staple diet in many parts of its range.

NICHE WIDTH

Because island communities often lack some of the species found on mainlands, it is possible to look at the behaviour of certain species in the absence of some of their mainland competitors. In most Swedish conifer forests there are breeding Crested, Willow, Marsh and Coal Tits, each of which tends to feed in a different place in the forest. On the island of Gotland, however, Crested, Willow and Marsh Tits are absent; there, the Coal Tit has a much wider range of feeding sites, and has expanded into many of those used elsewhere by the other three species. It is difficult to escape the conclusion that Coal Tits on the Swedish mainland are prevented from feeding in such sites by the presence of the other species, and their population is thus limited.

This evidence, and that in other similar cases, suggests that at least some species will make use of certain feeding sites under certain conditions, but not when a competitor is present. The inference is that the competitor is better at foraging in such sites, and that it is not therefore worthwhile for the other species to compete. But in the absence of such competition it becomes profitable for a bird to broaden its niche.

It would be logical to suppose that, since there are fewer species present on an island, those species that *are* present would occur at higher densities. Indeed, this is the case with the Coal Tits on Gotland, compared with those on the Swedish mainland where they have to co-exist with three other tit species.

Small populations, such as those on very small islands, depend on frequent immigration.

Distance of island from a major land mass
If a species can exist only in small numbers on an island and is likely to go extinct, the numbers present at any given time depend largely on the frequency with which new colonists arrive from the mainland. Hence the number of species on an island is greatly affected both by the island's size (the larger the island the greater the numbers of any given species, and so the more stable the population) and its distance from the nearest large land mass (the further away, the less frequent are new colonists).

Habitat variety
While these factors explain much of the variation in numbers of species on small islands, they are less convincing for large islands such as England

PROTECTION AND CONSERVATION

The small population of resident Dartford Warblers in England can be seriously affected by hard weather, or by the destruction of its habitat.

Man has had a greater effect on the landscape than any other agent since the Ice Age. Many natural habitats have almost disappeared. There is almost no truly natural woodland left over most of Europe, and much concern is now being shown over the rapid disappearance of tropical rain forests. In an attempt to prevent too great a loss of wildlife, many bodies are now concerned with various aspects of conservation. There is a great shortage of resources for such activities, and of land for nature reserves; so it is imperative that we make the best use of what is available by making sure that we understand the key needs. In one sense, this is stating the obvious; but it is by no means always clear what the priorities should be.

PROTECTION OF INDIVIDUALS

We have seen that, normally, populations of birds have a natural ability to maintain their numbers without our help. They possess a resilience which enables them rapidly to make good their numbers after natural disasters. Therefore we should not usually worry unduly about the effect of natural disasters, such as cold winters, on species that are well-established.

It is necessary, perhaps, to stress the difference here between caring for individual birds and being concerned for the well-being of populations as a whole. Cold winters result in an increased mortality of individuals, but they do not endanger the population. Should we therefore interfere with nature by providing food to help the weaker individuals to survive? Since the populations of most garden birds decline markedly in cold winters, even though a lot of people feed them, it must be doubted whether our feeding achieves much anyway!

For species that have only small populations in restricted areas, a natural disaster may have a more marked effect and even lead to the extinction of some local populations. The species may then be absent, briefly or for a long time, until such areas are recolonised by birds from elsewhere. Species such as the Dartford Warbler in Britain and the Fan-tailed Warbler in southern France, both of which are severely affected by hard winters, have patchy and restricted ranges. The more reduced and dissected populations become, the longer recolonisation may take. It might never happen. Putting effort into ameliorating the effect of natural disasters on such species is likely to produce more useful results than with common species.

The protection of rare species takes up a great deal of the conservationist's time. One difficulty is that it is not always easy to define what is a rare species and what is not. It could be argued that there are no rare birds in Britain. All the species that the British consider rare are, in fact, reasonably common somewhere else in Europe. None of them could be considered extremely rare on a world scale. All are birds that are on the edge of their range – a place where, almost by definition, a species finds it difficult to survive. In this sense, perhaps, bird watchers are like gardeners, forever trying to persuade species to flourish in places where they cannot easily do so.

Similarly, there are not very many rare birds in Europe: the majority of those that we consider rare are well-distributed further east or south. Perhaps the only birds that can really be classified as rare on this basis are the Corsican Nuthatch, a species not merely restricted to Corsica, but limited even there to montane woodlands, and the Cyprus Warbler, a species restricted to Cyprus. This is not to say that there is no reason to be concerned for any of our European birds, for many of those with extensive

populations outside Europe are under greater threat there than in Europe. However, if we use world numbers as the main criterion of scarceness, few European birds are at this moment greatly endangered.

The important thing about such a form of ranking is that it might change the priorities of what we are doing. Research on wildfowl is already well-organised along these lines. Sites are recognised as important for certain species in relation to the percentage of the world population of that species which they hold. Very probably, we would be well-advised to apply this criterion to all other groups of birds. The seabird populations of Britain, for example, contain significant proportions of the world population of Gannet, Manx Shearwater and Storm Petrel.

VULNERABLE SPECIES

Although healthy populations of most species can withstand natural disasters, and quite a few can withstand concerted onslaughts by man (p. 295), other species which take longer to make good their numbers after a disaster are particularly vulnerable to changes. There are perhaps five groups of birds which have shown themselves to be particularly threatened by man's activities and which need the greatest protection. These are:

Species with limited distributions
Such species are plainly at risk because any changes occurring within their range may affect the whole population. Small populations are also in greater danger of extinction than larger ones (p. 294).

If we look at the species which have become extinct in recorded history, almost all are birds with restricted ranges. Most were restricted to small islands. So, indeed, are many of the species that are listed as endangered at the present time. There are not many in Europe, but the Corsican Nuthatch and the Cyprus Warbler mentioned above are in this category.

The rare, endemic Cyprus Warbler

Species where individual pairs need large areas

Some species such as the larger eagles and vultures need very large areas for hunting. A pair of Golden Eagles may need to hunt over areas of 100 square kilometres or more. Clearly it is not possible to maintain nature reserves which can hold more than a few pairs of such a species. In order for a large population of such species to be maintained, the birds must be able to hunt, unmolested, over areas outside reserves. The continued pressure on land makes life progressively more difficult for such species. The Short-toed Eagle is a specialist snake- and lizard-eater, and habitats suitable for it have become greatly reduced. Not surprisingly, the species has declined markedly in Europe in this century. The Black Vulture is a carrion feeder, which soars over large areas of country to find its food. The reduction in wild habitats, and the reduction in the populations of the wild animals which provide the carrion, have made life particularly difficult for this species.

Seabirds also require large areas. Although individual pairs do not defend feeding territories, colonies of seabirds require very large areas of sea from which to get their food.

Colonial species

Although colonial species may not necessarily be particularly scarce, many have rather few nesting places. They are vulnerable for two reasons. In the past, they have been particularly susceptible to persecution, for they were easy to locate and kill. Many egret populations were greatly reduced by hunters who collected their plumes. Second, even when they became scarce, the remainder were still concentrated into a few places and so worth hunting. One of the few really abundant land-birds that has been exterminated by man was the Passenger Pigeon of North America. which nested colonially.

Although it may be hoped that such types of persecution are now a thing of the past in most of Europe. concern is still felt for the safety of

The Short-toed Eagle specialises in reptile prey.

species which nest in only a few places. The number of large colonies of some seabirds is quite limited. For example, there are only some 28 colonies of Gannets in Europe, and eleven of these contain over 90% of the population. The majority of the world's Manx Shearwaters breed in the British Isles, yet of the estimated 300,000 breeding pairs, perhaps in excess of 75% breed on four islands, two of them only about 3 km apart. A major oiling incident in the breeding season could result in the deaths of a significant proportion of the world population of such a species.

Many seabirds are highly colonial; so are many of the herons. The Flamingo, which nests in enormous colonies, now only has one regular breeding site in Europe, the Camargue in southern France. Other sites where this population of birds breed irregularly are found in Spain and Tunisia. but none of these is considered wholly safe.

Species with low reproductive rates

Birds which have high reproductive rates and which breed at an early age can recover from a natural disaster within a year or two. It is for this reason that, if they are pests, such species are so difficult to control. In contrast, those species with long periods of immaturity, and low reproductive rates, are much more vulnerable to changes in the environment. If their numbers are reduced for some reason, they take several or many years to make good their numbers. Puffins and Fulmars both produce a single chick per year and take many years to reach adulthood (p. 216). When the Fulmar was increasing rapidly in Britain, it did so at about 7% per annum; and in a recent increase in the Puffin in Scotland, the birds were also increasing at about this rate (though some Puffin colonies increased more rapidly because of immigration). In these two species, if these rates are anything to go by, it would take many years to make good a substantial reduction of the population.

For the larger birds of prey the threats have not so much been occasional disasters, but rather a lowered overall breeding success and survival, the former brought about to some extent by toxic pesticides (p. 313), and the latter by persecution. Such species are less able to maintain their numbers, in the face of small changes in reproductive rates and survival, than are the smaller species with naturally higher reproductive rates. It is for this reason that the big birds of prey, such as the eagles, have been among the birds most easily exterminated by man.

The Great Auk was also exterminated by man. This bird was vulnerable on many counts; it bred in colonies in a restricted number of places, had a low reproductive rate and probably a long period of immaturity – and it was flightless!

PROTECTION OF HABITATS

In contrast to the fact that healthy populations may need little or no protection, the preservation of suitable habitat is of prime importance. Even small environmental changes may be important, because they tend to be permanent, rather than happening once in a while as is the case with natural disasters. To this end, it might be more important to our garden birds to plant trees and bushes for them, or to buy and protect more woodland, than to provide food for them in winter.

In recent years there has been greater recognition of the problems which arise from trying to protect a single species. Conservation now tends to put much of its emphasis on preserving representative areas of a wide range of habitats. In many cases this has the desired effect of protecting many of the rarer birds anyway, and brings the added bonus of giving protection to all the other flora and fauna which occur in such habitats.

Even so, there are problems associated with trying to maintain

The last Great Auk was shot in 1844; its breeding colonies probably looked like this.

natural habitats. Even if one can obtain, and give protection to, large areas this does not guarantee success, since it is not possible to keep the birds in such areas in total isolation. Certain threats to birds' populations cannot be eliminated just by setting up reserves. Many species have been affected by the use of poisons aimed primarily at insects, but which also poison birds. These, such as DDT and related substances (often referred to as the chlorinated hydrocarbons), are applied to fields to protect crops. Since they do not break down readily, they have slowly spread into all habitats, partly by the movements of animals carrying them. For example, a finch may eat the treated seeds, fly to roost in the woods, where it is eaten, chemicals and all, by a Sparrowhawk. Chemicals have also been washed out of the soils and carried down rivers into the seas, where they have built up in the marine food-chains and hence in the seabirds. Such is their persistence, and so great the quantities used, that they have even been found in the Antarctic – many thousands of kilometres from where they were originally applied.

HABITATS FOR MIGRANTS

One of the most difficult problems in the conservation of birds concerns the migrant species. At the very simplest, these usually require *two* areas of safe habitats – in quite different areas. In many cases their requirements are much more complex than this.

Those species which breed in the Arctic and spend the winter in Europe – such as many of the geese and waders – are perhaps among the easiest to deal with. At the moment, most of their breeding grounds are still relatively unaltered. And in the case of many of the geese which winter in Europe, their wintering grounds, too, are relatively safe, many being nature reserves. The situation for the waders is less secure. Most spend the winter on the coast, especially in estuary mouths where there is abundant food. Many of these areas are under threat in one way or another – often from plans to build barrages. A major wintering area in Holland, the Ijsselmeer, has been reclaimed, as have large parts of the Schelde estuary; there have even been plans to reclaim the Waddensee, the wintering ground for many hundreds of thousands of waders.

Waders in the Waddensee

Many of the waders have very complex lives. They may well rely on finding good feeding grounds in Europe, but only for a few weeks in the autumn while they moult and fatten up for their next journey which, as in the case of the Sanderling, may take them southwards to some African coast. Many other species of migrants also need two or three good feeding areas between their breeding and their wintering grounds. Many small warblers and flycatchers, for example, migrate as far south as Spain and Portugal before fattening up for the long crossing of the Mediterranean and the Sahara (p. 239); they are consequently very dependent on finding good feeding grounds there.

Migrants may therefore be dependent on the maintenance of several suitable areas in different parts of the world. The chances that one or more of these will be altered becomes greater the higher the number of places that are necessary. The birds most at risk from man-made changes are probably those species which inhabit wetlands, since it is these habitats which have been, and are being, most drastically damaged (p. 308).

DIVERSITY AND SIZE OF RESERVES

A conservationist has to decide what his aims should be. This may sound simple; but nature reserves need to be managed, and the aims of management can differ. There is often a temptation to try to maintain as diverse a set of habitats as possible; this should certainly provide a wide range of species present for people to see. But it also results in there being fewer individuals of any one species than if the reserve were a uniform habitat, and this in turn may mean that the reserve is not large enough to hold viable populations of many of the species. (In primeval habitats, untouched by man, most habitat-types would have occurred in large, unbroken sheets.)

Another question that has been much discussed of late concerns what size reserves should be. Some people, noting that big islands have more species than smaller ones (p. 298), have extended this observation to claim that it is better to have a few large reserves than several smaller ones. This argument, however, assumes that the reserves are close together and of identical habitat. When they are spread out and vary somewhat in character, then it may not be true that a single large area is the one which holds the largest numbers of species. However, it is still true that large areas make better reserves than many smaller ones since, as mentioned above, they are more likely to hold populations of individual species which are large enough to sustain themselves.

THE CHANGING SCENE

A BRIEF HISTORY OF EUROPEAN HABITATS

The European habitats have changed markedly during the last 15,000 years or so, since the peak of the last glaciation. This glaciation was not an isolated incident. During the last two million years there have been several glaciations, interspersed by warmer periods. Indeed there is every reason to suppose that we are living in just one such inter-glacial period and that yet another Ice Age will, in the course of the next few thousand years, descend on Europe.

During these glacial periods, the Arctic ice-cap covered vast areas of Europe, extending down to southern Britain and much of central Europe. These areas were of little or no interest to birds. To the south lay the arctic tundra, usable, as it is today, by waders, geese and a few other species during the summer months.

The habitats which we see today in Northern Europe were not eliminated during the Ice Ages; rather they moved southwards and northwards with the changes in climate. As the climate got colder, the plants in any given habitat would die out on the northern edge, but spread on the southern edge. As the climate warmed up, this pattern was reversed.

Botanists have built up a good understanding of the movements of the habitats. Ornithologists do not have comparable information on the birds, but it seems reasonable to assume that these stayed in the habitats that they prefer today, and that they too moved as their habitats shifted back and forth.

The habitats did not always stay intact. Barriers such as the Pyrenees and the Mediterranean barred the way southwards and caused many of the habitats to become fragmented, a factor which was probably responsible for much of the speciation which occurred (p. 54). Living in these habitats was not quite the same as living in the ones we know today. For example, the birds that breed on the arctic tundra today can make use of one asset of that habitat – continuous daylight during the breeding season. When this habitat was at its southern limit, the birds would have had only sixteen or eighteen hours of daylight even at the height of summer. How much difference did this make to their ability to prosper in the tundra?

About 6,000 years ago the habitats stopped moving northwards. They settled into a pattern which, if things had followed the pattern of the previous inter-glacials, would have remained unchanged until the ice began to move southwards once again. But the current inter-glacial (if that is what it is) differs from all previous ones in that a new factor intervened to make other changes to the habitats. Man arrived on the scene.

Middle-spotted Woodpecker and Thrush Nightingale; two of the birds whose populations and distributions have been affected by the elimination of the natural forest which is their preferred habitat in Europe.

THE NATURAL HABITATS AND THE ARRIVAL OF MAN

Before man, most of Europe was covered by a forest of oak, ash, beech, spruce and pine. River valleys were clogged with fallen trees and debris, and so wide areas were flooded, forming extensive marsh-lands. Only the tops of mountains, the far north where the tundra still exists today, and some drier areas in the south, were forest free. Grassland was almost non-existent. The only open lowland areas, apart from marshes, were sand-dunes and temporary clearings where there had been fire or where large trees had fallen and left small glades.

Until about 5,000 years ago, Meso-lithic men lived in tune with their habitat. They had a niche which was rather like that of other predatory mammals and had only limited effects on the forests and the marshes. Marked changes occurred with the advent of the Neolithic agriculturists. These people were not nomadic hunters, but settlers who cleared patches of forests in order to grow crops. At first they were only able to clear the lightly-wooded ridges, but later, with improved tools, they were able to deal with the larger trees of lowland forests. As the size of the flocks of grazing animals increased, so did the size of the clearings. Grassland started to appear.

Today, in many parts of Europe only a tiny proportion of the original forest remains. Only in recent years has any attempt been made to reverse the trend by re-afforestation, though the new forests are often of alien tree species.

Even those forests which have survived have been greatly changed, for man has removed many of the valuable species and the largest trees. Such losses affect the bird population directly, because these are the very trees that tend to produce the heaviest crops of seeds.

Only one or two areas of almost natural forest remain in central Europe: in Poland and in Hungary. Some of the scrub forest in the drier parts of southern Europe, or on mountains near the limit of the tree-line, is probably fairly unchanged, though many of even these have been heavily felled or grazed. The birch and conifer forests of the far north are also probably little altered.

Man did not make a great impres-sion on the marshes until much later, for to do so required more organisa-tion and technical skill than tree-felling. First, the main streams of the rivers were cleared to make them suitable for navigation. Later, it became possible to speed up the flow from minor streams and tributaries, and reduce the flooding of the low-land meadows which were valuable for farming. Marshland has now been even more seriously reduced than forest. Parallel with the extensive removal of forests and marshes, there has been an enormous expansion of open country of all sorts. Primarily this has been for agricultural pur-poses, but a varied range of heath, moor and grassland and other open country now exists where there was virtually none before.

CHANGES IN THE BIRD-LIFE

The changes which man has made to the environment have been covered in some detail because they have had very profound effects on the bird fauna of Europe. Indeed they could be said to be the dominant factor in the distribution of many of the birds we have today.

The Losses

Perhaps the greatest surprise is to find that very few European birds have become totally extinct as a result of these extensive changes. As far as is known, only the Great Auk and the Demoiselle Crane have disappeared from Europe, and perhaps Steppe Eagle.

Nonetheless, many other species have been greatly reduced in numbers and have disappeared from large parts of their former ranges. The birds that are in greatest danger tend to be the larger ones. Many of these are heavily hunted; but for most species habitat destruction is probably at least as important a factor. Large birds need large territories and a given area of woodland or marsh can support far fewer large birds than small ones. Hence the danger of local extinction tends to be higher for a large bird than a small one.

Two of the forest species that have declined markedly throughout much of their range are the Black Grouse and the Capercaillie. The latter was exterminated from Scotland and Ireland in about 1770, probably more from the massive deforestation for sheep farming than by hunting. After some re-afforestation in the early 1800s, large numbers were introduced to Scotland from Scandinavia, and the species is once more fairly widespread in the new forests.

Other species which have declined as a result of deforestation include birds of prey such as the Goshawk and the Honey Buzzard which are now absent from or very scarce in much of their former range. Loss of habitat and persecution are probably responsible for their decline.

Many of the woodland species have been able to make at least some use of farmland, parks and gardens. Indeed, most of the birds that occupy these habitats are basically birds of woodland or woodland edge.

The marshland birds have been less fortunate, for few have been able to make use of man-made habitats. As a result, marshland species have probably suffered greater reductions in populations than many of the wood-

Widespread drainage of marshland has reduced drastically the populations in Europe of Marsh Harrier, Bittern, Bearded Tit and Savi's Warbler.

land ones. The decline of the White Stork over much of western Europe (p. 289) is the result of drainage of wet habitats. The Crane was also once widespread over much of central Europe. Other marshland birds affected by drainage, include Bittern, Marsh Harrier, Avocet, Black-tailed Godwit, Black Tern, Ruff and Savi's Warbler. All these became extinct in Britain as breeding species, though all are back again in small numbers. The Bearded Tit also declined catastrophically, and became extinct over much of its former range.

The dabbling ducks have also become very reduced in numbers. For them, extensive marshlands were not only important as breeding grounds; they were also winter quarters for many migrants from the north and east. The only goose native to Britain, the Greylag, also possibly became extinct as a breeding species, though because of the presence of domestic stock, the exact status of this species is hard to ascertain.

The gains

Man's changes have not just brought about reductions. A number of species must have found man-made habitats to their liking.

Many of the birds which live in

although it nests in trees. Originally it probably lived on the edges of steppe, nesting in trees and flying out to open country to feed.

Like the Rook, the Starling nests in trees; but it feeds, for most of the year, on areas of short grass. However, it also nests in holes in cliffs, and feeds along the shore-line. Was this its natural habitat in Europe before man? Similarly, the Chough in Britain feeds mainly on the short grass turf maintained by the presence of grazing sheep. Where was it before sheep?

The primeval European countryside may also have been unsuitable for the Buzzard, Red Kite and Kestrel, all nesting in trees, but feeding over open country. Did they exist along the edges of marshes? Where were the grassland habitats for Quail and Grey Partridge? Where would Skylarks, Meadow Pipits or Whinchats have been found? All must have been very much less numerous than they are today.

The same is probably also true of some of the birds which we think of as common in wet meadows – Lapwing, Ruff, Redshank, Black-tailed Godwit and Snipe. Almost all the extensive wet meadows of Europe are man-made; some of these species presumably existed on salt-marshes. Similarly, the birds of lowland heaths, like Stonechat and Curlew, must have had much more restricted areas available to them. Although upland heaths and moors existed, they were restricted to high altitudes above the tree-line, or to high latitudes beyond the tree-line's northern limits.

Open heather moorland did not exist as we now know it – except in some areas under pine forest. Was this where the Red Grouse lived? Or was it confined to poorer heather country above the tree-line, eking out an existence in competition with the Ptarmigan? Did the Dartford Warbler live in forest-covered heather, or was it confined to gorse-covered cliffs?

A particular puzzle surrounds many of the aerial insectivores. Nowadays, virtually all the swallows, House Martins and swifts nest in or on

towns and gardens, were originally occupants of the extensive forests; many individuals still live there. Such species include the thrushes (the Blackbird, Mistle Thrush and Song Thrush), the tits (especially Great and Blue Tits), Robin, Chaffinch, Greenfinch and, in larger areas of parks and gardens, Woodpigeon, Great Spotted Woodpecker and Tawny Owl. These birds may even have preferred woodland *edge* to the deep forest. Moving into farmland hedgerows and into gardens may not have seemed a great change to them.

Some very common garden birds, such as the Starling, House Sparrow and Rook, are not woodland species. It is difficult to say where they lived before man opened up the countryside, or to imagine the House Sparrow without man; most of its relations (Ploceidae) live in dry, open, savannah country, and presumably it originally did too. It might have survived the last Ice Age in parts of southern Spain, where there was some rather open steppe-like country. Surely, however, it would not occur in most of Europe today were it not for man's activities. Much the same may be said of the Rook; this species needs open country for feeding,

Before man appeared and made buildings,
House Martins presumably nested on cliffs.

man's buildings. Even the Sand
Martin is largely dependent on man
for its nest-sites. Most of them are in
the banks of gravel diggings; even the
small cliffs along river banks are
created by the wash from boats. In
the primeval, water-logged marshes
such vertical banks would have been
absent. Of all the European swifts and
swallows, only the Crag Martin
remains in truly natural sites. Are
these species much commoner today
than they were before man appeared
on the scene?

CHANGES OF HABITS

Some of the birds which occupy man-
made habitats may well have been
able to colonize them with little or no
change of behaviour, since the habitats were sufficiently similar to the
ones which they lived in already.

In other cases the birds may well
have changed their habits somewhat;
and this enabled them to increase
their numbers markedly.

This is what happened with the
Collared Dove (p. 289). Many of the
European birds have had 2,000
generations or more to adapt to the
changes man has made. Since some
small changes can be observed in 100
generations or less, major changes in
habits could have taken place since
man started to change the face of
Europe.

Several species of gulls have learned

to take food provided by man.
Herring, Lesser Black-backed, Black-
headed and Common Gulls in particular visit rubbish dumps in large
numbers, and also follow the plough,
collecting worms. These species are
commoner inland in Europe than
they used to be, and many winter
further north than they could have
done formerly. The provision of these
extra sources of food must be an
important factor.

NEW FORESTS

In addition to the entirely new
habitats, such as open country,
man has produced new forests.
Although much used by birds, the
forests are usually of different trees
from those that were there before, so
the benefits have often been to bird
species different from those which lost
their natural habitats.

In southern Europe there has been
much planting of eucalypts from
Australia. These tend to have poor
insect fauna, and are of little use to
most birds for feeding. Over the rest
of Europe, most new forests are of
conifers. Sometimes these are of
species which are endemic to Europe,
but often they are exotics and seem to
be of little value to birds, except for
nesting.

A very large part of the European
woodland bird community is primarily adapted to live in broad-
leaved, deciduous forests. Blue and
Marsh Tits tend to avoid conifers, at
least during the breeding season. In
Great Britain, the situation is even
more marked than on the Continent.
As the forests were spreading back
across Europe after the Ice Age, the
English Channel opened up to
separate Britain from the Continent
and prevented spruce and fir from
reaching Britain. Consequently, the
only conifer woodland in Britain was
the pine forest in Scotland.

Nonetheless, some species *have*
benefited from the planting of conifer
forests. Coal Tit, Crested Tit, crossbills, Goldcrest and Firecrest may all
have increased in parts of Europe as a
result of the new plantations.

Few species of bird are at home in coniferous woodland; but Coal Tit and Goldcrest are two that are.

NEW WETLANDS

New wetlands take the form of reservoirs and gravel pits. These large bodies of water can provide valuable habitat for birds; but, as with the new forests, they do not always benefit the species which lost the original habitats. The low-lying, shallow marshes were used by a wide range of species including the dabbling ducks, and many other birds lived in the thick reeds and other vegetation. The deep, open waters of the new habitats, often devoid of fringing vegetation, provide a home for a different group of species, in particular diving ducks

such as the Tufted Duck and Pochard. The new deep waters also provide a safe roosting site for large numbers of gulls.

In southern Europe a few extensive areas of high salinity have been built for the extraction of salt. It is on these that the Flamingos breed in the Camargue. Other birds such as Avocets, Black-winged Stilts and Kentish Plovers use them; more species would doubtless use these areas for nesting if more islands were provided.

INTRODUCTIONS

Species introduced by man play a conspicuous part in the bird-life of some parts of Europe.

One of the most important of them is the Pheasant. The stock was brought into Europe by man a very long time ago, reaching Britain with the Normans in about the eleventh century, and Ireland, Wales and Scotland about five or six centuries later. More recently Golden and Lady Amherst's Pheasants have been introduced, and both are now well established in several parts of Britain.

The early attempts to introduce the Red-legged Partridge to Britain were not successful; but a massive intro-

Many species of duck (Pochard and Tufted Duck here) and gulls (Black-headed and Lesser Black-backed here) use man-made reservoirs for resting and roosting.

duction in about 1790 succeeded, and the species is now widespread in Britain. Many are still reared in captivity and released to augment the wild stock. Included among these released birds are Chukar which now interbreed with the Red-legged in some areas.

The Little Owl bred naturally on the other side of the Channel. Several attempts were made to introduce it, but without marked success until large numbers were released in about 1890. This introduction seems to have formed the basis for the British stock. It has been suggested that the Romans brought the Mute Swan to Britain. But this species bred in nearby Europe, and it seems almost certain that it was well-established in the extensive British marshlands before man came on the scene.

Other species have been released intentionally or accidentally in Europe with varying results. The Canada Goose is now found in several parts of Europe including Britain, Scandinavia, Holland and Germany. There seems every likelihood that this goose will continue to spread, since it is still increasing steadily in many areas. Other species of wildfowl with wild populations that seem to be maintaining themselves in Europe include Ruddy Duck, Egyptian Goose and Mandarin Duck. The latter is particularly well-established in areas to the south of London and the population is now probably well in excess of 1,000 birds.

After escaping from captivity Ring-necked Parakeets breed quite successfully around London.

It is perhaps surprising that so few species of introduced birds have become established in the warmer parts of southern Europe. The Common Waxbill and some other small finches have occurred in certain areas, but none has yet become clearly established, though the Waxbill may be close to doing so in Portugal. Ring-necked Parakeets seem to be increasing steadily around London. The birds have survived several severe winters and are breeding quite successfully. They may be entirely dependent on food put out at bird tables during periods of snow. If they do become established, they may well spread to warmer areas.

PERMANENT DAMAGE TO HABITATS

Many of the changes brought to Europe by man have been deleterious to some species, but beneficial to others. There are however, two types of changes that are particularly undesirable.

First, if we were to cover the whole of Europe with buildings and cities, there might still be large numbers of birds present. But there would be large losses in diversity. Many species would be unable to cope with such alterations; it would be the Starling,

Little Owl; introduced in Northamptonshire in the late nineteenth century.

the House Sparrow and the feral pigeon that would flourish. If we are to enable a wide range of species to thrive in Europe, then we must see that a wide range of habitats remains.

The other way in which an avifauna can be impoverished is to damage its habitats in such a way that the birds living in them cannot survive well enough, or produce sufficient surviving young, for the populations to maintain their numbers. One way in which this happens is by the widespread use of pesticides, especially the highly persistent ones. These may be used in one habitat but be spread to others by sick and dying birds or other animals. The clearest case of this type of habitat damage in Europe occurred in the late 1950s and 1960s, when farmers dressed seeds with some of the chlorinated hydrocarbons, especially dieldrin, as a protection against crop damage. Seed-eating birds such as the finches and the pigeons picked these up. Even though in many cases *these* birds may not have been seriously affected by the amounts of poison that they picked up, many of them were later caught and eaten by predators, the finches by Sparrowhawks, the pigeons by Peregrines. These birds of prey gradually acquired large doses of the poison as it accumulated in their bodies from many different prey. This either killed them or greatly reduced their breeding success. The numbers of both species crashed over wide areas. Eventually, after much argument, the use of these poisons as seed dressing was largely phased out. Both species of predator are steadily regaining their former numbers.

But these poisons are persistent, and will remain in the environment for very long periods. Although the lesson has been partly learnt in Europe, the error is being perpetuated in many other parts of the world with equally severe effects on the wildlife. In parts of Africa this wildlife includes migrants from Europe.

Oil on the sea has also increased in recent years. It gets into seabirds' plumage and destroys its waterproofing and insulation. Since many seabirds are long-lived, and reproduce only slowly, a small increase in the proportion dying each year can have serious implications for their populations.

Seabird populations may also suffer if man overfishes the seas. Overfishing reduces the average age of the fish stock. Initially, this may be beneficial to the birds: there are more small fish for them to eat. However, now that stocks of several species have been seriously depleted, man is turning his attention to the very small fish which can be converted into fishmeal for poultry and other domestic animals.

In recent years the Puffin populations of northern Norway have had a series of disastrous breeding seasons: almost all the young birds have died of starvation, because their parents could not bring in enough food for them, probably because we have depleted the stocks of their main prey, the herring.

RE-INTRODUCTIONS

Bird populations might be increased by re-introducing them to places where they have become extinct. But it is not much use trying to re-introduce a bird to an area unless one is fairly certain that the problem that caused the extinction in the first instance has been overcome. If, for example, the bird was hunted to extinction and hunting can be prevented, then re-introduction might work. But if the habitat has deterio-

Puffins

313

White-tailed Eagles

OVERALL CHANGE: THE FUTURE

The result of all these changes is difficult to summarise. We have lost many species from certain areas, though few from the whole of Europe. Many are much less numerous than they once were. Contrariwise, many that were scarce must now be much commoner than they were before man made his mark upon the scene.

To some extent, the changes wrought by man are similar to those that have always been going on; new species have arisen while others have evolved new adaptations to new situations. In one important way however, man's alterations are different from most of those wrought by nature: they occur much faster. Our increasing technological skills enable us to make ever swifter, more marked changes. In many areas of the world, especially the tropical rain-forests, where birds are closely adapted to highly specialised forest types, changes are occurring very much faster than they have in Europe. These changes bring about huge losses of plant and animal species.

Equally, the future is not particularly rosy for many animals in Europe; changes will almost certainly occur more rapidly in the future than they did in the past. In spite of the growing awareness of the need for a greater ecological conscience, financial pressures are still very powerful and, in the Third World, where there are the unsolved needs of rapidly growing human populations, wise long-term planning may be pushed aside by short-term expediency.

It is to be hoped that the growing appreciation of the need for wildlife – not just for its aesthetic merits, but also as evidence of a healthy world – will make our successors more careful and more clever in the ways in which they handle our natural resources than we have been so far. This does not mean that there will be no further changes. Even if we are able to avoid further serious alterations to the world, natural selection will still remain a powerful active force.

rated, or been altered, then attempts at re-introduction are unlikely to succeed.

The Capercaillie became extinct in Scotland, as a result of deforestation; it was successfully re-introduced after much reforestation.

The White-tailed Eagle has been re-introduced to western Scotland, and the birds are starting to breed. This species was originally hunted to extinction, and there is every hope that this can now be prevented. Since western Scotland used to hold a sizeable population of these eagles, and since they are threatened in many other parts of their range, this seems a constructive thing to do.

A more difficult case concerns the attempt to re-introduce the Great Bustard to Britain. This bird used to breed in many areas of Britain, but became extinct in the middle of the last century, and is seriously threatened over large parts of its range. The Great Bustard could only have spread to Britain after man rendered huge tracts of English downland treeless during the height of the Wool Trade. With the increase in tree planting and intensive agriculture the habitat became less favourable again.

314

INDEX

This index is restricted to names of species and groups of species. Figures in **bold** refer to the main entry in the 'Directory'. No distinction is made between entries referring to illustrations and those referring to mentions in the text.

The DIRECTORY includes all species which breed in Europe, plus those which visit, as non-breeders, in reasonable numbers, e.g. the arctic-breeding geese. It does not include vagrants from elsewhere, such as some of the North American waders, even though a few of these occur (in very small numbers) in most years.

In order to present as much information as possible for each species in the space available, some of the facts have been presented in an abbreviated form. The codes have been devised in such a way that the reader will learn rapidly to read off the information with little difficulty.

The brief introduction to each family or group outlines the common characteristics of the species within it. This is followed by some general information about identification, and a final sentence directs the reader to the *key points to look for in order to distinguish between the species within that group*.

In each species account, the English vernacular name appears at the beginning of the entry in bold capitals, followed by the scientific name (see p. 58) in italics, e.g.

WOOD SANDPIPER *Tringa glareola*

As a quick check, a symbol in the margin indicates the likelihood of the species being seen in Britain and Ireland:

● Regular breeder in significant numbers
○ Irregular breeder, or regular breeder in very small numbers
■ Regular outside the breeding season in significant numbers
□ Vagrant or regular outside the breeding season in very small numbers

The absence of a symbol means that the species has not been recorded in Britain or Ireland.

The average length of the adult bird is expressed in centimetres from bill-tip to tail-tip when the bird is stretched out. Even though this only happens to dead specimens, it is nevertheless a useful standard, e.g.

20cm.

Weights of birds fluctuate greatly with feeding conditions, season, geographical race, and with many other factors; in particular, birds lay down large amounts of fat before migration, and some small birds double their weight just before starting on a long flight. A normal range of summer weights is given, e.g.

50–80g.

Following these measurements is a comment on the bird's status in Britain and Ireland, which includes an 'order' of abundance, which can be interpreted as follows:

During the breeding season

order 1	under 10 breeding pairs
order 2	10–99 breeding pairs
order 3	100–999 breeding pairs
order 4	1,000–9,999 breeding pairs
order 5	10,000–99,999 breeding pairs
order 6	100,000–999,999 breeding pairs
order 7	over 1,000,000 breeding pairs

Outside the breeding season

order 1	under 20 records in an average year
order 2	20–199 records in an average year
order 3	200–1,999 birds probably in Britain and Ireland per year
order 4	2,000–19,999 birds probably in Britain and Ireland per year
order 5	20,000–199,999 birds probably in Britain and Ireland per year
order 6	200,000–1,999,999 birds probably in Britain and Ireland per year
order 7	over 2,000,000 birds probably in Britain and Ireland per year

Such records may be of individuals which spend the whole of the non-breeding season, or long periods of it, in Britain, or of birds which merely pass through briefly while on migration.

Diagnostic features of the species are given. These are the most obvious and useful points by which the bird may be recognised in the field: most of them concern plumage, but typical behaviour is also mentioned if it helps in identification.

VOICE: the usual call(s) and song(s) are described. Most species give a variety of different calls, and only the most characteristic are given.

The habitat (HAB) normally occupied by the bird in summer (SUM), i.e. the breeding habitat, and in winter (WIN), i.e. between breeding seasons, are given.
NB: many birds on migration are found in atypical habitats (particularly on the coast).

NEST: If the mating system is other than monogamous, this is mentioned first. Otherwise, the information concerns the usual nest site, the materials used in its construction, and which of the sexes is involved in building it. The following abbreviations are used:

♂	Male only builds
♀	Female only builds
♂♀	Both sexes share the building
♀(♂)	Female does most of the work; male may help

For EGGS the usual clutch size is given; figures in brackets are less common clutches, and others further outside the normal range may occur. A brief description of the colour and markings is followed by the average length of the egg in millimetres.